Evolution and Learning

Life and Mind: Philosophical Issues in Biology and Psychology
Kim Sterelny and Rob Wilson, editors

Evolution and Learning

The Baldwin Effect Reconsidered

edited by Bruce H. Weber and David J. Depew

A Bradford Book
The MIT Press
Cambridge, Massachusetts
London, England

MIT Press books may be purchased at special quantity discounts for business or sales promotional use. For information, please email <special_sales @mitpress.mit.edu> or write to Special Sales Department, The MIT Press, 55 Hayward Street, Cambridge, MA 02142.

This book was set in Sabon by Achorn Graphic Services Inc. and was printed and bound in the United States of America.

Library of Congress Cataloging-in-Publication Data

Evolution and learning : the Baldwin effect reconsidered / edited by Bruce H. Weber and David J. Depew.
  p. cm. — (Life and mind)
Based on a conference held in Nov. 1999 at Bennington College.
"A Bradford book."
Includes bibliographical references and index.
ISBN: 978-0-262-23229-6 (hardcover : alk. paper)—ISBN: 978-0-262-73181-2 (pbk. : alk. paper)
1. Genetic psychology. 2. Learning, Psychology of. 3. Baldwin, James Mark, 1861–1934. I. Weber, Bruce H. II. Depew, David J., 1942– . III. Series.

BF701.E59 2003
155.7—dc21

2002031992

10   9   8   7   6   5   4   3   2

Contents

Contributors

Terrence W. Deacon
Department of Anthropology
University of California, Berkeley

Daniel Dennett
Center for Cognitive Studies
Tufts University

David J. Depew
Department of Communication
Studies
University of Iowa

Stephen M. Downes
Department of Philosophy
University of Utah

Scott F. Gilbert
Department of Biology
Swarthmore College

Peter Godfrey-Smith
Department of Philosophy
Stanford University

Paul E. Griffiths
Department of History and Philosophy
of Science
University of Pittsburgh

Brian K. Hall
Department of Biology
Dalhousie University

Jesper Hoffmeyer
Department of Biological Chemistry
University of Copenhagen

Kalevi Kull
Department of Semiotics and Institute
of Zoology and Botany
Tartu University, Estonia

Celia L. Moore
Department of Psychology
University of Massachusetts, Boston

Susan Oyama
Department of Psychology
John Jay College of Criminal Justice
and The Graduate Center,
City University of New York

Ruben R. Puentedura
Division of Science
Bennington College

Bruce H. Weber
Division of Science
Bennington College
Department of Chemistry and
Biochemistry
California State University, Fullerton

Preface

The genesis of this volume lies in a week-long, interdisciplinary conference held at Bennington College in November 1999 on the subject of the emergence of mind from both evolutionary and developmental perspectives. A major, though not exclusive, focus of the conference was the so-called Baldwin effect, taken as a starting point for thinking about learning and evolution generally. The papers collected in this volume represent revisions of some of the papers first presented at the conference and new papers specifically prepared for this volume, either by participants in the conference or others who were invited to contribute. Several papers were published in preliminary versions elsewhere, as indicated in the specific papers.

In recent years philosophers and theorists with strikingly different ontological and epistemological commitments, such as Daniel Dennett or Terrence Deacon, have made use of something called the "Baldwin effect" in their accounts of the evolutionary emergence of mind and/or how mind, through behavior, might affect evolution. At the close of the nineteenth century several evolutionary theorists, James Mark Baldwin, Conway Lloyd Morgan, and Henry Fairfield Osborn, responding to the challenge of Weismannian inheritance, independently speculated that learned behaviors could affect the direction and rate of evolutionary change. As several contributions to this volume show, the Baldwin effect was not a clear-cut concept, phenomenon, or mechanism. Neither can it be articulated and applied apart from the theoretical context within which it has been variously deployed. One goal of this volume is to bring together historical and philosophical analyses of what was originally proposed, how it was modified and redefined over time, and what it might mean in contemporary evolutionary theory. Another goal is to explore how something called the Baldwin effect, or something like it, might be useful to present-day empirical and theoretical evolutionary studies. Several contributors explore the possible role of the Baldwin effect in emergence of mind and reflect on the kind or kinds of emergence so engendered.

The papers arrayed in Part I, Baldwin Boosters, Baldwin Skeptics, examine the historical context of the original proposals of the "Baldwin effect" as well as the arguments for and against such an effect. In particular they examine the effect of the modern evolutionary synthesis on the notion of the Baldwin effect when it became assimilated to Conrad Waddington's notion of "genetic assimilation." This section ends with contributions by Daniel Dennett and Terrence Deacon, in which they review how they conceive and use the Baldwin effect in their work. A special feature in this section is a "Postscript" to Deacon's contribution in which there is an exchange in which Peter Godfrey-Smith, Dennett, and Deacon exchange views about the nature and role of "niche construction" in contemporary evolutionary theory.

The middle section of the book, Baldwinism and Development, explores at an experimental and theoretical level, as well as in historical perspective, the role of developmental processes in anything that can count as Baldwin effect, and the ways such processes could affect the evolutionary trajectory of a lineage. Susan Oyama and Paul Griffiths place the Baldwin effect in the context of developmental systems theory. This conceptual framework takes the Baldwin effect to be less problematic than strictly-constructed neo-Darwinism does. The notion of the Baldwin effect as an aspect of niche construction that contributes to the selection of certain life-cycles over others is explored by Griffiths.

The third part, Beyond Baldwinism, takes the Baldwin effect as a starting point for exploring computational cognitive science, bio-semiotics, and the emergence of consciousness and language. This section closes with an exploration of the nature of emergence and an argument that the Baldwin effect may have contributed to the emergence of mind, but was itself an emergent phenomenon.

The editors hope that this collection of essays and explorations will help clarify not only what the Baldwin effect has been, but how the circle of ideas at which it points might prove useful to evolutionary theory in the future. We wish to thank all of our contributors and look forward to a lively discussion generated by this book.

I

Baldwin Boosters, Baldwin Skeptics

1

Baldwin and His Many Effects

David J. Depew

1 Introduction: The Very Idea of the Baldwin Effect

In recent years, a number of evolutionary theorists have spoken well of a turn-of-the-twentieth-century idea that since the nineteen fifties has gone by the name of "the Baldwin effect" (Hinton and Nowlan 1987; Dennett 1995; Deacon 1997). The general thrust of the idea is to urge that, under some conditions, learned behaviors can affect the direction and rate of evolutionary change by natural selection. In such cases, cultural inheritance of a learned behavior across an indefinite number of generations creates a "breathing space" (Godfrey-Smith, chap. 3, this volume) in which inherited factors favorable to the adaptive behavior in question that either already exist, happen to crop up, or can be stimulated by the change in question—there is some dispute about this—will move along the channel already cut by culture, thereby converting learned behaviors into genetic adaptations or, alternatively, supporting learned behaviors by related genetic adaptations. In either case, natural selection will have ratified evolutionary vectors that learning began.

It was George Gaylord Simpson who in a 1953 article gave the Baldwin effect the name it has borne ever since (Simpson 1953). He named it after James Mark Baldwin, an American child psychologist who claimed to have introduced the idea in articles appearing in a paper given in late 1895 and in publications in the *American Naturalist* and *Science* in 1896 (Baldwin 1896a,b). The Baldwin effect might just as easily, however, have been called the "Lloyd Morgan effect." For the British animal ethologist Conwy Lloyd Morgan, who addressed academic audiences in the United States during winter of 1895–1896, proposed the same idea in a paper delivered to a February 1896 session of the New York Academy of Science at which Baldwin also spoke (Lloyd Morgan 1896b; see Richards 1987: 398–399). For that matter, the hypothesis might also have been called "the Osborn effect," after the American paleontologist H. F. Osborn, who, also in 1896, published a paper that he titled "A Mode of Evolution Requiring Neither Natural Selection Nor the Inheritance of Acquired Characteristics" (Osborn 1896).

The subsequent fortunes of the Baldwin effect have varied considerably. Julian Huxley was a Baldwin booster in *Evolution: The Modern Synthesis* (Huxley 1942: 114). Simpson, by contrast, was something of a Baldwin skeptic. In his 1953 articles, he admitted that the idea is theoretically coherent, that is, not inconsistent with the fundamental principles of the Modern Evolutionary Synthesis. But Simpson doubted whether the alleged effect is empirically instantiated very often, and, if it is, whether this can be definitively shown. By the early sixties, a deeper skepticism had set in. In *Animal Species and Evolution,* Ernst Mayr recommended "discarding this concept altogether" as either a trivially true example of normal natural selection at work or a flatly false regression to Lamarckism (Mayr 1963: 611). Theodosius Dobzhansky soon followed suit (Dobzhansky 1970: 211).

Against this hardening mid-century hostility, it is striking that a rather diverse lot of contemporary evolutionary theorists, most of whom regard themselves as supporters of the Modern Synthesis, have of late become "Baldwin boosters." One reason is not hard to find. In contrast to the original Baldwin boosters, who were interested in saving some aspects of Lamarckism in the wake of the post-Weismannian turn to hard inheritance, but who differed from one another about what and how much to save, today's Baldwin boosters are typically evolutionary psychologists who are searching for scenarios in which a population can get itself by behavioral trial and error onto a "hard-to-find" part of the fitness landscape in which human brain, language, and mind can rapidly co-evolve. They are searching for what Daniel Dennett, a Baldwin booster, calls an "evolutionary crane," an instrument to do some heavy lifting fast. What Dennett calls "a Good Trick"—potato washing initiated by an individual, perhaps, which is subsequently spread by imitation among a population of monkeys—can serve as such an evolutionary crane so long as gene frequencies also change in a way that supports the behavior (Dennett 1991, 1995).

The attention of those who, like Dennett, are looking for mechanisms for rapid evolution was first turned to "Baldwinesque" scenarios by a series of publications that appeared in 1987. The most important of these was G. E. Hinton and S. J. Nowlan's "How Learning Can Guide Evolution," which, in the course of reporting on genetic algorithms that seemed to do precisely what the title of their paper suggested, not only referenced Baldwin's 1896 papers, but claimed that Baldwin had already demonstrated what their computer simulations now illustrated (Hinton and Nowlan 1987; see also Ackly and Littman 1992; and Puentedura, chap. 11, this volume). Equally significant was the fact that John Maynard Smith, doyen of contemporary British Darwinian, not yet chastened by the scorn he subsequently displayed for treating simulations of complex adaptive systems as actual biological knowledge, gave his blessing to Hinton and Nowlan's results in an article in *Nature* in October of the same year (Maynard Smith 1987). The year 1987 also saw the publication of Robert Richards' *Darwin and the Emergence of Evolutionary Theories of Mind and Behavior*, which gave a lucid account of the Baldwin effect in its original setting (Richards 1987). The concerted flurry of interest in the Baldwin effect that first manifested itself in 1987 apparently stimulated Dennett to endorse the idea in *Consciousness Explained* (1991) and later in his best-selling tract *Darwin's Dangerous Idea* (1995). Dennett implies that the orthodoxy of the Baldwin effect had never been in much doubt, and that even if it had been, "Hinton and Nowlan and Maynard Smith have shown clearly and succinctly how and why it worked," thereby rendering the Baldwin effect "no longer a controversial wrinkle in orthodox Darwinism" (Dennett, chap. 4, this volume). Terrence Deacon too has made significant use of what he takes to be Baldwinian themes in his *The Symbolic Species* (Deacon 1997). As we will see, however, his approach differs from Dennett's.

In this chapter, I propose to elicit some reasons why the very idea of the Baldwin effect appeared promising in its original setting, increasingly unpromising to the founders of the Modern Synthesis, and why in recent years it has seemed promising once again. I will do so by reconstructing the arguments of the original Baldwin boosters, their mid-century critics, and contemporary advocates in terms of the quite different theoretical assumptions that each party took, or takes, for granted. My claim will be that the history of the general idea that "learning guides evolution by natural selection" reveals that the Baldwin effect does not reliably refer either to a theory-neutral empirical phenomenon, or to a single hypothesis, or to an identifiable mechanism, and that these facts explain why the Baldwin effect has been so diversely received. Because it has never been shown to be a theory-neutral phenomenon, articulations and assessments of the general idea depend on different contrasts and on different, often contradictory, theoretical backgrounds. They depend, in the first instance, on what you are arguing against—Lamarckism, for example, or slow-poke balancing selection. But they also depend on what brand of Darwinism you are presupposing. It is possible that the Darwinian frameworks of today's Baldwin boosters differ from Simpson's by about as much as Simpson's differed from Baldwin's or Lloyd Morgan's. If so, it should come as no surprise that characterizing the Baldwin effect, deducing it from principles, verifying it in fact, explaining how it works, and recommending it as important, depends primarily on a variety of shifting and contested theoretical ideas.

Let me add that I do not say this in order to join forces with Baldwin skeptics. The reasons that deter me from becoming a Baldwin booster on Baldwin's terms also deter me from becoming a Baldwin skeptic on the word of anyone who simply presupposes Simpson's or Mayr's assumptions. Admittedly, I would hate to buy into the contemporary enthusiasm for Baldwinism if it commits me to an unacceptable explanatory scheme. On the other hand, I would hate to have a good idea go unused simply because it does not fit a presupposed theoretical framework. For as many philosophers and historians of science have shown, it is as profitable under some conditions to call a conceptual scheme into question as it is to dismiss an idea for its lack of fit with received assumptions (Lakatos 1970; Laudan 1977).

2   Baldwin's Baldwin Effect—and Lloyd Morgan's Too

Baldwin's argument for the Baldwin effect has the following steps:

1. In the course of their life-cycles, "excess," "overproduced," largely random, movements and behaviors of organisms are shaped into adaptive habits by a process of selective reinforcement under the influence of physical, neurological, and "intelligent" forces, the latter including imitation, reinforcement by pleasure and pain, and in some cases means-end reasoning. (Baldwin calls these "ontogenetic adaptations.")

2. Ontogenetic adaptations adapt the inherited instincts that permit them to environmental contingencies.

3. Ontogenetic adaptations enhance the life chances of the organisms that possess them by making them more responsive to the challenges of contemporary environments. The more ontogenetically adapted an organism, the more it can "stand the stress and storm" of environmental challenge and "rise to the occasion" (Baldwin 1896c: 445, 443).

4. The more ontogenetically adapted an organism, the greater the probability that it will leave offspring. ("This sort of adaptation on the part of the creature keeps the creature alive by supplementing his reflex and instinctive actions, and so prevents the operation of natural selection itself" [Baldwin 1896c: 440]).

5. In some species, ontogenetic adaptations are made more effective by "social heritability." ("By imitation the little animal picks up directly the example, instruction, mode of life, etc. of his private family circle and species" [Baldwin 1896c: 440].)

6. Socially heritable ontogenetic adaptations can be maintained indefinitely in a population until germinal elements that coincide with their influence turn them into congenital instincts.

7. Newly evolved congenital instincts provide a platform for further ontogenetic adaptation.

Baldwin used the phrase "organic selection" to refer to the process by which an organism "selects" spontaneous movements and behaviors so that they form ontogenetic adaptations, or what he sometimes called "individual accommodations" (Steps 1 and 2). In *Mental Development in the Child and the Race,* and in his subsequent papers, he used the notion that organisms select movements and behaviors in accord with environmental rewards and punishments in order to find a mean between Spencer's stress on the role of an impinging environment in physically conforming the organism to its environment and the neo-Lamarckians' tendency to think of instincts as "lapsed intelligence," that is, as the residual effects of conscious choice (Baldwin 1895, 1896a). The former, even when it works on "overproduced" nervous discharges, renders organisms too passive to account for the fact that they learn; the latter treats them as too active in a rational, means-end way. Baldwin called attention to the interplay between novel adaptive responses and preformed congenital instincts by his careful observation of the ways in which the young are instinctively prone to imitate parents and other adults, while at the same time parents and other adults, who form a large part of the neonate's environment, encourage some movements and behaviors and discourage others.[1]

In a paper delivered to the New York Academy of Sciences in February 1896, and in articles published later in the same year (Baldwin 1896b,c), Baldwin asserted that "organic selection" is also a "new factor in evolution." The social heritability of learned behaviors that intensifies and preserves ontogenetic adaptations opens up a transgenerational "breathing space" in which, through the action of natural selection working on whole organisms, ontogenetic adaptations will eventually be fixed by germ-line shifts that reduce the contingencies to which a presumably adaptive learned behavior is exposed. This process is a "new factor in evolution" not only because it explains the formation of congenital instincts that support ontogenetic adaptations, but because it putatively constitutes the leading edge of evolutionary change more generally. In opening the way to further ontogenetic adaptations, organic selection is an engine of phylogenetic progress.

Baldwin was eager to assert that he had already discerned the phylogenetic implications of organic selection in his 1895 book in order to lay a claim of priority for this idea over Lloyd Morgan and Osborn. As both Richards and Paul Griffiths point out, however, Baldwin could do so only by overlooking statements he had explicitly made in 1895 to the effect that the organic selection of behaviors by individual organisms across a series of generations is neutral between Weismannian hard inheritance and neo-Lamarckian soft inheritance (Griffiths, chap. 10, this volume; Richards 1987: 488). Nor could he have used anything in his 1895 book as the basis for such an argument. For the only relatively clear reasons that Baldwin and his contemporaries ever gave for thinking that phylogenetic shifts will predictably move in the direction first marked out by Baldwin's ontogenetic adaptations depend on August Weismann's hard account of inheritance, which was not only inconsistent with Lamarckism, but was apparently suggested to Baldwin by Lloyd Morgan in 1896 (Richards 1987: 493).

So-called simultaneous discoveries are, I suppose, like that. Nevertheless, it is not hard to understand why a simultaneous discovery of this sort would have occurred in the mid 1890s. Baldwin, Lloyd Morgan, and Osborn were all responding to the same exigency—the appearance in the 1880s of Weismann's empirical proof, as it was almost universally taken to be, that traits acquired by an organism in its lifetime could not be passed directly to offspring.[2] What made this observation compelling was its connection to a causal mechanism, namely, the early developmental sequestering of germ line cells—those original "immortal replicators"—from somatic cells. This explanation had a revolutionary effect on evolutionary thought. It instantly broke the connection between Darwinism and evolutionary mechanisms other than natural selection that Darwin himself had sought to keep open. Darwinism henceforth meant "neo-Darwinism," namely, the claim that evolutionary change was to be based exclusively on natural selection and that natural selection was to be based exclusively on hard inheritance. The origins of the Baldwin effect lie in the sudden need of "Darwinians" in the widest sense, as well as neo-Lamarckians like Osborn, either to bring their leading ideas into conformity with this set of parameters or perish. Spencerian Social Darwinism, for example, hitherto a leading account of the evolutionary process, more or less perished on the spot, or at least retreated to the redoubts of popular ideology.

Osborn provides an example of the panic induced by Weismannism. The sudden ascendancy of hard inheritance and the all-sufficiency of natural selection stimulated him to find a way to protect his directional, progressivist, endogenously-driven view of the evolutionary process ("aristogenesis") without relying quite as directly as he had on the heritability of characteristics acquired by intelligence and effort (Osborn 1896). Unlike his fellow neo-Lamarckian Edward Drinker Cope, however, who attempted to refute Baldwin simply by claiming that "it is impossible to believe that Weismann's doctrine is true" and by reasserting strenuously that "Lamarckism *is* true" (Cope 1896: 430), Osborn thought that his version of organic selection evaded both the direct inheritance of acquired characteristics and Darwinian natural selection.

In view of Osborn's neo-Lamarckian flirtation with something like organic selection, it is of great importance to recognize that the Baldwin effect attracted Baldwin and Lloyd Morgan for quite different reasons. Like Weismann, they were proud to call themselves Darwinians not only in the wide evolutionary sense, but in the selectionist sense as well, although like everyone else they had hitherto not distinguished very clearly between hard and soft inheritance and in some cases had to be dragged kicking and screaming to the cause. Like William James, a fellow Darwinian psychologist, they now rejoiced that Weismann's "neo-Darwinism" strengthened the hand of natural selection against Darwinism's evolutionary rivals in explaining the origin of instincts (James 1890: 684). Like James too, Baldwin and Lloyd Morgan were delighted that Weismannism afforded them a way of pillorying Herbert Spencer, who thought of something like germ-line adaptations as arising in a single generation from the direct effects of an impinging environment combined with the direct heritability of characteristics acquired in this brute way (James 1890: 686; Baldwin 1896a,b,c; Lloyd Morgan 1896a,b).[3] Lloyd Morgan and Baldwin were especially delighted to be able to accuse Spencerians and neo-Lamarckians alike of being, paradoxically, extreme "naturists," since the view that acquired characteristics are immediately heritable implied a loss of phenotypic flexibility. "Such inheritance would tend so to bind up the child's nervous substance in fixed form that he [sic] would have less or possibly no plastic substance left to learn with" (Baldwin 1902: 55; see Hoffmeyer and Kull, chap. 13, this volume).

In arguing that organic selection is a "new factor in evolution," both Baldwin and Lloyd Morgan asserted nonetheless that there is a natural tendency for a learned trait to become phylogenetically entrenched or supported *as a learned trait*. Indeed, Baldwin and Lloyd Morgan thought that something even stronger must be true, namely that "the direction at each stage of a species' development *must* be in the direction ratified by intelligence" (Baldwin 1896c: 447–448, my italics). To discover why Lloyd Morgan, followed it would seem by Baldwin, came to this conclusion, we must first sketch in a bit more detail about the sort of Darwinism to which they subscribed. To do so, we must see how they understood not only organic selection, but also natural and germinal selection.

Natural Selection

Organic selection, even when it is considered as a "new factor in evolution," is contrasted with "the natural selection of whole organisms" (Baldwin 1896c: 445, n. 3). Rather than a creative force that accumulates the results of many generations of small directional changes, natural selection is for Baldwin and Lloyd Morgan a negative, rather indiscriminate, force. It illustrates well what one wag has called "the fly-swatter theory of natural selection." It sentences whole organisms that cannot compete for scarce resources to death without issue. Baldwin wrote:

If we suppose, at first, organisms capable of reacting to stimulations . . . we may suppose the stimuli to which they react to be some beneficial and some injurious. If the beneficial ones recur more frequently to some organisms, these would live rather than others. . . . The former would therefore be selected. . . . This is the current Darwinian position. (Baldwin 1902: 163)

To reinforce the view that this was indeed the "current Darwinian position" in these years, consider the following passage from Lloyd Morgan:

Now, what is natural selection, at any rate as understood by the master—Darwin? It is a process whereby, in the struggle for existence, individuals possessed of favorable and adaptive variations survive and pass on their good seed, while individuals possessed of unfavorable variations succumb—are sooner or later eliminated, standing therefore a less chance of begetting offspring. (Lloyd Morgan 1896b: 735)[4]

Modern Darwinians will doubtless be disconcerted by Baldwin's and Lloyd Morgan's conception of natural selection, and by their ascription of this view to "the master." Natural selection as conceived by the Modern Synthesis, and in its view by Darwin as well, does not consist in swatting down whole organisms, but in pumping up slightly divergent reproductive rates. It is not, or not crucially, negative selection of whole organisms, but positive, creative selection for minutely discriminated traits carried by organisms and underwritten by genes. On the modern view, you do not have to die young if you belong to a population whose phenotypic traits are being selected against. You merely have to be part of a population with a statistically lower reproductive output than a relevant comparison population. Baldwin and Lloyd Morgan do not share this view.

Germinal Selection

Baldwin's notion of "organic selection" is also intended to mark a contrast with Weismann's notion of "germinal selection," that is, with the differential survival of germ-line variants as they struggle *in utero* for scarce maternal resources. Germinal selection, not natural selection, is for Weismann the creative force in evolution. It protects hard inheritance by working exclusively on the sequestered germ line; and it conforms to the demand that natural selection must be "all-powerful" by ensuring that nothing that an organism can do in its lifetime to affect its external environment, or be stimulated by its parents to do, can stay the unforgiving demands of natural selection. That is because the organism itself rather than the external world constitutes the environment in which germinal selection occurs.

Using these three concepts—organic, natural, and germinal selection—Baldwin and Lloyd Morgan argued that organic selection, wherever it occurs, must form the leading edge of evolution by natural selection both within species and between them. It is Lloyd Morgan, however, who is much clearer on this point, and who probably instructed Baldwin that "the incidence of natural selection" has an effect in moving evolution in the direction pointed by organic selection. Germinal selection, Lloyd Morgan noted in *Habit and Instinct*, is not necessarily correlated to the natural selection of whole organisms at the organism-environment interface (Lloyd Morgan 1896a). There can, accordingly, be a variety of possible relationships between the three kinds, or, if you will, levels, of selection. Lloyd Morgan argues that there are three, and only three, such possible relationships when the organism-environment interaction is mediated by the organic selection of ontogenetic adaptations and the incidence of negative natural selection.

(i) Germinal selection can occur in a way that opposes the direction of individual accommodations or ontogenetic adaptations. In this case, more effort will have to be poured into learning to compensate for what is going on at the germinal level. This will involve a greater expenditure of energy and a greater vulnerability to contingencies. This in turn entails a greater likelihood that the effort will fail at some point, and that individuals and populations bearing such inherited factors will be swatted down by negative natural selection. As Lloyd Morgan puts it, "Any congenital variations antagonistic in direction to [organic] modifications will tend to thwart them and render the organisms in which they occur liable to elimination" (Lloyd Morgan 1896a: 320).

(ii) There might be a neutral relationship between germinal and organic selection, in which neither supports nor hinders the other. In this case, there will be no correlation at all between the two levels. Both will go their merry way, the former at the germ line level, the later at the level of culture. So the case is irrelevant to questions about the effect of learning on adaptive and evolutionary vectors.

(iii) If, finally, germinal variants are fixed in the germ line in a way that coincides with the direction of learned behavior, the adaptive behavior will be reinforced by inherited factors.

Lloyd Morgan writes:

By their innate plasticity the several parts of an organism implicated by their association with the varying parts are modified in individual life in such a way that their modifications co-operate with germinal variation in producing an adaptation of a double-origin, partly congenital, partly acquired. The organism then waits, so to speak, for a further congenital variation, when a like process of adaptation again occurs. Thus race progress is effected by a series of successive variational steps, assisted by a series of cooperating individual modifications. (Lloyd Morgan 1896a: 315)

Assuming the relevant definitions of key concepts, what Lloyd Morgan is describing is a logically valid inference to a win-win situation. The scythe of natural selection will eventually shift the populational mean in successive generations toward a situation that makes the behavior in question more widespread in the population and screens off any contrary tendencies that may originate in the sphere of germinal selection. In the long run only the germinal elements that reinforce the direction of organic selection by increasing its heritability are retained "because natural selection kills off the others" (Baldwin 1896b: 447). Baldwin's inference that "the future development at each stage of a species' development must be in the direction ratified by intelligence," where intelligence means a variety of ways of responding flexibly to environmental contingencies, including anticipation of likely consequences, is thus grounded in an argument that eliminates any other possibility. Note that on this view no violation of Weismann's injunctions against the inheritance of acquired characteristics will have been incurred. Nonetheless, the agency-accentuating effects that had hitherto been monopolized by Lamarckism, some of which Baldwin and Lloyd Morgan are concerned to preserve, would have been reaffirmed within a decidedly Darwinian framework. Note too that Baldwin and Lloyd Morgan are not arguing that a phenotype is driven into the genotype. Their idea is that germinal and organic selection coincide to evolve a congenital instinct that is stable enough to buffer the organism's efforts to respond to environmental pressures, but at the same time open enough to allow further modification by ontogenetic adaptation. What we would call a feedback loop between instincts and behaviors has been expanded to embrace a wider loop between organisms that are ontogenetically adapted and the arrow of evolution.

3   The Baldwin Effect and the Modern Synthesis

The original explanatory framework in which the Baldwin effect was formulated—a complex of concepts in which organic selection of ontogenetic adaptations produces individual "adaptations," negative natural selection swats down whole organisms before reproduction, germinal selection plays a creative role producing heritable adaptations, and phylogeny is decidedly progressive—is wholly abandoned by the Modern Synthesis. Physiological and behavior adaptiveness, even when reinforced, is not an adaptation, but merely the instantiation of genetically underwritten inherited adaptations; natural selection affects reproductive rates of populations, and only indirectly relies on the life or death of individuals; the variant alleles that are the creative material of natural selection code for phenotypes at the organismic, not at the germinal, level (at least until the rise of gene-level selection); and, finally, evolution by natural selection is not inherently directional. These differences pose questions about whether the Baldwin effect could survive in any recognizable way in the new theoretical environment. My suggestion is: not very well.

The makers of the Modern Synthesis of the 1940s and '50's varied a good deal among themselves about the answer to this question. Huxley, as I have mentioned, was something of a Baldwin booster. "The principle of Baldwin and Lloyd Morgan," he wrote in *Evolution: The Modern Synthesis*,

shows how Lamarckism may be simulated by the later replacement of adaptive modifications by adaptive mutations . . . In areas outside the normal habitat of the species . . . the extension of habitat may in the first instance be dependent on a non-inherited modification of behavior, mutation and selection later stepping in to fix the change genetically. (Huxley 1942: 17, 114)

For his part—and it was a considerable part indeed—Simpson was not entirely negative. For him, the effect meant that "characters individually acquired by members of a group of organisms may eventually, under the influence of selection, be re-enforced or replaced by similar hereditary characters" (Simpson 1953: 110). So understood, Simpson thought that the Baldwin effect is "fully plausible under current theories of evolution" (Simpson 1953: 115). It can happen, however, only where several contingently related circumstances coincide. First, since adaptations are by definition based on gene frequencies, an adaptive novelty can occur in individuals within a population only if a gene or gene complex codes for a trait that has a fairly wide "norm of reaction" at the phenotypic level. In this analysis, Simpson was following the lead of the Russian Darwinian I. I. Schmalhausen, who, in struggling to defend Darwinism against state-sponsored Lysenkoism as intently as Baldwin and other Darwinian psychologists had once struggled against Social Darwinism and neo-Lamarckism, rested his case for a Darwinian mimicry of the inheritance of acquired characteristics on the notion that genes typically have a range of phenotypic effects, and that what looks like the heritability of acquired characteristics is merely a shifted norm of reaction of genes that are already there (Simpson 1953: 115–116; Schmalhausen 1949).[5] Second, a behavior or habit preserved across generations by cultural transmission can causally lead to changes in gene frequencies only if "there occur in the population genetic factors producing hereditary characteristics similar to the individual modifications . . . or having the same sorts of adaptive advantages" (Simpson 1953: 112). This is roughly Baldwin's and Lloyd Morgan's idea of a concurrence between germinal and socially inherited factors. But—and this is the crucial point—it is Baldwin's and Lloyd Morgan's idea shorn of any theoretical reasons why in the long run such a concurrence *must* form the leading edge of evolutionary change.

Indeed, given the theoretical framework of the Modern Synthesis there are good reasons to think that such a concurrence will seldom, if ever, occur at all. If learned behaviors are so effective in getting a useful trait passed from generation to generation at the cultural level, there will presumably be no selection pressure for the spread of genetic factors favoring that trait. Simpson claimed that in circumstances where flexible responses are required to meet the challenges of changing environments learning can be presumed to be more effective than hard-wired responses. To show this, he deployed against Baldwin the same argument that Baldwin had used against the Lamarckians. If learned behaviors do become genetically underwritten, a population will be swapping "short term and more plastic [learned behaviors] for long term, but more rigid adaptations," thus subverting the very point of the Baldwin effect (Simpson 1953: 116). On an even more skeptical note, Simpson added that it would be very difficult to tell for sure if it *had* happened, since the theoretical presumption must always be that existing adapted gene complexes with wide norms of reaction are merely surfacing under new selection pressures rather than that learning is antecedently causing or guiding a shift in gene frequencies. Given the variety of nature, as well as an analogy between the Baldwin effect and C. H. Waddington's "genetic assimilation" to which I will turn momentarily, Simpson was loathe to deny that the phenomenon might have occurred at some time or another (Simpson 1953: 115). Still, he concluded that there is "singularly little concrete ground for the view that [the Baldwin effect] is a frequent and important element in adaptation" (Simpson 1953: 115).

Simpson's interest in the Baldwin effect was stimulated by Conrad H. Waddington's mention of it in connection with "genetic assimilation," which was the subject of an article by Waddington in the same issue of *Evolution* as Simpson's 1953 article (Waddington 1953). Waddington had reliably and replicably shown that strong shocks to fruit flies will produce phenotypes that subsequently, and often quite rapidly, become genetically heritable in later generations, even those not subjected to the initiating shock. In Waddington's view, as well as that of other respectable Darwinians of the Modern Synthesis, this happens because the shock "destabilizes a developmental system and reveals genetic variation that was previously concealed" at a much deeper level than, say, alternative alleles for darker and lighter pepper moths (Waddington 1962: 226–227). Presumably, this is what is happening in cases that one might be tempted to chalk up to the Baldwin effect. In contrast to the genetic-variation-preserving thrust of adaptation at the genetic level and the presumed plasticity at the phenotypic level that a flexible genetic inheritance favors, the Baldwin effect, as redescribed by Simpson, applies at best to unusual cases in which a population under very strong selection pressure (at the margins of its range, for example, as Huxley suggests) genetically "assimilates" a culturally transmitted phenotype by narrowing the genetic norm of reaction to a vanishing point. So described, Simpson wrote, "The Baldwin effect would ensue when selection for the ability to acquire an adaptive character so narrows the developmental range that the character would usually or invariably appear" (Simpson 1953: 116). Presumably, this will take place under conditions where loss of genetic and phenotypic flexibility is a small cost to pay under dire circumstances for basic survival. Any port will do in a storm. Leaving aside the troublingly disanalogous fact that phenotypes under genetic assimilation are not necessarily adapted, this scenario forms the basis for comparing the Baldwin effect to genetic assimilation within the framework of the Modern Synthesis. Even here, a genetic basis, albeit a newly scrambled one, precedes the expression of an adapted phenotype and so preserves the insistence of the makers of the Modern Synthesis that genetic change both precedes and causes adaptations.

This view of the conditions under which something that might be called the Baldwin effect could conceivably occur was, I want to suggest, influential in the subsequent dismissal of the putative phenomenon altogether. This negative reading is registered most clearly in Ernst Mayr's 1963 *Animal Species and Evolution*. In reviewing Simpson's version of the argument, Mayr pronounced the very idea of the Baldwin effect incoherent. For Mayr, the Baldwin effect falls between two stools. Baldwin's original version, he asserts, "has no validity" at all. In assuming that "organic selection" is an alternative to natural selection, Baldwin implies not a reconciliation of Darwinism and Lamarckism, but a disguised or cryptic form of Lamarckism in which phenotypic innovation is said actually to cause new genotypes rather than to favor a new arrangement or unconcealment of already existing genetic variation (Mayr 1963: 610). This was a pointed remark in light of the recent Lysenko affair. But even under Simpson's redescription, Mayr could not imagine *any* circumstances in which there would be an adaptive advantage to genetically fixing a previously flexible phenotype in a way that is comparable to genetic assimilation. As a universal rule, Mayr writes, "Those genes will be selected . . . which produce genotypes with an optimal modifiability of the phenotype" (Mayr 1963: 612). There is no reason to think that adaptive natural selection could play a role, then, in collapsing norms of reaction, even in cases where stress is involved. Indeed, it is just such cases that led Mayr to assert that his pet theory of allopatric speciation by means of wholesale genetic reorganization at the periphery of an isolated population is actually paradigmatic of adaptive natural selection at work.

Dobzhansky seems to have agreed (Dobzhansky 1970: 211). The premium placed by his theory of "balancing selection" on retaining vast amounts of genetic variation in natural populations was designed to highlight the presumption that adaptive natural selection favors plastic phenotypes, phenotypes with very wide norms of reaction. Both Mayr and Dobzhansky thought that selection, in favoring the evolution of phenotypic plasticity, also favors the development of cultural transmission. As the philosopher Robert Brandon puts the point, "One would expect a species subjected to [changing] conditions to become highly plastic and to develop culture" (Brandon 1996: 82). For the makers of the Modern Synthesis, culture is natural selection's greatest achievement. But the very reasons for thinking this also imply that there is no path back from culture to a world in which behavior is governed directly by natural selection. It was this strongly autonomous view of culture that in my view turned the modest retreat proposed by E. O. Wilson's "sociobiology" into a full-scale crisis in evolutionary biology in the 1970s.

To describe the Baldwin effect in ways that made it analogous to, or even a "special kind of," genetic assimilation was, then, bad news for the Baldwin effect. Simpson's choice of the term "effect," whether intentionally or not, could not have been better calculated to expose the general idea that learning guides evolution to obloquy. The term "effect" is associated with a theory-neutral phenomena that is waiting to be explained by this or that theory. Genetic assimilation is an effect in this sense. But the Baldwin effect is not. No straightforward, theoretically neutral case of the Baldwin effect has ever been reported or agreed on. Rather, the Baldwin effect is a hypothesis that might be used to explain this or that phenomenon, such as the mix of learning and instinct in bird song, foot calluses, or lactose tolerance. Even then, however, Baldwinian explanations are no better than the theoretical background that licenses them. They were favored by the version of Darwinism assumed by Weismann, Baldwin, and Lloyd Morgan. They were at a considerable disadvantage, however, in a conceptual environment dominated by Simpson, Dobzhansky, Mayr.

This disadvantage can be seen clearly in the fact that, much to Waddington's annoyance, repeated comparisons of the Baldwin effect to genetic assimilation in the 1950s and 1960s were soon casting a shadow over the genetic assimilation itself. While no one doubted that it happened sometimes, it was generally treated as at most a peripheral, and not very important, mechanism of possible evolutionary change. Dobzhansky was even more dismissive. He called it a "tour de force," but one "achieved by manipulation of the external rather than the genetic environment" (Dobzhansky 1970: 211). Dismissing genetic assimilation in this way also meant driving a stake through the heart of the Baldwin effect. Comparison between genetic assimilation and "alleged Lamarckian inheritance is superficial," Dobzhansky proclaimed (Dobzhansky 1970: 211). This reading became the dominant one because the makers of the Modern Synthesis, having marginalized developmental biology from the outset, could not see why Waddington had fancied the comparison between the Baldwin effect and genetic assimilation in the first place. In large part, that is because on-togenetic processes were off their screen; what Dobzhansky and Mayr saw was only natural selection operating on adult phenotypes in populations. It was quite otherwise for Waddington. While he admitted that genetic as-similation is the manifestation of preexisting genetic variation, Wadding-ton's point was that whether and when variation is triggered depends on the crucial role of formed and forming tissues in "transferring competence" during the embryological process. Because Dobzhansky, Mayr, and Simp-son considered the values of only two variables, genotypes and phenotypes, rather than attending to the role of embryology, which Waddington took to be the most proximate causal factor, they were inclined, according to Scott Gilbert, to put Waddington on the side of the Lamarckians and so to call his Darwinian credentials into question (Gilbert 1991: 205, n. 53).

4   Two Contemporary Baldwin Boosters

In view of the growing hostility of Simpson, Mayr, and Dobzhansky that I have recounted, it is odd that the Baldwin effect, or evolutionary scenarios that choose to go by that name, should have come into vogue again. For his part, Deacon acknowledges the tension; he speaks of either "Darwinian *or* Baldwinian" explanations (Deacon 1997: 328). Dennett, on the other hand, claims that the Baldwin effect is "a no longer controversial wrinkle in orthodox Darwinism" (Dennett, chap. 4, this volume). This conflict re-quires some explanation, especially in view of the fact that it is Deacon, I will suggest, whose version of the Baldwin effect is closer to the spirit of the mid-century Modern Synthesis than Dennett's. Dennett's approach reflects the influence of post-Synthesis versions of Darwinism in which game-theory and genetic algorithms are deployed in conjunction with selfish genes to trace the evolution of optimimally adapted functional modules, in-cluding, perhaps, a "module" for language.

In *The Symbolic Species,* Deacon invokes the Baldwin effect in the course of trying to explain the same things that Dennett wants to explain: the rapid evolution of brain, language, and representationally mediated intentional activity. The details of his case are not relevant in the present context, ex-cept to note that Deacon thinks that the acquisition of even a minimal ca-pacity for using symbols creates a niche in which very strong selection pressures were brought to bear against members of human populations who failed to acquire this capacity. Rather than being a mere side effect of an enlarged brain, protolinguistic capacities may well have helped (in a co-evolutionary way) cause the brain's expansion, as well as other species-specific adaptations, such as changes in the position of the larynx that permit enhanced vocalization.

In developing this argument, Deacon prepares the way by putting a Baldwinian spin on two well-known stories: lactose tolerance among herding populations, and selection in favor of heterozygotes that confer some protection against malaria. Deacon is aware that orthodox neo-Darwinian stories are available for both phenomena. In human populations that follow herds, alleles that allow infants to digest milk are not shut down immediately after weaning, as is normally the case, but instead remain operative at increasingly deferred points in the life cycle. The Modern Synthesis can easily interpret this by saying that members of the relevant subpopulations deferred shutting down genes for breaking down lactose *before* they became radically dependent on milk products, not (or at least dominantly) the other way around. The case of sickle-cell anemia and resistance to malaria has an even more canonical explanation. It is a virtual paradigm of Dobzhansky's theory of balancing selection, not of the Baldwin effect. The benefit conferred by having an allele that sickles blood cells, thereby conferring some degree of resistance to malaria, far outweighs the resulting illness in circumstances where the alternative is death, and so spreads rapidly through the population. (The cost-benefit ratio changes, of course, when these populations migrate to, or in this case were transported to, malaria-free environments.) Nonetheless, Deacon puts a decidedly Baldwinian accent on these cases by stressing the initiating and sustaining, and hence *causally primary,* role of cooperating human agents in creating and maintaining the environmental conditions down which cascades of gene frequency changes by means of natural selection can, and, in his opinion, must have proceeded to support the new dependence on an environment shaped by human activity. This is what Deacon calls "niche construction." "Whether Darwinian or Baldwinian," he writes, "the evolution of genetically based adaptations is a function of the long-term invariance of conditions that affect reproductive success" (Deacon 1997: 328). Accordingly, Deacon writes that

It is no coincidence that the human populations with the highest percentage of lactose-tolerant adults are those where animals have been herded for the longest time, and those with the least lactose tolerance are those where herding was introduced most recently or not at all. (Deacon 1997: 323)

and that the

sickle cell trait spread quite rapidly in Africa in recent prehistory because of human activity. . . . Probably the critical historical event that catapulted malaria to an epidemic disease was the introduction of agriculture and animal husbandry into Africa between five and ten thousand years ago. This culturally transmitted practice modified the tropical environment to create the perfect breeding ground for mosquitoes. . . . The human population was thrust into a context in which powerful selection favored reproduction of any mutation that conferred some resistance to malaria. (Deacon 1997: 323)

Deacon calls these cases "Baldwinian *rather than* Darwinian" in part because he explicitly dissents from the insistence of the lions of the mid-century Synthesis that adaptive natural selection always favors phenotypic flexibility (Deacon 1997: 323). About that they were just wrong. In some cases, he argues, it makes sense to lose phenotypic flexibility in order to ensure environmental stability and adaptedness to that stable environment. Soon enough the disadvantage conferred on members of a population that cannot more or less effortlessly acquire the behavior in question will be felt. An environment in which maintaining a learned behavior has become a matter of life and death survival for the population in question (shades of fly-swatter selection) will thus incur "costs in terms of learning times, costs for failing to learn, or learning incorrectly, and costs for simply being inefficient" (Deacon 1997: 326). In these conditions, Deacon argues, "any predisposition that even remotely contributes to producing a more reliable and efficient response will be positively selected" (Deacon 1997: 326). Deacon sees this dynamic at work in the progressive autonomization of language acquisition abilities.

In recent work, Deacon has had new thoughts, some of which he shares in the present volume (Deacon, chap. 5, this volume). His stress on the agency of organisms, especially of organisms that possess culture, in constructing environments that in turn exert their own selection pressures remains a central theme in his work. But Deacon has become increasingly insistent that the learned traits in question—herding in the case of lactose-tolerance, slash-and-burn agriculture in the case of sickle-cell anemia, and language-acquisition coincident upon an enlarged brain—are not genetically assimilated. They require learning, and plenty of it. Nonetheless, to the extent that the new behavior becomes absolutely necessary for survival and reproduction in a cultural niche, gene frequencies do change radically in favor of all manner of *supportive* adaptations that render the learned behavior more easily and universally acquired. There are no genes for herding cows, or for planting crops—or, indeed, for a "language instinct," at least of the sort postulated by Steven Pinker (Deacon 1997: 328). Nonetheless, as populations become dependent on herding, even at the cost of some digestive distress, regulatory genes that defer the shutting down of lactose-digesting metabolic pathways spread quickly and thoroughly through the population. So do genes that confer protection against malaria. An even more telling case is the dependence of modern humans on agriculture to supply ascorbic acid. Although ascorbic acid is obligatory, selection pressures that would unmask buried metabolic pathways that supply this vital nutrient metabolically are screened off by the construction and maintainance of cultural practices that ensure it by other means. Still, peripheral genetic adaptations that support the relevant learned behaviors, such as the proclivity to attend visually to yellow and orange oval shapes against a green background, do spread quickly and pervasively through the population. So too with the traits that support language acquisition.

Since writing *The Symbolic Species,* Deacon has resisted thinking of his account of language-acquisition as straightforwardly Baldwinian. The Baldwin effect refers, in his view, to the unmasking of previously hidden genetic variation under conditions in which strong selection pressures, and collapsed norms of reaction, are in play (Deacon, chap. 5, this volume). That is essentially Simpson's mid-century interpretation, to which Deacon cleaves. By this standard, language acquisition, which on Deacon's view deflects natural selection from fixing a trait genetically by favoring supportive adaptations, is a kind of Baldwinism in reverse. Nothing is in the genome that doesn't have to be. But what is there supports an obligatory dependence on learning by way of supportive genetic adaptations that often go to fixation. Accordingly, language acquisition is even further from genetic assimilation, which the makers of the Modern Synthesis conflated with the Baldwin effect simply because from the perspective of their conceptual scheme both seemed to have in common a certain "pseudo-Lamarckism" (Deacon, chap. 5, this volume). Having teased these concepts apart, however, we might profitably recall from our earlier discussion that Simpson's and Mayr's reconstruction of the Baldwin effect involved recasting it in something other than its original conceptual framework. This being so, Deacon's "reverse Baldwinism" might actually be closer, ceteris paribus, to Baldwin's and Lloyd Morgan's original concept of the relation between organic selection and evolutionary change than it would seem from a mid-century perspective. Baldwin and Lloyd Morgan too required strong selection pressures, sometimes at the cost of death; a collapse of norms of reaction; a conception of organisms as agents that are able to construct and maintain their own environments; and the (anti-Spencerian) notion that germ-line modifications support and reinforce, rather than actually replace, phenotypic plasticity.

These reflections reveal a certain continuity between Deacon and the Modern Synthesis. This impression is reinforced by noting that Dobzhansky's heir, Richard Lewontin, has also stressed the causal primary of niche construction, not only in the human case, but in the case of most organisms (Lewontin 1983; 1992: 32)—although, unlike Deacon, Lewontin will not retreat an inch from the view that natural selection has produced in humans full cultural autonomy and phenotypic plasticity, as his implacable hostility to sociobiology, evolutionary psychology, and to what he regards as the fatuous promises of the Human Genome Project shows (Lewontin 1992). In the matter of evolving genetic adaptations that help make certain kinds of learning obligate, moreover, Deacon appeals to the vastly enlarged supply of genetic variation that gene-reduplication and exon-shuffling have made available. But the insistence on new sources of genetic variability that can be maintained in human populations has since the 1940s been the hallmark of Dobzhansky's version of Darwinism. Here too Deacon reveals his continuity with received theory. It is also possible, however, that Deacon's "reverse Baldwinism," which increasingly stresses the interaction between cultural and genetic evolution, might resonate with something like Developmental Systems theory, which does not countenance privileging genes as developmental resources, but instead treats niche construction by human activity, Waddington-style embryology, and genes as mutually reinforcing, and presumptively causally equal, developmental resources (Griffiths, chap. 10, this volume). These developments will appear non-Darwinian only if the term Darwinism is exclusively reserved for the optimization thinking that has become increasingly well known in recent decades. (See Weber and Depew and 2001.)

In contrast to Deacon, who takes note of his differences with the Modern Synthesis because he shares a good deal of its conceptual background, Dennett tends to downplay the discontinuity between the orthodox Synthesis and his version of Darwinism, at least when it comes to the legitimacy of the Baldwin effect. In *Darwin's Dangerous Idea,* Dennett admits that the Baldwin effect has "typically been shunned by overcautious thinkers, because they thought it smacked of the Lamarckian heresy" (Dennett 1995: 80). We can guess that he means Simpson, Mayr, and Dobzhansky. After the work of Hinton, Nowlan, and Maynard Smith, however, Dennett argues that the Baldwin effect should be considered "no longer a controversial wrinkle in orthodox Darwinism" (Dennett, chap. 4, this volume). He appears to conclude that it was a merely contingent fact—lack of access to computational machines, programs, and models—rather than conceptual disagreement that led people like Simpson, Dobzhansky, and Mayr to fail to understand that the Baldwin effect can be part of the "orthodox" Synthesis itself. (In a similar way, Dennett argues that Darwin himself failed to grasp fully the nature and consequences of what Dennett still takes to be *his,* namely Darwin's, Dangerous Idea [Dennett 1995].)

It is no doubt true that Dennett would like to recruit the authority of Modern Synthesis for his version of genetic Darwinism. Nonetheless, the differences between his version and the Modern Synthesis are fairly large. Dennett turns to the Baldwin effect as a way of accounting for the rapid co-evolution of the physiological, mental, linguistic, and behavioral characteristics that mark off our quite young species from other hominids, and perhaps hominids from primates. Dennett has Baldwin, as reconstructed by Richards, holding that a "species will evolve faster because of its greater capacity to discover design improvements in the neighborhood" through a process of behavioral trial and error (Dennett 1995: 79). ("Design improvements" is Dennett's concept, not Richards's or Baldwin's.) As Dennett makes clear in his contribution to this volume, however, it is not just evolutionary tempo that is in question, but the need to ensure that natural selection moves in a concerted direction as it explores fitness landscapes in what Dennett calls the "design space" that lead toward big brains, behavioral plasticity, and speech (Dennett, chap. 4). Dennett's scenario for the

Baldwin effect relies on the lucky hard-wiring of the neural system of an individual (or perhaps small group of individuals) who happens to perform a "Good Trick," which, if it were to spread in a population, would solve a significant, pressing adaptive problem. "With this Good Trick," Dennett writes, "comes a minimal capacity to 'recognize' (in scare quotes) a tiny bit of progress, to 'learn' something by blind trial and error" (Dennett 1995: 78–79). The required spread through the population is assured by reinforcing the behavior in offspring and other members of the population. Dennett then relies on Hinton and Nowlan, as glossed by Maynard Smith, to show that such learned and relearned tricks will be favored by reiterated bouts of natural selection moving in the direction pointed by learning. The assumption must be that these selection pressures are very strong, that they move in a concerted direction, and that subsequent gene frequency changes both optimize and autonomize the behaviors in question.

Whether this scenario, or the mechanism on which it rests, is the same as that proposed by Deacon is a matter of dispute. The issue is explored in a subtle three-way exchange among Godfrey-Smith, Dennett, and Deacon in this volume (Godfrey-Smith, Dennett, and Deacon, chap. 6, this volume). On the descriptive surface, however, it is for Dennett a neurological, or perhaps even a genetic, variant rather than wide norms of reaction that is causally responsible for the initial behavior; and learning is seen as capable of marking off evolutionary vectors not because a shared environment brought into existence by the spread of the novel behavior exerts a new selection pressure on the population as a whole, but because competition among individual members of society for the reproductive benefits brought by the Good Trick is very stiff. This individualist picture accords well with Dennett's own theoretical framework, according to which natural selection itself is a negative feedback process, an "algorithm" for generating and testing variations (Dennett 1995). It accords less well than Dennett might like to admit, however, with the way in which the Baldwin effect was reconstructed by Simpson and other mid-century figures.

Construing natural selection as an algorithm encourages the reader to think of natural selection itself, and not just the adaptations it brings forth, as operating in a concerted, end-oriented, optimizing way, and so justifies Dennett's confidence that the results of genetic algorithms can be read directly into nature's ways. So concerted is the effect of a Good Trick that, according to Dennett, it confers on those who possess it a tiny bit of "look ahead" not only into what is immediately necessary for task at hand, but into the direction of evolution (at least in their lineage) itself. This claim, if interpreted in this way, may well echo Baldwin's and Lloyd Morgan's view that evolution marches in the direction marked off by organic adaptations, or, roughly, learned behaviors. If interpreted charitably, it might be a good account of adaptive dynamics. Nonetheless, the conceptual scheme that permits the first uncharitable interpretation is not, as we have seen, one that could be countenanced by the orthodox Modern Synthesis. While wide arrays of genetic variation in populations allow novel, potentially imitable behaviors to occur in populations of social animals, and in addition confer on populations the genetic plasticity that allows them to remain adapted to changing environments, this very stress on genetic variety and phenotypic plasticity—a conception that is at the core of the fully articulated Modern Synthesis—blocks any sort of "look ahead" that foreshadows, either at the phenotypic or genotypic levels, the direction of evolution itself (Downes, chap. 2, this volume). It was for just this reason that the Baldwin effect was placed under suspicion by the Modern Synthesis. It is also why Deacon, in his second thoughts, has retreated from thinking of the role of learning in evolution as straightforwardly Baldwinian. If the Baldwin effect, under this redescription, does not fall under suspicion in Dennett's work, it is perhaps because his version of genetic Darwinism, while it might very well be superior, differs from that of the Modern Synthesis.

5 An Encouraging Conclusion

In this essay, I have argued for two theses. The first is that there is no theory-neutral empirical phenomenon that can be named "the Baldwin effect." The second is that the term "Baldwin effect" cannot name even a theoretical concept that maintains fixity of reference between Baldwin's version of Darwinism, Simpson's version, and either Dennett's or Deacon's, which themselves diverge. The moral I wish to draw from these claims, however, is a cautionary, and perhaps even an encouraging, one. Just as there was considerable conceptual slippage between the so-called Baldwin effect in its first and second reconstructions, so too there might very well be slippage between the fate of Baldwinism in a new, post-Synthesis framework and how it appeared to Simpson and the other framers of the Modern Synthesis. The very fact that Deacon's version of the Baldwinian idea calls into question what it takes to be arbitrary dogmas of Modern Synthesis—its prohibition on collapsed norms of reaction, for example, or its a priori insistence that gene frequency changes must always precede phenotypic heritability—reinforces the observation that the Modern Synthesis is being buffeted by many challenges, and may, taken as a totality, be a thing of the past. So too does Dennett's refiguring of natural selection, in the age of computation, as a cybernetic process. Admittedly, there is some irony in the circumstance that, if I am right, Deacon's version of the Baldwin effect remains closer to the central principles of orthodoxy than Dennett's. For it is Dennett who professes himself to be drawing out implications of the tradition, while, in dissenting from subsidiary, but influential, hypotheses that were presumably insisted upon by the makers of the Modern Synthesis, Deacon downplays the degree of continuity between his theory and the fundamental principles of orthodoxy. The main lesson, however, is this. The fact that we may be entering into a post-Synthesis period need not be an objection to creative appropriations of the Baldwinian idea by Deacon, Dennett, or anyone else. If the history of Darwinism generally, and of the Baldwin effect specifically, is any guide, we should be wary of dismissing hypotheses just because they do not fit with received interpretive schemes. For it is possible that new appropriations of the general Baldwinian idea may go hand in hand with the emergence, if sometimes obscurely and *in statu nascendi,* of theoretical frameworks that may in the end prove more empirically satisfactory than their predecessors.[6]

Notes

1. It would be possible to argue that Baldwin discovered the principle of operant conditioning. Since Baldwin habitually claimed priority for new ideas in biological psychology, he would have been gratified by this attribution. This is a point made by Paul Griffiths (chap. 10, this volume).

2. Weismann's argument first became known in the English-speaking world in 1889 with a translation of his *Essays upon Heredity and Kindred Biological Problems* (Weismann 1893). They became far more widely known to the reading public, however, and charged with political meaning, only with the appearance in 1893 of an article in *Contemporary Review* entitled "The All-sufficiency of Natural Selection: A Reply to Herbert Spencer" (Weismann 1893).

3. James, who had been attracted to it in his youth, rejected Spencerism, and despised Social Darwinism. In an 1878 letter to his boss, Harvard president Charles Norton Eliot, he had written, "My quarrel with Spencer is not that he makes much of the environment, but that he makes nothing of the glaring and patent fact of subjective interests which cooperate with the environment in molding intelligence" (James to Eliot, November 22, 1878; quoted in Richards 1987: 426–427). James's fidelity to Darwinism is evident in the support he gives Weismann in the final pages of the second edition of his *Principles of Psychology* (James 1890: 678–680). In the same place, however, James reiterated his belief that it would be helpful "if habits could bear fruit outside individual life, and if the modification so painfully acquired by parents' nervous systems could be found ready made at birth in those of the young" (James 1890: 680–681). Alas, James was unclear how this might happen under the exclusive regime of hard inheritance—the very point on which Baldwin and Lloyd Morgan profess to give an answer. Thus James could do little more comfort himself in the final sentenced of his revised masterpiece with the thought that "the actual course of psychogenesis" may be forever occluded as "the slowly gathering twilight closes into utter night" (James 1890: 689).

Dewey's early Darwinism shows signs of having profited from Baldwin's 1895 book, from the press battle in *Science* and the *American Naturalist* that followed in 1896, and perhaps from Lloyd Morgan's lecture tour, which brought him to Illinois. Dewey's earliest recorded thoughts about natural selection stress Baldwin's notion that behavior is shaped by a process of organic selection. He alludes in a review written in 1896 to

those having competent knowledge of details have good reason [for claiming that] not only is one form of life as a whole selected at the expense of other forms [for a population], but one mode of action in the same individual is constantly selected . . . by the success or failure of special acts—the counterpart, I suppose of physiological selection so called. We do not need to go here into the vexed question of the inheritance of acquired characters. We know that through what we call public stimulated and encouraged, while other types are as constantly objected to. . . . What difference in principle exists between this mediation of the acts of the individual by society and what is ordinarily called natural selection I am unable to see. (Dewey, *Early Works* 5:50)

Dewey's insouciant solution to the problem that vexed James, Baldwin, and Lloyd Morgan is to redefine organic selection as itself a form of natural selection, and to think of Baldwin's ontogenetic adaptations simpliciter in the case of humans, because the social environment, and social heredity of humans, constitute, in his view, their species-specific biotic environment. That is why Dewey wrote at the same time, "The unwritten chapter in natural selection is the evolution of environments" (Dewey 1971: 5: 52). This bracketing of what Dewey calls "extreme Weismannism" (Dewey 1971: 4: 212) provides, I suspect, the foundations of his "instrumentalist" brand of pragmatism, and of the opinions about "the influence of Darwinism on philosophy" that he set down in his 1910 essay of the same name (see Godfrey-Smith 1996). I suspect that Dewey neither changed his view nor defended it in subsequent decades, but merely assumed it in all of his work.

4. I am not entirely sure how to reconcile this conception of natural selection with Lloyd Morgan's earlier proposal, cited by Richards (1987): 390, to distinguish between natural selection and "natural elimination," and to identify something close to Baldwin's ontogenetic adaptation as natural selection—the same proposal made by Dewey, except that it seems to be a general claim rather than a special claim about humans.

5. Schmalhausen recognizes that "development is determined not only by the genotype but by environment factors. Therefore, the genotypic expression of both normal organisms and mutants is different in diverse environments" (Schmalhausen 1949: 4). Schmalhausen's term "norms of reaction" names the width of such responses. Schmalhausen does not, however, think that all norms of reaction are either adaptive or adaptations. They include "adaptive modifications of the organism to different environments" (7), but also include "nonadaptive modifications . . . which have not yet attained an historical basis." Indeed, Schmalhausen claims that "all really new reactions are never adaptive" (8). These are, he says, "very unstable," in contrast to "adaptive modifications," which are stable precisely because they have fairly wide norms of reactions, and thus can adjust to all environmental changes that are not so random and capricious that they could never become historical, or adaptive, responses. This has become a fundamental principle of contemporary genetic Darwinism, especially through the work of Dobzhansky (Dobzhansky 1970) and Lewontin (Lewontin 1974). Along the way, however, the term seems to have become ever more restricted to norms of reaction that are adaptations. Schmalhausen's openness on this point may well have influenced Waddington's and even Simpson's comparison of the Baldwin effect with genetic assimilation. For genetic assimilation is sometimes indeed nonadaptive. I owe this point to Allan Love.

6. I am grateful to audiences at Bennington College, the Center for Philosophy of Science, University of Pittsburgh, and the University of Iowa for many good suggestions. An earlier, much different version of the argument in this paper appeared in *Cybernetics and Human Knowing* 7 (2000) 7–20. I am grateful to Soren Brier for comments on that version. I am also grateful to Terry Deacon for helpful comments on the present version.

References

Ackly, D. and M. Littman. (1992). Interaction between learning and evolution. In C. G. Langston, C. Taylor, J. D. Farmer, and S. Rasmussen (eds.), *Artificial Life II*, pp. 487–509. Redwood City, Calif.: Addison-Wesley.

Baldwin, J. M. (1895). *Mental Development in the Child and the Race.* New York: Macmillan.

Baldwin, J. M. (1896a). Heredity and instinct. *Science* 3 (March 20–April 10): 438–441, 558–561.

Baldwin, J. M. (1896b). Physical and social heredity. *American Naturalist* 30 (May) 353, 422–428.

Baldwin, J. M. (1896c). A new factor in evolution. *American Naturalist* 30 (June) 354, 422, 441–451, 536–553.

Baldwin, J. M. (1902). *Development and Evolution.* New York: Macmillan.

Brandon, R. N. (1996). Phenotypic plasticity, cultural transmission, and human sociobiology. In R. N. Brandon, *Concepts and Methods in Evolutionary Biology.* Cambridge: Cambridge University Press.

Cope, E. D. (1896). *Primary Factors in Organic Evolution.* Chicago: Open Court.

Deacon, T. (1997). *The Symbolic Species.* New York: W. W. Norton.

Dennett, D. (1991). *Consciousness Explained.* Boston: Little, Brown.

Dennett, D. (1995). *Darwin's Dangerous Idea.* New York: Simon and Schuster.

Depew, D. J. and B. H. Weber (1995). *Darwinism Evolving: Systems Dynamics and the Genealogy of Natural Selection.* Cambridge, Mass.: Bradford Books/MIT Press.

Dewey, J. (1971). *Early Works,* vols. 4, 5. Edited by Jo Ann Boydston. Carbondale: Southern Illinois University.

Dobzhansky, T. (1970). *Genetics of the Evolutionary Process.* New York. Columbia University Press.

Hinton, G. E. and S. J. Nowlan (1987). How learning can guide evolution. *Complex Systems* 1: 495–502. Reprinted in R. K. Belew and M. Mitchell (eds.), *Adaptive Individuals in Evolving Populations,* pp. 447–453 (Reading, Mass: Addison-Wesley, 1996).

Huxley, J. (1942). *Evolution: The Modern Synthesis.* London: Allen and Unwin.

Gilbert, S. (1991). *A Conceptual History of Modern Embryology.* Baltimore, Md.: Johns Hopkins University Press.

Godfrey-Smith, P. (1996). *Complexity and the Function of Mind.* Cambridge: Cambridge University Press.

James, W. (1890). *The Principles of Psychology,* revised edition. New York: Henry Holt.

Lakatos, I. (1970). Falsification and the methodology of scientific research programmes. In I. Lakatos and A. Musgrave (eds.), *Criticism and the Growth of Knowledge,* pp. 91–195. Cambridge: Cambridge University Press.

Laudan, L. (1977). *Progress and Its Problems: Toward a Theory of Scientific Growth.* Berkeley and Los Angeles: University of California Press.

Lewontin, R. (1974). *The Genetic Basis of Evolutionary Change.* New York: Columbia University Press.

Lewontin, R. (1983). Gene, organisms and environment. In D. S. Bendall (ed.), *Evolution from Molecules to Men,* pp. 273–285. Cambridge: Cambridge University Press.

Lewontin, R. (1992). *Biology as Ideology.* New York: Harper/Perennial.

Lloyd Morgan, C. (1896a). *Habit and Instinct.* London: Arnold.

Lloyd Morgan, C. (1896b). Of modification and variation. *Science* 4 (99) (November 20): 733–739.

Maynard Smith, J. (1987). Natural selection: when learning guides evolution. *Nature* 329: 761–762. Reprinted in R. K. Belew and M. Mitchell (eds.), *Adaptive Individuals in Evolving Populations*, pp. 455–457 (Reading, Mass: Addison Wesley, 1996).

Mayr, E. (1963). *Animal Species and Evolution*. Cambridge, Mass: Harvard University Press.

Osborn, H. F. (1896). A mode of evolution requiring neither natural selection nor the inheritance of acquired characteristics. *Transactions of the New York Academy of Science* 15: 141–148.

Richards, R. J. (1987). *Darwin and the Emergence of Evolutionary Theories of Mind and Behavior*. Chicago: The University of Chicago Press.

Schmalhausen, I. I. (1949). *Factors of Evolution*. Translated I. Dorick, ed. T. Dobzhansky. Philadelphia: Blackison Press.

Simpson, G. G. (1953). The Baldwin effect. *Evolution* 7: 110–117.

Waddington, C. H. (1953). "The Baldwin effect," "genetic assimilation," and homeostasis. *Evolution* 7: 386–387.

Waddington, C. H. (1962). *New Patterns in Genetics and Development*. New York: Columbia University Press.

Watkins, J. (1999). A note on the Baldwin effect. *British Journal for the Philosophy of Science* 50: 417–423.

Weber, B. H. and D. Depew (2001). Developmental systems, Darwinian evolution, and the unity of science. In S. Oyama, P. Griffiths, and R. Gray (eds), *Cycles of Contingency*, pp. 239–253. Cambridge, Mass.: MIT Press/Bradford Books.

Weismann, F. (1891). *Essays on Heredity and Kindred Problems*. Edited by E. Poulton et al. Oxford: Clarendon Press.

Weismann, F. (1893). The all-sufficiency of natural selection: A reply to Herbert Spencer. *Contemporary Review* 64: 309–338, 596–610.

2

Baldwin Effects and the Expansion of the Explanatory Repertoire in Evolutionary Biology

Stephen M. Downes

1 Introduction

The specific focus of this essay is the Baldwin effect. I construe various defenses of the Baldwin effect as attempts to expand the explanatory repertoire in evolutionary biology. There have been numerous proposals to expand the explanatory repertoire in evolutionary biology; some have stuck and have become part of the standard evolutionary story and others have been rejected. Usually such proposals are introduced in the face of phenomena that appear to call for a new kind of explanation. An obvious illustration is Gould and Elredge's proposal that punctuated equilibrium had to be taken seriously to account for a range of data in the fossil record (see Gould 1980). Often the explanatory repertoire expands with less fanfare and in a more piecemeal way. Sometimes the expansionist will only settle for a complete overturning of the old corpus. I argue that there are not sufficient grounds to add the Baldwin effect to our evolutionary explanatory repertoire.

The term "Baldwin effect" has been used by different people to mean different things. In this essay I present several definitions of the Baldwin effect and attempt to show that each can be understood as characterizing a range of phenomena. Most of these classes of phenomena can readily be accounted for by what I take to be a standard evolutionary story. Here I assume a somewhat simple-minded distinction between phenomena and explanatory mechanisms. The Baldwin effect was proposed as a mechanism of evolution that was consistent with Darwinian principles. As such we might expect that the mechanism is invoked to account for ranges of perplexing phenomena that are not satisfactorily accounted for by existing evolutionary mechanisms. My sense of the attempts to revive the Baldwin effect since Baldwin's time is that they can involve a confusion between phenomena and mechanism. Some authors who discuss the Baldwin effect assume that it is an explanatory mechanism and yet they do not even provide an example of a phenomenon that calls for such special explanation. Of course, such assumptions may be entirely theoretically grounded and as a result I look into some of the theoretical arguments that are taken to support the postulation of Baldwin effects.

There are two crude parameters that guide my considerations about expansion in accounting for issues relevant to mind and evolution. An expansionist move that remains consistent with evolutionary principles can neither endorse Lamarckism nor progressivism. The kind of Lamarckian view that I have in mind is that an individual organism's needs lead to that organism striving to serve them, resulting in morphological modifications to the organism that are passed on to its offspring. The kind of progressivism I have in mind is to take the perfection of the human mind and brain to be the culmination of evolution.[1] Many progressivists also hold that conscious intelligent action has a hand in directing evolution. Most expansionists steer clear of Lamarckism but some contemporary expansionists appear to adhere to a version of progressivism.

I start by introducing Baldwin's original definition of the Baldwin effect and then I examine various definitions since his. In this survey of the terrain I distinguish between definitions that emphasize the role of mind or consciousness in evolution versus those that emphasize more general phenotypic plasticity. Next I attempt to clarify the relation between Waddington's genetic assimilation and Baldwin effects. I go on to critically review two recent examples of explanatory appeals to the Baldwin effect: Daniel Dennett's (1995) and Terrence Deacon's (1997). I then turn to the idea of speeding evolution up and argue that an appeal to Baldwin effects cannot be motivated simply by a demonstration of the existence of high rates of evolution. I argue that there appears to be no clear empirical evidence for Baldwin effects construed as mind-directed evolution and that there are no satisfactory theoretical grounds so far for proposing the Baldwin effect as a new evolutionary mechanism. Several types of phenomena have been clustered under the Baldwin effect label and although they may share some features at a high level of generality, they are not examples of the same effect. I argue that various effects of behavior on evolution have been empirically characterized and that a start can be, and has been, made on providing evolutionary explanations of them without appealing to an independent Baldwin effect mechanism.

2   The Baldwin Effect

Baldwin's name is associated with the idea that "biological evolution operated not as a blind mechanical process but as one governed by mind" (Richards 1987: 451).[2] Baldwin was writing at a time when Lamarck was still considered a viable option. The pull of Lamarck was strong for many in the late nineteenth and early twentieth century and Baldwin was clear to emphasize his Darwinian commitments. Baldwin in fact was clearer than Darwin himself about his commitment to a non-Lamarckian approach to evolution. The phenomena Baldwin was most interested in accounting for were human behavioral patterns. He was ultimately interested in developing what we might now call a Darwinian social psychology. The route to this was via an account of the relation between acquired behavior and instinctual behavior. Darwin had set up the problem, and left himself open to the charge of Lamarckism, in *The Descent of Man*. He wrote: "I am ... very far from wishing to deny that instinctive actions may lose their fixed and untaught character, and be replaced by others performed by the aid of the free will. On the other hand, some intelligent actions, after being performed during several generations, become converted into instincts and are inherited, as when birds on oceanic islands learn to avoid man" (1871: 69). The appeal to the will had a Lamarckian air to it, as Lamarck had said that change in individual need led to change in individual striving resulting in modification that was passed on to offspring. But later in the same passage Darwin sounds more Darwinian: " ... the greater number of more complex instincts appear to have been gained in a wholly different manner, through the natural selection of variations of simpler instinctive actions" (1871: 69). This is the kind of account Darwin usually provides for the origin of intellectual and emotional faculties in humans in *The Descent of Man*. Baldwin foresaw a problem here. He thought that the unit of selection was not the "congenital variations taken alone," for example, Darwin's inherited instincts, but the combination of congenital characters and acquired modifications. His intuition was that what made an organism successful was the whole constellation of its physiological and behavioral traits, whether the behavior was acquired or instinctual. Hence, selection acted upon acquired as well as congenital traits.

Baldwin confuses his readers by quoting his own works, or slipping into previous works in his various elaborations of his view. I find one of the more readable accounts to be in *Darwin and the Humanities* (1909) and much of Robert Richards's (1987) useful characterization of Baldwin's view is derived from *Development and Evolution* (1902). Here is Baldwin:

The variations which we find available for physical inheritance are congenital changes; the utility of individual modifications is confined to their influence in screening, supplementing and preserving the natural equipment of individuals and species, and thus directing the course of evolution. We have no reason to depart from this position in the matter of mental variations and the education of the individual. Mental characters already congenital are inherited; and the plasticity, which intelligence carries with it, is a congenital character. There is no evidence of the transmission of the results of mental education or experience; but both physical and mental endowments and the variations arising in them are subject to continuous physical transmission. So far the consistent application of Darwinian principles. (1909: 27–28)

So intelligence is a form of plasticity that is heritable and although the results of experience or education cannot be passed on, the advantages gained by heritable plasticity can be. These advantages may ultimately be translated into distinct heritable characteristics over time.

Baldwin is in a more progressivist mode in the following passage: We see in these functions [imitation and play], as in the more developed intelligent functions, ways in which many of the organic processes . . . may be directly supplemented, by the creature's efforts consciously directed, to the actual saving of its life. This becomes then a capital instance of the operation of 'organic selection;' of the union and joint utility of congenital and acquired characters, for the incidence of natural selection. *Since the utility attaches to the combination* [emphasis in original], it is the combination that has survived in various forms, reaching its culmination in the mind and brain of man. (1909: 25)

And more succinctly, ". . . evolution has advanced by the aid, and in the direction, of conscious adjustment" (1909: 20). Richards nicely summarizes Baldwin's intent in the following passage:

Baldwin envisioned as the paradigm for his principle animals' acquiring innate behaviors similar to behaviors they originally had to learn. If a group of animals migrates into a new environment for which they initially lack congenital adaptations, those plastic enough to accommodate themselves through conscious learning will survive. Their ontogenetic behaviors will buffer them against the winnowing hand of natural selection. This safety net, according to Baldwin, will allow natural selection opportunity to accumulate chance variation that follow the path laid down by the acquired behaviors, which indeed have already been favored by selection. (Richards 1987: 482)

A few points of clarification are in order here. Baldwin was an unabashed progressivist. Progressivists (see Ruse 1999) take the perfection of the human mind and brain to be the culmination of evolution. Many also hold that our conscious intelligent action has a hand in directing evolution. Baldwin's progressivism is evidenced in part by his view that we could develop higher moral principles by practicing them enough so that natural selection could take over. It was reasonable for him to have thought this a Darwinian view since Darwin expressed a similar view about morals and intelligence in *The Descent of Man* (1871: 129). Baldwin was interested in promoting the role of conscious intelligence in directing evolution without collapsing into a Lamarckian view.

The history of the Baldwin effect from this point on has been a history of attempts to define it coherently. Discussion of the Baldwin effect appeared in literature on birdsong and in other discussions of adaptive behavior but current discussion has been directed by an influential paper of Gaylord Simpson's that appeared in *Evolution* in 1953.[3] Simpson may not have coined the term "Baldwin effect" but he puts it to good use and rejects the misleading term "organic selection" that Baldwin favored. Simpson takes the Baldwin effect to be that "characters individually acquired by members of a group of organisms may eventually, under the influence of selection, be reinforced or replaced by similar hereditary characters" (1996: 99). This is an important expansion of the view from Baldwin's consideration of mental traits or conscious effort to the influence of any ontogenetic adaptation on selection.[4] According to Simpson, the relevant traits are "behavioral, physiological, or structural modifications that are not hereditary as such but that are advantageous for survival, i.e., are adaptive for the individuals having them" (1996: 103). The new definition characterizes the Baldwin effect as the influence of ontogenetic adaptation on selection. We will delay further discussion of this point until later but it is worth mentioning now that Simpson was not defining the Baldwin effect simply out of passing interest, he was defining it in order to argue it did not exist as an independent factor from natural selection.

Another influential account of the Baldwin effect comes from Hinton and Nowlan's (1996) paper in which they claim to have demonstrated a context in which Baldwin effects have a role in speeding up evolution. Hinton and Nowlan present a computational model that they claim shows that simple organisms that can learn to deal with a fixed environment evolve faster than those that cannot learn. They put the point as follows: "... learning organisms ... evolve much faster than their non-learning equivalents, even though the characteristics acquired by the phenotype are not communicated to the genotype" (1996: 447). They stress that they have only modeled this phenomena computationally and that some of their biological assumptions are highly unrealistic, but perhaps the nice summary and endorsement Maynard Smith provided of their results in *Nature* helped some to think that they conclusively demonstrated the effect in action.

Maynard Smith defines the Baldwin effect in a characteristically clear and concise way: "If individuals vary genetically in their capacity to learn, or to adapt developmentally, then those most able to adapt will leave most descendants, and the genes responsible will increase in frequency. In a fixed environment, when the best thing to learn remains constant, this can lead to the genetic determination of a character that, in earlier generations, had to be acquired afresh in each generation" (1996: 456). Maynard Smith betrays an allegiance to a Simpson type construal of the effect in his locution "adapt developmentally." In contrast Hinton and Nowlan focus on learning rather than the broader issue of ontogenetic adaptation. Maynard Smith also says "Hinton and Nowlan show that there are contexts in which learning (or developmental flexibility) speeds up evolution" (457).

Let us look at two further definitions before tabulating them with respect to their fundamental assumptions. Dennett says that "what Baldwin discovered was that creatures capable of 'reinforcement learning' not only do better individually than creatures that are entirely hardwired; their species will evolve faster because of its greater capacity to discover design improvements in the neighborhood" (1995: 79); and that Baldwin demonstrated that "animals, *by dint of their own clever activities in the world* [emphasis in original], might hasten or guide the further evolution of their species" (1995: 77). These definitions focus more on the influence of conscious intelligence on evolution and are consistent with the account that Dennett provides in earlier work (1991), but he also alludes to a broader conception of the effect: "In the long run, natural selection—redesign at the genotype level—will tend to *follow the lead of* and *confirm* [emphasis in original] the directions taken by the individual organisms' successful explorations—redesign at the individual or phenotype level" (1995: 78). On one construal, Dennett's "successful explorations" could be ontogenetic adaptations of any kind.[5]

Finally, Deacon calls the effect "Baldwinian evolution." He defines it as follows: "Baldwin suggested that learning and behavioral flexibility can play a role in amplifying and biasing natural selection because these abilities enable individuals to modify the context of natural selection that affects their future kin" (1997: 322). And further ". . . Baldwin's theory explains how behaviors can effect evolution, but without the necessity of claiming that responses to environmental demands acquired during one's lifetime could be passed directly on to one's offspring . . ." (322). This definition focuses on learning or acquired behavior but is more general in the sense that it ambiguates the actual relation between behavior and evolution. For example, if an organism moves to a new niche, its behavior has effected the context of selection, but this is presumably not what Baldwin had in mind. I will have more to say on this point below.

Here is a classification of the content of various definitions of the Baldwin effect and an attribution of the definitions to the authors considered here:

A. Selection acts on the organism as a whole, including its ontogenetic adaptations.

B. Selection acts on the organism including its learned behavior.

1. Ontogenetic adaptation directs evolution.

2. Behavior has a direct effect on evolution.

3. Learning alters the rate and direction of evolution.

4. Mind or consciousness alters the rate and direction of evolution.

Baldwin: A, B, 1, 3, 4.

Simpson: 1, 3.

Hinton and Nowlan: B, 3.

Maynard Smith: B, 1, 3.

Dennett: 3, 4, 1.

Deacon: A, B, 2, 4.

So we have a general and a specific claim about organisms as the unit of selection and then three different claims about the relation between onto-genetic adaptation and selection. Definition 2 seems to be the most general and uninteresting here. An example of 2 is the above example of moving to a new niche. I will argue later that these kinds of cases are ubiquitous and hardly need precipitate the search for a new agent of evolutionary change. Claim 1 is the more general case of 3 that Simpson and Maynard Smith add to the definition. Claim 4 is what Dennett argues that Baldwin established in a way consistent with Darwin. Before discussing rates of evolution and specific examples, I first want to turn to another issue of terminology.

3   Baldwin and Waddington

Godfrey-Smith introduces a distinction between two further issues at stake in the discussion of the Baldwin effect, and related effects, that is relevant here (1990; chap. 3, this volume). He takes the important components of Baldwin effects to be: (i) the evolutionary value of plasticity and (ii) genetic assimilation. If we combine this distinction with my breakdown of the definitions of the Baldwin effect from above, we can shed some light on the relation between genetic assimilation and the Baldwin effect.

Several authors refer to the Baldwin effect as if it is genetic assimilation. Dawkins (1982) refers to the Baldwin/Waddington effect and provides a definition of this combined concept in his glossary (44; 284). Deacon (1997) and Plotkin (1988) both seem to assume that the Baldwin effect and Waddington's genetic assimilation are the same phenomenon. I think that this collapse is a mistake that arises from conflating two distinct meanings of the term "genetic assimilation." Waddington proposed the term genetic assimilation for the phenomenon of an acquired trait, for example, a trait produced by environmental shock during early development, becoming genetically determined in subsequent generations (see, e.g., 1996). Waddington believed that there was existing genotypic variation in the genome of the relevant organism and that this variation could be exploited in the event of extreme environmental change, for example, heat shocks in early development. Hinton and Nowlan and Dennett appeal to another construal of genetic assimilation. This is the idea that genetic change may ultimately take place as a result of fortuitous mutations. This is genetic assimilation in a different sense. On this view the trait ultimately becomes heritable due to being coded for by the newly produced gene.[6]

There are a few further points of contrast between Waddington's genetic assimilation and Baldwin effects. Claims 1 and 3 above are examples of the claim that plasticity has evolutionary value, and they are both claims about adaptive traits. Neither constrain our account of how a previously acquired trait becomes fixed. In contrast, as Williams forcefully argued, Waddington's genetic assimilation does not necessarily describe adaptive traits (Williams, 1966).[7]

Second, there are several ways to account for the phenomenon of Waddington-style genetic assimilation. Waddington's (1996) own approach appealed to canalization, and more recent support for this kind of view has been derived from experiments that show that Waddington's results cannot be produced in inbred Drosophila populations without genetic variation (Futuyma 1998: 441). Genetic assimilation can also be accounted for by appealing to reaction norms (Simpson 1996). In both the appeal to canalization and reaction norms, the apparent passing of acquired traits into the genome is explained by existing genetic variation.

Genetic assimilation was Waddington's name for the phenomenon of the apparent fixing of acquired traits. The connection many draw between genetic assimilation and the Baldwin effect is that genetic assimilation can be appealed to in accounting for Baldwin effects. This situation is confused by the two distinct concepts of genetic assimilation and the other problems mentioned above. It may be safer to say that the non–Waddington style concept of genetic assimilation may account for a subclass of phenomena labeled as Baldwin effects.

4   Two Recent Defenses of the Baldwin Effect

Dennett and Deacon both present the Baldwin effect as an established mechanism that can be appealed to in explaining phenomena that appear to go against what one would expect from an evolutionary standpoint. I argue that both their defenses of the Baldwin effect as an independent explanatory mechanism fail, but each fail for different reasons.

First let's consider Dennett. Dennett initially introduces the Baldwin effect as a mechanism that can help explain the evolution of consciousness

(1991: 184) but has more recently appealed to the Baldwin effect to show that mind can effect evolution without violating strict Darwinian assumptions (1995). In both *Consciousness Explained* (1991) and *Darwin's Dangerous Idea* (1995), Dennett relies on the same account of the Baldwin effect, which he derives mostly from Hinton and Nowlan with some modifications. His definitions are presented in section 1 above. In *Consciousness Explained* Dennett introduces us to the problem of the evolution of learning and then turns the discussion to the effect of learning on evolution. He says "amazingly, [the capability of learning] not only gives the organisms who have it an edge over their hard-wired cousins who cannot redesign themselves, but also reflects back on the process of genetic evolution and *speeds it up*" (1991: 184). He then says that this phenomenon is known as the Baldwin effect. The conclusion of his section on the Baldwin effect is that learning can speed up evolution, which is a restatement of one of the definitions of the Baldwin effect.

In the discussion in *Darwin's Dangerous Idea,* Dennett emphasizes the mindless and blind character of Darwinian selection and introduces his terminology of a crane: "a sub-process or special feature of a design process that can be demonstrated to permit the local speeding up of the basic, slow process of natural selection, and that can be demonstrated to be itself the predictable product of the basic process" (1995: 76). He then says that Baldwin discovered the Baldwin effect, which is just such a crane. What is being accounted for in this discussion shifts as the account develops. What Dennett appears to conclude is that the Baldwin effect is a mechanism that provides the blind process of selection with some look-ahead, which goes against his own Darwinian position. Dennett agrees with Williams, for example, who says that "[selection] is not a mechanism that can anticipate possible extinction and take steps to avoid it" (1966: 32). There are two problems here: First, Dennett claims that the Baldwin effect is a well-established mechanism of a particular kind, which implies that the mechanism has been invoked in successfully explaining various phenomena, and, second, he appears to claim that it serves a role that conflicts with his own Darwinian picture.

Dennett provides no examples of phenomena that call for explanation by appeal to the Baldwin effect. Rather, he argues for the theoretical plausibility of the Baldwin effect (see Dennett, chap. 4, this volume) for an elaboration of this point). So rather than saying that Baldwin "discovered" the Baldwin effect, perhaps Dennett should say that he is following Baldwin, who also argued for the theoretical plausibility of the Baldwin effect, and providing additional theoretical considerations. My sense is that the decision whether or not to appeal to a new explanatory mechanism is driven, at least to a large extent, by the phenomena we hope to explain. Now it is certainly reasonable for Dennett to argue that if the Baldwin effect, construed as a possible mechanism, is not characterized in a way that is clearly inconsistent with evolutionary theory, then it may be a viable theoretical mechanism. But it would seem that a successful explanation of phenomena that do not succumb to standard evolutionary explanations is still needed to seal the deal in favor of the Baldwin effect. And further, it may be that Dennett's Baldwin effect is consistent with evolutionary theory, because it is an example of an already established evolutionary mechanism, rather than a new independent mechanism. I turn to one particular kind of purely theoretical defense of Baldwin effects below when I discuss changes of evolutionary rate.

The second problem with Dennett's account that I mention above may end up resulting from terminological issues. Dennett makes liberal use of terms such as "design" and "guide." We could take this usage as indicating a compromise of Dennett's Darwinian principles or we could take a more charitable line. For example, in the animal behavior literature, researchers refer to animals' "choices," "intentions," "plans," "strategies," and so on, but the same researchers are careful to point out that these terms are to be understood instrumentally at best. This caveat is especially relevant in the case of ants or bees. When Dennett says that a creature's clever activities "guide the further evolution of their species," "guide" should perhaps be read as shorthand for something like "provide new opportunities for selection." Perhaps Dennett's liberal use of such terminology arises from his interdisciplinary mixing of results, terms, and findings from artificial intelligence and artificial life with those from evolutionary biology.

Deacon has a particular explanadum in mind for the Baldwin effect to explain: how the human brain evolved. He proposes to account for this by appealing to Baldwinian evolution. He argues that "an idea changed the brain" (1997: 322) by which he means symbolic representations directly effected the evolution of the human brain. Language use changed the context of selection leading to the rapid evolution of a large and complex brain. To support this view Deacon appeals to examples that he believes demonstrate the Baldwin effect in action. He relies on a kind of argument from analogy that aims to show that language bears the same relation to brain evolution in general as behavior bears to evolution in the case of his specific examples. The nature of Deacon's examples may be where the problems originate from in his view. For him, some of the best examples of Baldwinian evolution come from cases where "human behaviors have changed natural selection in unexpected ways" (1997: 323). This is consistent with Claim 2 above and, as I have pointed out, 2 seems consistent with numerous relations between behavior and evolution that need not be Baldwin effects, strongly construed. For example, as I pointed out above, if a population moves to a new niche, that behavior can have an evolutionary effect.

Deacon takes some of the relevant examples from Durham's (1991) work on coevolution. The first is the development of lactose tolerance. Durham argues that lactose tolerance developed in populations who engaged in animal husbandry partially as a result of the ingestion of animal milk. Now let's assume for argument's sake that this is true; it has little to do with mind directing evolution or learning changing evolutionary rates. The relevant details are probably best spelled out in the molecular biology of enzyme production. All this aside, the case is hardly analogous to the effect of language use on the evolution of the brain.

Deacon's second example of a Baldwin effect is the spread of sickle-cell anemia. The spread of sickle-cell anemia provides an example of "Baldwinian evolution," because human behavior ultimately led to the rapid proliferation of the trait. Changing agricultural practices in Africa led to an increase in available breeding grounds for the mosquito carrying malaria, and possession of one of the alleles for the sickle-cell trait renders most individuals immune from malaria. This may be the case but it does not motivate an explanatory appeal to nonstandard evolutionary mechanisms. The interesting fact usually focused on about sickle-cell alleles is that having one of them renders the person immune to malaria. As a result, the way the distribution of sickle-cell alleles is accounted for is by appeal to heterozygote selective dominance, a well-understood mechanism. Deacon provides good examples of unusual causal chains leading to the construction of new niches, but similarly effective niches could also have been constructed by climate change or change in the organisms' geographical location. As a result, neither of Deacon's examples strike me as cases where learning altered the course or rate of evolution. And neither seem to be analogous with the effect producing a language might have on the evolution of the brain. The relevant connections still remain to be made.

Neither Dennett nor Deacon is able to defend a viable role for the Baldwin effect as an independent explanatory mechanism. Dennett's Baldwin effect collapses into other standard evolutionary mechanisms, and Deacon examples do not reveal connections between human behavior and evolution that call for the proposal of an independent new mechanism.

5 Rates of Evolution

One way in which the Baldwin effect has been defined is in terms of evolutionary rates. The advantages provided to the organism by learning, for example, change the context of selection so as to speed up the process of fixing on a hereditary solution to the problem previously solved by learning. I want to briefly forestall the idea that evolutionary rate increase alone indicates something unusual or special going on and hence motivates the proposal of a new and independent mechanism such as the Baldwin effect.[8]

Following Hinton and Nowlan, Dennett puts the point about evolutionary rate changes in terms of hill climbing. He compares the situation of hitting upon a needle in a haystack to moving up a nice gradient (1995: 78–79). The idea is that a random search for the one genetic solution to a problem, the needle in the haystack, would take considerably more time than the relevant population moving up a smooth gradient to an adaptive peak. Maynard Smith explains this situation with respect to rates of evolution: In the Hinton and Nowlan model there are alleles labeled 0 and 1 that combine at 20 loci to form one "correct" genotype. This means that there are approximately 10^6 genotypes, one of which has a fitness of 20 and the rest a fitness of 1. "In a sexual population of 1,000 with initial allele frequencies of 0.5, a fit individual would arise about once in 1,000 generations" (1996: 457). (This ignores drift and population sub-division.) But mating would disrupt the optimum genotype and offspring would lose the adaptation, so in fact a sexual population could never evolve the relevant genotype. In the Hinton and Nowlan model, learning can improve the organism's situation and many organisms with the correct genotype were produced in as few as twenty generations. Hence evolution speeds up.

So in a computer model with many idealizations, we can simulate a huge increase in the speed of evolution. But does an increase in the rate of evolution force us to propose a new evolutionary mechanism? The answer to the question is "no." There are many examples of rapid evolution. If we rule out asexual cases, we still have numerous examples. Recent work on transplanted lizards indicated that in as short as a 10- to 14-year period the same species produced distinct, heritable, morphological traits in response to different environments (Losos et al. 1997). William Rice's (1999) work on intersexual interlocus contest evolution demonstrates what he calls "break-neck" evolutionary rates in the morphology of gonads of certain species of Drosophila. Specific examples aside, we encounter an enormous variety of evolutionary rates and numerous mechanisms to explain the very fastest and the slowest. The Baldwin effect cannot be supported as an independent evolutionary mechanism simply on the theoretical ground that it speeds up evolution.[9]

6   The Relations between Learning, Mind, and Evolution

There are many calls to arms to study the relations between learning and evolution or to study the effects of behavior on evolution and Baldwin was probably among the first to attempt to systematically address the issue. I want to modify Simpson's appeal that there are no Baldwin effects, conceived of as independent mechanisms of evolution, while maintaining that there is room to discuss the effect of behavior on evolution. We can make a start on this by appealing to the definitions of the Baldwin effect I listed above.

First, we can see that A and B have been widely discussed under different headings than the Baldwin effect. For example, Lewontin (e.g., 1985) has long argued that A should guide our approach to evolutionary explanation in general. Maybe surprisingly, Dawkins (1982) has examined versions of B while investigating the products of learned and instinctual behavior in his discussions of extended phenotypes. I have already mentioned Claim 1 as guiding work on speciation, for example Mayr leans on this kind of consideration (see Futuyma 1998: chap. 20). Also, there are cases from the bird behavior literature that illustrate particular behavioral patterns in evidence as phylogenetic precursors of associated morphological traits (Alcock 1989). For example, Futuyma introduces Prum's work on courtship displays in Manakins in which Prum demonstrates that plumage traits evolve after the behavior in which they are involved (1998: 581).

The contentious cases that need to be established are those that fit definitions 2, 3, and 4. Definition 2 can appear to be happening in numerous cases. It could even be considered the problem in accounting for adaptation. For example, the lizards Losos (1997) introduced to new islands appeared to adapt ontogenetically and then selection followed. Why would these kinds of cases not have researchers like Losos running for new explanatory mechanisms? I think that no such new mechanisms are sought because an appeal to norms of reaction or to the exploitation of existent genetic variation will do the trick adequately. This is not to say that such appeals have given us the whole story in the relevant case but I think that there are no obvious reasons why these kinds of approaches will not be productive.

What kinds of empirical grounds would it take to convince me that there were Baldwin effects? David Sloan-Wilson (personal communication) tried to convince me by suggesting a scenario that I elaborate on here: If some members of a population of rats could learn how to open Coke cans and some could not, and twenty or so generations down the road the descendants of the Coke can openers could open cans without any instruction, then we might want to say that the learned behavior had become hereditary. The problem here is that Sloan-Wilson and I made up this scenario. Perhaps similar-looking cases in the animal behavior literature make the case. For example, it looked for a while, from around the 1920s, that British Blue Tits were passing on the skill of opening milk bottles to their young. This skill clearly originated from learned behavior given the relative newness of milk bottle tops in the phylogenetic history of Blue Tits. Unfortunately, there was not enough time for selection to get into the act, because milk distribution and packaging changed at the time of World War II and so disrupted the relevant constant feature of the environment for the tits to work on.

I do not have a case of 3 as clear as the imaginary rat case but there are cases, for example derived from the study of bird songs, where acquired behavioral traits do appear to become fixed. I do not find these cases alarming and they do not seem to cry out for explanation by a new mechanism. One obvious point is that a fine-grained study of a behavioral pattern over time in a particular species or cluster of related species would reveal minute differences in the patterns of behavior, even if the behavior ostensibly solved a similar problem. Apparently fixed behavioral solutions could be under the control of quite different genomic sequences than those that coded for the plasticity that produced the learned behavior in the first place (see Dawkins 1982: 25).[10] If one bird transports a seed in flight by piercing it with its thin sharp beak and another carries it by grabbing it between its bills, they have both solved the same problem at one level of analysis. If one form of seed carrying was learned and subsequently the other is demonstrated to be instinctive, we only have a case of the inheritance of an acquired trait at a coarse-grained level of analysis. A further problem is that in a case such as the Blue Tit one, the relevant trait may be passed on by social learning or some such mechanism. Discerning the mode of transmission for such traits requires a great deal of observation and experimental work and often an element of luck, for example, a fortuitous population subdivision.

Definition 4 is the toughest to deal with and the hardest to imagine developing a hard and fast case for. If the claim is weakened to definition B, it seems fair enough. Early humans affected their environment in numerous ways, often, no doubt, as a result of learned behavior. It is also clear that selection regimens are different among language users than among the mute. But the version of 4 that I resist is the idea that consciousness gives an organism a capacity of second-guessing evolution or the capacity of look-ahead. Perhaps such locutions are better replaced by the claim that learned activities enabled by our conscious minds have presented changes in our niches that sometimes have presented significant selection pressure.

7   Conclusion

In summary, there are several ways in which the Baldwin effect has been understood. I have urged that none of the cases in which the Baldwin effect could be appealed to in explaining a range of phenomena warrant the proposal of a new mechanism of evolution. Also, purely theoretical defenses of the Baldwin effect as an independent mechanism are not decisive. The strongest version of the Baldwin effect that Baldwin proposed, encapsulated in my definition 4, always was the most interesting, is still the most contentious, and should be the most suspect. As yet there are no good examples of robust empirical phenomenon that exemplify this mechanism in action.

Acknowledgments

Some of the research for this paper was supported by a fellowship from the Tanner Humanities Center at the University of Utah; the final version was prepared while on a University of Utah Faculty Research Fellowship. Versions of this paper were presented at the ISHPSSB conference in Oaxaca, Mexico and at the University of Minnesota. I am grateful to both audiences for their helpful comments. A subsequent draft was presented at Bruce Weber's Bennington Conference and I am grateful to students and other conference participants. This version has benefited from discussion with Dan Dennett and comments from Mateo Mammeli, Ram Neta, and Rasmus Winther.

Notes

1. This is a view that Lamarck also held.

2. The Baldwin effect was also called "organic selection" and was introduced as a new evolutionary mechanism by both Lloyd Morgan and H. F. Osborn independently from Baldwin.

3. Belew and Mitchell (1996) contains a useful collection of papers on the Baldwin effect and related issues. They include both historically important contributions to the discussion of adaptive behavior and recent approaches in biology, computer science, and psychology.

4. "Ontogentic adaptation" is Sober's term (Sober 1993: 85).

5. This is the construal Dennett prefers (personal communication).

6. Brian Hall provides a detailed and helpful discussion of this point (2001; chap. 8, this volume).

7. Experiments performed since Williams's discussion have produced results consistent with Waddington's work for adaptive traits in Drosophila but this fact need not distract us here (Futuyma 1998: 441).

8. Elliott Sober pointed out that learning and the ability to learn slows down evolution in specific cases. Also Peter Godfrey-Smith pointed out that I should at least agree that learning can have some effect on evolutionary rate. These two points are consistent. If we take the influence on evolutionary rate to be in the direction Sober indicates, my agreeing with Godfrey-Smith need give no support to proponents of Baldwin effects.

9. A further comment is relevant here. Often in popular discussions of evolution there is a presupposition that evolution is of necessity an incredibly slow process. This claim taken at face value is misleading. Claims about evolutionary rates need to be made in relation to particular cases and the relevant levels of explanation need to be made specific.

10. One problematic idealization in the Hinton and Nowlan model is that there is only one genotype that produces the relevant behavior. A more likely scenario is that learned behavior can be replaced by a hereditary trait in subsequent generations that is similar but under different genetic control.

References

Alcock, J. (1989). *Animal Behavior*. Sunderland, Mass.: Sinauer.

Baldwin, J. M. (1902). *Development and Evolution*. New York: Macmillan.

Baldwin, J. M. (1909). *Darwin and the Humanities*. Baltimore, Md.: Review.

Belew, R. K. and M. Mitchell (eds.) (1996). *Adaptive Individuals in Evolving Populations: Models and Algorithms*. (Santa Fe Institute Studies in the Sciences of Complexity, vol. 26.) Reading, Mass.: Addison-Wesley.

Darwin, C. (1998/1871). *The Descent of Man*. New York: Prometheus Books.

Dawkins, R. (1982). *The Extended Phenotype*. Oxford: Oxford University Press.

Deacon, T. (1997). *The Symbolic Species*. New York: W. W. Norton.

Dennett, D. (1991). *Consciousness Explained*. Boston: Little, Brown.

Dennett, Daniel (1995). *Darwin's Dangerous Idea*. New York: Simon and Schuster.

Durham, W. H. (1991). *Coevolution*. Stanford: Stanford University Press.

Futuyma, D. J. (1998). *Evolutionary Biology*. Sunderland, Mass.: Sinauer.

Godfrey-Smith, P. (1990). Ph.D. dissertation. *Teleonomy and the Philosophy of Mind*. University of California, San Diego.

Gould, S. J. (1980). Is a new and general theory of evolution emerging? *Paleobiology* 6: 119–130.

Hall, B. K. (2001). Organic selection: proximate environmental effects on the evolution of morphology and behaviour. *Biology and Philosophy* 16: 215–237.

Hinton, G. E. and Nowlan, S. J. (1996). How learning can guide evolution. In R. K. Belew and M. Mitchell (eds.), *Adaptive Individuals in Evolving Populations*, pp. 447–454. Reading, Mass.: Addison-Wesley.

Lewontin, R. (1985). The Organism as Subject and Object of Evolution. In R. Levins and R. Lewontin (eds.), *The Dialectical Biologist*, pp. 85–108. Cambridge, Mass.: Harvard University Press.

Losos, J. B. et al. (1997). Adaptive differentiation following experimental island colonization in *Anolis* lizards. *Nature* 387: 70–73.

Maynard Smith, J. (1996). Natural selection: when learning guides evolution. In R. K. Belew and M. Mitchell (eds.), *Adaptive Individuals in Evolving Populations,* pp. 455–457. Reading, Mass.: Addison-Wesley.

Peirce, C. S. (1955). *Collected Works.* J. Buchler (ed.). New York: Dover.

Plotkin, H. C. (ed.) (1988). *The Role of Behavior in Evolution.* Cambridge, Mass.: MIT Press.

Rice, W. R. (1999). Adaptation and coevolution of the sexes: Gender-specific fitness, interlocus contest evolution (ICE), and sexually antagonistic genes. Presentation at Human Behavior and Evolution Society Meetings, Salt Lake City, Utah.

Richards, R. J. (1987). *Darwin and the Emergence of Evolutionary Theories of Mind and Behavior.* Chicago: The University of Chicago Press.

Ruse, M. (1999). *Mystery of Mysteries: Is Evolution a Social Construction?* Cambridge, Mass.: Harvard University Press.

Simpson, G. G. (1996). The Baldwin effect. In R. K. Belew and M. Mitchell (eds.), *Adaptive Individuals in Evolving Populations,* pp. 99–110. Reading, Mass.: Addison-Wesley.

Sober, E. (1993). *Philosophy of Biology.* Boulder: Westview Press.

Waddington, C. H. (1996). Canalization of development and the inheritance of acquired characters. In R. K. Belew and M. Mitchell (eds.), *Adaptive Individuals in Evolving Populations,* pp. 91–98. Reading, Mass.: Addison-Wesley.

Williams, G. C. (1966). *Adaptation and Natural Selection.* Princeton, N.J.: Princeton University Press.

3

Between Baldwin Skepticism and Baldwin Boosterism

Peter Godfrey-Smith

1   Introduction

A "Baldwin skeptic" is someone who thinks the Baldwin effect is no big deal. "Baldwin boosters" think the Baldwin effect is a distinctive and important evolutionary phenomenon. Terrence Deacon and Daniel Dennett are recent examples of Baldwin boosters (Deacon 1997, Dennett 1995).[1] George Gaylord Simpson's 1953 article is a famous piece of Baldwin skepticism. Stephen Downes and Paul Griffiths, among others, carry on the skeptical tradition (chaps. 2 and 10, this volume). I have always counted myself a skeptic, but in the course of writing this paper my skepticism has been somewhat reduced, partly by one aspect of Deacon's argument in *The Symbolic Species* (1997). So I am less of a Baldwin skeptic than before.

However, I am still a long way from Baldwin boosterism. I hold that the Baldwin effect is often misunderstood and misdescribed. The Baldwin effect proper is also often conflated with a motley collection of other ideas about plasticity and the evolutionary role of behavior. (On this point, see also Depew, chap. 1, this volume.)

The main aim of this chapter is to break the classical Baldwin effect down into its component pieces and look closely at the relation between them. I will try to extract some kernels of real theoretical interest in the Baldwin effect from the often confused mass of discussion.

2   The Baldwin Effect, as Originally and Narrowly Conceived

The Baldwin effect, as is well known, provides a way for Darwinian selection to mimic the "Lamarckian" inheritance of acquired characteristics.

Baldwin has done well to have become the namesake for the effect, as it was described simultaneously by three people, Baldwin, Lloyd Morgan, and Osborn, around 1896 (see Griffiths, chap. 10, this volume). Baldwin largely has G. G. Simpson to thank for this element of immortality (Simpson 1953). This is ironic, as Simpson's paper was intended to *deflate* interest in the "effect." But his deflation included giving the effect a catchy name, which stuck.

Here is my understanding of the original "effect." Suppose a population encounters a new environmental condition, in which its old behavioral strategies are inappropriate. If some members of the population are plastic with respect to their behavioral program, and can acquire in the course of their lifetime new behavioral skills that fit their new surroundings, these plastic individuals will survive and reproduce at the expense of less flexible individuals. The population will then have the chance to produce mutations that cause organisms to exhibit the new optimal behavioral profile without the need for learning. Selection will favor these mutants, and in time the behaviors which once had to be learned will be innate.

This "effect" involves two transitions. The first has to do with the evolutionary value of plasticity, or some particular form of plasticity such as learning. Plastic individuals are able to develop new behaviors to deal with new situations. That leads to natural selection, not for the behavior itself, but for the capacity to learn.

The second is the "genetic assimilation" of the learned trait. The trait that once had to be acquired by each individual through learning comes to be produced in the normal course of development without learning.

Baldwin called this process "a new factor in evolution." But is the Baldwin effect no more than the "sum of its parts"? Is the effect a theoretically interesting phenomenon when taken as a whole, or is the whole just a trivial combination or concatenation of two phenomena, each of which is independently important? It is always hard to answer such questions. I used to think the Baldwin effect is *at most* the sum of its parts, where these parts are (i) the usefulness of learning, and (ii) ordinary natural selection for specific traits. These are important phenomena, but whether the combination of them in the Baldwin effect is important is a further question.

I say "at most" the sum of the parts because the parts can work *against* each other. One way to make this point is with an objection that Robert Richards attributes to Darwin's disciple Romanes, in an 1895 discussion anticipating the formulation of the Baldwin effect proper (Richards 1987). Consider the point at the intersection of the two key parts of the process. The population is using learning to adapt to its new circumstances, and with time, genetic mutations arise that would make possible an innate basis for the new behaviors. But if the other individuals in the population are *already* doing the right thing, why should there be selection favoring the mutants? Why should the second transition, the "genetic assimilation" of the trait, ever occur?

The assimilation might occur if, for some reason, the strategy of learning the behavior has costs that are avoided by genetic control of a more inflexible kind. Learning takes time, and can go astray if individual experience is misleading. The cognitive machinery underlying learning also has its own associated costs; brains are expensive to set up and to run. These extra factors might give us reason to expect the second part of the process in some circumstances. On the other hand, if the task being learned is such that each individual does best to learn it for itself, tailoring its behavior to the details of its circumstances, and the costs of plasticity are not too high, then the process should stop at the first stage.

So the original Romanes question can be answered—sometimes we have reason to expect the second step. However, we can also formulate a more general analogue of Romanes's question.

Before asking the question, I will give a more detailed outline of the relevant stages in the story:[2]

Stage 0   A new environmental condition has arisen. The population has not yet undergone any evolutionary change as a consequence.

Stage 1   Natural selection favors learning, as a consequence of the challenge posed by the new environmental condition. Genotypes associated with the effective learning of suitable behaviors proliferate in the population.

Stage 2   Mutation, recombination, and selection lead to the proliferation of genotypes that are able to produce the best available behavioral response without learning.

Assuming an environmental change in stage 0 makes some versions of the effect, especially Baldwin's own, easier to describe. But a change in stage 0 is not strictly necessary. We can also just think of stage 0 as the prior state of the population.

Now the question: Suppose we have a population that does make it to stage 2 after going through stage 1. What role does the sojourn in stage 1 play in the passage to stage 2? Why does the fact that the population goes through stage 1 make it more likely that it also gets to stage 2? Why couldn't the population go just as well, and just as quickly, from stage 0 to stage 2? Given that genetic control of the trait is supposed to be superior to learning, and superior also to not producing the trait at all, why should we believe that a transition from stage 0 to 1 to 2 has any particular importance here?

The question can be answered. As I count them, there are three possible mechanisms that might lead us to expect transitions to stage 2 that go via stage 1.

(i) Breathing space—Baldwin's mechanism   Learning keeps the population alive long enough for it to get to stage 2. This mechanism is unlikely to be important.

(ii) The similarity relations between genotypes—Waddington's mechanism   The genotypes associated with the optimal state—reliable genetic control of the trait—are more genetically accessible from a state in which the population is mostly comprised of good learners than they are from a prior state in which the population is not mostly comprised of good learners. Getting to stage 1 makes stage 2 more genetically accessible for the evolving population.

(iii) Niche construction—Deacon's mechanism   The transition to stage 1 changes the social ecology of the population. In this new ecology, the transition to stage 2 is selectively favored. But prior to stage 1, there is no selection (or much weaker selection) for these stage 2 traits.

These three mechanisms are not exclusive of each other; each can work with the others. In the discussion that follows I will sometimes (though not always) use "learning" as a short-hand for all facultative mechanisms for acquiring adaptive traits. So the examples I will discuss will generally involve behavior, even though some of the phenomena are not restricted to behavioral cases.

3   Breathing Space—Baldwin's Mechanism

In Baldwin's 1896 "New Factor" paper, he argues that learning helps the population get to stage 2 by keeping it alive. The problem is presented as one in which individuals who do not produce the right trait for their altered circumstances will die as a result. If all the individuals die before reproducing, the population itself will disappear. But learning gives the population a breathing space; it enables some individuals to produce a good enough version of the required behaviors to keep the population alive. "Thus kept alive, the species has all the time necessary to perfect the variations required by a complete instinct" (1896, p. 63).

Baldwin is right that in some circumstances, this will explain why stage 2 can only be approached by stage 1. If the situation at stage 0 is sufficiently dire, then the only way the population can survive is if some individuals in the population already have some capacity to learn the right behavior. These individuals will do well, and learning may then increase in frequency. Once the population is at a healthy stage 1 state, mutations may arise that will take it to stage 2.

If this mechanism is required, the Baldwin effect is unlikely to be important. Baldwin's story makes several strong assumptions. First, we should note that although a few learners present at stage 0 will indeed save the population, so will a few individuals with the stage 2 genotypes. (In either case, the genetics of the favored trait must also be such as to allow it to increase in frequency from a rare state.) Baldwin might reply that there are lots of reasons for the population to contain some good learners, and no particular reasons for it to contain individuals with stage 2 genotypes. Fair enough. Note, however, that the second stage of the Baldwin effect is supposed to *reduce* the prevalence of plasticity. If learning is still around, that is no thanks to previous instantiations of the Baldwin effect in that population.

A more important fact is that the majority of evolution does not involve the extreme "do-or-die" challenges to populations that Baldwin assumes here. Baldwin's explanation requires that without a specific response to the new challenge, the life of the population as a whole is drastically shortened. However, evolution by natural selection is a comparative matter; some do better than others in a population, and gene frequencies change as a result. Evolutionary explanations in general do not require life-or-death threats to a population as a whole. Those are rather special cases.[3]

Still, in those special cases, learning populations may do better. So might one suggest that a process of species selection could explain the maintenance of learning in a population? After all, the populations that cannot learn do not get the "breathing space," and might go extinct. Maybe in some cases the explanation could be filled out in a plausible way. But this has little to do with the Baldwin effect. After a population has benefited from learning, if it follows the path of the Baldwin effect, it is supposed to then lose flexibility with respect to the behaviors in question. Genetic assimilation renders inflexible what was once flexible. The loss of this dimension of flexibility does not entail the loss of other kinds of flexibility, but it certainly *does not help* other kinds of flexibility! Genetic assimilation is the enemy of flexibility, and the friend of canalized production of phenotypes. In Baldwin's scenario, an environmental challenge makes the population first get smarter (stage 1) . . . and then get dumber again (stage 2).

4   The Similarity Relations between Genotypes—Waddington's Mechanism

Waddington's famous experiments on genetic assimilation can be seen as showing another way in which a special path from stage 0 to 1 to 2 can exist (see, e.g., Waddington 1953). The path derives from the similarity relations between different genotypes. The genotypes associated with stage 2—reliable genetic control of the trait—might be more genetically accessible from a state in which the population is mostly comprised of good learners of that trait than they are from a prior state. Getting to stage 1 might make stage 2 more accessible to the processes of genetic change. If this were so, then we might at least expect a transition via stage 1 to greatly speed up the passage from stage 0 to stage 2. If we made extra assumptions, the only possible way to get to stage 2 might be via stage 1.[4]

Waddington's mechanism is interesting because he showed that it actually works in some cases. He did not show that the mechanism works for cases involving behavior, though, and we cannot describe the role of plasticity in his experiments as a case of learning or intelligence. What Waddington did show is that for some morphological traits, such as the absence of a cross-vein on a fruit fly's wing, or a double thorax, one can select for reliable, nonfacultative expression of a specific mutant form by first selecting for less reliable, environment-specific, or facultative expression of the form. If one selects for the propensity to produce a trait in specific environmental conditions, one can eventually produce individuals that produce the trait across a wide range of normal environments. What once was only elicited by a very specific environmental condition can now arise in the normal course of development.

The production of a morphological trait as a response to specific environmental conditions is often taken to have some analogy to learning. If Waddington's mechanism were to work in cases of behavior, what would be required is for genotypes that make an individual apt to learn the trait (stage 1 genotypes) to be closer to genotypes that produce the trait without learning (stage 2 genotypes) than these stage 2 genotypes are to stage 0 genotypes. As one traverses genetic space through genotypes that are more and more effective at learning a given behavior, one is also moving closer to genotypes that tend to produce the behavior without a need for learning. Waddington's mechanism would work for behavioral traits if this genetic assumption was true in the case of behavior-influencing genetic combinations. It would not work if the proliferation during stage 1 of genotypes enabling behavioral flexibility had the effect of making mutations for direct, genetically controlled production of the behavior less accessible than they were before, or if stage 1 made no difference to the accessibility of stage 2 genotypes.

I don't know if experimental work has been done that demonstrates for behavior what Waddington was able to demonstrate for some morphological traits. Because the mechanisms by which plastic individuals acquire the traits that Waddington worked on are in no sense "smart" mechanisms, there seems little reason to extrapolate from his cases to cases involving real learning. In Waddington's cases, initial rounds of selection pick out genetic variants that happen to have some tendency to produce an unusual form as a consequence of an unusual stimulus. Subsequent rounds of selection uncover individuals whose developmental patterns have more and more tendency to go down this unusual path. The kinds of plasticity involved in the early rounds of Waddington's experiments have only a very superficial analogy with mechanisms enabling adaptive plasticity of the kind seen in learning.[5]

The most famous computer simulation of the Baldwin effect does incorporate Waddington's mechanism, however, and does not incorporate either of the other two mechanisms. This is the simulation by Hinton and Nowlan (1987). The simulation is worth discussing in detail, as it makes the role of Waddington's assumption very clear.

Hinton and Nowlan place a population of simple neural nets in an environment that is extremely hostile to normal evolutionary search. If the creatures cannot learn, there is exactly one genotype with high fitness, and all other genotypes are equally poor. That is, the adaptive landscape has a needle at one point, and there is no information elsewhere in the landscape about the location of the needle. In their model, each neural net has 20 connections, controlled by 20 genes. For nets unable to learn, each connection is set at 1 or 0. The spike of high fitness is where all 20 connections are set at 1, though this is unimportant to the model. There are then 2^{20} possible genotypes, and the only way to find the right one is to search exhaustively until it is hit upon.

If the nets are capable of simple learning, however, the task is easier. In this case the connections are initially set at 1, 0 or ?. The ? connections are those that can be modified by a simple form of learning. Each learning net has 1000 trials, in which it produces a random combination of 1s and 0s in place of its ?s. If a net ever hits upon the right phenotype (all 1s), it stops guessing, and is rewarded at the end of the day with reproductive success. Obviously only the nets with a combination of 1s and ?s have a chance of getting the right phenotype; a single 0 makes it impossible. Although each individual net is "looking" for 1s, it cannot build up 1s during its lifetime cumulatively. Its overall phenotype is either right or wrong on each trial. Though the search is still not easy, the effect of learning is, as Hinton and Nowlan say, to put "shoulders" on the needle of high fitness. The adaptive peak can now be ascended from nearby points.

At the close of each generation the nets reproduce sexually and variation arises by recombination. Parents are chosen randomly, but a net that succeeded in finding the right phenotype has a higher chance of reproducing than normal. Its chances are proportional to $1 + 19n/1000$, where n is the number of learning trials that remained after the net hit on the right combination. So a net that learned early does better than one that learned late.

Figure 3.1 shows the relative frequencies of the alleles 1, 0, and ? through the generations in a typical run. The diagram is a bit unusual as all the 1 alleles at different loci (and all the 0 alleles, etc.) are represented with a single overall frequency. The details of the Hinton and Nowlan model have the effect of downplaying stage 1 of the process. The initial frequency of the ? allele is 0.5, which is high. So a typical stage 0 net has 10 learnable and 10 fixed connections. During the Hinton and Nowlan analogue of stage 1 (up until a bit after generation 10), there is not much increase in the frequency

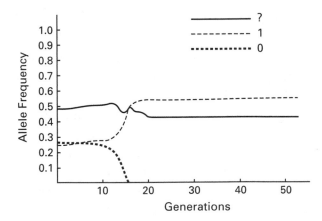

Figure 3.1
Hinton and Nowlan's simulation of the Baldwin effect (from Hinton and Nowlan 1987).

of ? alleles, though there is some. Then once the 0 alleles are gone from the population, there is a very slow replacement of ? alleles with 1 alleles; this is stage 2, genetic assimilation.

The decline in ? is driven by the fitness function's sensitivity to the number of trials a net takes to guess the right phenotype. The fewer trials it takes to guess the combination, the higher the fitness. This amounts to a cost of plasticity; a net born with all 1s always has higher fitness than a learner. The pressure becomes weaker over time as the learning task becomes very easy for a net with only a few ?s, and not much distinguishes it from an all-1 net. Different fitness functions would allow a quicker replacement of the last ?s with 1s. For example, all learners might be penalized by a fixed amount of fitness that represents the metabolic costs of learning mechanisms.

The Waddington requirement is met here, because the genetic path leading through better and better learners is also a path leading to a well-adapted nonlearner. The slow cementing of 1 connections by the genes during stage 2 does not affect the ability of the net to guess the other connections specified by ? alleles.

This assumption is substantial. Consider the result if, for example, in order to be able to learn *at all* one must have (say) three ? alleles in one's genotype. Then there will be a barrier to genetic assimilation. In Hinton and Nowlan's model, the best learners are not just almost as fit, but *almost the same* as systems that don't learn at all.

5   Niche Construction—Deacon's Mechanism

Terrence Deacon's book *The Symbolic Species* is a recent example of Baldwin boosterism, and one that describes a third mechanism bearing on stage 1/stage 2 transitions (Deacon 1997).

Deacon uses the term "Baldwinian" in a rather vague way that covers a lot of different ideas. Some of the phenomena he discusses under the "Baldwinian" heading are not cases of the Baldwin effect at all. The evolution of lactose tolerance and of blood proteins that provide partial malaria resistance, such as the sickle cell anemia protein, are not cases of the Baldwin effect. They are cases in which behavioral capacities and choices affect the course of evolution by natural selection, but they do not involve the genetic assimilation of a previously acquired trait. Deacon recognizes that these are not cases in which evolution produces an "innate replica" of an acquired trait (p. 327), but he sees them as "Baldwinian" anyway. I would say that Baldwin has done quite well enough in having his name attached to the "Baldwin effect," given its multiple discoverers; there is no justification for attaching Baldwin's name to *all* cases in which behavior has an effect on evolution.

Once we restrict our discussion to the Baldwin effect itself, it turns out that Deacon's book makes a significant contribution to this topic. He outlines a third mechanism by which a population might tread a special path from stage 0 through stage 1 to stage 2, a path that cannot be cut short by going from 0 to 2 directly. He discusses this mechanism as if it is what Baldwin himself had in mind. I see no evidence for this in Baldwin's "A New Factor in Evolution" (1896). But I have not read all of Baldwin's discussions, and there may be presentations of the third mechanism elsewhere in Baldwin's work, or in the work of others. (Griffiths's contribution to this volume, chap. 10, makes it seem that Baldwin came close but did not make the key connection.)

This third mechanism involves not the underlying genetics of the stage 0-1-2 relationships, but changes made to *selection pressures* by the population itself. The transition from stage 0 to stage 1 occurs because some facultatively acquired behaviors are advantageous. These behaviors are accessible to some smarter individuals during stage 0, but selection increases the frequency of genotypes adept at learning the behaviors in question.

That takes us to stage 1. But the existence of these behaviors, which become common in stage 1, changes the selection pressures bearing on the population; the transition from stage 0 to 1 has changed the social ecology that individuals confront. Deacon's mechanism requires that the facultatively acquired behaviors become *entrenched in the social life of the population.* Once they are common, individuals that are unable to produce the behavior at all have reduced fitness. This advantage will exhibit positive frequency dependence—the behavior becomes more and more important to individual fitness the more common it gets.

This frequency dependence concerns the capacity to produce the behavior at all. But in addition, individuals able to produce the behaviors easily are favored because of the demands the behavior exerts on cognitive and behavioral mechanisms. And individuals able to display sophistication or inventiveness in this behavioral domain might be favored as well.

In these circumstances, any new mutations that enable individuals to produce the behavior with less learning, a lower demand on cognitive mechanisms, or both, should be favored. Genotypes that predispose individuals to acquire these behaviors rapidly and reliably will increase in frequency. That is what takes the population from stage 1 to stage 2. There is no need for the similarity relations among genotypes discussed in section 4 above; the process will work even if the population has to take a partial genetic "U-turn" in moving from stage 1 to stage 2. And as the population comes to contain individuals with higher and higher proficiency in this behavioral domain, mutations that enable yet more reliable acquisition and yet more sophisticated performance will be favored. And so on, until the self-reinforcing nature of the process is halted by other constraints. Crucially, the genotypes that are favored during stage 2 are only advantageous in the circumstances created by stage 1. If such a genotype appeared during stage 0, an individual with that genotype need have no selective advantage, and might have a behavioral profile poorly adapted to the stage 0 social ecology. A Proust appearing in the Pleistocene would probably have had a life that was indeed nasty, brutish, and short.

So in a stage 0 population, there is no selection for stage 2 genotypes, while there is such selection in stage 1. Such selection leads to less and less learning—to more and more genetically controlled special-purpose wiring—associated with the behavior as time goes by.

Deacon is describing a process of "niche construction," a phenomenon that is in no way limited to behavioral traits. (For general discussions, see Lewontin 1983, Laland, Odling-Smee, and Felman 2000, and Sterelny 2001.) Not all niche construction has any connection to genetic assimilation, and Baldwin's own "breathing space" mechanism is not a case of niche construction.

Deacon has in mind a particular kind of behavior in his discussion of Baldwin: linguistic behavior. His claim is that the earliest proto-linguistic behaviors, which were produced via a nonspecialized apelike brain, conditioned the subsequent evolution of the human brain. Linguistic behavior places great demands on learning, processing, and motor mechanisms. And in the social ecology that Deacon imagines for early humans, the role of symbolic behavior in social coordination becomes extremely important. So selection will favor any mutations that predispose human brains for language acquisition.

It is a further question which particular kinds of language-friendly neural structures were selected for. Deacon does not think that the standard Chomskian candidates for innate specification, the principles of "universal grammar," are likely to be the targets of this kind of selection. Instead, Deacon thinks that the best candidates are some of the mechanisms for producing and hearing speech, and some general structural features of the computational mechanisms associated with symbolic thought and speech analysis.

The Baldwinian mechanism that Deacon describes is also quite independent of the speculative story he goes on to tell about how exactly linguistic behavior and symbolic thought helped early humans. Deacon argues that language and symbolic thought were part of the means by which early humans solved a foraging problem. The effective utilization of meat by early humans required both group hunting and some way to ensure that the food made its way back to females and infants. Marriage-like contracts were the solution to the distribution problem, and language was the means by which these complex social arrangements were established and maintained. Sexual rights and exclusions would be otherwise hard to maintain in a group-living species.

We might call this the "meat and marriage" theory. The meat and marriage theory is one of a large number of speculative stories about the origins of high human intelligence. Not being an anthropologist or primatologist, I don't know how well it compares with its rivals.

Aside from language, the best candidate traits for a Baldwin effect using Deacon's mechanism are other social behaviors. G. G. Simpson's original skeptical discussion includes a rather favorable assessment of Lloyd Morgan's proposal that bird song could sometimes become genetic via a Baldwin effect. If this were to occur, it would probably work via a Deacon-style story, at least in part. The early facultative production of particular songs might come to change the social ecology in ways that put a premium on faster and more reliable mechanisms that are less dependent on learning. Other mating displays and behaviors might also provide examples, especially in cases where there is both (i) some standardization in the population of a behavior that is hard to learn, and (ii) an advantage in extra sophistication in the production of the behavior.

In sum, Deacon outlines a third mechanism by which a nontrivial Baldwin effect could occur. The mechanism involves niche construction, and a process of positive feedback. The further stories Deacon tells, including the meat and marriage theory of intelligence, are largely independent of this basic point. Indeed, it would not be hard to graft Deacon's handling of the Baldwin effect onto a more conventional "social intelligence" hypothesis about the origins of human cognitive capacities (Whiten and Byrne 1997).

6   Conclusion

Fifty years ago, Simpson wrote the concise article that both named and deflated the Baldwin effect. I had long thought that Simpson's arguments, and a close scrutiny of how the "effect" is supposed to work, reveal that the Baldwin effect has little or no real interest. Parts of Deacon's discussion have convinced me that I was being too skeptical. Without being committed to any of the details of his story, I suggest that the general shape of Deacon's account does put a bit of real substance into the Baldwin effect. And no one can claim he picked a trivial trait to explain.

Simpson made the following claim in his paper:

If the Baldwin effect occurs, either there is or is not a causal connection between an individual accommodation [acquired adaptive trait] and subsequent genetic change in a population. If there is no such connection, then the truly genetic change must occur wholly by mutation, reproduction and natural selection, and the accommodation may be irrelevant. If there is a causal connection, the neo-Lamarckian argument is as much supported as supplanted. (1953, p. 106)

This is a nicely expressed point, but I suggest that the dichotomy is either false, or else Simpson is wrong that a causal connection of the kind he describes is not compatible with mainstream Darwinism. There are at least three mechanisms that do establish something like the kind of connection Simpson requires here. The most significant of the three is likely to be the third one discussed here, which involves niche construction.

Acknowledgment

Thanks to all those present at the Bennington conference for helpful comments. Thanks also to Brian Hall and Lisa Lloyd for correspondence and discussion.

Notes

1. Dennett is more moderate than Deacon, but I'd put him with the boosters (1955 pp. 77–80). Carl Schlicting and Massimo Pigliucci's recent book about phenotypic evolution also inclines toward Baldwin boosterism (1998). The standard textbook in evolutionary biology by Douglas Futuyma (second edition1986, third edition 1998) exemplifies the skeptical view by not mentioning Baldwin or his effect at all, although there is a discussion of Waddington's work on genetic assimilation (1998, pp. 441–442).

2. This breakdown of the process is not quite the same as Simpson's 1953 account, though it is close.

3. The term "hard selection" is now, as far as I can tell you, only used to describe multi-niche situations or cases of population subdivision (Futuyma 1998, p. 386). My impression is that an earlier and more informal use of the term was to describe cases in which a particular selection pressure determines noy just the genotypes but also the size of the next generation. If so, Baldwin is assuming very intense hard selection.

4. Brian Hall (in correspondence) pointed out tome that for Waddington, recombination acting on existing genetic variation is sufficient to produce genetic assimilation of a formerly acquired trait. So in my discussions of Waddington here, I have tried to be neutral on the respective roles of mutation and recombination as sources of variability. In much of the rest of the chapter I assume that mutation is the source of variation, as this is the simplest way to present the core issues.

5. That is one reason for G. C. Williams's skepticism about genetic assimilation (Williams 1996). Williams argued that Waddington refused to distinguish between mere *susceptibility* to environmental conditions and adaptive *response* to environmental stimuli (pp. 71–83). This distinction is indeed important in discussions of the analogy between learning and the more general category of phenotypic plasticity. Williams also used a separate argument based on informational consid-

erations, which is less convincing and less important here. (The informational argument has been criticized in detail by Sober 1984, chap. 6.)

References

Baldwin, J. M. (1896). A new factor in evolution. *American Naturalist* 30: 441–451, 536–553. Reprinted in Belew and Mitchell (1996).

Belew, R. K. and M. Mitchell (eds.) (1996). *Adaptive Individuals in Evolving Populations: Models and Algorithms.* (Santa Fe Institute Studies in the Sciences of Complexity, vol. 26.) Reading, Mass.: Addison-Wesley.

Deacon, T. (1997). *The Symbolic Species: The Co-Evolution of Language and the Brain.* New York: Norton.

Dennett, D. C. (1995). *Darwin's Dangerous Idea.* New York: Simon and Schuster.

Downes, S. (unpublished). Do minds speed up evolution? Paper presented at the 1999 ISHPPB Meetings, Oaxaca, Mexico.

Futuyma, D. (1998). *Evolutionary Biology,* third edition. Sunderland, Mass.: Sinauer. (Second edition, 1986.)

Hinton, G. and S. Nowlan (1987). How learning can guide evolution. *Complex Systems* 1: 495–502. Reprinted in Belew and Mitchell (1996).

Laland, K., F. J. Odling-Smee, and M. Feldman (2000). Niche construction, biological evolution and cultural change. *Behavioral and Brain Sciences* 23: 131–175.

Lewontin, R. C. (1983). The organism as the subject and object of evolution. Reprinted in R. Levins, R. and R. C. Lewontin, *The Dialectical Biologist,* pp. 85–106 (Cambridge, Mass.: Harvard University Press, 1985).

Lloyd Morgan, C. (1896). On modification and variation. *Science* 4 (99) 733–740.

Richards, R. (1987). *Darwin and the Emergence of Evolutionary Theories of Mind and Behavior.* Chicago: University of Chicago Press.

Schlichting, C. and M. Pigliucci (1998). *Phenotypic Evolution: A Reaction Norm Perspective.* Sunderland, Mass.: Sinauer.

Simpson, G. G. (1953). The Baldwin effect. *Evolution* 7: 110–117.

Sober, E. (1984). *The Nature of Selection.* Cambridge, Mass.: MIT Press.

Sterelny, K. (2001). Niche construction, developmental systems, and the extended replicator. In S. Oyama, P. Griffiths, and R. Gray (eds.), *Cycles of Contingency,* pp. 333–349. Cambridge, Mass.: MIT Press.

Waddington, C. H. (1953). Genetic assimilation of an acquired character. *Evolution* 7: 118–126.

Whiten, A. and R. W. Byrne (eds.) (1997). *Machiavellian Intelligence II: Extensions and Evaluations.* Cambridge: Cambridge University Press.

Williams, G. C. (1966). *Adaptation and Natural Selection.* Berkeley: University of California Press.

4

The Baldwin Effect: A Crane, Not a Skyhook

Daniel Dennett

1 Introduction

In 1991, I included a brief discussion of the Baldwin effect in my account of the evolution of human consciousness, thinking I was introducing to non-specialist readers a little-appreciated, but no longer controversial, wrinkle in orthodox neo-Darwinism. I had thought that Hinton and Nowlan (1987) and Maynard Smith (1987) had shown clearly and succinctly how and why it worked, and had restored the neglected concept to grace. Here is how I put it then:

> If we give individuals a variable chance to hit upon (and then "recognize" and "cling to") the Good Trick in the course of their lifetimes, the near-invisible needle in the haystack ... becomes the summit of a quite visible hill that natural selection can climb. ... Over generations, the competition becomes stiffer: eventually, unless you are born with (or very nearly with) the Good Trick, you are not close enough to compete. If it weren't for the plasticity, however, the effect wouldn't be there, for "a miss is as good as a mile" *unless* you get to keep trying variations until you get it right.
>
> Thanks to the Baldwin effect, species can be said to pretest the efficacy of particular different designs by phenotypic (individual) exploration of the space of nearby possibilities. If a particularly winning setting is thereby discovered, this discovery will *create* a new selection pressure: organisms that are closer in the adaptive landscape to that discovery will have a clear advantage over those more distant. This means that species with plasticity will *tend* to evolve faster (and more "clearsightedly") than those without it. (Dennett 1991: 186)

I now discover that there are still "Baldwin skeptics" (Downes, Godfrey-Smith, chaps. 2 and 3, respectively, this volume) who do not so much doubt the possibility of the Baldwin effect as doubt its importance as what I have called a *crane:* "a subprocess or special feature of a design process that can be demonstrated to permit the local speeding up of the basic, slow process of natural selection, *and* that can be demonstrated to be itself the predictable (or retrospectively explicable) product of the basic process" (Dennett 1995: 76). This is what I claimed:

It shows how the "blind" process of the basic phenomenon of natural selection can be abetted by a limited amount of "look-ahead" in the activities of individual organisms, which create fitness differences that natural selection can then act upon. (Ibid.: 80)

So the question is: Does the Baldwin effect really occur, and if it does, how much "local lifting" can it do? Can it make a significant difference in the trajectories through Design Space that species have traversed? Part of the problem is a relatively unimportant wrangle about naming and boundaries: shouldn't the Baldwin effect be named after somebody else, and is the Baldwin effect just a special case of Waddington's (or somebody else's) "genetic assimilation," and if so, how special is it, if at all? The rest of the problem concerns the soundness or realism of the (idealized, oversimplified) models and explanations, and the more directly empirical question of whether in fact there are demonstrated cases of Baldwin effects in nature. As so often happens in evolutionary controversies, the empirical questions of most interest have to be traded in for something more practical if we want to test them experimentally. We'd love to know about the role of language-learning abilities in *H. sapiens* and its ancestors, but we have to settle for the more modest learning (if that's not too strong a term) abilities of something like *E. coli* or *D. melanogaster* if we want to look at hundreds or thousands of generations. I expect that experiments will eventually shed light on this, if they haven't already done so (I confess that I am not up to date on the literature), but in the meantime, several commentators have expressed objections to the more strictly theoretical discussions that I want to answer.

2   Peering Through the Fog of Battle

These theoretical objections are valuable because they expose a vein of misdirection that continues to haunt evolutionary thinking a century and more after Baldwin mounted his campaign to claim the discovery as his own. That campaign finally succeeded more than a half century after it started, when George Gaylord Simpson (1953) dubbed it the Baldwin effect, but it was presumably a pyrrhic victory, since, as Downes (chap. 2, this volume) notes, Simpson coined the term "in order to argue it did not exist as an in-dependent factor from natural selection." In fact, Simpson does not so much argue for this deflationary conclusion as simply express his (expert) opinion. He demonstrates that the Baldwin effect is possible, calling it "an interesting, but, I would judge, relatively minor outcome of the theory" (Belew and Mitchell 1996: 107), and goes on to remark that Waddington's genetic assimilation represents "a broader principle of which the Baldwin effect may be considered a special case" (ibid.). The last sentence of Simp-son's short paper reveals that his main target in writing the paper has been to dump cold water on a misguided enthusiasm: "It does not, however, seem to require any modification of the opinion that the *directive force* in adaptation, in the Baldwin effect or in any other particular way, is natural selection" (108).

From the outset, Baldwin had advertised the effect as an instance of what Downes calls "mind-directed" evolution, and it was gullibility about this prospect that Simpson was trying to squelch; but Baldwin's own account (see especially his discussion of the possible mechanisms of "selection" in what he calls "neurogenetic" modifications, p. 61 in Belew and Mitchell 1996) shows that he was always alert to the requirement that his commit-ment to Darwinism obliged him to postulate a crane, not a *skyhook* ("a 'mind-first' force or power or process, an exception to the principle that all design, and apparent design, is ultimately the result of mindless, motiveless mechanicity," Dennett 1995: 76). Baldwin's own presentation of the issue was thus Janus-faced: he seemed to promise a skyhook to the eager buyers but was careful to deliver an orthodox crane, a fact underappreciated by some who took up the cause. Godfrey-Smith closes his paper by noting that Simpson, in his eagerness to preserve orthodoxy from contamination, also seems to have overshot his target somewhat in the opposite, compensatory direction: "the dichotomy is either false, or else Simpson is wrong that a causal connection of the kind he describes is not compatible with main-stream Darwinism."

The same tug of war distorts the rhetorical setting of Stephen Downes's latter day skepticism: if the Baldwin effect is "just" a special case of genetic assimilation, then it is not a "new evolutionary mechanism" (Downes, this volume) and hence no big deal; if, on the contrary, it is supposed to be an *alternative* to natural selection, an independent source of "mind-directed evolution," then it is (deservedly) suspect and contentious. My claim continues to be that the Baldwin effect is not at all an alternative to natural selection, but it is nonetheless an important extrapolation from, or extension of, orthodox theory that potentially can explain the origins of many of the most challenging adaptations. And so when Downes goes on to say (this volume) "It may be safer to say that the non-Waddington style concept of genetic assimilation may account for a subclass of phenomena labeled as Baldwin effects," he is not disagreeing with me, with Dawkins, with Deacon, or with Simpson. That is the bland position that we, too, take.

Downes (this volume) tries to manufacture a conflict between my claim that this provides a limited "look-ahead" and my agreement with Williams (and orthodoxy) that there is no foresight in natural selection, but this charge of inconsistency readily collapses: design explorations by phenotypic trial and error are just as mechanical and nonmiraculous as explorations by genetic natural selection; they just occur more swiftly and at less cost, and once design improvements are thereby discovered, genetic assimilation can incorporate them gradually into the genome. I wonder: does Downes think that the existence of genetic engineers is a problem for orthodox neo-Darwinism? These people now second-guess evolution on a broad front (with mixed results, of course, but surely it is better than a coin toss, better than random). How are these people capable of any foresight when they do this? Are they themselves gods, not products of natural selection? Of course not. It is obvious, I would have thought, that this look-ahead is itself the product of conscious and deliberate human reasoning and analysis, which is itself a product of earlier evolutionary processes. Our capacity to look ahead is as uncontroversially real as our capacity to breathe and metabolize. It had to evolve.

Moreover, contrary to Downes's discussion, my point has always been to stress that learning is just a particular case (not in any other way special) of ontogenetic adaptation. The continuity between learning and other purported varieties of self-redesign is taken as given in the circles in which I converse; learning is adaptive, functional change of one's cognitive (or control) mechanisms, as contrasted with one's digestive mechanisms, reproductive mechanisms, and so on. Hence no part of my purpose was to propose any sort of threshold distinguishing learning as a distinct phenomenon. (Godfrey-Smith, chap. 3, this volume, follows the same familiar policy when he says he is "going to use 'learning' as a short-hand for all facultative mechanisms for acquiring traits.") Wherein lies the importance of the Baldwin effect, then, if it is "just" business-as-usual ontogenetic adaptive plasticity leading the way to genetic adaptation?

It is not that the Baldwin effect accounts for otherwise inexplicable differences in tempo in evolution, but that it accounts, as Maynard Smith so crisply shows, for the evolution, in sexually reproducing species, of traits that theory would otherwise declare to be all but unevolvable—those needles in a haystack that would otherwise be invisible to natural selection. The importance of this issue does not loom large for either Godfrey-Smith or Downes. I don't know why. Perhaps it is because they, like many others, have been taught at least to feign discomfort when adopting the adaptationist perspective, or perhaps because they have not encountered much of the bizarre skepticism regarding the evolution of language (and "language acquisition devices") that has haunted the corridors of linguistics and philosophy of mind over the years. Putting the best interpretation on this skepticism (that is to say, ignoring the sometimes highly tempting diagnosis of closet Creationism), it amounts to a general conviction that something as specialized as the imagined "language acquisition device" is just such a needle in the haystack, something that could not evolve gradually but would have to be an almost miraculous saltation, a cosmic accident of good luck—what a Creationist would call a gift from God. Nonsense, say we Baldwin effect supporters. A practice that is both learnable (with effort) and highly advantageous once learned *can* become more and more easily learned, can move gradually into the status of not needing to be learned at all. It is instructive to note the parallel between this battlefield and the ground on which Waddington mounted his campaign for genetic assimilation: how *could* the embryonic callosities on ostrich legs (and human soles) be explained by orthodox Darwinism without appeal to Lamarckian mechanisms? In both cases, the initial, superficially plausible incredulity or skepticism must give way to an appreciation that evolution has a few more tricks up its sleeve than heretofore imagined; *there are* paths of (non-Lamarckian) orthodoxy leading from adaptative phenotypic adjustments to inherited genetic arrangements.

3   Trade-offs between Learning and "Instinct"

As Godfrey-Smith and others have noted, the purported outcome of Baldwin effects is *reduced* phenotypic plasticity (for the trait in question), so the Baldwin effect cannot be trundled out to explain the evolution of learning. Nevertheless, there is need for an account of the relationship between selection pressures in favor of enhanced learning abilities and selection pressures in favor of driving a new trick into the genome. Consider the generalized case in which the Baldwin effect is supposed to operate.

When a new Good Trick is discovered (by some member or members of a population), any genetic variation in the population that makes the learning swifter or more probable should have a fitness advantage, other things being equal. Different sorts of variation may happen to exist simultaneously in the gene pool, operating in two quite different ways:

(A) giving a leg up: starting the individual off in a state closer *in learning space* to the mature practice, so there's simply less to learn (this is the Hinton and Nowlan variation); and

(B) putting more spring in the legs: enhancing the learning capacity itself, so that the "lifting" distance is more swiftly and surely covered (this is variation in learning ability or adaptability).

Of these two "opposite" paths—one heading toward creating a new "instinct" and the other heading toward creating greater "general intelligence"—which will be favored? Presumably the incidental costs and benefits in each case will tip the scales one way or the other, and this is plausibly a highly sensitive variable. If the Good Trick has a fairly stereotypic set of releasers and conditions in the prevailing environment, and there are few *other* Good Tricks in the neighborhood it behooves one to learn, then probably the path to adding a new instinct is favored. In a more volatile environment, the costs of working harder to get the Good Trick may have enough incidental side payoffs to favor maintaining, and enhancing, the learning machinery instead. In some circumstances a species would be wise/lucky to "pay" for this increased learning *speed* by moving the neonate *farther* away, in learning space, from the Good Trick. This tidy picture is no doubt complicated in reality by dozens of other effects that might swamp this underlying consideration: perhaps a particular anatomical detail in some brains makes certain sorts of learning (or instinct) particularly expensive; perhaps there's an interaction with metabolism or growth rate or who knows what else. In any event, this saddle in Design Space must have often confronted species, for we see a host of instances in which what is fixed and instinctual in one species is variable but learnable in another.

Godfrey-Smith makes the point that Hinton and Nowlan's model has a particularly strong idealization in it, which he calls the Waddington requirement: "the genetic path leading through better and better learners is *also* a path leading to a well-adapted nonlearner" (this volume). The learning space is simply declared to be superimposed on the genetic space, so that there is a one-to-one mapping of mutations onto lessons-learned. This simplifies the phenomenon, since it treats the paths of learning and genetic transition as common and interchangeable; an organism can be *n* bits away from the Good Trick, a distance that can be traversed by any combination of learning and mutation. "As one traverses genetic space through genotypes that are more and more effective at learning a given behavior, one is also moving closer to genotypes that tend to produce the behavior without need for learning" (this volume). This may seem to be a huge and deeply unwarranted oversimplifying assumption, since it ignores what might seem to be a very real, even likely possibility: in order to "traverse genetic space" in the direction of more and more effective learning, you might have to leapfrog around in actual genetic distances. There is no guarantee, it might seem, that genotypes that are neighbors in genetic space are also similar in learning space. But in fact, Hinton and Nowlan's simplification is, so far as I can see, innocent, since it generalizes over the more realistic cases. To see this, suppose that there are, in some instance, three genetically distinct peaks in the adaptive landscape (rather distant from each other in genetic space)—three "different ways" to have an *instinct* for a specific behavior that is, at the outset, a *learned* behavior of some value. If there is selection pressure for learning the Good Trick *one way or another,* there will be simultaneous selection pressure felt on the slopes of all three peaks. The fact that there is no gradual upward path connecting all regions of genetic space to a single summit (Hinton and Nowlan's idealization) means only that there is no guarantee that there aren't suboptimal dead-end paths that must be traversed and then eventually discarded (unless a dimorphism or multimorphism happens to be stable). But we can be sure that there are *local* gradients in favor of heightened ease-of-learning because, if we imagine holding the learning mechanism constant (whatever it is), any small change in genetic space that changes the starting point in a way that happens to shorten the distance in learning space must be simultaneously a (small) step in the right direction both genetically and phenotypically. If there are *no* such changes, then, of course, there will be no genetic assimilation, but it does not seem extravagant to suppose that there will often be a winding upward path of small steps in genetic space that have the effect of shortening the distance in learning space one way or another. Where the genetic path stops, leaving the rest of the redesign trajectory to individual learning, is then a matter that can vary indefinitely.

A thought experiment can highlight the point at issue.[1] Imagine an obsessive Skinnerian who has joined forces with an evolutionary biologist in order to create a subspecies of African gray parrots with the *innate instinct* for uttering, without any special training, without so much as hearing an exemplar, "Boo Chomsky!" There is plenty of genetic diversity among African gray parrots, and no doubt some of it is in the desired direction of a bird who would be born wanting to utter "Boo Chomsky!" at its earliest opportunity, but how on earth could the birds with these alleles be identified? How could evolution, even with a helping hand from our artificial selector, find the leverage to steer a lineage in this direction? This is where the Baldwin effect comes to the rescue. We know that African gray parrots, like mynah birds and a few other species, are particularly trainable, and even self-trainable, aural mimics, so there is no question that any Skinnerian who set himself the task of creating a flock of parrots who all said "Boo Chomsky!" would soon be able, by the "shaping" method of operant conditioning, to create an avian chorus of adult birds with just this talent.[2] Having done so, he could begin, with the help of the evolutionary biologist, to raise the bar: only those birds who were particularly trainable, the champion learners of this phrase, would be allowed to reproduce in the next generation. There would be, as we have just seen, no guarantee that this would head in the right direction. It might be that there was no way to select for the talent for saying "Boo Chomsky!" (path A) that wasn't just selecting for virtuoso trainability in general (path B). But if there were any variability down path A, if (in other words) some of the accessible genotypes were not better learners in general but just more likely to learn to say "Boo Chomsky!" (and perhaps a few other phrases unimagined and untested by the selectors) easier than their rivals, they would be identified by this new selection pressure *that comes into existence only when the learned adult competence is discernible in the population.* They could then be selected for exactly this proclivity, which could, in due course, go all the way to a hairtrigger utterance of "Boo Chomsky!" in need of no training at all.

Is this impossible? Who knows? It may just be, perhaps, that in the Vast catalogue of possible but as yet unrealized African gray parrot genomes, not a single one yields a bird (under normal developmental conditions) that squawks "Boo Chomsky" as soon as it squawks anything. But if there is even one such genome, the beauty of the Baldwin effect is that it shows that there is no theoretical reason to rule out the otherwise astonishing feat of finding such a genetic needle in the haystack. Anyone who was tempted to assert that there is simply no way for natural selection to produce an African gray parrot whose "instinctual call" is "Boo Chomsky!" would be ignoring a path of orthodoxy, an unappreciated mechanism, but not a new or revolutionary one. This thought experiment of mine will have to suffice for the time being as my response to Downes's challenge for me to produce an actual example of "phenomena that do not succumb to standard evolutionary explanations" (this volume). If any funding agency wants me to turn my thought experiment into a real experiment, I'm sure I can still find a behaviorist or two who would enjoy coming out of retirement and setting this in motion. It will take quite a few years, and be quite expensive, but it might be worth it, if it would convince the diehard skeptics. The important point is that the chances of selectively breeding such a bird depend on the bird's having enough of a "mind" to be *trainable* to utter the sounds. There might also be an unrealized genome in the Vast catalogue of possible blue jay genomes that would yield the same vocalization instinct, but it is hard even to imagine a feasible path that could take us there, since there would be no adaptive slope to guide our search.

I take it that I am so far just elaborating the standard presumption about how the Baldwin effect works, not breaking new ground. But I have learned to be cautious about this. Is Godfrey-Smith right that Deacon, in his discussion of the Baldwin effect, has added a new mechanism? Now it is my turn to play skeptic; I think Deacon is right about the heightened selection pressure brought about by the prevalence of the Good Trick in the population, but I thought that was implicit all along in the earlier discussions—in Hinton and Nowlan, in Maynard Smith, and in my own remark (quoted above): "Over generations, the competition becomes stiffer: eventually, unless you are born with (or very nearly with) the Good Trick, you are not close enough to compete." Perhaps Deacon spelled it out better, or perhaps he has indeed proposed a new mechanism, but if so, I don't yet see what it is.

Finally, I was puzzled by Downes's dismissive suggestion regarding the evolution of lactose tolerance among people engaged in herding: "The relevant details are probably best spelled out in the molecular biology of enzyme production." But surely the difference between human subpopulations that plays the major role in explaining the observed differences in "enzyme production" is the large difference in diet, which is itself explained by a food-gathering practice that is learned, not genetically transmitted. This is not yet the Baldwin effect, but it is definitely an instance, contrary to what Downes says, of "mind directing evolution" in the bland but important sense of a learned, culturally transmitted practice having dramatic genetic consequences. Moreover, the case is pretty strong for an *indirect* Baldwin effect arising from such practices in another species involved in them. A border collie puppy hardly has to be taught to herd sheep—its instinctual skills are merely honed by training (unlike, say, the children of Basque shepherds who are not similarly genetically equipped with herding instincts!). What drove the evolution of herding instincts in border collies? The learned human Good Trick of animal husbandry. Dogs that could more readily learn to herd had a huge selective advantage, but only because of their interactions with their foresighted, looking-ahead "masters." In this case, it was the "mind-directed" activities of another species that created the gradients up which first unconscious, and later, artificial selection could drive the genomes of those wolf-kins.[3]

Acknowledgments

I am indebted to Mateo Mameli and Stephen Downes for valuable discussion on an earlier draft of this paper.

Notes

1. Since devising this case, I have been delighted to discover that a strikingly similar example with a slightly different emphasis was invented over a century ago by

Spalding (1873) quoted in Avital and Jablonca (2000): 321, a striking case of convergent evolution. Spalding's version has some variations of its own that are particularly amusing, since he supposes that sexual selection maintains the instinct long after the death of the Crusoe, the behaviorist trainer in his version. This is genuine possibility, I think.

2. A better technique that classical operant conditioning would be the ingenious imitation method used by Pepperberg (2000) in training her virtuoso vocalizer, Alex, who watches a rival being trained and competes for her attention and approval. But for the sake of my example it is important to recognize that the "flock" of parrots may be kept isolated from each other; the Baldwin effect depends on individual trainability and discernible differences therein, not on imitation or social learning, which are further effects of considerable power.

3. On the relation of unconscious and artificial selection (Darwin's terms) to natural selection, see Dennett (2001).

References

Avital, E. and E. Jablonka (2000). *Animal Traditions: Behavioural Inheritance in Evolution.* Cambridge: Cambridge University Press.

Baldwin, J. M. (1896). A new factor in evolution. *American Naturalist* 30: 441–451, 536–553. Reprinted in Belew and Mitchell (1996).

Belew, R. K. and M. Mitchell (eds.) (1996). *Adaptive Individuals in Evolving Populations: Models and Algorithms.* Reading, Mass.: Addison-Wesley.

Dawkins, R. (1982). *The Extended Phenotype.* Oxford: Oxford University Press.

Dennett, D. (1991). *Consciousness Explained.* Boston: Little, Brown.

Dennett, D. (1995). *Darwin's Dangerous Idea.* New York: Simon and Schuster.

Dennett, D. (2001). The evolution of culture. *Monist* 84 (3): 305–324.

Hinton, G. E. and S. J. Nowlan (1987). How learning can guide evolution. In Belew and Mitchell (1996), pp. 447–454.

Maynard Smith, J. (1987). Natural selection: When learning guides evolution. *Nature* 329: 761–762. Reprinted in Belew and Mitchell (1996).

Pepperberg, I. M. (2000). *The Alex Studies: Cognitive and Communicative Abilities of Grey Parrots.* Cambridge, Mass.: Harvard University Press.

Simpson, G. G. (1953). The Baldwin effect. In Belew and Mitchell (1996), pp. 99–110.

Spalding, D. (1873). Instinct with original observations on young animals. *MacMillan's Magazine* 27: 282–293. (Reprinted with an introduction by J. B. S. Haldane in 1954 in the *British Journal of Animal Behaviour* 2: 1–11.)

5

Multilevel Selection in a Complex Adaptive System: The Problem of Language Origins

Terrence W. Deacon

1 Introduction: Recipes for Failure

Theories of language origins have almost universally been embarrassments to empirical science. This is because they are typically like narratives exemplifying certain linguistic theories and deep philosophical commitments rather than efforts to understand the processes involved in generating this uniquely complex phenomenon. The reasons for this tendency are not hard to find. There is an almost complete absence of direct evidence of the process itself; an incomprehensibly complex organ (the brain) underlying the capacity to acquire and use language; and many competing philosophical preconceptions that all make strong claims about the nature of language and its role in human cognitive uniqueness. These are serious constraints and biases (though in at least one of these areas—neuroscience— there has been considerable progress in developing critical tools and compiling relevant evidence). These limits have licensed the acceptance of considerably more speculation in this field than in many others. But even as some of these limitations are becoming removed, as relevant comparative and developmental linguistic and neurological data are becoming available, I believe we are still crippled in a more fundamental way by theoretical biases and naivete.

In my opinion the greatest failure in this enterprise has been a failure to appreciate the full complexity of the evolutionary problem it poses. This is reflected in the remarkably simple evolutionary logic typically offered by standard accounts of language competence in humans. Indeed, I believe that much useful neurological and linguistic data are ignored in this enterprise, while other spurious features are considered important, precisely because we tend to conceive of language in a way that ignores the complex self-organizing and evolutionary dynamics that form the very essence of its design logic.

The tendency to ignore the evolutionary complexity of the problem is reflected in the plethora of scenarios based on (a) extrapolations of what are presumed to be general evolutionary trends or else on (b) one-of-a-kind special causes, which I will refer to as "magic bullets."

In the first category are theories based mostly on a presumed evolutionary *trend* toward increasing general intelligence. It is perhaps the oldest and least questioned assumption about human evolution that it is characterized by increasing intelligence resulting from an increase in brain size. A great many scenarios have been offered to explain this presumed advance—from the demands of hunting and tool manufacture, to the Machiavelian demands of competing for social status in large groups, to the importance of mother-infant communication for insuring care for a helpless human infant—however, there has been little critical reflection on the underlying assumption itself. That hominid brains have enlarged with respect to the common African ape ancestor and with respect to australopithecines is without question. The assumption that this must somehow reflect an increase in intelligence is in my opinion supported only by "just so" argumentation and precious little direct evidence. Moreover, even the evidence that is cited tends to make different and contradictory predictions, typically confounding absolute and comparative measures of brain size, and extrapolating the concept of human IQ (which is based on a collection of mostly symbolic tasks) to species unable to comprehend symbols altogether.

My intention in bringing these issues into focus is not to spend time criticizing the details of these assumptions (for this, see arguments in Deacon 1997), but to examine the role it has been given in language origin theories. The most common assumption along these lines is that the appearance of language in *Homo sapiens* is simply an expression of this increase in intelligence. The fact that there is not a *scala naturae* of languages correlated with species' intelligence is problematic; though this is often side-stepped by postulating some threshold effect such that only above some minimal intelligence is language possible. But this move undermines the simple extrapolation argument and requires explaining these special restrictions. More troublesome is the fact that language itself contributes to our effective intelligence. Considering that our common understanding of "general" intelligence derives from symbol-centric tests, the logic of the argument is somewhat circular.

To be fair, there are also a handful of theories suggesting that large brain size in humans evolved for some other reason than cognitive advance (including theories that it provided redundancy under conditions of failure due to heat stress, or that prior species have been limited in brain size for other reasons such as problems of heat dissipation, dietary support, or maternal pelvic limitations). Notably, however, all of these apparently noncognitive theories are smokescreens hiding the same ultimate functional claim. They all make the assumption that once brains were released from these constraints, or else enlarged for other reasons, their large size would have become advantageous because of the increased neural computational power this offered. So the difference is a matter of the order of events in the scenario rather than functional assumptions about brain size.

The second class of fallacious assumptions, which lead to what I have dubbed "magic bullet" theories, have also proliferated recently. The increase in the number of language origin theories that claim to trace the human language faculty to a unique neural mutation producing some specialized mental "organ" probably reflects the enormous influence of the innate grammar hypothesis initially made popular by the linguist Noam Chomsky. This speculation about the predominance of innate versus acquired knowledge about language structure has all but become the default dogma in the field. Unfortunately, not only are the specifications of this "faculty" in question, but any hints about how we are to translate the linguistic requirements into predictions about a neurological "organ" are completely vague. Such problems of evolutionary implausibility will be argued below, but here I want to focus on its influence on the study of human brain evolution. Notably, I think it has in effect become the standard-bearer for the much older philosophical speculation that there is some "essence" present in humans that is absent in other species: a human Rubicon.

If language is made possible in humans because only we possess an innate language faculty, incorporated into human brains at some point in hominid prehistory, then it should be possible to identify this critical distinguishing feature in human brains and correlate its first appearance with the introduction of modern human behavior. It is my belief that this intuitively compelling belief bolstered by linguistic speculation has created a theoretical vacuum that causes us to fall easy prey to exaggerating the significance of any apparently unique and unprecedented structures in humans that might be relevant to language. It has produced the cognitive and neural equivalent of a search for the proverbial "missing link"—that one bridge structure that allowed a primate species to become human, or, in this modern variant, allowed a mute and uncomprehending ape to become empowered with language.

Hypothetical missing-link claims for anatomical changes (many of which have not withstood scrutiny or have turned out not to be uniquely human) have included the descent of the larynx, the addition of Broca's language area to the brain, the cerebral asymmetry of the planum temporale, enlargement of the hypoglossal nerve, "mirror neurons" (controlling the tongue), as well as a diversity of hypothetical new mental faculties such as a "theory-of-mind" module, and "cerebral coherence," to list a very few. Each purported discovery of a missing link is heralded in the popular press as key to explaining the transformation of an ape into a human. They offer the promise of simple, single causes, an obvious before and after (without and then with language), and a "something" that embodies this critical difference. If only the solution were this simple and the difference this concrete! But it is precisely the curiously abstract nature of language structures and the enigma of their lawlike systematicity, despite the fact that they are evolved and not designed, that should warn us away from this sort of greedy reductionism in this case.

Language is not a trait of simple inheritance like sickle cell anemia, and it is not even a trait of complex inheritance like nose shape. Unlike the majority of adaptations one typically reads about in introductory textbooks on evolution, language presents us with an evolutionary problem that cannot be adequately handled by single cause caricatures of the evolutionary process. The "structures" we need to explain are not things but high-level abstractions. They are regularities of behavior and cognition that cannot even begin to be characterized in terms of the sounds and movements of vocal muscles that fleetingly embody them. The units of these "structures" are semiotic entities and their geometry is entirely relational.

Language didn't just evolve in the standard sense of that term. Language is an "emergent" biological phenomenon in ways unlike almost any other biological product (see Deacon, chap. 14, and Weber, chap. 15, both in this volume). Many biologists (see, e.g., Maynard Smith and Szathmáry 1997) have been forced to conclude, as I have, that language is as unprecedented in biology as was the very origins of the molecular genetic code. Imagining that explaining it would not require significant augmentation of existing evolutionary theory is, in my opinion, naive. Attempting to understand its emergent character by reducing it to a mere change in anatomy, an increase in intelligence, or a special case of computation inevitably obfuscates this central emergent nature. Because of this special status among evolved phenomena, the mystery of language forces us to explain it on different terms than say the evolution of upright posture or color vision. It is a problem analogous to explaining the evolution of an evolutionary process.

There are three additional considerations that I believe are indispensable to devising an adequate evolutionary approach to this mystery: (1) an appreciation of the role of self-organizing dynamics in the production of the complex systematicity recognized in language structures; (2) an evolutionary analysis that takes into account the multilevel interactions between biological evolutionary processes and nonbiological linguistic evolutionary processes; and (3) an analysis of the semiotic infrastructure of language that is sufficient to articulate its ultimate functional constraints. Though the following discussion will focus on the second of these considerations, it will become clear that each of the others becomes implicated at every level of analysis. Ultimately, the emergence of language offers a puzzle that requires us to rethink the concept of evolution itself in many significant ways, and demonstrates that it is intimately linked with processes of self-organization and semiosis.

2   Coevolution and Language

Language is not exactly a biological phenomenon subject to the sorts of constraints affecting organic matter, and yet neither is it simply a human tool designed for communication. It is a phenomenon subject to both kinds of influences. This is reflected in the evolutionary processes that have produced the human language capacity. Like living organisms themselves, languages have evolved, and continually evolve (though this often goes under the name "language change" or "drift"). Although it is unlike genetic evolution in many ways, it is nonetheless a form of "evolution" in the modern sense. Sensitivity to the use of this term dates to the nineteenth-century progressivist conceptions of evolution, in which "primitive" forms were supposedly inevitably to be replaced by ever more "advanced" forms. Comparative linguists long ago recognized that there were no obvious progressive tendencies in language change, and no consistent basis for ranking languages on their degree of sophistication. But *linguistic evolution* (as I will call it to distinguish it from the evolution of language abilities, e.g., involving changes in genes and brains) is an evolutionary process, even if it appears not to produce any obvious trend. It spontaneously occurs in the generation-to-generation replication of certain aspects of a language so long as some of these are favored over others, irrespective of whether this has a bearing on general language improvement. Biologists mostly recognize natural selection as a factor maintaining functional stabilization and counteracting spontaneous tendencies toward degradation and drift. The same can be expected for selective forces in linguistic evolution. Their predominant effects should be maintenance of internal functional stability in the face of constant forces of cross-linguistic diffusion, structural simplification, the spontaneous generation of lexical and syntactic variant forms, and the whims of historical chance. The selection factors driving linguistic evolution must include cognitive language "processing" constraints, communicative function requirements, frequency-dependence effects, and learnability. In this view of evolution, human brains, with their processing limitations, and human cultures with their special communicative contexts, can be considered the "environments" within which languages evolve.

In a paper titled "Brain-language co-evolution," I argued that language structure must have arisen in a long and drawn-out coevolutionary process in which both brain and language structures would have exerted selection pressures on one another (Deacon 1992). In my book *The Symbolic Species,* I elaborated this argument and suggested that because of this we should expect to find that human brains exhibit species-unique modifications that tend to "fit" the unique processing demands imposed by language learning and use (Deacon 1997). Reciprocally, we should expect languages to exhibit structures that appear "fitted" to human processing constraints. For example, languages should exhibit structures that optimize limits in human working memory and incorporate global architectures that are well suited for learning by immature brains with their reduced mnemonic capacities, even if this made them more difficult for adults to acquire, because these features would be favored by linguistic evolution. These predictions are still in direct contradiction to claims by generative linguists that language structures are intrinsically difficult to learn (in the absence of considerable innate foreknowledge of what are the allowed structures). I believe that this latter position arises due to a misguided conception of linguistic theory on the model of computational and engineering design. The appropriate model for language is not, however, a formal rule system nor a set of algorithms, no matter how closely this can come to modeling some linguistic functions. Language is an evolved biological phenomenon, and its core architectonic logic must be conceived in evolutionary terms, although as I hope to demonstrate, our conception of the relevant evolutionary processes may need to be considerably broadened to deal with the complexities involved.

In a paper entitled "Natural language and natural selection," Steven Pinker and Paul Bloom made a superficially similar argument, but came to opposite conclusions (Pinker and Bloom 1989; 1990). This argument was further elaborated by Pinker in his book *The Language Instinct* (Pinker 1994). They argued that those language principles characterized as "universal grammar" by generative linguists, and presumed to be part of an innate human language faculty, could have arisen via natural selection processes. This view ran counter to most accepted claims by advocates of innate universal grammar. It had been argued previously that both the thoroughly integrated systematicity of syntax and the apparent ubiquity of nontransparent syntactic operations (which appear to be neither computationally nor functionally optimal) were signs of a system that could not have evolved incrementally under selection for functional effectiveness. Of course, similar features in organisms that in the nineteenth century were cited as evidence against Darwinian theory—such as the design of the image-forming eye or the elaboration of costly ornamentation as in male peacock tail feathers—have long since been successfully explained and incorporated into evolutionary theory. So Pinker and Bloom felt they were on solid ground arguing that similar features of language design could likewise have been accomplished via the operation of natural selection. The incremental evolution of interdependent syntactic operations could be understood, they argued, on the analogy of "parity" constraints in computational systems, which forces mutual agreement between communicators on the choice of otherwise arbitrary alternative signal markers.[1] The existence of apparently nonoptimal structures and operations in language could be compared with similarly compromised functional organization exhibited in organisms. Such non-optimal compromises usually reflect competing functional demands on the same structure. Many physiological compromises balance the competing demands of functional integration, developmental "construction," metabolic support, and phylogenetic "inertia."

When it came to an account of exactly how evolution would be able to generate such atypical and abstract "traits" as linguistic operators, Pinker and Bloom found it necessary to appeal to some nonstandard evolutionary approaches. Evolution is "descent with modification," as Darwin encapsulated it in his elegantly simple phrase. Prior structures become progressively modified by forces of selection. The ultimate source of novelty, according to this well-tested orthodoxy, is noisiness in the design specification in some structure or function. This serendipitous variation can ultimately be captured and amplified by natural selection to the extent that it provides some better fit to the demands imposed from without. But what were the prior structures modified to give rise to the abstract language structures that are grammatical relationships and syntactic operations? Presumably they would have to be something like behavioral, perceptual, or mnemonic instincts of some kind, perhaps as applied to innate calls or gestural communication. However, nowhere in the works I have surveyed advocating this evolutionary origin of universal grammar (UG) is any candidate antecedent proposed.

Instead of attempting to homologize these abstract and idiosyncratic language structures to anything nonlinguistic that could be "shaped up" into innate language instincts, advocates of an evolved UG have suggested the plausibility of a different kind of antecedent: a learned habit. They suggest that there may have been a gradual evolutionary internalization of initially (in protolinguistic prehistory) learned language habits that over the course of evolution became "assimilated" as innate knowledge of grammar. Presumably, communicative regularities acquired and developed by learning and social transmission in our distant ancestors became progressively replaced by innate counterparts. On the surface, this sounds like a blatantly Lamarckian argument. In fact, however, there is a striking difference. Advocates of an evolved UG mostly invoke the twin concepts of the Baldwin effect and genetic assimilation to explain this transformation from habit to innate knowledge (e.g., Pinker 1994).

This superficially fits an interpretation of James Mark Baldwin's (1896) and Conrad Waddington's (1957) theories as Darwinian surrogates for Lamarckian evolutionary processes. Both of these processes have been characterized as the transformation of a set of acquired habits or physiological responses to a set of instinctual, ineluctable products of development by virtue of progressive replacement of one mechanism (learned or environmentally stimulated production) by the other (developmental genetic production). Historically, both theories were offered as counterparts to Lamarckian accounts, and were intended to demonstrate the plausibility (and in Waddington's case, the existence) of a parallel evolutionary transition from acquired to innate adaptations that could be explained in a roughly Darwinian way. In this sense, they can be characterized as pseudo-Lamarckian rather than crypto-Lamarckian, as some critics have charged.

These two theoretical mechanisms have been the subject of much controversy in evolutionary biology, and as this volume demonstrates, they have not yet achieved the status of well-accepted biological processes. In part, this is because many mechanistic details necessary to empirically ground these theoretically plausible processes have not been worked out. And, in part, this is because until very recently no presumed examples had been identified and studied to determine what is occurring. In addition, differences between Baldwin's conception of "organic selection" and Waddington's "genetic assimilation" are also often overlooked, especially when both are characterized in pseudo-Lamarckian terms. Because of this intrinsic vagueness of theory, it has not been obvious how to specify the conditions under which such processes will or will not occur, what physiological and genetic mechanisms would be recruited in the process, and whether this pseudo-Lamarckian characterization is consistent with the underlying mechanisms.

Pinker's intention has merely been to argue for the evolutionary biological plausibility of innate universal grammar. So if a Lamarckian trend can be achieved by Darwinian means then at least plausibility is not at issue. But there are good reasons to be cautious about accepting the plausibility of this assumption before the mechanisms that can explain these special cases of multilevel evolutionary processes are better understood.

3   Breaking the Pseudo-Lamarckian Mold

The Symbolic Species developed the details of such a coevolutionary argument, suggesting that extensive use of symbolic communication would have constituted something analogous to a novel niche, imposing novel selection pressures on human cognition and vocal systems (Deacon 1997). This was a subtle, but important, variant on the kind of process thought to occur in organic selection and genetic assimilation. The concept of niche construction has indeed been independently described in some greater detail and applied to a number of other nonhuman evolutionary phenomena (Laland et al. 1996). The logic of the niche construction effect is somewhat different than either Baldwinian or Waddingtonian models suggested, although in my original account I did not adequately discriminate between them. In some ways the theory of niche construction is more general than either of these other two theories, in other ways it is more limited.[2]

But I also argued (also outlined below) that many of the grammatical computational "structures" imagined to be evolvable, according to the plausibility argument of Pinker and Bloom, would in fact not be biologically evolvable. Though there is nothing "in principle" that makes it an impossibility, in order for this to occur one would need to make some exceedingly unrealistic assumptions about the nature of the link between language functions and brains, and regarding the requirements for natural selection.

So to the inevitable irritation of linguists, who had claimed "it couldn't be otherwise," I concluded that the structure of UG would not yield to a biological evolutionary solution, nor would it have a neurological explanation, although I had very little to say regarding how else grammatical knowledge might arise (Deacon 1997). However, the restrictions on evolvability that exclude a biological solution to the problem of explaining grammar do not apply to processes of *linguistic evolution*. It is in this realm of nonbiological evolutionary processes that I suggested we might look to find the most important factors contributing to language structure. Elsewhere I have outlined a number of potential influences that might have affected the linguistic evolution of features of syntactic form, as well as the neurological supports for representing them (Deacon 1992). These include semiotic constraints and processing constraints, as well as requirements of communicative function, and perhaps even certain cognitive predispositions for linguistic "schemas" such as those suggested by cognitive linguists (e.g., see Langacker 1990). All of these must be understood analogous to the way we understand selection pressures operating in evolutionary biology. Over time languages are constantly being shaped by them, self-organize with respect to them, and compensate to them as simultaneous and not necessarily concordant boundary conditions.

In *The Symbolic Species* I focused on two other capacities necessary for language that should be evolvable as well as language-specific (Deacon 1997). These are the special cognitive demands imposed by comprehending symbolic representation itself, and the neural circuitry enabling precise cortical control over vocalization. These adaptations would be invariant across the most diverse languages, would make the same cognitive and neurological demands irrespective of individual differences, and would provide significant reproductive consequences across great spans of evolutionary time, so long as linguistic communication in some form is present. I suggested plausible, specific, testable neural correlates for these: (1) early disproportionately increased cell production in the cerebral cortex, which would (2) alter the pattern of developmental competition for axonal targets in many linked structures, including (3) shifting proportions of projections to cortical regions favoring expansion of prefrontal cortex, and (4) increasing projections from cortex to brainstem vocal nuclei. The connectional changes in these brain structures, achieved by this developmental mechanism, would be evolvable as a response to selection pressures favoring symbol learning and phonological control, respectively. In other words, the selection pressure is generated by language use itself, as then expressed in protolinguistic form.

At first glance, the logic of this argument, like that proposed by Pinker and Bloom for UG, may appear to have a pseudo-Lamarkian character. But on closer inspection this turns out not to be so. It differs not just with respect to what is and is not evolvable, but with respect to how the evolutionary mechanism is itself conceived and what it produces. Contrary to Pinker and Bloom, I think the evolutionary logic we must invoke to explain language is quite unlike its Lamarckian counterpart, even as "Darwinized" by Baldwin and others. In fact, I think it is the converse of a Lamarckian process in both mechanism and direction of change. Rather than producing innate language knowledge or predispositions for certain grammatical constructions that replace their presumably less efficient learned antecedents, the learning component has become, more important (e.g., the relative importance of working memory). Nor has vocal control become more innately prespecified. Again, just the opposite. Innate control of vocalization has diminished and learning has come to play a crucial role. In neither case does evolution genetically assimilate what was previously an acquired habit. Nothing is made more innate.

In this regard the process is quite different in consequence from what either Baldwin or Waddington might have predicted. In some ways, the evolutionary dynamic linking language behavior and brain evolution had the opposite effect: the *de*-differentiation of innate predispositions and an *increase* in the contribution by a learning mechanism. In addition, I am convinced that a suite of additional supports for the acquisition and use of language were likewise augmented, from an enhancement of automatization capabilities to an increase in the motivation to imitate, among others. But, again, these do not replace or assimilate an ancestral acquired function. They are modifications of ancillary systems that make the acquisition by learning far more facile.

The key concept for understanding this logic is what I will call "masking." I am using this term to refer to shielding or protecting something from natural selection. Selection is often viewed as a negative or subtractive factor in evolution. This is explicit, for example, in Baldwin, and in part motivates his theory as a means to introduce a "positive factor" (Baldwin 1896). But this is an oversimplification. Selection is generated by any bias affecting reproduction of genes or traits, positively or negatively. What links all these multilevel coevolutionary theories together is that they involve differential exposure to selection: either as something is shielded from natural selection or else is unshielded and newly exposed to selection by virtue of some action of the organism itself.

In recent years, especially following the comparative analysis of protein and gene sequence change in evolution, it has become obvious that selection cannot reach into all or even most aspects of physiology. Much genetic change is either unexpressed ("silent"), has its effect masked by more "dominant" alleles, or is expressed as altered protein structure but has no functional consequence at the level of the whole organism, where selection operates. In fact, with the advent of transgenic research and the study of animals with "knocked-out" genes, it is becoming clear that the self-regulatory and self-organizing capacities of the organism can often compensate for the absence of what were once believed to be essential genes.

Moreover, under ecological conditions where competition is relatively reduced or alternative supports are provided, even normally deleterious loss-of-function mutations may be effectively invisible to (masked from) selection. Examples of masking by virtue of reduced competition would include founder species populating a new island ecosystem. This should result in diverse patterns of genomic degradation (a prediction that could be tested) as well as rapid diversification. The rapid replacement of dinosaurs by placental mammals after the KT boundary event could also be an example. Examples of masking by generally reduced selection are ubiquitous in domesticated species, though also paired with human selection for certain distinctive traits. Thus, domestication should also produce extensive genomic degradation, including some reduction of innate specification and a generalized dedifferentiation of behavioral traits. An example of extrinsic masking appears to be provided by fruit-eating primates (anthropoids) in which the gene for the protein l-gulono-gamma-lactone oxidase (LGO)—the final enzyme in the metabolic pathway for endogenously synthesizing ascorbic acid (vitamin C) in mammals—has degraded as selection for its function was masked by the ubiquity of vitamin C available in fruit (see Nishikimi et al. 1994).

Both masking and unmasking have been involved in the evolution of human language abilities. The social evolution and transmission of symbolic communication, along with the parallel elaboration of stone tools, created a radically different niche than that experienced by our non-symbolic ancestors, the australopithecines and other apes. As this communicative tool evolved through a sequence of progressively more elaborate, more vocalized, more systematic forms, and as it became ever more essential to successful reproduction, novel selection pressures unmasked selection on previously "neutral" variants and created advantages for certain classes of mutations that might not otherwise have been favored. It also masked selection on traits made less vital by being supplemented by the consequences of this cultural niche.

For example, there appears to have been a significant reduction in the number and the innate specificity of our species-typical calls (e.g., laughter and sobbing) as compared to the other African apes. This has probably been directly influenced by vocal language, because of competitive interference. Masking may have led to their reduced specificity and structural simplification and to the ease of recruitment of their component tonal, temporal, and emotional correlates for language functions, in the form of prosodic features. There are likely many other effects of masking in humans, such as reduction of olfactory structures. There may even have been a global dedifferentiation of a variety of other cognitive tendencies that has produced what might be described as a more paedomorphic cognitive style, by virtue of which exploratory play and other forms of non-instrumental activity (i.e., "entertainment") have become disinhibited as compared to other species. Our biologically atypical aesthetic predispositions may be reflections of this. In general, we are a self-domesticated species in these many regards.

So, in a way not radically dissimilar to the way the construction of beaver dams led to an evolutionary change in beaver anatomy and physiology, making them more aquatic, the human-created niche we call culture had its primary influence on neurologically based systems. I have argued that the major neuroanatomic differences that distinguish humans from other apes, other primates, and from mammals in general, are the anatomical effects produced by this radical niche modification (Deacon 1997). It's hard to imagine any more robust, ubiquitous, sex-independent, and unprecedented source of selection pressures than would be provided by this unusual, symbolic, cultural niche. And it seems almost ludicrous to suggest that some nonspecific increase in the need for general intelligence could have generated most of these changes while symbolic culture is attributed only a post hoc role in human cognitive evolution. This is one reason I have argued that some form of symbolic cultural communication must have been in place right from the point that neuroanatomical changes (e.g., increasing relative brain size) become evident in hominids (Deacon 1997).

We are then, I believe, a "symbolic species" in a deeply physiological sense. But note that this is not because we have genetically assimilated symbolic knowledge. It is because symbols have played a major role in shaping our cognitive capacities in ways that are complementary to their special functional demands, not that we are made in their image in any sense. Our physiology has not assimilated these symbolic habits themselves. We have changed with respect to them. They must still be acquired. *It's just that everything about us has made this acquisition almost automatic and inevitable.*

In summary, the process I have described has all the hallmarks of the processes of organic selection and genetic assimilation, but without the pseudo-Lamarckian consequence. It is the result of the effects of adaptive physiological capacities and learning abilities complicating the simple logic of natural selection, in ways that Baldwin and Waddington would have felt comfortable with. It's just that these pressures do not work the way they imagined. The reverse should in fact be the general rule. Perhaps the failure to appreciate this was a result of thinking in nonsystemic ways, in terms of simple traits and individual genetic determinates. Organisms are not this simple. Masking or unmasking may indeed affect specific systems and specific gene loci (e.g., the LGO locus in the frugivory example above), but the consequences are inevitably distributed widely within the complex system of the organism and the population.

The most ubiquitous effect of masking selection is dedifferentiation and degradation of function, analogous to what we observe in the case of cave fish, whose eyes have degenerated. But when one system is degraded, it often shifts selection and the burden of the masked and degraded adaptive function to other functional loci within the genome and body. In the case of frugivory and vitamin C, for example, I suspect that the evolution of three-color vision in anthropoid primates was evolutionarily coupled with the new and ineluctable need to accurately identify ripe fruit. Thus, a variant capacity in this otherwise totally unrelated organ system for vision became unmasked with respect to this novel selection pressure. And there are within the systems of the body potentially dozens of capabilities that might exhibit some variants that overlap with the features of these unmasked selection pressures. In other words, masking leads to degradation leads to unmasking. And the unmasking can have highly distributed parallel synergistic consequences—with the potential to significantly amplify adaptations. This latter effect is further enhanced by population effects that ultimately account for the appearance of genetic assimilation, which I will now turn to.

Unmasking previously neutral variations in a population has a similar distributed influence, though in this case it tends to play a collecting rather than distributing role. Consider the case of Waddington's experiments showing genetic assimilation of fly-wing vein patterns induced in response to heat (Waddington 1953). Recent developmental genetic studies suggest that this changed environment unmasked a variety of susceptibilities (associated with heat shock protein variants) that initially were scattered diffusely in different individuals in the population (e.g., see Rutherford and Lindquist 1998). By unmasking these "risk factors" (so to speak) and breeding only individuals that expressed one of these now exposed variants, Waddington progressively inbred individuals carrying these various factors that produced similar phenotypic consequences and ended up co-assorting them in the genome. As a result, in later generations there were individuals who carried multiple risk factors, and so crossed some threshold of synergistic effects to produce the trait ineluctably.

Taken, as Waddington intended, as an analogue to the context-sensitive expression of adaptive traits, it similarly suggests that the supports for an unmasked adaptive response may be drawn widely from resources in the organism and the population. Waddington focused on single morphological traits, and only bred with respect to them, but evolution tends to have a more systemic and less trivial "focus" on the traits selected. In the case of language adaptations (as opposed to any unitary "language faculty"), the demands of symbolic communication unmasked selection on a widely diverse set of traits whose independent modifications collectively and convergently provided adaptations to this demand. Any support was accepted.

Finally, it should be noted that these two classic efforts to explain pseudo-Lamarckian processes by Darwinian means, namely those of Baldwin and Waddington, are inverses of one another regarding this mechanism. Whereas Baldwin implicitly attributed the effects of organic selection to the masking of selection by behavioral adaptation, Waddington implicitly attributed genetic assimilation to the unmasking of variants, otherwise unexpressed, by the introduction of new selection pressures in the form of environmental stresses.

4   The Tangled Hierarchy of Linguistic Selection

The story of the origin of language structures does not stop with the reformulation of the logic of evolutionary assimilation. Where I disagree most
from previous theories is with regard to the role played by evolution at
many levels. This positions me somewhat with developmental systems theorists emphasizing nongenetic sources that contribute a significant fraction
of the biological information reflected in organism structure and function.
A major emphasis of *The Symbolic Species* was the importance of self-
organization processes and *intra*selection processes that contribute to the
final structure of the developing brain. This does not mean that I consider
genetic evolution to play a minor role. Nor does it mean that I find any reason to abandon a fairly strict interpretation of natural selection. Indeed, as
the above discussion indicates, I find no reason to entertain even the
pseudo-Lamarckian interpretations of Baldwin and Waddington. But in
the context of such reformulation of classic multilevel selection theories, it
opens up a whole domain of circuitous and multilevel means by which evolution can operate. The complexity of these multilevel interactions is,
again, epitomized by language evolution. The origins of language is not
simply a two-tiered evolutionary problem, but involves a many-tiered
complex system of self-organizing and selection processes nested within
each other. One of the most important elements of this is the emergence of
a new level of evolutionary dynamic out of biological evolution. With the
emergence of language a second-order level of evolutionary process begins
at the level of symbols themselves: linguistic evolution. This changes
everything.

Selection "pressures" affecting language must be considered as nested
within one another to the extent that language evolution is nested in biological evolution. On the human side of this equation, the processing
demands of symbolic reference, symbol combination, and symbolic communication in real-time provide novel selection pressures affecting the
brain and vocal tract. As the language-mediated niche (the symbolic cultural environment) became more and more ubiquitous in human prehistory, these selection pressures would have become correspondingly more
important and powerful, producing evolutionary changes in these structures in response. On the language side of this equation, the human-derived

requirements of learnability, automatizability, and maintaining consistency with the constraints of symbolic reference provide selection pressures that affect language structures. These ultimately determine the relative viability of different morphological and syntactic regularities with respect to their human environment, and the likelihood that they will be passed on to succeeding generations. One might conceive of these as the linguistic analogues to the selection pressure that affect reproductive success, only in this case it is the differential "reproduction" of alternative language features that is affected—in other words, the fecundity and fidelity of their transmission across generations.

I have repeatedly argued that probably the most important of these constraints are those that arise from the semiotic infrastructure implicit in symbolic reference itself (Deacon 1992, 1997). This has almost entirely been ignored by linguists and cognitive scientists alike, largely because it has been assumed that symbolic reference contributes no constraint on the form of language other than arbitrariness. I believe that this is an unwarranted assumption based on the fallacy of generalizing from individual symbol-object relationships to systems of symbols. As I will argue below, there are indeed constraints that are implicit in symbol use. The point I want to emphasize here, however, is that such semiotic constraints as involve symbol systems are neither located in brains nor in society, per se. They are a bit like the formal constraints that have shaped the development of mathematics (and yield such curious universal phenomena as prime numbers). Though I leave it to philosophers to argue over the nature of the "existence" of such formal constraints, I believe it cannot be denied that mathematics has had to evolve with respect to them. Similarly in the case of language, semiotic constraints have acted as selection pressures on the evolution of both language and brain structures.

To see how this can be so, we need to dissect the symbolic reference relationship, such as exemplified by words and sentences, to see in what ways it is not merely unconstrained arbitrariness.[3] Though the common meaning of this term has been diluted to refer to any arbitrarily correlated sign and its reference, this obscures the subtlety of a more traditional and discriminative meaning by which linguistic signs were thought to differ from more "natural" signs, such as icons and indices. In language, the fundamental symbolic units—words and morphemes—derive their reference not merely by being conventionally assigned some correspondence with an object in the world, but from a kind of indirect systemic reference. This is not immediately reflected in symbol-object associations, but is implicit in what we recognize as "valences" for word combinations. These implicit valences indicate that the referential power of words is vested in and mediated by a system of indexical (or pointing) relationships between symbol tokens (e.g., words) themselves. Symbols implicitly indicate other symbols. This is reflected in the implicit word-word networks captured differently by a dictionary, a thesaurus, or an encyclopedia. Their relationships with one another constitute a system. This systematicity determines their possibilities of concatenation, substitution, alternation, and so forth, which constrains their useful combinations, and creates a structured space of relationships in which each becomes a marker of semantic position. But because there is also a conventional correspondence between words and things in the world, the topologies of these two "spaces" (i.e., the system of word-word valence relationships and some systematization of the regularities linking certain physical objects) can potentially be mapped one to the other. The result is that "positional" relationships within semantic space can be taken as corresponding to physical relationships. Symbolic reference is thus reference mediated by reference to a system, and by that system's relationship to a perceived systematicity in the world. This system embeddedness of symbols is reflected in the way linguistic utterances can still refer to objects of reference in the complete absence or nonexistence of these objects; a feature that is often called "displacement." So the combination of systematicity and indirectness of reference allows words without simple reference, and with reference that has no real-world counterpart. Symbolic reference is thus *irreducibly systemic*.

This implicit abstract infrastructure can have real physical effects because it makes special demands on learning. The discovery that certain sign tokens (e.g., words) refer to things symbolically (instead of by likeness or simple conventional correlation), requires the language learner first to learn these correlations (by rote), and then to sort through a large number of possible systemic correspondence patterns in order to discover the one symbol-symbol system that best maps to some logic of object-object relationships. Though correspondences also exist between words and objects, and recognizing these must precede recognizing that there is a system "behind" them, it is this shift in referential strategy that transforms simple correspondence into meaning. Sorting through the evidence of correspondences and regularities to find the one relevant topology that bisociates these two realms is an intrinsically difficult task. In this way, symbolic reference is the archetypal encryption relationship; a fact that is evident in any attempt to interpret a foreign language or ancient script.

In *The Symbolic Species*, I argued that the most extensive modification to take place in human brain evolution—the disproportionate expansion of the cerebral cortex, and specifically of the prefrontal cortex—reflects the evolutionary adaptation to this intensive working memory processing demand imposed by symbol learning (Deacon 1997). This correspondence is inferred from the additional fact that this kind of cognitive sorting task— and the related abilities to maintain attention on multiple relationships, suppress stimulus drive, and shift attention to nonsalient stimulus features—is impaired by prefrontal damage in many species and is associated with prefrontal activation in *in vivo* imagery studies when tasks of this sort are presented to human subjects. So the very nature of symbolic reference, and its unusual cognitive demands when compared to nonsymbolic forms of reference, is a selection force working on those neurological resources most critical to supporting it. In the context of a society heavily dependent on symbol use—as is any conceivable human society, but no nonhuman societies—brains would have been under intense selection to adapt to these needs. This, then, is a case of selection pressure affecting the evolution of a biological substrate (the brain) and yet which is imposed, not by the physical environment, but ultimately from a purely semiotic realm.

Grammar and syntax are also affected by selection pressures having to do with processing demands that are distinct from these semiotic constraints. Like brains, language structures are also under selection to maintain structural conformity to these restrictions, but at the same time the structures of a language are also subject to selection with respect to the neural processing demands imposed by symbolic communication in real time. Linguistic forms that failed to conform to these semiotic constraints and created regular ambiguity or failure of reference would face extinction, as would forms that overburdened working memory or could not take advantage of cognitive automatization shortcuts.

In summary, I believe that many structural features of language are derived from sources of "information" other than nature or nurture. The demands of symbol learning can ultimately be construed as selection pressures over and above those that are contributed by genetic, neural, social, or ecological sources. They may in fact play the dominant role in shaping the fine structure of languages, at least at the symbolic level, although the actual physical features of language may be even more affected by neural, physiological, and communicative constraints. Still, the demands imposed by symbol acquisition and symbolic analyses have, in my opinion, driven the major features of brain evolution in hominids.

Irrespective of my specific hypotheses, it seems beyond doubt that in order to develop an adequate account of the origins of symbolic abilities and of the grammatical regularities that languages exhibit, we are forced to consider a tangled hierarchy of interlocking evolutionary and self-organizing phenomena. It should no longer be considered radical to predict that much of the information behind language structure is derived via self-organizing and selection dynamics that proceed mostly independent of biological evolution. To ignore this vast web of organizing effects and these interweaving semiotic and neurological constraints and their role in shaping the dynamic processes that produce and sustain languages is to ignore most details of the problem.

5   Conclusions: Oh What a Tangled Web We Weave

To begin to sum up these arguments and relate all to the theme of this volume, let me step back from the details and consider how the logic of the original Baldwinian insight has been undermined and augmented by trying to apply it to the problem of language origins.

First, we have retained the insight that the diverse and flexible phenotypic products of a complex organism (especially including behavioral and cognitive products) contribute an important complication to the simple minimalist conception of natural selection. There is a kind of compound interest effect that comes from adaptations that significantly change the environment, or that more subtly restructure the niche that encapsulates the organism. This flexibility means that the virtual space of alternatives is always larger than what is actually snared by natural selection, and that the complexity of the organism itself is the origin of this wider range of potentially relevant "environments." Another metaphoric way to think of this is simply that because organisms are extended physical systems with causal circuits that reach out beyond their surfaces, they are a constituent part of the environment they inhabit and from which forces of selection may emerge.

Second, we have jettisoned any underlying Lamarckian gloss given to this kind of process and have shown that this interpretation is not consistent with its most likely consequences. Even a fully "Darwinized" interpretation of organic selection or genetic assimilation, as many evolutionary psychologists have accepted, turns out to have serious theoretical flaws once the underlying mechanism is somewhat more carefully fleshed out. This is a serious challenge to the speculation that universal grammar might have evolved to be an innate complement of the "language faculty" by anything like a Baldwinian or Waddingtonian mechanism.

Third, by unpacking the causal logic of these theories and recognizing the central role played by masking functions, and the way these distribute, collect, and reorganize selection factors, we have begun to glimpse the generality of these processes, and how they may actually contribute to such complex multilevel adaptations as language behavior. This can liberate us from the tendency to think in terms of single evolutionary causes and simple accounts of adaptive structures. It also creates a biological context within which to begin to consider the contributory roles of systemic self-organizing processes, without succumbing to the tendency to attribute Lamarckian functions to them, or in any way envisioning that they undermine the constraints and logic of natural selection. Natural selection is simply far more complex than is often appreciated. But it would be a mistake to imagine that we could reduce the logic of these processes to nothing but natural selection. The very topology of the process is fundamentally altered in this case. The simple feed-forward of phenotypic effects on reproductive success has become embedded in another feed-forward loop in which other features of the phenotypic effect come to be amplified and to play a significant role in the direction that evolutionary change takes. This kind of directional-biasing effect (although it does not imply that evolution is "directed" in any vague intentional sense) cannot be addressed by natural selection theory itself. Natural selection itself is agnostic with respect to any directionality of evolutionary processes, even with respect to complexification, despite the intuitive appeal of this link. But these sorts of second-order evolutionary dynamics can be directional, as the case of language suggests. Indeed, I suspect that biological complexification itself must be explained using a generalization of this second-order evolutionary logic.

Fourth, by recognizing that linguistic evolution (irrespective of gene evolution) likely contributes a significant fraction of the information determining language structure, and by identifying some of the selection factors that constitute the "niche" that language occupies, we are in a much better position to approach questions that are merely begged by innate grammar theories (and which are now undermined by this analysis). What determines that languages share certain abstract features in common? Why these and not others? How is it that we come to learn or discover them? How did they come into being? What determines how they are represented and processed in brains? This is where the greatest amount of theoretical, empirical, and simulation work needs to be done. It will require the combined efforts of linguists, computer modelers, evolutionary and developmental biologists, and neuroscientists to thoroughly unpack the details of the complex system from which grammar and syntax emerge.

Fifth, this multilevel evolutionary approach has for the first time implicated what is neither a genetic- nor a culture-derived source of selection acting on both brains and languages. Semiotic constraints are in my estimation the most critical part of this story. Leaving this out leaves the analysis ungrounded, without a prime mover of sorts. Although this representational trick had to be "discovered" socially, and it was indirectly via social factors that it had its biological evolutionary effects, these semiotic constraints aren't strictly speaking social phenomena. In the study of complex systems, many researchers have recognized the critical formative influence of what might be described as topological universals. Boundary conditions of various sorts—spatial constraints, temporal parameters, connectedness of graphs and networks, recursive or re-entrant, causal or representational geometries, and mere finiteness of systems—can determine the characteristic patterns and stable attractor configurations of dynamical systems. Semiotic constraints affect the evolution of language in much the same way that boundary conditions affect the dynamics of physical systems. This makes the argument a natural extension of developmental systems theory. Semiotic constraints have had a significant role in structuring both languages and brains, because these physical phenomena are embedded in complex dynamic evolving systems, made sensitive to these constraints by the discovery of what can be done when they are respected and embodied. This just touches the tip of an immense iceberg of a field that has yet to be brought to the surface, and which might be called evolutionary semiotics. Until a more principled analysis of the logic of these sorts of processes is understood, we will remain in a prescientific phase of cognitive and social science.

Finally, approaching evolutionary processes in a way that respects the complexity and self-organizing character of the substrates in which they occur can give us a glimpse at a higher-order logic of kinds of evolutionary processes. Additionally, we can begin to see the essential interplay that must exist between self-organizing and selection processes that constitutes evolution. Not only can we recognize that evolutionary processes include self-organizing processes, but they may also include nested levels of other evolutionary dynamics. To understand the details of language origins— including both the origins of language adaptations and the origins of language structures—we need to understand how one evolutionary dynamic can emerge from another, how linguistic evolution can emerge from molecular evolution, and how this can feed back to alter the very nature of the antecedent process. Language evolution was shown to be analogous to niche construction in some regards, and this was seen to introduce a complicated compound interest effect into evolution in which products of behavioral intervention in the environment can feed forward to become selection pressures in future generations. In one sense this is the essential dynamic captured by both Baldwin's and Waddington's insights. In many ways niche construction is far too narrowly conceived to capture all such phenotypic feed-forward effects, but by recognizing the phenotype as part of the niche, one can at least see how the analogy can be extended. Nevertheless, the evolutionary dynamic that gave rise to language and still plays a role in driving language change and maintaining linguistic systematic complexity, is incompletely characterized in this way. Language and symbolic culture do not merely constitute a niche. They are more than this. They are emergent and parasitic (or rather symbiotic) evolutionary processes whose independent dynamics (driven in part by semiotic factors never before relevant to biological evolution) have essentially become the tail that wagged the dog. These semiotic systems are active evolving systems that have their own self-organizing principles and evolutionary dynamics, and have imposed this on human biology. It is, in effect, a third-order evolutionary process, in which complex directionality effects are clearly evident. There is, literally, no telling where it will lead.

Notes

1. This argument is based on a misleading engineering metaphor in which independent parts preexist an assembled whole. In biologically evolved systems, however, the integration and complementarity of "parts" come as natural consequences of the progressive *differentiation* of an antecedent less differentiated whole structure, both phylogenetically and embryologically.

2. At the time of writing *The Symbolic Species* I was unaware of the work on "niche construction" as described in Laland et al. (1996).

3. The following condenses an argument presented in chapters 2 and 3 of *The Symbolic Species*.

References

Baldwin, J. M. (1896). A new factor in evolution. *American Naturalist* 30: 441–451, 536–553.

Deacon, T. (1992). Brain-language coevolution. In John A. Hawkins and Murray Gel-Mann (eds.), *The Evolution of Human Languages*. Santa Fe Institute Studies in the Sciences of Complexity, Proc. vol. 10, Redwood City, Calif.: Addison-Wesley.

Deacon, T. (1997). *The Symbolic Species*. New York: W. W. Norton.

Laland, K., F. Odling-Smee, and F. Feldman (1996). On the evolutionary consequences of niche construction. *Journal of Evolutionary Biology* 9: 293–316.

Langacker, R. (1990). *Concept, Image, and Symbol: The Cognitive Basis of Grammar*. Berlin and New York: Mouton de Gruyter.

Maynard Smith, J. and E. Szathmáry (1997). *The Major Transitions in Evolution*. London and New York: Oxford University Press.

Nishikimi, M., R. Fukuyama, S. Minoshoma, N. Shimizu, and K. Yagi (1994). Cloning and chromosomal mapping of the human nonfunctional gene for L-gulono-gamma-lactone oxidase, the enzyme for L-ascorbic acid biosynthesis missing in man. *Journal of Biological Chemistry* 269: 13685–13688.

Pinker, S. (1994). *The Language Instinct: How the Mind Creates Language*. New York: William Morrow.

Pinker, S. and P. Bloom (1989). Natural language and natural selection. Occasional paper no. 39, Center for Cognitive Science, MIT, Cambridge, Mass. Revised and reprinted with commentary in *Behavioral and Brain Sciences* 13: 707–784 (1990).

Rutherford, S. and S. Lindquist (1998). Hsp90 as a capacitor for morphological evolution. *Nature* 396: 336–342.

Waddington, C. H. (1953). Genetic assimilation of an acquired character. *Evolution* 7: 118–126.

Waddington, C. H. (1957). *The Strategy of the Genes*. London: Allen and Unwin.

6

Postscript on the Baldwin Effect and Niche Construction

Peter Godfrey-Smith, Daniel Dennett, and Terrence W. Deacon

Peter Godfrey-Smith

My essay credits Deacon's *The Symbolic Species* with a new version of the Baldwin effect that overcomes, at least in principle, accusations that the "effect" is trivial. Dennett objects that he cannot see much difference between what Deacon said and Dennett's own exposition in *Consciousness Explained*. Here is the difference. In Dennett's case, a learning individual hits on a "Good Trick" and "raises the bar" for getting by successfully in that population. "Over generations, the competition becomes stiffer: eventually, unless you are born with (or very nearly with) the Good Trick, you are not close enough to compete" (as quoted by Dennett). But this is not a "niche construction" phenomenon in the sense I associate with Deacon's proposal. The selection pressure in Dennett's case was there all along, but was "dormant" because of a lack of the right kind of variation in the population. Suddenly the right kind of variation appears (thanks to the learning individual) and selection is able to operate. In Deacon's cases something different is happening. Rather than a selection pressure being activated by the appearance of new variation in the population, the social life of the population changes in a way that creates a selection pressure that did not exist before. Note that in Dennett's case, an innately specified version of the Good Trick would do very well, if it happened to arise, at any stage in the process. (The population could jump from stage 0, to stage 2 without any particular role for stage 1.) In the Deacon case, it is only the change in the social ecology (due to stage 1 behaviors) that makes an innately specified, highly sophisticated version of the trait so advantageous. This version of the Baldwin effect may well not be original with Deacon, but I do not think the discussions cited by Dennett hit the same point.

Daniel Dennett

I can see that Deacon's proposal draws attention to a particularly interesting variety of Baldwin effect, but I still don't see that it is anything more than a special case (a particularly interesting one) of the phenomenon I took myself to be describing. I doubt if it is wise to talk about selection pressures that are present but "dormant" because the relevant phenotypes aren't present. If I understand Godfrey-Smith correctly, there are right now a kazillion dormant selection pressures on *H. sapiens*. Suppose smoking banana peels (remember the Mellow Yellow hoax?) provides protection against HIV. There is, then, a dormant selection pressure in favor of a proclivity to smoke banana peels even if nobody ever thinks to try it out. There are no doubt microbes in the depths of the ocean whose effects on human beings, were any ever to encounter them, would be variable; so right now there is a dormant selection pressure in favor of those human phenotypes that happen not to be vulnerable to those microbes. And so forth. Perhaps this is unobjectionable, since "dormant selection pressures" don't take up any space or energy, but I wonder.

Godfrey-Smith says that in the Deacon scenario, "the social life of the population changes in a way that creates a selection pressure that did not exist before." Really? Why shouldn't we say that the selection pressure in question existed, but was "dormant"? It just needed a double (or multiple) triggering to be awakened. If the selection pressure for smoking banana peels exists in dormant form (and is not created by the behavioral innovation that makes it visible to selection), why shouldn't we equally say that it takes a series of (social) actions and reactions to wake up a Deacon selection pressure?

I join Godfrey-Smith in appreciating Deacon's point that interaction between individuals creates (or awakens—this has not yet been shown to be importantly different) a novel (or heretofore dormant) selection pressure. But is something more being loaded into the term "social"? What is the importance of social interactions, in contrast with other interactions?

I take it that the Good Trick of picking up a stick and wielding it as a club against game would be just a boring old Baldwin effect with no new selection pressures (they were always there, just dormant). But what if the game starts turning on us and fighting back when we go at it with clubs? Is this a "social" interaction that can engender altogether new selection pressures? If not, then is wielding a club against conspecifics who wield back a novel, Deacon-style Baldwin effect? Or does the Deacon social interaction effect come into play only when, for instance, females start playing sexual selection games that favor males who carry big clubs (mine is bigger than yours, etc., etc.), an effect that arguably depends on there being a widespread new practice (just one club-wielder will not provoke or sustain female interest in club size)?

Good Tricks depend on the environments in which they can operate. Some environments are simple and others involve much layering of context to come into their own. Someone who would be an excellent bluffer in poker needs to find a poker game in which to display his superiority. At the end of his postscript, Godfrey-Smith points to what he thinks is a residual difference: "Note that in Dennett's case, an innately specified version of the Good Trick would do very well, if it happened to arise, at any stage in the process. (The population could jump from stage zero to stage 2 without any particular role for stage 1.) In the Deacon case, it is only the change in the social ecology (due to stage 1 behaviors) that makes an innately specified, highly sophisticated version of the trait so advantageous." But what Godfrey-Smith is pointing to is the existence of something like an arms race with a series of innovations and counterinnovations in it, and this is not restricted to *social* ecology. A club-wielding hunter with an innate propensity to plan a path of retreat in case his prey countercharges (stage 2) will similarly have no selective advantage in a world where the prey haven't yet learned to fight back (stage 1).

Terrence Deacon Responds

In my opinion both Godfrey-Smith (GS) and Dennett (DD) appear to miss the point, though they miss different points in each case and get things right in others, so I wonder how much of this is a "semantic" issue.

I would not at all want to suggest that we start to consider something like "dormant" selection pressures (though I have no problem with the ubiquitous presence of a sea of near-neutral variations). I have a suspicion, however, that GS introduces this unfortunate suggestion to make a different point than DD comments on, but which gets lost in this exchange. Dennett's caricature of a behaviorally implemented arms race of Good Tricks does not in my interpretation even quite qualify as an account that Baldwin would recognize. Baldwin at least recognized that selection could act on something like a norm of reaction for a trait. Although the concept was introduced later, Baldwin pretty accurately sketches it in 1896. In later formulations Baldwin seems also to be suggesting that something like a "frequency dependence" effect of a behavior (also in advance of his time) plays a role. Both of these are implicit in my *Symbolic Species* (SS) account, and at least the latter, frequency dependence, is implied in the paper by GS. This point is made by his persistent comparison of my argument to "niche construction" and his efforts to distinguish the argument in SS from that view, as well as from Baldwinian theory proper (even if I didn't do a great job of making either distinction).

I also want to accept DD's "cross-this-line" challenge to me about what I "might" mean by "social." I *do* indeed want to load something more into the term "social" than seems to be imagined here, certainly more than in his account, and which I believe gives us something more interesting than "cranes" even if quite a bit less interesting than "skyhooks."

The virtual future is limitless. The great value of the Darwinian evolutionary paradigm is the way it helps us understand how what once was "noise" (e.g., unselected-uncorrelated variation) can become new "signal" under changing circumstances. There is nothing revolutionary in my thoughts about this. I consider myself to be a pretty well committed Darwinian. Talking about "latent" or "dormant" selection will likely get us into the same kind of hot water that the term "preadaptation" gets us in, or that psychologists and philosophers find themselves in when talking about unexpressed predispositions. And I don't think "exaptation" is much better. Luckily there is something a bit more concrete to consider when talking about ranges of phenotypic variation, norms of reaction, canalization, and the fact that genetic and phenotypic random walks are constrained in interesting and relevant ways (note: most traits develop in the context of complex epigentic linkages, episases, and pleiotropies—all of which add more than just plausibility to such otherwise hollow concepts as "coordinating conditions," "phylogenetic inertia," or "adaptive potential."

All I am interested in are the ways that the brain-language coevolutionary dynamic might accomplish this "recruitment of new signal" differently than do simpler Darwinian mechanisms. One doesn't even have to stray from the so-called ultra-Darwinian fold to recognize that the formulation of natural selection theory is pretty generic, and that there is plenty of room for interesting tail-wagging-the-dog possibilities within its confines. The original Organic Selection conjecture was not after all about undoing Darwinism, but reinforcing it, as is my modest effort. No "skyhooks" please, and no Lamarckian loopholes. But there may be other kinds of hooks (not just cranes) from other directions that *do* merit consideration of a different kind. Hence my pleading guilty to Dennett's latter probe about how I think about the nature of at least certain "social" factors.

The social phenomenon in question—language—is not just a passively constructed niche, like a beaver dam, not just a sexually selected runaway effect like peacock feathers, but is a complex dynamic niche, with something like a "life of its own," or at the very least a powerful *self-organizing dynamic* that can't be reduced to mere social dynamics, much less passive caricatures of natural selection. Dennett should appreciate this more than anyone else in the group, and I was surprised that GS seems to drive this point while DD seems to dismiss it. The ability to symbolize things and relationships in the world, and the factors that allow symbolic systems to self-organize, are new elements that take evolution in unexpected directions. This is not just because language is subject to a partially uncorrelated evolutionary dynamic of its own, but also because of the way symbolic representational processes can recruit new kinds of "noise" into the larger symbol-gene system, which can provide both a whole new realm of variations and of reciprocal selection pressures. The transindividual and transgenerational niche-like effects of cultural-linguistic evolution introduce a complex system dynamic, which vastly complicates things. I refer to this as *co*evolution in the subtitle of SS for just this reason. It's not just Darwin or even Baldwin, as I think GS has accurately noted.

My sympathy for reintegrating systems thinking into evolutionary theory (though in my opinion to do so doesn't replace or even weaken the centrality of Darwinian processes) becomes a full-fledged endorsement once symbolic processes are brought into the mix. The extent of the feed-forward circularity of the selection processes linking brain and linguistic evolutionary/self-organizational processes requires us to take into account, or at least (in our current state of theoretical simplicity) appreciate, the way complex systems dynamics have been an inescapable factor in human evolution. There is a new level of "chaos" and "bias/noise amplification" that we must contend with, and for which our current intuitional models are inadequate. This is niche construction, but of a self-organizing asynchronously evolving all-encompassing niche. Who but the most unimaginative hyperreductionist could imagine that it's just "evolution as usual"?

II

Baldwinism and Development

7

Evolution, Development, and the Individual Acquisition of Traits: What We've Learned since Baldwin

Celia L. Moore

1 Introduction

James Mark Baldwin developed his concept of organic selection at the close of the nineteenth century, during a time when Lamarckian ideas about the inheritance of acquired characters were being dealt a death blow by Weismann's germ plasm concept (Baldwin 1895, 1896; Oyama 2000; Weismann 1893). Baldwin was a Darwinian, as that designation was understood a century ago. It is, therefore, unsurprising that he cast his developmental concept of organic selection in the Darwinian mold of overproduction and selective survival. He was well aware that organisms acquire traits as they go through ontogeny and that there was variation among individuals in the traits so acquired. Of all the diverse acquisitions in a population, some can be observed to work better than others. Individuals with more successful ontogenetic accommodations survive longer and leave more progeny. But can these ontogenetic gains accumulate across generations and have a directional effect on evolution? Baldwin thought they could, and his "new factor" was an effort to explain how this might work without recourse to the direct inheritance of acquired characters.

As a developmental psychologist, Baldwin's primary work centered on explaining how individuals change during ontogeny. He acknowledged that all of the organism develops over time, including those traits that grow and mature in ways common to the species, but he distinguished between what he saw as genealogically given traits and those that were acquired in individually variable ways. Organic selection had to do with the latter. He divided the sources of individually acquired traits into three categories: fluctuations in the physical environment (physico-genetic), the internalized effects of the organism's own neural and other activities (neuro-genetic), and the effects of learning and intelligence (psycho-genetic) (Baldwin 1896). Of these, he placed greatest emphasis on the survival benefits of psycho-genetic traits: ontogenetic plasticity gained through trial-and-error learning, imitation, instruction, and conscious intelligence. Baldwin's basic hypothesis was that individuals with greater ability to acquire traits that suited the demands of a novel environment would survive in disproportionate numbers in that environment, thus allowing for the eventual generation of novel adaptations that could be perpetuated through inheritance.

Recent discussions of the hypothesized Baldwin effect and Waddington's related concept of genetic assimilation have typically been conducted within the context of today's dominant view of evolution as genetic selection (see Depew, chap. 1, this volume, for a historical analysis). In this view, heredity is a matter for molecular genes—sequences of base-pairs along a portion of a DNA molecule—and it is these genes on which natural selection acts. Therefore, the success of Baldwin's organic selection as an agent of evolutionary change is seen to hinge on the occurrence in the population of new genetic mutations with phenotypic effects that mirror the successful traits acquired by individual effort in the pioneering forebears. Waddington's genetic assimilation mechanism would work somewhat differently (Waddington 1956). He proposed that novel environmental factors can uncover hidden genetic variations that are already in the genome, some of which might prove beneficial in the new environment. In both cases, natural selection would work to increase the favored genetic variants (see Hall, chap. 8, this volume).

On most interpretations, both Baldwin's and Waddington's mechanisms require natural selection to act on molecular genes (see Dennett, chap. 4, Downes, chap. 2, and Godfrey-Smith, chap. 6, all in this volume). However, there are broader views of inheritance; furthermore, the units of selection that are adopted change the evolutionary problem (Griffiths and Gray 1994; Gottlieb 1992; Lewontin 2000; Michel and Moore 1995; Oyama 2000). It is no longer necessary to assume that the change that has an adaptive consequence occurs at the genomic level. It is sufficient to postulate an adaptive change somewhere in the developmental system that has sufficient robustness and reliability to ensure recurrence of the adaptive phenotype in succeeding generations.

The emergence and growth of child development and learning psychology were fed during the late nineteenth and early twentieth centuries by a strong interest in educational applications (Bijou and Baer 1961). Education is goal-directed or goal-corrected change in a developing individual. The individual environment is deliberately rigged to produce desired goals. Education includes imitation, giving and following explicit instructions, learning to accomplish tasks specified in advance, and incorporating pre-existing cultural knowledge and norms. The goal in development and education is for children to acquire the knowledge and the skills that will enable them to be productive and constructive members of society.

Throughout the history of psychology, the concept of acquisition from the environment has been widely and generally applied in both learning and child development to the acquisition of something known in advance. Baldwin, a developmental child psychologist, worked within this tradition, and his examples of acquired traits were primarily those of forward-looking learning or intelligent actions. There is also the sense from his writings that he had in mind a fairly transparent and forward-looking connection between environmental agent and individual accommodation in the physico-genetic and neuro-genetic realms as well. He cites, for example, the law of use and disuse in discussing neuro-genetic acquisitions (Baldwin 1896). However, the concept of experience has undergone radical extensions from its educational roots during the past few decades. Learning is now recognized as only one type of change through experience. Environmental effects have been identified where the connection between input and phenotypic effect is anything but transparent even when, as is sometimes but not always the case, the mediating mechanism is classical conditioning or some other well-characterized form of learning. Furthermore, rather dramatic morphological effects of such experience on the nervous system and other organic structures have been observed (Michel and Moore 1995).

One of the many consequences of the new work on experience, heredity, and developmental systems is to reveal as arbitrary the historically accepted division between genealogically given, inherited traits that simply mature during ontogeny and acquired traits that come about through individual experience. Baldwin used this standard distinction, but he also suggested the potential ontogenetic importance of self-generated experience and called attention to the evolutionarily relevant fact that some environments are stably repeated across generations and can support the same acquisitions in successive generations. Both of these phenomena have been studied extensively in recent years and used to call the inherited/acquired distinction into question (Michel and Moore 1995).

2   Research Strategies for Investigating the Development of Organisms

Multicelled organisms offer an intriguing puzzle to developmentalists. Zygotes express few of the traits expressed by organisms at later ontogenetic stages. Traits are constructed anew during each organism's life. Understanding how this is done, and done with such fidelity to a species-typical theme, is a daunting scientific challenge. It is one of the great questions about life, clearly central to a comprehensive, synthetic biology. Despite this centrality, the developmental sciences were for quite some time relegated to a peripheral, supporting role in the grand biological synthesis. Neo-Darwinian selectionism and the broad acceptance of DNA as a sufficient explanation of inheritance conspired to confine interest to a rather narrow range of developmental questions circumscribed by that context. This is now rapidly changing, with theories about evolution and heredity reconceived on the basis of a deeper understanding of development (Gould 1977; Griffiths and Gray 1994; Ho and Saunders 1984; Michel and Moore 1995; Oyama 2000; Oyama, Griffiths, and Gray 2001).

Although learning and related processes are readily addressed experimentally, many processes in behavioral development have proved more difficult. It took longer to develop a successful experimental approach that could be applied to behavior outside the realm of learning. There is now such an epigenetic approach, which has become mainstream developmental psychobiology and is applied to a broad range of developmental questions in a large variety of species (Michel and Moore 1995). It has its roots in the early work of Schneirla and Lehrman (Lehrman 1953; Schneirla 1949, 1957). The approach includes the following assumptions and generalizations:

behavior, cognition, and psychological traits generally are properties of a whole organism functioning as a system with the proximate environmental milieu;

organisms are organized at multiple levels, with both top-down and bottom-up interactions across levels and a network of bidirectional interactions within levels;

development consists of successive reorganizations over time, incorporating raw materials previously assembled in the organism and new environmental inputs available for use by the organism at the relevant times;

material properties and available connections of elements constrain the kinds of interactions that can occur within an organism or between an organism and its environment, and, therefore, the kinds of developmental transformations that can occur; and

development results from epigenetic processes that can produce qualitative change, including the emergence of novel properties.

This list of core features, although not exhaustive, is sufficient to introduce some significant differences between this developmental approach and the prevailing synthesis of Darwinian selectionism and genetics. Here are three.

(a) If organisms are organized systems of multiple, interconnected parts, it will rarely be possible for selection to act on isolated traits. Selection on one trait is very likely to bring about correlated changes in several others, which may be favorable, neutral, or detrimental with respect to selection (Gould and Lewontin 1979; Nolan and Ketterson 1994).

(b) The functional demarcations of traits, which is so useful for discussing adaptation, lose usefulness in explaining development. This is because interactions frequently cross functional boundaries within developing organisms, and new functional capacities frequently develop from the raw materials left by functionally discontinuous earlier stages. Hence, prolactin, which was named for its effect on the mammary gland, plays an important role as neuromodulator in the central nervous system; vision builds on foundations left by the prior development of audition; and sexual behavior makes use of mechanisms that develop during mother-infant interactions (Brown 1994; Lickliter 1993; Moore 1992).

(c) Both genes and environment become relevant to development only when they contribute in material ways to organismic processes, that is, at the cellular level, after they are translated or transduced into the molecules that cells use to do their work. Therefore, questions about what genes do are likely to be raised in terms of developmental process rather than programming of outcomes. The same is true for questions about the environment.

3   Development Toward or Development From?

The epigenetic developmental theory outlined in the previous section is steadily gaining empirical support, but it is not the only developmental theory of behavior. One way to characterize the major difference among developmentalists is where they stand to ask their developmental questions. Do they stand at the developmental outcome and look backward in time, or at some earlier point in ontogenetic time, looking forward? Do they ask how the final state was shaped, or how the final state emerged? Do they seek potentials in earlier stages or consequences for later stages? These two stances lead to qualitatively different suites of questions that are pursued with different strategies and that are satisfied with different kinds of answers.

There is a long tradition of defining behavior in functional terms and starting developmental inquiry from these functionally defined, phenotypic endpoints. For workers in this tradition, the major task is to characterize how the behavior was shaped or guided during ontogeny. The field is filled with metaphors used to hypothesize developmental guides by which the endpoint is achieved from some isomorphic earlier condition: for gene, we have the metaphors of blueprint, code, program, and information; for environment, we have the metaphors of imprint, template, example, and practice. Because of the isomorphism that is assumed to exist in the instructional or mapping relationship between the first and final ontogenetic states, the difficulties of qualitative change are reduced to a straightforward problem of building the finished product according to instructions, using materials at hand. These hypothesized constructs satisfy developmental curiosity when the focus is on the apparent design properties of the outcomes, or the close fit of phenotypic endpoints with environmental demands.

Contrast those who look at a developmental endpoint and ask what it came from and how it got made. The task is to unravel the developmental process, following threads to find out how the behaving organism was put together. Metaphoric language is drawn mostly from construction: raw materials, resources, scaffolding, stages, levels. Developmental curiosity is satisfied by understanding the mechanisms underlying behavior and how they got built during ontogeny. Because these mechanisms include physiological, cellular, and molecular details of organic structure, behavioral scientists who approach development in this way typically move back and forth between levels of organization, weaving biological and psychological methods into their research programs.

Accounting for individual differences in outcomes is a major part of the developmental agenda. This is of utmost importance within evolutionary theory because heritable phenotypic variation is a necessary condition for evolution. There are also powerful social reasons for wanting to know how different outcomes might be achieved through modifications in ontogeny. The different developmental approaches to individual differences can be used to elaborate on the distinction between the "from" and "toward" perspectives. Those who begin with functionally defined outcomes are likely to search backward for the "difference that made a difference" (Goodwin 1984; van der Weel 1993). They will seek the ontogenetically original factor that diverted development down one path instead of another and attach particular significance to determining whether the originating difference is genetic or environmental. They may be content to accept this resolution as a sufficient developmental account. But this will not satisfy those who seek to reconstruct the full developmental history of the outcome of interest. They will want to know how the difference-provoking factor works along with other factors to produce the organized mechanisms on which the outcome rests. Indeed, independent of established or putative function, naturally occurring individual differences may be treated quite practically as loose strands that can be exploited as starting points for unravelling the underlying fabric of the organism by experimental means.

4   Individual Acquisition of Traits

In a very real sense, all but the handful of traits present in a fertilized egg are acquired by individuals as they go through ontogeny. But that is not how "individual acquisition" has typically been used and understood. Genetic determinists use acquired traits to refer to those that depend for their specificity on environmental input and that, therefore, will vary as a function of environmental differences. Acquired traits are contrasted with traits that preexist in a coded genotypic form, that are inherited by the organism during reproduction, and that are unaffected by environmental variation. Behavioral scientists usually equate individual acquisition with learning. Because learning theories were so strongly influenced by educational concerns, environments for behavior have generally been conceived in instructional, shaping, or formative terms. Thus, we have the old dichotomy of the innate and the acquired, which has been used since the ascendance of Mendelian genetics to sort sources of information for design of outcomes into two heaps: inherited from parents through genes or individually acquired from the environment.

As has been said many times, this dichotomy falls apart under a close developmental analysis that is embedded in physiological reality. We get a very different and fuller picture of how molecular-level genes contribute to development and ongoing physiological processes when we examine their activities within the integrated system of the organism (Lemke 1992; Singer and Berg 1991). Recent advances in molecular genetics have shown us that how genes work and what they do depend crucially on the rest of the cell and connections between the cell and the rest of the organism. Which genes are active, their rate of activity, and when and where they are active are all regulated by other genes, factors from neighboring cells, factors from remote parts of the organism, or factors transduced from stimuli in the external environment. Spliceosomes can splice a transcript in more than one way, thereby regulating what protein is translated from a particular gene; proteins can be cleaved, strung together, or phosphorylated into different functional molecules; and transport mechanisms can regulate which proteins are available at different locations in the organism.

When genes are looked at as material parts of cells instead of as coded phenotypes, it is possible to see more clearly how they participate with other molecules to produce organized activity at cellular to organismic levels. A parallel argument can be made for experience, which can also be analyzed at different levels from molar to molecular. Developmental psychobiologists have developed new methods for studying experience that are different from those traditional in learning and cognitive psychology, and they have identified diverse effects at cellular to organismic levels. These discoveries may not give definitive answers to the questions raised by Baldwin, Waddington, or Lamarck, but they do change the meanings of their questions by changing what it means to say that characters are acquired through individual experience.

5   Obvious and Nonobvious Experience: What's the Difference?

We are told that innate behavior is that which develops without obvious experience (e.g., McFarland 1999). But what is obvious experience? One answer is that it is experience that someone has made obvious by demonstrating how it affects behavioral development. This makes the relevant distinction one between what we know and don't know, a distinction that has nothing to do with nature but a statement about how far we have gotten with our developmental work. The only other answer that I have been able to come up with is that it is experience directly recognizable as relevant from knowledge of the developmental outcome. In the absence of experimental demonstration, a relevant experience is likely to be recognized as such only if there is some formal or functional similarity between the experience and the outcome, and this in turn requires the organism to have at least roughly similar sensory and motor systems at the acquisition and outcome stages.

Learned behavior is generally thought to be the most obvious developmental outcome of experience. In an influential effort to distinguish and then integrate innate and acquired aspects of animal behavior, Thorpe defined learning as "that process which manifests itself by adaptive changes in individual behaviour as a result of experience; or, to put it another way, the organisation of behaviour as a result of individual experience" (Thorpe 1962: 55). He goes on through example and explication to make clear that adaptive changes are those that make the behavior of greater use to the organism by achieving a greater fit with the demands of its environment. This is not an unusual definition of learning, and all the various forms of learning, from imprinting through instrumental conditioning, readily fit within it. The experiences that lead to learning are those that carry information about the outcome. They involve familiarity, as in imprinting or classical conditioning; practice, as in trial and error or song crystallization; or instruction, as in modeling or shaping.

But what makes learning an obvious form of experience? I suggest that it is because scientists study learning by starting with an adaptive outcome to achieve or explain and then searching for experiences that will lead to it. The experience becomes obvious because it is defined in terms of the outcome. It is only by having a clear way to identify potential experiences before they are encountered by an organism that such experiences can be ruled out to reveal innate behavior. Early criticisms of this line of reasoning have made people wary of concluding that all experience can be ruled out (see, e.g., Lehrman 1953). Just obvious experience.

If important experiential effects remain once obvious experience is eliminated, the concept of innate behavior and the experimental effort to partition behavior into the innate and the acquired have some serious problems. That appears to be the case. Those who study development by following its process from earlier to later stages have identified numerous instances of experience that have important consequences for the developing organism, including contributions to survival or reproduction, yet that almost certainly would never have been guessed from knowledge about the mature traits.

Some instances of "nonobvious" experience can be incorporated into learning paradigms, at least in retrospect. Take the example of a newborn rat pup that approaches, attaches, and sucks from the mother's nipple within minutes of birth. However, if the nipple region is carefully cleaned of odors, the pup will not grasp the nipple and suck. Thus, it seems that the pup uses odors that are naturally on the mother's ventral region to guide and elicit sucking behavior. As it turns out, these odors come primarily from maternal saliva, which has odorants in common with those found in amniotic fluid. By inserting citral, which is a tasteless lemony odor, into the amniotic fluid of developing fetuses and then observing their subsequent responses to nipples, it has been demonstrated that they learn about maternal odors in the uterus and use this learning to organize their neonatal suckling. Pups reared in the artificially scented prenatal environment readily attach to citral-scented nipples, whereas normally reared pups avoid them (Pedersen and Blass 1981).

The story of how male cowbirds develop song provides an example of a different type of experiential effect (West and King 1988). Cowbirds are brood parasites that hatch in the nest of other species and that are, therefore, not exposed to conspecific song models from parents in the typical songbird manner. Adult cowbirds are in the neighborhood, however, and juveniles join them after fledging to live a social life among conspecifics. During the time that developing males begin to produce their songs, females in the group prove an attentive and responsive audience. When they hear a song they like, they respond with a brief wing movement called a wing stroke. Males pay close attention to this audience. Wing strokes excite them, and careful observation reveals that they are likely to repeat songs that elicit wing strokes from females. In this gentle and rather subtle manner, females teach males which songs to keep and hone as oft-repeated standards in their vocal repertoire. Although the cowbird audience effect can be considered a form of shaping or reinforced learning and, therefore, to meet the criterion for "obvious" experience, it took intimate knowledge of the birds' behavior gained during years of observation and experimentation before the behavioral contingencies were detected by first-rate researchers.

It is not difficult to recognize mothers and other social companions as part of a developing organism's environment, despite the hidden quality of some of their influences. What is perhaps not so apparent is that the organism also generates some of its own environmental input that is then incorporated into new developmental achievements. These influences are often called self-stimulation or activity-dependent effects, depending on where the emphasis is placed. Baldwin recognized the potential importance of self-stimulation for development (Baldwin 1896). Kuo carried out the earliest thorough analysis of the self-stimulation hypothesis, and he was able to trace organic effects to earliest embryonic stages in avian embryos (Kuo 1932).

The first behavioral example that was worked out in detail starts with the observation that newly hatched ducklings direct their filial responses preferentially to maternal calls of their own species. By systematically observing and manipulating the environmental inputs available to the duckling before the time that the behavior first appeared, Gottlieb demonstrated that even a duckling isolated from all acoustic and other contact with mothers and siblings throughout embryonic and posthatching periods would show the preference (Gottlieb 1971, 1991). However, if both isolated and prevented from vocalizing (by transiently immobilizing the syrinx), it would not. Ducklings gain sufficient input from their own vocalizations to acquire preferential direction of filial responses to conspecific maternal calls. Self-stimulative effects such as these are not limited to early developmental periods. To take another example from birds, female ring doves undergo ovarian development and produce eggs when they are courted by a male. The effective courtship pattern is nest-cooing. This behavior involves a head-down postural adjustment and repeated cooing while remaining stationary (by preference, at a location with a concavity that might serve as a nest site). Nest-cooing is associated with small amplitude wing movements known as wing-flipping. Cheng analyzed the mechanisms behind the adult developmental transition from courtship to egg-laying and found that male courtship stimulation was only indirectly responsible for the endocrine response in females: a courting male stimulates the female to respond with nest-cooing, and it is her own nest-cooing behavior that stimulates her neuroendocrine system to produce the high levels of estrogen necessary for egg production (Cheng 1979). If brain mechanisms necessary for nest-cooing are surgically disabled, female ring doves will not progress to the egg-laying stage of the reproductive cycle.

The effects of self stimulation on filial behavior or on adult neuroendocrine changes are not readily brought within the purview of learning, although they describe developmental acquisitions that are shaped in large part by experience. Some recent studies of early human development extend this broadened concept of acquisition to the developmental roots of human cognition. The differences between left and right cerebral hemispheres have generated an extraordinarily high level of interest in cognitive neuroscience. Why are humans so asymmetrical with respect to the functioning of these brain regions, and why does the great majority of the population have the same asymmetry? Cortical asymmetries that have been observed in other mammalian species, including nonhuman primates, tend to be randomly distributed across individuals. This is quite unlike the biased asymmetry in humans that leads, for example, most of the population to be right-handed. One answer is that human newborns already exhibit various asymmetries, such as postural preferences, that give the left and right hemispheres predictably different sensorimotor input. This differential experience contributes to different developmental achievements in the two halves of the brain, setting foundations for continued differential development at later stages (Michel 1987).

But why are infants born with neurobehavioral asymmetries? At least some of the answer may lie in the predictably asymmetrical stimulation that fetal humans receive when the mother walks (Previc 1991). Unlike nonhuman primates, humans walk upright. Furthermore, the human uterus has an asymmetrical shape that in combination with gravity has the effect of orienting most fetuses head down with their dorsal surface to the mother's left side. This has the consequence of providing differential stimulation to the left and right otolith organs of the vestibular system because of differences in shearing forces on them as the mother walks forward. Because the vestibular system develops early and is active throughout much of gestation, these sensory organs and those parts of the CNS that receive input from them develop with different patterns of sensory input. Differential otolith organ sensitivity in combination with the effect of vestibular stimulation on head and trunk movements can account for neonatal postural preferences. This may not be all. Input from otolith organs projects to major neurotransmitter systems in the locus coeruleus and the raphe nuclei, which may lead to other widespread asymmetrical effects on CNS development during gestation (Previc 1991).

Developmental neuroscience has revealed numerous mechanisms that can account for cascading effects of sensory input, peptide production, and other products of early experience on neurobehavioral development. Many of these recent findings can be used to inform discussions of mind and brain evolution. But perhaps none are more provocative for evolutionary theory than discoveries of how the periphery of the body is used to construct the central nervous system (Purves 1988). The construction is achieved through a variety of mechanisms, including regulation by trophic factors from such target tissues as muscles, activity dependent processes involving input from the sensory and motor periphery, and hormonal effects from remote or regionally restricted parts of the body. Diverse cellular effects include those that lead to nonrandom survival of neurons, that support differential migration of cells, that affect differentiation of neuronal form or biochemistry, and that bias neuronal connections.

Striking individual differences in nervous system structure may result from morphological differences at the periphery. There is, for example, a large nucleus of motor neurons in the lumbar spinal cord of male rats which has known functions in their adult copulatory behavior. Females have a much smaller nucleus in the same location. The large nucleus in males develops because of an antecedent development of the striated muscles surrounding the base of the penis that are innervated by the motor neurons. The penile muscles develop in response to androgens that are secreted by males during prenatal and neonatal life. Trophic factors from the peripheral muscles in turn contribute to motor neuronal survival. Neonatal females lack endogenous androgen and therefore do not retain the peripheral muscles, do not have the same amount of trophic factors available to motor neurons in the lumbar nucleus, and, consequently, do not have the same number of neurons survive the early periods of cell death. The result is a predictably divergent structure in the lumbar spinal cord of males and females (Breedlove 1992; Forger, Hodges, Roberts, and Breedlove 1992). Acting through diverse cellular mechanisms, input from the periphery can account for the development of a close functional fit between the central nervous system and the requirements of the rest of the body it serves. These peripheral effects can also account for divergent developmental outcomes and for the origin of novel patterns in the brain.

When Lehrman wrote his seminal 1953 critique of instinct theory, he had only a handful of incompletely analyzed examples of experience outside conventional conceptions of learning with which to make his points. There was even less available to Baldwin as he grappled with the relation between individual acquisition and evolution at an earlier time. This has changed radically: the examples used here could easily have been replaced with a large number of equally persuasive studies (Blass 1986, 1988; Michel and Moore 1995). The picture of experience that emerges from the experimental work that has been done in the past half-century is not yet fully clear. Nevertheless, it is clear enough to see that it must be conceptualized in terms of the structures making use of it: it will have different qualities at earlier and later developmental stages and for micro and macro system levels. What we conventionally call learning is but a subset of experience used in the individual acquisition of traits. Schneirla made this point some time ago: "[Experience] denotes a wide range of phenomena, from the influence of biochemical changes and growth-induced activities to an afferent input variously aroused, with possible trace effects not usually classed as 'learning.'. . . It is only at later stages that learning, a higher order of process resulting from 'experience,' contributes to behavioral development" (Schneirla 1956: 150).

Despite the diverse mechanisms for environmental input and the diverse levels of the organism making use of it, there is a common theme in the examples described here. In each instance, the developing organism can count on getting the experience. It is a completely reliable part of its environment. It has been inherited as surely as its genome.

6   Making the Nonobvious Obvious

"Nonobvious experience" is not intended as an explanatory construct: the organism is unlikely to care how easy it is for experimenters to identify sources of experience that are important to it. It is practically useful, however, for pointing out that experimental efforts to rule out experience so as to reveal innate behavior are extremely likely to fail. It is also practically useful for drawing attention to the fact that research strategies different from those used to identify effects of "obvious" experience are needed to identify experiential effects that do not leap out as potentially important from knowledge of mature outcomes. As the examples described earlier make plain, developmentally important experience may be subtle or fleeting but with a nonlinearly large impact; it may be functionally, temporally, or formally remote from a developmental effect; or it may be so ubiquitous as to appear invisible.

Natural History Applied to Ontogeny
There are several strategies that have been used and that seem to work for identifying experiential effects that might otherwise be missed (Michel and Moore 1995). An important one is to start with a thorough description of the organism and its environments through ontogenetic stages prior to the one of interest (Alberts and Cramer 1988). The descriptive phase is used to identify available inputs or raw materials from which later developmental outcomes might be constructed and is followed by experimental manipulations to determine what effect, if any, they have. This seems straightforward enough, despite the fact that it has often been short-circuited in deprivation studies that eliminate large chunks of environmental input, making assumptions about what is of likely importance from knowledge of outcome (Lehrman 1953). What may not be so apparent, however, is that

"available" inputs will need to be characterized with respect to the organism's ability to use them at the available time. Of equal importance, "effects" need to be traced from their earliest appearance through ontogeny. These steps require physiological as well as behavioral methods.

What constitutes a natural developmental environment is different in different phyletic groups. A newly produced zygote may be stuck to the underside of a leaf on a tree, left to float in a gelatinous mass in a pond, or put inside a leathery shell and deposited in the warm sand of a beach. A mammalian zygote begins life inside the maternal uterus, where it remains through a series of embryonic and fetal transformations. After birth, the neonate necessarily remains in close connection with the mother; she is the source of warmth, food, and other life-supporting resources (Alberts and Cramer 1988). Of particular importance for behavioral difference, the mother is a major source of stimulation as well. As she nourishes and protects her offspring during prenatal and postnatal periods, she provides a wealth of environmental inputs that stem from her physiology and behavior. She is a source of hormones, immune factors, and other molecules that travel through the placenta and in milk and a source of stimuli that result from her movements, vocalizations, odors, and so forth. For these reasons, the maternal contribution to heritable variance is greater than the 50 percent predicted by her genomic contribution, a fact of heredity that is known by the descriptive label of maternal effects (Arnold 1987; Kirkpatrick and Lande 1989).

Developmental psychobiologists have found the maternal environment a rich field to mine for experiential effects on development. Much of the work that has been done in the past few decades has included a thorough exploration of this environment for the species under study, whether human or animal. This has included the discovery and refinement of techniques that allow investigations to extend to ever earlier stages without destroying or distorting normal processes (Shair, Barr, and Hofer 1991). The use of ultrasound in humans is one notable example. New experimental preparations for exteriorizing rat fetuses and maintaining them in environments that support life processes, including normal movements, have made it possible to explore their natural experiential world (e.g., Smotherman and Robinson 1991). This goal eluded earlier attempts because fetuses develop so deeply hidden within the maternal body. As the study of development had been pushed to earlier stages, it has become more and more necessary to work at more than one level of system organization. This means that both inputs and effects are likely to be specified in physiological as well as behavioral terms. It may be possible for developmentalists to elect to remain at the behavioral level when working with older organisms, but this is rarely possible for very young organisms. Thus, the physiological nature of early maternal-fetal interactions has promoted a multileveled system approach among developmentalists.

Exploiting Naturally Occurring Outcome Differences

Another strategy that seems to work is to correlate naturally occurring outcome differences with naturally occurring environmental variations as a preliminary to experimentation. This variation may be within an organism (as in differential input to the two hemispheres), between the sexes, between strains, between species, or between any identified groups of individuals.

Individual differences in reproductive traits play a critically important role in evolutionary theory. For obvious reasons, they top the list of traits that have been subjected to study within neo-Darwinian genetic selection theory. They have also been subjected to intense developmental study. For several decades, the developmental study of these differences centered on relating sex differences in early hormone exposure to sex differences in developmental outcomes—finding the early difference that made the difference (Moore 1985). Differences in prenatal or neonatal hormones (testosterone in males but not females) were found first to account for differences in peripheral anatomy, then for differences in behavior, and finally for differences in brain structure. These studies were readily interpreted within prevailing evolutionary and genetic concepts: testosterone was the mediating agent that turned on genes that had selective advantages in males. Through these means, it was credited with programming masculine brains.

In recent years, the hormonal study of sex differences has turned from a focus on identifying originating differences to an analysis of developmental process. Methods from both developmental neuroscience and behavioral neuroendocrinology have been incorporated into the research program, with the goal of understanding in detail how the cellular, anatomical, and physiological mechanisms underlying reproductive outcomes develop (e.g., Breedlove 1992). The goal of my own research program has been to analyze naturally occurring experiential input for contributions to these developmental processes (Moore 1992, 1995).

There is a major, reliable difference in the experience of developing male and female rats. Maternal rats spend a great deal of time licking and handling their young pups throughout early development, and they direct substantially more of this activity to the males in their litter (Moore and Morelli 1979). Maternal licking is focused on the perineum, which results in the release of urine that she then consumes. This has the functions of removing waste products from the young, keeping the nest clean, and recycling water and salts to the lactating dam (Alberts and Gubernick 1983). It also has the more remote developmental consequence of contributing to the development of the nervous system and adult reproductive behavior (Moore 1992).

There are several redundant mechanisms that ensure relatively high levels of stimulation for neonatal males. The dam is more attracted to odors in male urine, male pups more readily assume a posture that promotes maternal licking and they produce more urine, and the sensory nerve that carries afferent input from the perineal region has more and larger myelinated axons in males (Clark, Bone, and Galef 1989; Moore and Chadwick-Dias 1986; Moore and Samonte 1986; Moore and White 1996). Testosterone, acting on a variety of tissues during early development, contributes to the differences among pups that dams use to discriminate among pups (Moore 1995). Experimental reduction of maternal stimulation by making the dam unable to smell the odors that elicit licking, or by giving her dietary salt that reduces her motivation to lick salty pups, has developmental consequences for the adult sexual behavior of male offspring and its neural mechanisms. In particular, males from low stimulating dams are less likely to perform intromissions and the penile reflexes used in sperm competition (Moore 1995). They also have fewer motor neurons in the lumbar nucleus that innervates penile muscles used in these copulatory movements (Moore, Dou, and Juraska 1992). In order for the extrinsic input from the maternal stimulation to affect cellular survival, it must be transduced into the kinds of things that cells use to regulate survival. From what we know about developmental cell death, this is likely to involve activity-dependent regulation of calcium channels or access to trophic factors—the same kinds of things that hormones affect (Oppenheim 1991). The experience of the young pup in the nest with his dam must be reconceived at the same cellular system level at which testesterone acts on development. For the developing system, it is the material factors that matter, not where they originated.

Not all strains of rats provide equally high levels of maternal licking. Most rats, including the Long-Evans strain used in the studies described above, like salt, but the F344 strain has a salt aversion. Likely for this reason, dams of this strain also engage in low levels of maternal licking (Moore, Wong, Daum, and Leclair 1997). When reproductive competitions between adult males of the two strains are staged, Long-Evans males father most of the offspring. This is because they are better at removing sperm plugs set by other males and replacing them with sperm plugs of their own. Cross-fostering studies reveal that the mother contributes to these behavioral differences. Long-Evans males reared by F344 dams are apparently less able to remove sperm plugs than males reared by a Long-Evans foster dam (Moore 1995).

The maternal effects on reproductive behavior of male offspring demonstrate that the behavior is acquired during development in part through experience provided by the mother. Individual differences in copulatory mechanisms that affect competitive reproductive success among males can be traced to individual differences in their maternally provided experience during infancy. Through their contributions to a nexus of reliable developmental events, female rats can affect the number of grandpups they will have through male offspring. Thus, the acquisition process is subject to natural selection. However, as the strain difference in maternal stimulation makes plain, there may be heritable factors in females that affect their maternal behavior, and therefore the development of their male offspring, that arose for unrelated reasons. The salt aversion in F344 rats is part of a cascade of metabolic effects having to do with adrenal function that just happens also to affect the amount of stimulation they give to their salty pups.

7 Conclusion

If experience is everywhere in development, acting on the system at multiple levels and in diverse ways throughout the course of ontogeny, the distinction between development and individual acquisition becomes meaningless. In order for acquisitions through experience to become a part of the organism, they must be converted into the material of the organism: into the fabric of cells and their organization into larger structures. Even the specialized, higher-order experience we call learning changes the brain in material ways (Greenough and Black 1992).

The distinction between genetic and environmental sources of information for development also sits on a slippery slope. If developmental analysis is carried far enough, factors arising from genomic action or from environmental input become identical in material terms. Furthermore, factors arising from genomic action regulate availability of environmental input, and factors arising from environmental input regulate genomic action. The distinction is difficult on practical grounds as well: experimental procedures for separating the two do not work. The information metaphor used to characterize genetic contributions to development makes us leave out much of what genes do and fails to capture what development is (Oyama 1985). The information metaphor applied to the study of experience likewise restricts us to a subset of experience, learning or learninglike experience that seems obvious from knowledge of outcome. As developmental analysis proceeds, more and more processes are discovered without reference to genetic or environmental codes.

Despite all these difficulties, there is heredity. Evolution includes both descent and modification of organismic traits. There is overwhelming evidence of characters that have been conserved over very long stretches of time and equally overwhelming evidence of new variants introduced and then conserved in different phyletic lineages. How can there be heredity of traits without a code?

One suggestion that has been made from time to time is that heredity should be considered as the first developmental stage of an organism. Perhaps it is time to take this suggestion seriously. There are not two compartments in this first stage, as is often assumed, but three. In addition to the genome and the environment, there is an organized cell with organelles and system properties. Outcomes that are not either specified in advance by a genetic code or designed by a shaping environment may grow as this system grows. Reliable outcomes can result from reliable starting points, the organizing properties of cells, the organizing properties of organisms at successive ontogenetic levels, and a reliable succession of environments during development.

Baldwin was right to put an emphasis on the developing organism as a contributor to evolution, but he had available to him only a limited understanding of experience. With what we have since learned about experience, in conjunction with a reconception of heredity in developmental terms, there is new meaning in Baldwin's question: Can gains through ontogeny be incorporated into heredity? Such incorporation does not require genomic changes (although such changes through the mechanisms suggested by Baldwin and Waddington might occur), but could involve reliable changes in other parts of the developing system.

Acknowledgments

I am grateful to the National Science Foundation (awards IBN-9121238 and IBN-9511325) for support of my research. I also thank the students of Bennington College and the members of the Bennington International Conference on Development, Evolution, and Cognition for a stimulating week of discussions that helped to shape the ideas in this chapter.

References

Alberts, J. R. and C. P. Cramer (1988). Ecology and experience: Sources of means and meaning of developmental change. In E. M. Blass, ed., *Handbook of Behavioral Neurobiology, vol. 9: Developmental Psychobiology and Behavioral Ecology,* pp. 1–67. New York: Plenum Press.

Alberts, J. R. and D. J. Gubernick (1983). Reciprocity and resource exchange: A symbiotic model of parent-offspring relations. In L. A. Rosenblum and H. Moltz (eds.), *Symbiosis in Parent-Offspring Interactions,* pp. 7–44. New York: Plenum Press.

Arnold, S. J. (1987). Genetic correlation and the evolution of physiology. In M. E. Feder, A. F. Bennett, W. W. Burggren, and R. B. Huey (eds.), *New Directions in Ecological Physiology,* pp. 189–215. Cambridge: Cambridge University Press.

Baldwin, J. M. (1895). *Mental Development in the Child and Race*. New York: Macmillan.

Baldwin, J. M. (1896). A new factor in evolution, *American Naturalist* 30: 441–451, 536–553.

Bijou, S. W. and D. M. Baer (1961). *Child Development: A Systematic and Empirical Theory*, vol. 1. New York: Appleton-Century-Crofts.

Blass, E. M. (ed.) (1986). *Handbook of Behavioral Neurobiology, vol. 8: Developmental Psychobiology and Developmental Neurobiology*. New York: Plenum Press.

Blass, E. M. (ed.) (1988). *Handbook of Behavioral Neurobiology, vol. 9: Developmental Psychobiology and Behavioral Ecology*. New York: Plenum Press.

Breedlove, S. M. (1992). Sexual dimorphism in the vertebrate nervous system. *Journal of Neuroscience* 12: 4133–4142.

Brown, R. E. (1994). *An Introduction to Neuroendocrinology*. Cambridge: Cambridge University Press.

Cheng, M.-F. (1979). Progress and prospect in ring dove research: A personal view. In J. S. Rosenblatt, R. A. Hinde, C. G. Beer, and M.-C. Busnel (eds.), *Advances in the Study of Behavior*, vol. 9, pp. 97–129. New York: Academic Press.

Clark, M. M., S. Bone, and B. G. Galef, Jr. (1989). Uterine positions and schedules of urination: Correlates of differential maternal anogenital stimulation. *Developmental Psychobiology* 22: 389–400.

Forger, N. G., L. L. Hodges, S. L. Roberts, and S. M. Breedlove (1992). Regulation of motoneuron death in the spinal nucleus of the bulbocavernosus. *Journal of Neurobiology*, 23: 1192–1203.

Goodwin, B. C. (1984). Changing from an evolutionary to a generative paradigm in biology. In J. W. Pollard (ed.), *Evolutionary Theory: Paths into the Future*, pp. 99–120. New York: John Wiley.

Gottlieb, G. (1971). *Development of Species Identification in Birds*. Chicago: The University of Chicago Press.

Gottlieb, G. (1991). Experiential canalization of behavioral development: Results. *Developmental Psychology* 27: 35–39.

Gottlieb, G. (1992). Individual Development and Evolution: *The Genesis of Novel Behavior*. New York: Oxford University Press.

Gould, S. J. (1977). *Ontogeny and Phylogeny*. Cambridge, Mass.: Harvard University Press.

Gould, S. J. and R. C. Lewontin (1979). The spandrels of San Marco and the Panglossian paradigm: A critique of the adaptationist programme. *Proceedings of the Royal Society of London, B* 205: 581–598.

Greenough, W. T. and J. E. Black (1992). Induction of brain structure by experience: Substrates for cognitive development. In M. Gunnar and C. A. Nelson (eds.),

Behavioral Developmental Neuroscience, vol. 24. *Minnesota Symposia on Child Psychology,* pp. 35–52. Hillsdale, N.J.: Erlbaum.

Griffiths, P. E. and R. D. Gray (1994). Developmental systems and evolutionary explanation. *Journal of Philosophy* 91: 277–304.

Ho, M. and P. T. Saunders (eds.) (1984). *Beyond Neo-Darwinism: An Introduction to the Evolutionary Paradigm.* London: Academic Press.

Kirkpatrick, M. and R. Lande (1989). The evolution of maternal characters. *Evolution* 43: 485–503.

Kuo, Z. Y. (1932). Ontogeny of embryonic behavior in Aves. IV. The influence of embryonic movements upon the behavior after hatching. *Journal of Comparative Psychology* 14: 109–122.

Lehrman, D. S. (1953). A critique of Konrad Lorenz's theory of instinctive behavior. *Quarterly Review of Biology* 28: 337–363.

Lemke, Greg (1992). Gene regulation in the nervous system. In Z. W. Hall (ed.), *An Introduction to Molecular Neurobiology,* pp. 313–354. Sunderland, Mass.: Sinauer.

Lewontin, R. (2000). *The Triple Helix: Gene, Organism, and Environment.* Cambridge, Mass.: Harvard University Press.

Lickliter, R. (1993). Timing and the development of perinatal perceptual organization. In G. Turkewitz and D. A. Devenny (eds.), *Developmental Time and Timing,* pp. 105–123. Hillsdale, N.J.: Erlbaum.

McFarland, D. (1999). *Animal Behaviour: Psychobiology, Ethology, and Evolution,* third ed. Harlow, Essex: Longman Scientific and Technical.

Michel, G. F. (1987). Self-generated experience and the development of lateralized neurobehavioral organization in infants. *Advances in the Study of Behavior* 17: 61–83.

Michel, G. F. and C. L. Moore (1995). *Developmental Psychobiology: An Interdisciplinary Science.* Cambridge, Mass.: MIT Press.

Moore, C. L. (1985). Another psychobiological view of sexual differentiation. *Developmental Review* 5: 18–55.

Moore, C. L. (1992). The role of maternal stimulation in the development of sexual behavior and its neural basis. *Annals of the New York Academy of Sciences* 662: 160–177.

Moore, C. L. (1995). Maternal contributions to mammalian reproductive development and the divergence of males and females. In P. J. B. Slater, J. S. Rosenblatt, C. T. Snowdon, and M. Milinski (eds.), *Advances in the Study of Behavior,* vol. 24, pp. 147–118. New York: Academic Press.

Moore, C. L. and A.-M. Chadwick-Dias (1986). Behavioral responses of infant rats to maternal licking: Variations with age and sex. *Developmental Psychobiology* 19: 427–438.

Moore, C. L., H. Dou, and J. M. Juraska (1992). Maternal stimulation affects the number of motor neurons in a sexually dimorphic nucleus of the lumbar spinal cord. *Brain Research* 572: 52–56.

Moore, C. L. and G. A. Morelli (1979). Mother rats interact differently with male and female offspring. *Journal of Comparative and Physiological Psychology* 93: 677–684.

Moore, C. L. and B. Samonte (1986). Preputial glands of infant rats (*Rattus norvegicus*) provide chemosignals for maternal discrimination of sex. *Journal of Comparative Psychology* 100: 76–80.

Moore, C. L. and R. H. White (1996). Sex differences in sensory and motor branches of the pudendal nerve of the rat. *Hormones and Behavior* 30: 590–599.

Moore, C. L., L. Wong, M. C. Daum, and O. U. Leclair (1997). Mother-infant interactions in two strains of rats: Implications for dissociating mechanism and function of a maternal pattern. *Developmental Psychobiology* 30: 301–312.

Nolan, V., Jr. and E. D. Ketterson (1994). Hormones and life histories: An integrative approach. In L. A. Real (ed.), *Behavioral Mechanisms in Evolutionary Ecology*, pp. 327–353. Chicago: The University of Chicago Press.

Oppenheim, R. W. (1991). Cell death during development of the nervous system. *Annual Review of Neuroscience* 14: 453–501.

Oyama, S. (1985). *The Ontogeny of Information: Developmental Systems and Evolution*. Cambridge: Cambridge University Press.

Oyama, S. (2000). *Evolution's Eye: A Systems View of the Biology-Culture Divide*. Durham, N.C.: Duke University Press.

Oyama, S., P. E. Griffiths, and R. D. Gray (eds.) (2001). *Cycles of Contingency: Developmental Systems and Evolution*. Cambridge, Mass.: MIT Press.

Pedersen, P. E. and E. M. Blass (1981). Olfactory control over suckling in albino rats. In R. N. Aslin, J. R. Alberts, and M. R. Petersen (eds.), *Development of Perception, vol. 1: Audition, Somatic Perception, and the Chemical Senses*, pp. 359–381. New York: Academic Press.

Previc, F. H. (1991). A general theory concerning the prenatal origins of cerebral lateralization in humans. *Psychological Review* 98: 299–334.

Purves, D. (1988). *Body and Brain: A Trophic Theory of Neural Connections*. Cambridge, Mass.: Harvard University Press.

Schneirla, T. C. (1949). Levels in the psychological capacities of animals. In R. W. Sellars, V. J. McGill, and M. Farber (eds.), *Philosophy for the Future*, pp. 243–286. New York: Macmillan.

Schneirla, T. C. (1956). Interrelationships of the "innate" and the "acquired" in instinctive behavior. In P.-P. Grassé (ed.), *L'Instinct dans le comportement des animaux et de l'homme*, pp. 387–452. Paris: Masson.

Schneirla, T. C. (1957). The concept of development in comparative psychology. In D. B. Harris (ed.), *The Concept of Development*, pp. 78–108. Minneapolis: University of Minnesota Press.

Shair, H. N., G. A. Barr, and M. A. Hofer (eds.) (1991). *Developmental Psychobiology: New Methods and Changing Concepts.* New York: Oxford University Press.

Singer, M. and P. Berg (1991). *Genes and Genomes: A Changing Perspective.* Mill Valley, Calif.: University Science Books.

Smotherman, W. P. and S. R. Robinson (1991). Accessibility of the rat fetus for psychobiological investigation. In H. N. Shair, G. A. Barr, and M. A. Hofer (eds.), *Developmental Psychobiology: New Methods and Changing Concepts,* pp. 148–163. New York: Oxford University Press.

Thorpe, W. H. (1962). *Learning and Instinct in Animals: A Study of the Integration of Acquired and Innate Behavior.* Cambridge, Mass.: Harvard University Press.

van der Weel, C. (1993). Explaining embryological development: Should integration be the goal? *Biology and Philosophy* 8: 385–397.

Waddington, C. H. (1956). Genetic assimilation of the *Bithorax* phenotype. *Evolution* 10: 1–13.

Weismann, A. (1893). *The Germ Plasm: A Theory of Heredity.* New York: Scribner's.

West, M. J. and A. P. King (1988). Female visual displays affect the development of male song in the cowbird. *Nature* 334: 244–246.

8

Baldwin and Beyond: Organic Selection and Genetic Assimilation

Brian K. Hall

Thus the Baldwin Effect, the concept proposed by Schmalhausen, and genetic assimilation of Waddington are the same in that they propose the proximate environmental effect on morphogenesis and the ultimate process of natural selection in the study of evolution, and they agree, in essence, with the evolutionary thinking in the late nineteenth century after Darwin (1859).
(Matsuda 1987: 45)

1 Introduction

Organic selection (the Baldwin effect as it became known) as a mechanism mediating proximate environmental effects on the evolution of morphology and behavior is the topic of this chapter. Organic selection describes the situation by which an environmentally elicited phenotypic adaptation comes under genotypic control following selection.[1] It was proposed independently in 1896 by the psychologists James Baldwin and Conwy Lloyd Morgan. An essentially similar mechanism—coincident selection—was proposed by the paleontologist Henry Fairfield Osborn a few months later. Modified forms of organic selection were proposed as autonomization by Ivan Ivanovitch Schmalhausen in 1938 and as genetic assimilation by Conrad Hal Waddington in 1942. More recently, the Canadian entomologist Ryuishi Matsuda invoked organic selection as an explanation for evolution in changing environments, while West-Eberhard saw how different adaptive phenotypes and behavioral programs in the same life history stage could explain evolution in changing environments or speciation (Matsuda 1982, 1987; West-Eberhard 1986). The use and elaboration of organic selection as a mechanism mediating proximate environmental effects on the evolution of morphology and behavior is the topic of this chapter. I discuss the context in which organic selection was proposed, Lamarckian or neo-Lamarckian implications of organic selection, Waddington's experimental studies demonstrating the existence and efficacy of genetic assimilation, stabilizing selection, and norms of reaction favored by Schmalhausen, and Matsuda's search for a mechanism of organic selection in endocrine changes and heterochrony.

Baldwin was seeking a synthesis of evolution by inheritance of acquired characters (neo-Lamarckism) and evolution by natural selection (neo-Darwinism).[2] Osborn (1896, 1897a,b) sought a principle distinct from Lamarckian inheritance of acquired characters that would accommodate his strongly progressive, orthogenetic views, and that would reconcile Lamarckian and Darwinian approaches.[3] Morgan and Baldwin were more strongly neo-Darwinian (Morgan 1896a,b, 1900). Matsuda regarded organic selection as neo-Lamarckian, although this label cannot be applied uncritically to the Baldwin effect or to organic selection as proposed by Morgan and Osborn (Matsuda 1982: 745; 1987: 43–44). Genetic assimilation and autonomization are certainly not neo-Lamarckian, nor should they be uncritically equated with the Baldwin effect, although they often are.[4]

2   The Baldwin Effect

In one of those fascinating coincidences of time and place akin to the announcement in 1884 in Australia by William Hay Caldwell and William Haacke that monotremes lay eggs (Hall 1999a), Baldwin and Morgan announced their theories of organic selection independently in back-to-back presentations at a meeting of the New York Academy of Science in late December, 1895. Osborn published similar ideas several months later. Baldwin acknowledged that John T. Gulick, an American naturalist and missionary to Japan, had developed the same concept as nonadaptive speciation (discriminate isolation, segregate breeding, indiscriminate isolation, separate breeding—the species-differentiating effect of isolation) ten years before (Baldwin 1925, vol. 2: 215).[5]

Far from being outside the mainstream of evolutionary thinking, organic selection was viewed by contemporary biologists as an important evolutionary mechanism (Richards 1987). Baldwin proposed organic selection

as an extension of selection theory to accommodate behavioral modification as a directing force in evolution. Organic selection stresses plasticity of
phenotypes, behavior, and embryonic development (Baldwin 1896, 1902).
The essential elements of organic selection therefore are:

- animals choose a new habitat or life style and adapt to it;
- mutations occur that favor the changes; and
- selection favors those individuals best adapted to that new habitat or life
style, and the adaptation spreads through the population.

   Baldwin denied that organic selection was inheritance of acquired characters but used acquired characters to show how selection could be increased by a positive organismal response to the environment. In effect, the
adaptive shift "holds the strain in an environment where mutations tending
in the same direction will be selected" (Huxley 1942: 304), or as neatly
summarized by Milner in *The Encyclopedia of Evolution:*

There is a real distinction between transmission from parental experience directly
to offspring and species "experience" mediated by Mendelian Inheritance. The
irony is that neither Darwin nor Lamarck made that distinction. Therefore the
"Baldwin Effect" can equally claim to be Lamarckian and Darwinian. (Milner
1990: 32)

At the very least, a process by which animals choose different habitats
or habits, adapt, and are then subject to selection, blurs the distinction
between natural selection and Lamarckism. Changes that have been regarded as classic examples of the operation of organic selection are the
evolution of food-plant preferences in insects, host selection associated
with sympatric speciation in the true fruit flies of the Tephretidae, and habitat selection and sympatric speciation in Australian fruit flies (Thorpe
1930, 1940, 1945; Bush 1969, 1973; Huettel and Bush 1972; Parsons
1981). G. G. Simpson argues this, although adaptation to a new host may
occur by individual adaptation or by genetic selection (Simpson 1953).
Thorpe's studies do not demonstrate replacement of the nonhereditary
adaptation by hereditary adaptation, as would be required if organic selection were operating (see Gillespie 1990 for a detailed analysis of Thorpe's
ethology, including connections to the Baldwin effect, which Thorpe initially embraced but later dropped).

   Julian Huxley argued that organic selection played a role, albeit a minor
one, in the origin of races and in speciation (Huxley 1942). As discussed in

the last section, West-Eberhard assigned organic selection a more substantive role. Hardy regarded organic selection as an important evolutionary force, and behavior as an important selective force (Hardy 1965). Ernst Mayr came out against sympatric speciation and therefore against the Baldwin effect (Mayr 1973). The Baldwin effect, however, does provide a plausible mechanism for the initiation of sympatric speciation.

Much influenced by Schmalhausen's *Factors of Evolution: The Theory of Stabilizing Selection,* Simpson also came out against the Baldwin effect, although he hedged his bets, being willing to accept that the Baldwin effect was "fully plausible," that "it probably has occurred," that "the ability to 'acquire' a character has, in itself, a genetical basis," and that the reaction norms of Schmalhausen provide the most reasonable approach to how genetic systems deal with environmental change (Simpson 1953: 115–116). As Simpson emphasized, each of the three phases invoked in the Baldwin effect—adaptation, mutation, selection—is known to occur separately. His argument is that they have rarely been shown to occur in sequence as required by the Baldwin effect.

Simpson considered that three conditions had to be met to demonstrate the Baldwin effect as an evolutionary mechanism:

• the ability to acquire the character must have a genetic basis;

• development has adjusted to selection for the ability to acquire an adaptive character so that the character invariably appears; and

• developmental ranges and reaction norms are balanced and labile.

All three conditions are met in a quantitative model of what has been called "the Simpson-Baldwin effect" (Ancel 1999).

Two points were telling for Simpson and Mayr: a direct effect of any modification of the phenotype on the genotype would be Lamarckism, while without such a feedback from phenotype to genotype, the Baldwin effect is no more than the operation of natural selection. In 1973, Mayr raised additional objections: the Baldwin effect relates to individuals, but variability within populations allows a response to selection; and the ability to modify the phenotype is itself under genetic control. By 1976, however, Mayr was less troubled by genetic assimilation:

Experiments on the "revealed genotype" [genetic assimilation] shed new light on the so-called Baldwin effect and indicate the possibility that a modification of the phenotype is of evolutionary significance only if it is due to concealed polygenes and will lead to their accumulation in the gene pool. (Mayr 1976: 320)

3 Genetic Assimilation

As a result of his studies in genetics and development, and as expressed in such pioneering books as *Organisers and Genes,* Conrad Waddington adopted an epigenetic viewpoint that saw development in strictly genetic and deterministic terms and formed the basis for his approach to evolution (Waddington 1940). To Waddington, organismal evolution resulted from the evolution of developmental systems. Much of his motivation for integrating genetics, development, and evolution stemmed from what he viewed as the inability of population genetics to provide a realistic model of the operation of genes in development and evolution (Waddington 1975), an approach that has reemerged as the integrative field of evolutionary developmental biology (Raff 1996; Hall 1999b; Robert et al. 2001; Hall and Olson 2002).[6] Waddington launched his attacks on prevailing evolutionary theory from the two platforms of *canalization* and *genetic assimilation.*

Waddington coined the term canalization for those features of developmental pathways that lead to the production of standard and discrete phenotypes despite environmental or genetic influences that would otherwise disrupt development (Waddington 1940). Canalization buffers development against environmental and genetic perturbations. Buffering is especially significant, and was central to Waddington's thinking. Canalization allows genetic variability to build up within the genotype, even though such variability is not expressed phenotypically. Concepts that also emphasized buffering were developed by Lerner as genetic homeostasis and by Sewall Wright as universal pleiotropy (Lerner 1954; Wright 1968).[7]

To canalization Waddington added the concept that hidden genetic variability can be brought to light and subjected to selection through genetic assimilation, which he defined as an organism's genetic capability to respond to environmental perturbations (Waddington 1942, 1953a,b). Waddington used genetic assimilation to relate hidden genetic variability, development, adaptation, and heritable phenotypic responses to environmental perturbations. Genetic assimilation has been defined as:

the process by which a phenotypic character initially produced only in response to some environmental influence becomes, through a process of selection, taken over by the genotype, so that it is formed even in the absence of the environmental influence that at first had been necessary. (King and Stansfield 1985)

Waddington provided experimental evidence; phenotypic changes were induced in *Drosophila* exposed to an environmental shock such as heat or ether, followed by selection for the induced phenotype in the absence of the environmental stimulus. Production of crossveinless and bithorax flies are the paradigmatic examples. Genetic assimilation does not, however, rest on Waddington's experiments alone, but has been demonstrated by other workers using other model systems.[8] In addition, it is now known that selection of the differential sensitivity to induction of the bithorax phenotype by ether is correlated with loss of expression of the gene *Ultrabithorax* (*Ubx*), and that much of the genetic variability underlying genetic assimilation of the bithorax phenotype lies in the *Ubx* locus (Gibson and Hogness 1996). Genetic assimilation has a genetic basis and in no way smacks of Lamarckian inheritance of acquired characters.

Phenocopies, genetic assimilation, and canalization document the hidden genetic variability that can be evoked following exposure of organisms to an environmental stimulus. Genetic assimilation is thus the expression of previously hidden genetic variability in response to selection following an environmental stimulus. As Waddington was aware, genetically assimilated phenotypes have a polygenic basis, involving genes on several chromosomes, in contrast with the Baldwin effect, which relies on chance mutations (Waddington 1956a,b, and see the summary in table 8.1). Nevertheless, many saw genetic assimilation as an extension of the Baldwin effect. Even today, many regard the two processes as synonymous, which they are not (see below).

In a letter to Sir Alister Hardy, Waddington claimed that he was unaware of the prior formulations by Baldwin or Morgan when he conceived genetic assimilation in 1942 (Waddington 1975: 279). The Baldwin effect came to Waddington's attention while he was preparing the first paper containing experimental evidence of genetic assimilation (Waddington 1953a). That paper, and Simpson's paper on the Baldwin effect, appeared back to back in the journal *Evolution*. Waddington subsequently published a note in *Evolution,* in which he indicated that he had intended to include a discus-

Table 8.1
A summary of the steps in the Baldwin effect and genetic assimilation to show the major differences between the two processes.

Baldwin effect	Genetic assimilation
1. Interaction with the environment results in phenotypic changes in structure, behavior, and/or function that are adaptive	Interaction with the environment results in phenotypic changes in structure, behavior, and/or function that are adaptive
2. Mutations occur that lead to the same adaptive phenotypic changes; existing genetic variability is insufficient	Existing genetic variability is expressed in an assimilated phenotype which appears in the absence of the environmental signal; mutation is not required
3. Selection favors the mutations, which spread through the population; the environmentally induced phenotype is now inherited.	Selection favors the previously unexpressed genetic variability; the number of individuals with the assimilated phenotype increases

sion of organic selection in his experimental paper, but omitted it for reasons of space (Waddington 1953b).

Waddington argued that genetic assimilation and the Baldwin effect were different in one fundamental respect: the initial adaptation to the environment as explained by the Baldwin effect was nongenetic, and therefore not subject to selection (Waddington 1961). Waddington saw genetic assimilation as selection of existing genetic variation. But genetic assimilation might also have been thought to have an initial nongenetic step had it too been proposed before the rediscovery of Mendelian genetics, as the Baldwin effect was. Conversely, the Baldwin effect might have placed more emphasis on the natural genetic variation within a population had it been articulated in the twentieth rather than in the nineteenth century.

Matsuda saw genetic assimilation as "an experimental demonstration of the Baldwin Effect" (Matsuda 1982: 745); indeed, because of its emphasis on the evolution of behavioral changes that lead to structural evolution, Matsuda saw genetic assimilation as broader than the Baldwin effect (Matsuda 1982: 745). He defined the essence of the Baldwin effect, and related it to Morgan's principle and genetic assimilation, as follows:

Characters acquired in individuals due to the influence of the environment they selected remain as they are when favored by natural selection [accommodation].

Such modified characters may, under the influence of natural selection, become reinforced or replaced by similar hereditary characters [the coincidental variations of Lloyd Morgan 1900 and Baldwin 1902]. (Matsuda 1987: 43–44)

In fact there are more fundamental differences between the Baldwin effect and genetic assimilation, especially the requirement for mutations to genocopy the phenotype (Baldwin effect) versus the expression of preexisting genetic variability for the phenotype in genetic assimilation (table 8.1). The phenotypes produced by genetic assimilation are phenocopies of known phenotypes normally produced in response to mutations. The term "genocopy" was used by Hovasse for situations in which the genotype copies nongenetic effects (Hovasse 1950). A genocopy is then the opposite of a phenocopy. A second and later usage of genocopy is for the production of the same phenotype by different mimetic nonallelic genes.

Drosophila respond to the environmental agents to produce the phenocopy at the same stage of embryonic development as mutant genes act to produce a genocopy; both phenocopies and genocopies activate equivalent developmental pathways (Hadorn 1961, and see Hall 2001c for a discussion of gene action in context). Ho and colleagues demonstrated that genetic assimilation involves an extension of the critical time period during which the phenotype is normally induced (Ho et al. 1983). As critical periods are times of heightened susceptibility to genetic and/or environmental perturbations, a longer critical period means that the time during which development is susceptible to, and able to respond to, environmental influences is also longer (Hall 1977, 1985, 1999b; Hall and Miyake 1997).

Genetic assimilation applies as much to the evolution of behavior as to the evolution of structures:

the Baldwin Effect differs from genetic assimilation only in the emphasis that animals select the environments that influence their development, and habitat or host selection occurs before the process of genetic assimilation.... Hence the behavior is an integral part of genetic assimilation.... (Matsuda 1987: 44–45)

Waddington knew this. However, the link to behavior was first demonstrated by Jean Piaget in his doctoral studies with observations on 80,000 specimens of the snail *Limnaea stagnalis* (Piaget 1929a,b). Piaget found that individuals with elongate shells were replaced by individuals with shorter shells, these individuals being better adapted to the turbulent waters of many of the lakes in Switzerland. A shortened shell develops if snails are raised in turbulent water but continues to be produced when these snails are bred in still water. The proximate mechanisms are thought to be contraction of the columnar muscles to allow developing snails to adhere to the substrate, and subsequent reduced growth of the shell. A behavioral response is also assimilated; snails with shorter shells prefer shallow water. Thus, both a morphological and a behavioral trait are assimilated. Piaget observed a similar phenomenon in an Alpine stonecrop, *Sedum parvulum*, that fails to modify its morphology when transplanted from a harsh to a more benign environment (Piaget 1966, 1980). Hereditary fixation has occurred.[9]

By the early 1960s, if not earlier, Waddington himself had come to recognize the central importance of behavior in evolution (Waddington 1975: 280). Piaget saw both the relationship between the Baldwin effect and genetic assimilation and the link between behavioral modification and a changed environment, or a new environment that the organisms entered:

But the interesting point for our purposes is that by eking out the selection accomplished by the environment with his "organic selection," Baldwin opened the door to the idea of the organism itself affecting the inception and canalization of new hereditary forms, and this as a consequence of its exploratory behavior. (Piaget 1978: xv)[10]

An inability to learn therefore reduces the fitness of the organism. Indeed, for Morgan (1896a,b), organisms that could not learn, or populations that lacked individuals with an ability to learn, had no fitness in a new environment. Learning allows time for mutations to arise in the population and for the population to change.

Behavioral changes may lead to learning and acceleration of evolutionary change without resorting to interpretations of Lamarckian inheritance. This view has gained some support from recent studies on the role of learning in real and simulated populations and from studies in artificial intelligence and robotics (Hinton and Nowlan 1987; Maynard Smith 1987; French and Messinger 1994; Papaj 1994; and Frank 1996; see too the final pages in Gerhart and Kirschner 1997 for the importance of behavioral changes and evolutionary change). The ethology literature is also a source of examples of habits that become instincts and of learned songs or repertoires that become innate. Morgan used the example of learned songs in birds becoming innate as a prime example of organic selection (Morgan 1896b). A minority of workers argue that we should abandon the distinction between inherited and acquired characters when seeking to explain phenotypic change. Consequently, even though they give primacy to developmental changes as leading evolutionary modifications, they see no need either for organic selection or for genetic assimilation. (Gottlieb 1987b, 1992; Johnston and Gottlieb 1990).

There was nothing Lamarckian about genetic assimilation as far as Waddington was concerned, although he had to battle mightily to convince others. The genetic basis underpinning genetic assimilation lies in the genetic capability of organisms to respond to environmental changes, unexpressed genetic variability, and the ability of selection to increase the frequency of individuals expressing that previously hidden genetic potential (table 8.1). The initial stimulus is environmental, the response is genetic; see Hall (1999b) for a recent discussion. Genetic polymorphism for the phenotype, an environmental signal, and selection to alter gene frequency in the population are the essential elements of genetic assimilation (Stern 1958, 1959).

A conceptually similar situation exists with the maintenance of balanced or seasonal polymorphisms or cyclomorphosis, in which environmental cues elicit the developmental program for one morphological type or another. Selective shifts in gene expression in response to different environments are shared as basic mechanisms by genetic assimilation, seasonal polymorphism and cyclomorphosis; see the last section of this paper.[11]

Waddington argued that genetic assimilation could produce adaptive change in nature, citing Piaget's experiments on the European snail *Limnaea* as a prime example (Waddington 1956a, 1975). Genetic assimilation is certainly a plausible basis for seasonal polymorphism as it is based on unexpressed but available genetic variability, canalization of development, a genetic capability to respond to environmental changes and selection for new gene combinations. Discussions of the prime examples—shell shape in *Limnaea,* permanent loss of leaves in xerophytic plants, and effects of altered egg size in amphibians, sea urchins and lizards—can be found in Matsuda (1987) and Hall (1999b).

4   Autonomization

Schmalhausen is associated with three interconnected evolutionary processes: autonomization, stabilizing selection, and norms of reaction. His views, first published in Russian in 1938 and 1942, became known to the English-speaking scientific world after the publication of *Factors of Evolution: The Theory of Stabilizing Selection* in 1949. As is clear from the epigraph, Matsuda regarded Schmalhausen's autonomization as equivalent to organic selection and genetic assimilation. I have considered the closeness between autonomization and genetic assimilation in detail elsewhere (Hall 1999b), and so will only comment briefly here.[12]

Schmalhausen saw adaptation to a new environment as the first step toward destabilizing development and allowing previously hidden genetic variability to be expressed phenotypically:

The *stabilizing form of selection* is based upon the selective advantage under definite and especially, fluctuating conditions possessed by the normal organization over variations from the norm. (Schmalhausen 1949: 73)

Norms of reaction exist in those developing systems in which a single genotype can give rise to different phenotypes, as occurs in cyclomorphosis or seasonal polymorphism.[13] Schmalhausen cited both Baldwin and Morgan as representative of Darwinian animal psychologists who saw the evolutionary importance of adaptive modification from a Darwinian rather than a Lamarckian point of view.

Just as Waddington was unaware of Baldwin's work when he formulated genetic assimilation, so Schmalhausen was unaware of Waddington's when he formulated autonomization. Just as Waddington dismissed Baldwin's organic selection, so Waddington dismissed Schmalhausen, either by failing to cite his work, or when he did (as in his 1961 review of genetic assimilation), by dismissing it on the dual grounds of lack of original experiments and lack of any process to explain the concepts. Waddington's criticisms are not overwhelming, often consisting of no more than accusing Schmalhausen of using the name "stabilizing selection" in a number of different senses (Waddington 1953a).

Schmalhausen proposed stabilizing selection and norms of reaction as mechanisms linking development and evolution. History is on Schmalhausen's side; stabilizing selection has been much more readily assimilated into mainstream evolutionary thought than has genetic assimilation and remains a potent force in evolutionary analysis of phenotypic modification. Wagner and his colleagues proposed a population genetics model of canalization reinforced by stabilizing selection, and drew a distinction between genetic and environmental canalization (Wagner et al. 1997; see also

Wilkins [1997] for a genetic perspective on canalization). In distinguishing genetic from environmental canalization, models of RNA folding have been used to provide a molecular illustration for the Simpson-Baldwin effect (Ancel and Fontana 2000).

5   Matsuda, Genetic Assimilation, and Evolution in Changing Environments

Matsuda invoked organic selection (genetic assimilation) as an explanation for evolution in changing environments (Matsuda 1982, 1987). Few seem to have appreciated or cited Matsuda's use of genetic assimilation.[14] The contexts of these citations varies from the role of developmental change in evolution, through species recognition and learning in birds, to sympatric speciation, the evolution of oysters and of viviparity in reptiles.

His first reference to organic selection was in a footnote in his review of abnormal metamorphosis and arthropod evolution (Matsuda 1979: 226). In discussing loss of wings in ancestral members of the Psocoptera (booklice), Matsuda recognized that settlement on hosts would have been the first step in their transformation into the parasitic lice that we recognize as members of the Phthiraptera. Settlement on the host provokes increased release of juvenile hormone, modification of development, and loss of the wings. Aptery was advantageous, persisted, and was accompanied (or followed) by adaptive changes in the mouth parts and thoracic segments as the organisms became neotenic:

> This [retention of aptery] is superficially akin to the "Baldwin Effect." In the context of this work, however, alteration in hormonal milieu directly induces alteration in the reaction norm of the genotype, so that aptery can occur; this situation may be comparable to the genetic assimilation of Waddington (1961), in which a phenotype initially produced in response to certain environmental stimuli is taken over by the genotype. In the Baldwin Effect (see Mayr 1963: 610), however, mutation occurs later in such a population in producing the favored phenotype. (Matsuda 1979: 226n)

Matsuda linked environment (settlement on the host), changes in endocrine balance, phenotypic modification and evolutionary change, and was aware of reaction norms, organic selection and genetic assimilation, and of the subtle differences between them. An important element of his approach was that alteration in organismal physiology (including endocrine status) is the inevitable first response to environmental change. Indeed, in any approach to genetic assimilation, the basis of the ability of the organism to respond to the environmental stimulus must be determined. Matsuda uses lability of hormonal status, and altered responsiveness of that status to signals associated with the new environment, to "explain" the immediate response of the organism to the altered environment. The physiological-endocrinological change is not inherited, but the capacity to elicit the change in response to the altered environment is a heritable feature, so that individuals continue to display such adaptive changes over subsequent generations. Genetic fixation of the response requires either genetic assimilation or that mutations favoring the same changes arise and spread through the population.

Matsuda makes it clear that genetic assimilation can only be inferred, not proven, although he does equate phases of genetic assimilation of crossveinless in *Drosophila* with phases in the progression to neoteny in salamanders (table 8.2). This aspect is worth exploring. There are circumstances

Table 8.2
Comparability of stages of genetic assimilation of crossveinless in *Drosophila* with phases of a classification of neoteny in salamanders according to Matsuda (1982).[a]

Genetic assimilation	Neoteny
1. Crossveinless appears in a few individuals of the upward selection line in generation 14 after crossveinless was induced with an environmental (temperature) shock in the parents	Phase 1, seen in *Ambystoma tigrinum*: neoteny dependent on an environmental stimulus (cold) and selection
2. Genetic assimilation of crossveinless as the number of individuals with crossveinless is increased with further selection	Phase 2, seen in *A. gracilis* and *A. mexicanum*, in which the number of genetically determined neotenous individuals has increased under selection[b] Phase 3, in which genetically determined neoteny occurs in all the individuals of a population in response to selection

a. Gottlieb (1989b) laid out a conceptually similar parallel set of stages in which development plays the leading role
b. The genetic change is a mutation affecting secretion of thyroxine

under which genetic assimilation can be demonstrated to have been the mechanism responsible for evolutionary change. Furthermore, genetic assimilation can be verified experimentally.

The first stage of genetic assimilation is the appearance of individuals with the phenotype after generations of upward selection in the absence of the environmental stimulus that was used to induce the phenotype in the parents. For example, Waddington induced crossveinless in *Drosophila* with a temperature shock in the first generation but then obtained a few assimilated crossveinless individuals in generation 14 after selection but without the temperature shock. Matsuda equates this with facultative neoteny in *Ambystoma tigrinum* (which is temperature-induced) and with caste differentiation in termites, in which presence of different morphs in the population influences the status of juvenile hormone and therefore caste differentiation.

The second phase of genetic assimilation is the spread of the assimilated phenotype through the population in response to further selection (table 8.2). Matsuda equates this phase with neoteny in such salamander species as *Ambystoma gracile* and *A. mexicanum,* in which neoteny is the normal condition; phase 2 is a condition of few individuals with the condition; phase 3 has many more individuals in the population exhibiting the condition. He offers microptery in crickets of the species *Nemobius yezoensis*—which is genetically fixed in some individuals but environmentally induced in others—as a further example of phase 2. Matsuda also offers numerous examples of constitutive wingless insects (including a reanalysis of those presented in his 1979 review) as evidence for phase 3, in which most or all members of the population display the phenotypic change without environmental elicitation.

Despite numerous examples brought forth by Matsuda, it is difficult to detect genetic assimilation as the mechanism of evolutionary change once assimilation has taken place, although a strong case has been made for genetic assimilation of a physiological response—retention of eggs within the oviduct—as the basis for the over 100 occurrences of the evolution of viviparity in reptiles (Shine and Guillette 1998). Once assimilated, the character will appear no different from a character that was fixed by mutation, unless we can analyze the genetic constitution of the species before and after the event; see below and chapter 19 in Hall (1999b).

Matsuda devoted Part One of his 1987 book to a review of metamorphosis, heterochrony, genetic fixation (genetic assimilation), and evolutionary change, and Part Two to an extensive, phylum by phylum, discussion of examples of evolution in changing environments, including: modification of shell shape in the mollusk *Limnaea;* altitudinal variation in egg size and egg number in the wood frog, *Rana sylvatica;* seasonal variation in butterfly wing color patterns; winglessness in various insects; and neoteny in salamanders.

Matsuda favored a mechanism by which changes initiated in response to an environmental stimulus could be genetically assimilated through heterochrony affecting individual organ systems, or through neoteny affecting the entire organism (Matsuda 1982, 1987).[15] His unique contribution was to identify hormonal mediation of the environmental stimulus as the developmental response. Hormonal states normally requiring environmental induction become genetically fixed. Unlike Waddington but like Baldwin, Matsuda invoked mutation to transform the environmental signal into a gene-based signal or genocopy; Waddington invoked expression of existing genetic variability to respond to changes in the environment.

Matsuda argued that genetic assimilation is the basis of the origin and preservation of any behavioral or phenotypic trait that is adapted to a particular environment but produced in a different environment. He relied heavily on an analysis of interesting experiments on relationships between altitudinal variation, egg size, and number in the wood frog *Rana sylvatica,* undertaken by Berven (1982) and discussed below.

Larger body size and delayed reproduction are advantageous at high altitudes. *Rana sylvatica* lays larger and fewer eggs at higher latitudes than it does at lower latitudes. Berven undertook an experimental analysis in which he transplanted juveniles from high to low altitudes and *vice versa.* At the next reproduction, egg size and egg number followed parental type and not altitude—in other words, size and number are appropriate to the environment in which individuals usually reside, not to the new environment. Failure to respond to the new environment was taken by Matsuda as evidence for genetic assimilation of egg size and egg number; assimilation had already occurred in response to the original environment. It would be nice to have rather more direct evidence.

West-Eberhard sees alternate adaptations—different adaptive phenotypes in the same life history stage—establishing a precondition and basis for speciation preceding reproductive isolation (West-Eberhard 1986). She supports her concept of epigenetic divergence (by which developmental or behavioral programs bifurcate to establish intraspecific alternative adaptations) with the work of Matsuda, stressing the importance of sudden regulatory changes brought about by heterochrony as common sources of new alternative adaptations.[16] In 1989 she argued strongly against phenotypic plasticity being considered nongenetic. The significance of Matsuda's body of work for her is that heterochronic changes that lead to altered metamorphosis create a polymorphic population in which the new phenotypes are especially sensitive to the environment.

Despite these examples, there is a fundamental problem with detecting evidence for genetic assimilation in nature, a problem tackled most directly by Matsuda. The only distinctive features of genetic assimilation are the environmental stimulus that initiates genetic and selectional processes that produce the new phenotype. If the assimilated phenotype is expressed in the absence of the environmental signal that originally evoked it—as it is by definition—then distinguishing a genetically assimilated character that arose following selection for preexisting genetic variability from one that arose through selection of a mutation would not be possible. We might only expect to detect genetic assimilation when it was occurring and through a multi-generational study that includes the generation exposed to the originating environmental perturbation. Alternatively, one could find two sister taxa or two local populations of the same species, one with the original character and one with the derived putative genetically assimilated character, and determine whether the reaction norm of the derived character lay within the reaction norm of the original character.

Such optimism notwithstanding, and despite the passage of over 100 years since organic selection was proposed, we neither know how many genetically fixed, dimorphic, and environmentally adaptive characters arose through genetic assimilation, nor the full force of genetic assimilation as a mechanism for animal evolution in changing environments. The challenge posed by the proponents of organic selection remains just that—a challenge.[17]

Acknowledgments

My thanks to Roy Pearson (University for Toronto) who prompted me to compare organic selection and genetic assimilation more critically than I had in the past. My research is supported by NSERC of Canada (grant A5056) and the Killam Trust of Dalhousie University.

Notes

1. A history of the terms "organic selection"—which Baldwin promoted—and the "Baldwin effect"—which Simpson (1953) promoted—may be found in Richards (1987): 489ff. Depew (2000) argues that the "Baldwin effect" is not an effect but rather a hypothesis and possibly a mechanism, neither of which reconcile Baldwin and Simpson with respect to natural selection; but see the chapter by Depew in this volume, in which he sees himself as "more of a Baldwin booster than a Baldwin sceptic." Indeed, some authors argue that the Baldwin effect should be set aside (Watkins 1999, and see chapter 4 in this volume by Godfrey-Smith). A quantitative model of the "Simpson-Baldwin effect" was provided by Ancel (1999). For the relationship between the Baldwin effect and developmental systems theory (DST), see Weber and Deacon (2000). For the relationship between DST, epigenetics, evolution, and development, see Robert et al. 2001.

2. Baldwin was a founding father of experimental psychology, having created the first laboratory for experimental psychology when he was appointed to the University of Toronto in 1889. By 1896 his reputation as an experimentalist, author, and editor was firmly established. His career ended in disgrace and his influence was almost entirely lost, when in early 1909 it was discovered, after a police raid and subsequent charges had been laid and then quashed, that Baldwin had visited a black house of prostitution in Baltimore in the early summer of 1908 (Richards 1987: 496 ff.).

3. For an analysis of Osborn's approach to evolution in the context of the influence of embryology on palaeontology, see Hall (2002b).

4. For detailed analyses of the life and work of Baldwin, see Sewyn (1945), Richards (1987), Sinha (1984), and Dennett (1995); for Osborn, see Rainger (1991); for Morgan, see Clarke (1974) and Richards (1987). For Baldwin's evaluation of the independent development of "organic selection," see the appendix in Baldwin (1902). For comparisons of the views of Baldwin, Osborn, and Morgan—including photographs of all three—see Gottlieb (1992). Daniel Dennett acknowledged Richards's account of the history of the Baldwin effect to "have been one of the major provocations and guides to my thinking in this book [*Darwin's Dangerous Idea*]" (Dennett 1995: 79 n.7). Matsuda (1987: 53) proposed the term "pan-environmentalism" for his concept of environmental effects on development and evolution, where environment consisted of both morphogenetic and selective factors. However, he made no further use of the term in his book; see also the review by Pearson (1988).

5. For analyses of Gulick's contribution to evolutionary theory—especially adaptation and speciation—and his role in the often vociferous debates between Alfred Wallace and George Romanes on the mechanism of speciation, see Kellogg (1908), Jordan (1923), Gulick (1932), Watanabe (1966), Lesch (1975), Provine (1986),

Gould (1987), and Amundson (1994). I have become intrigued by Gulick's Darwinism and plan a subsequent paper on his theories on isolation and speciation.

6. For analyses of how Waddington came to his integrated (epigenetic) view of genetics, development, and evolution, see Thom (1989), Robertson (1977), Polikoff (1981), Yoxen (1986), Gilbert (1994, 2000), Hall (1992, 2001b), and Stern (2000).

7. Canalization has resurfaced in evolutionary studies in the concept of developmental stability and constraint; see Maynard Smith et al. (1985), Scharloo (1991), Rollo (1995), Schwenk (1994/1995), Wagner and Altenberg (1996), Wilkins (1997), Hall (1999b), and Wagner and Schwenk (2000). For genetic variation, genetic buffering, and hidden genetic variability associated with canalization, see Gibson and Wagner (2000).

8. For his studies with *Drosophila,* see Waddington (1953a, 1956a,b, 1958, 1959, 1961). For other experimental demonstrations of genetic assimilation, see Bateman (1959a,b), Rendel (1968), Capdevila and Garcia-Bellido (1974), Thompson and Thoday (1975), Ho et al. (1983) and Ho (1984); and see Hall (1999b) for an extensive discussion.

9. For discussions of the genetic assimilation of both morphological and behavioral traits, see Messerly (1996) and Hall (1998). For studies of assimilation of behavioral and morphological traits in *Limnaea,* see Boycott et al. (1930), Boycott (1938), and Piaget (1929a,b, 1978, 1980). For critical evaluations of hereditary fixation in Piaget's biological and psychological studies, see Boden (1980), and the chapters by Changeux and Danchin in Piattelli-Palmarini (1980).

10. For an analysis by Piaget of organic selection as proposed by Baldwin, see chapter 2 in Piaget (1978). For connections and contrasts in the approaches of Baldwin and Piaget to what has variously been termed epigenetic psychobiology, epigenetic naturalism, or socially oriented epigeneticism, see Russell (1978), Vonèche (1982), Cahan (1984), and Sinha (1984).

11. For seasonal polymorphism, see Gilbert (1966, 1980), Greene (1989), Dodson (1989a,b), Stearns (1989), Harvell (1990), and Hall (1999b). For experimental evidence of similar genetic mechanisms in assimilation and polymorphism, see Dun and Fraser (1959), and Fraser and Kindred (1960). For discussions see Grant (1963), Arthur (1984), Thomson (1988), and Hall (1999b).

12. Schmalhausen's work is discussed in some depth by Adams (1980, 1994), Vorobyeva (1987, 1989), Allen (1991), Gilbert (1994), Wake (1986, 1996), Mikhailov (1997), and Van der Weele (1999). *Reaktionsnorm* has been traced by Sarkar (1999) from Waltereck who coined the term in 1909, through the central role that reaction norms played in Russian science, to the adaptive norms of the 1960s.

13. For analyses of the literature on norms of reaction and polymorphism, see West-Eberhard (1986, 1989), Matsuda (1987), Stearns (1989, 1992), Rollo (1995) and Hall (1999b).

14. Studies that cite both Matsuda and Waddington in relation to genetic assimilation (from a total of nine citations between 1983 and 1996) include Gottlieb

(1987a,b), Shine and Guillett (1988), West-Eberhard (1989), Gillespie (1990), Johnston and Gottlieb (1990), and Hall (1992).

15. For the developmental basis of heterochrony, see Hall (1984, 1990, 2001d, 2002a), chapter 24 in Hall (1999b), and the chapters in Zelditch (2001).

16. For an insightful analysis of heterochrony and modification of behavior, see chapter 7 in McKinney and McNamara (1991).

17. This chapter is adapted and updated from a paper ("Organic selection: Proximate environmental effects on the evolution of morphology and behaviour") published in *Biology and Philosophy* (Hall 2001a) with the permission of the Publisher, Kluwer Academic Publishers, Dordrecht, Netherlands and after payment of the required fee.

References

Adams, M. B. (1980). Severtzov and Schmalhausen: Russian morphology and the evolutionary synthesis. In E. Mayr and W. B. Provine (eds.), *The Evolutionary Synthesis: Perspectives on the Unification of Biology*, pp. 193–225. Cambridge, Mass.: Harvard University Press.

Adams, M. B. (ed.) (1994). *The Evolution of Theodosius Dobzhansky: Essays on His Life and Thought in Russia and America*. Princeton, N.J.: Princeton University Press.

Allen, G. E. (1991). Mechanistic and dialectical materialism in 20th Century Evolutionary Theory: The Work of Ivan I. Schmalhausen. In L. Warren and H. Koprowski (eds.), *New Perspectives on Evolution*, pp. 15–36. New York: Wiley-Liss.

Amundson, R. (1994). John T. Gulick and the active organism: Adaptation, Isolation, and the Politics of Evolution. In R. MacLeod and P. E. Rehbock (eds.), *Darwin's Laboratory: Evolutionary Theory and Natural History in the Pacific*, pp. 110–139. Honolulu: University of Hawai'i Press.

Ancel, L. W. (1999). A quantitative model of the Simpson-Baldwin effect. *Journal of Theoretical Biology* 196: 197–209.

Ancel, L. W. and W. Fontana (2000). Plasticity, evolvability, and modularity in RNA. *Journal of Experimental Zoology (Molecular and Developmental Evolution)* 288: 242–283.

Arthur, W. (1984). *Mechanisms of Morphological Evolution: A Combined Genetic, Developmental, and Ecological Approach*. London: John Wiley.

Baldwin, J. M. (1896). A new factor in evolution. *American Naturalist* 30: 441–451, 536–553.

Baldwin, J. M. (1902). *Development and Evolution*. New York: Macmillan.

Baldwin, J. M. (ed.) (1925). *Dictionary of Philosophy and Psychology*. New edition with corrections, 3 vols. New York: Macmillan.

Bateman, K. G. (1959a). The genetic assimilation of the dumpy phenotype. *Journal of Genetics* 56: 341–351.

Bateman, K. G. (1959b). The genetic assimilation of four venation phenocopies. *Journal of Genetics* 56: 443–474.

Benjafield, J. G. (1996). *A History of Psychology*. Boston: Allyn and Bacon.

Berven, K. A. (1982). The genetic basis of altitudinal variation in the wood frog, *Rana sylvatica*. 1. An experimental basis of life history traits. *Evolution* 36: 962–983.

Boden, M. A. (1980). *Jean Piaget*. New York: Viking.

Boycott, A. E. (1938). Experiments on the artificial breeding of *Limnaea involuta*, *Limnaea burnetti* and other forms of *Limnaea peregra*. *Proceedings of the Malacological Society of London* 23: 101–108.

Boycott, A. E., C. Diver, S. L. Garstang, and F. M. Turner (1930). The inheritance of sinestrality in *Limnaea peregra* (Mollusca: Pulmonata). *Philosophical Transactions of the Royal Society of London* (B) 219: 51–131.

Bush, G. L. (1969). Sympatric host race formation and speciation in frugivorous flies of the genus *Rhagoletis* (Diptera, Tephretidae). *Evolution* 23: 237–251.

Bush, G. L. (1973). The mechanism of sympatric host race formation in the true fruit flies (Tephretidae). In M. J. D. White (ed.), *Genetic Mechanisms of Speciation in Insects*, pp. 3–23. Dordrecht: Reidel.

Cahan, E. (1984). The genetic psychologies of James Mark Baldwin and Jean Piaget. *Developmental Physiology* 20: 128–135.

Capdevila, M. P. and A. Garcia-Bellido (1974). Development and genetic analysis of *bithorax* phenocopies in *Drosophila*. *Nature* 250: 500–502.

Clarke, E. (1974). Morgan, Conwy Lloyd. *Dictionary of Scientific Biography* 9: 512–513.

Dennett, D. C. (1995). *Darwin's Dangerous Idea: Evolution and the Meaning of Life*. New York: Simon and Schuster.

Depew, D. (2000). The Baldwin effect: An archaeology. *Cybernetics and Human Knowledge* 7: 7–20.

Dodson, S. (1989a). Predator-induced reaction norms: cyclic changes in shape and size can be protective. *BioScience* 39: 447–452.

Dodson, S. (1989b). The ecological role of chemical stimuli for the zooplankton predator-induced morphology in *Daphnia*. *Oecologia* (Berlin) 78: 361–367.

Dun, R. B. and A. S. Fraser (1959). Selection for an invariant character, vibrissa number, in the house mouse. *Australian Journal of Biological Science* 21: 506–523.

Frank, S. A. (1996). The design of natural and artificial adaptive systems. In M. S. Rose and G. V. Lauder (eds.), *Adaptation*, pp. 451–505. San Diego, Calif.: Academic Press.

Fraser, A. S. and D. M. Kindred (1960). Selection for an invariant character, vibrissa number, in the house mouse. II. Limits to variability. *Australian Journal of Biological Science* 13: 48–58.

French, R. M. and A. Messinger (1994). Genes, phenes and the Baldwin effect: Learning and evolution in a simulated population. In R. A. Brooks and P. Maes (eds.), *Artificial Life IV*, pp. 277–282. Cambridge, Mass.: MIT Press.

Gerhart, J. and M. Kirschner (1997). *Cells, Embryos, and Evolution: Toward a Cellular and Developmental Understanding of Phenotypic Variation and Evolutionary Adaptability*. Malden, Mass.: Blackwell.

Gibson, G. and D. S. Hogness (1996). Effect of polymorphism in the *Drosophila* regulatory gene *Ultrabithorax* on homeotic stability. *Science* 271: 200–203.

Gibson, G. and G. P. Wagner (2000. Canalization in evolutionary genetics: a stabilizing theory? *BioEssays* 22: 372–380.

Gilbert, J. J. (1966). Rotifer ecology and embryological induction. *Science* 151: 1234–1237.

Gilbert, J. J. (1980). Female polymorphism and sexual reproduction in the rotifer *Asplanchna*: evolution of their relationship and control by dietary tocopherol. *American Naturalist* 116: 409–431.

Gilbert, S. F. (1994). Dobzhansky, Waddington, and Schmalhausen: Embryology and the modern synthesis. In M. B. Adams (ed.), *The Evolution of Theodosius Dobzhansky*, pp. 143–154. Princeton, N.J.: Princeton University Press.

Gilbert, S. F. (2000). Diachronic biology meets evo-devo: C. H. Waddington's approach to evolutionary developmental biology. *American Zoologist* 40: 729–737.

Gillespie, N. C. (1990). The interface of natural theology and science in the ethology of W. H. Thorpe. *Journal of the History of Biology* 23: 1–38.

Gottlieb, G. (1987a). Development of species identification in ducklings: XIV. Malleability of species-specific perception. *Journal of Comparative Psychology* 101: 178–182.

Gottlieb, G. (1987b). The developmental basis of evolutionary change. *Journal of Comparative Psychology* 101: 262–271.

Gottlieb, G. (1992). *Individual Development and Evolution: The Genesis of Novel Behaviour*. New York: Oxford University Press.

Gould, S. J. (1987). The process whereby species originate. *BioScience* 37: 715–720.

Grant, V. (1963). *The Origin of Adaptations*. New York: Columbia University Press.

Greene, E. (1989). A diet-induced developmental polymorphism in a caterpillar. *Science* 243: 643–646.

Gulick, A. (1932). *Evolutionist and Missionary John Thomas Gulick, Portrayed through Documents and Discussions*. Chicago: The University of Chicago Press.

Hadorn, E. (1961). *Developmental Physiology and Lethal Factors*. London: John Wiley.

Hall, B. K. (1977). Thallium-induced achondroplasia in the chicken embryo and the concept of critical periods during development. *Teratology* 15: 1–16.

Hall, B. K. (1984). Developmental processes underlying heterochrony as an evolutionary mechanism. *Canadian Journal of Zoology* 62: 1–7.

Hall, B. K. (1985). Critical periods during development as assessed by thallium-induced inhibition of growth of embryonic chick tibiae *in vitro*. *Teratology* 31: 353–361.

Hall, B. K. (1990). Heterochronic change in vertebrate development. *Seminars in Developmental Biology* 1: 237–243.

Hall, B. K. (1992). Waddington's legacy in development and evolution. *American Zoologist* 32: 113–122.

Hall, B. K. (1998). Epigenetics: Regulation not replication. *Journal of Evolutionary Biology* 11: 201–205.

Hall, B. K. (1999a). The Paradoxical Platypus. *BioScience* 49: 211–218.

Hall, B. K. (1999b). *Evolutionary Developmental Biology*, second edition. Dordrecht: Kluwer.

Hall, B. K. (2001a). Organic selection: Proximate environmental effects on the evolution of morphology and behaviour. *Biology and Philosophy* 16: 215–237.

Hall, B. K. (2001b). Essay review of *Images of Development. Environmental Causes in Ontogeny*. Cor van der Weele, State University of New York Press, Albany, 1999. *Evolutionary Development* 3: 223–224.

Hall, B. K. (2001c). The gene is not dead, merely orphaned and seeking a home. *Evolutionary Development* 3: 225–228.

Hall, B. K. (2001d). Foreword to *Beyond Heterochrony: The Evolution of Development* (M. Zelditch, ed.), pp. vii–ix. London: John Wiley.

Hall, B. K. (2002a). Evolutionary developmental biology: Where embryos and fossils meet. In K. J. McNamara and N. Minugh-Purves (eds.), *Human Evolution through Developmental Change*. Baltimore, Md.: Johns Hopkins University Press.

Hall, B. K. (2002b). Palaeontology and evolutionary developmental biology: A science of the 19th and 21st centuries. *Palaeontology* 45: 647–669.

Hall, B. K. and T. Miyake (1997). How do embryos tell time? In K. J. McNamara (ed.), *Evolution through Heterochrony*, pp. 1–20. London: John Wiley.

Hall, B. K. and W. M. Olson (eds.) (2002). *Keywords and Concepts in Evolutionary Developmental Biology*. Cambridge, Mass.: Harvard University Press.

Hardy, A. (1965). *The Living Stream: A Restatement of Evolution Theory and Its Relation to the Spirit of Man*. London: Collins.

Harvell, C. D. (1990). The ecology and evolution of inducible defenses. *Quarterly Review of Biology* 65: 323–340.

Hinton, G. E. and S. J. Nowlan (1987). How learning can guide evolution. *Complex Systems* 1, pp. 495–502. Technical Report CMU-CS-86–128, Carnegie Mellon University.

Ho, M.-W. (1984). Environment and heredity in development and evolution. In M.-W. Ho and P. J. Saunders (eds.), *Beyond Neo-Darwinism: An Introduction to the New Evolutionary Paradigm*, pp. 267–289. London: Academic Press.

Ho, M.-W., E. Bolton, and P. T. Saunders. (1983). The bithorax phenocopy and pattern formation. 1. Spatiotemporal characteristics of the phenocopy response. *Experimental Cell Biology* 51: 282–290.

Hovasse, R. (1950). *Adaptation et Évolution*. Paris: Hermann.

Huettel, M. D. and G. L. Bush (1972). The genetics of host selection and its bearing on sympatric speciation in *Procecidochares* (Diptera, Tephretidae). *Entomology, Experimental and Applied* 15: 465–480.

Huxley, J. S. (1942). *Evolution: The Modern Synthesis*. London: Allen and Unwin.

Johnston, T. D. and G. Gottlieb (1990). Neophenogenesis: A developmental theory of phenotypic evolution. *Journal of Theoretical Biology* 147: 471–495.

Jordan, D. S. (1923). John Thomas Gulick, Missionary and Darwinian. *Science* 58: 509.

Kellogg, V. L. (1908). *Darwinism To-Day. A discussion of present-day scientific criticism of the Darwinian selection theories, together with a brief account of the principal other proposed auxillary and alternative theories of species-forming*. New York: Henry Holt.

King, R. C. and W. D. Stansfield (1985). *A Dictionary of Genetics*, third edition. Oxford: Oxford University Press.

Lerner, I. M. (1954). *Genetic Homeostasis*. Edinburgh: Oliver and Boyd.

Lesch, J. E. (1975). The role of isolation in evolution: George J. Romanes and John T. Gulick. *Isis* 66: 483–503.

Matsuda, R. (1979). Abnormal metamorphosis and arthropod evolution. In A. P. Gupta (ed.), *Arthropod Phylogeny*, pp. 137–256. New York: Van Nostrand Reinhold.

Matsuda, R. (1982). The evolutionary process in Talitrid amphipods and salamanders in changing environments, with a discussion of "genetic assimilation" and some other evolutionary concepts. *Canadian Journal of Zoology* 60: 733–749.

Matsuda, R. (1987). *Animal Evolution in Changing Environments with Special Reference to Abnormal Metamorphosis*. London: John Wiley.

Maynard Smith, J. (1987). When learning guides evolution. *Nature* 329: 761–762.

Maynard Smith, J., R. Burian, S. Kauffman, P. Alberch, J. Campbell, B. Goodwin, R. Lande, D. Raup, and L. Wolpert (1985). Developmental constraints and evolution. *Quarterly Review of Biology* 60: 265–287.

Mayr, E. (1973). *Animal Species and Evolution*. Cambridge, Mass.: The Belknap Press of Harvard University Press.

Mayr, E. (1976). *Evolution and Diversity of Life*. Cambridge, Mass.: The Belknap Press of Harvard University Press.

McKinney, M. L. and K. J. McNamara (1991). *Heterochrony: The Evolution of Ontogeny*. New York and London: Plenum Press.

Messerly, J. G. (1996). *Piaget's Conception of Evolution: Beyond Darwin and Lamarck*. Foreword by Richard J. Blackwell. Lanham, Md.: Rowman and Littlefield.

Mikhailov, A. T. (1997. Epigenesis versus preformation: first chapter of the Russian embryological research. *International Journal of Developmental Biology* 41: 755–762.

Milner, R. (1990). *The Encyclopedia of Evolution. Humanity's Search for Its Origin.* New York: Facts on File.

Morgan, C. Lloyd (1896a). Of modification and variation. *Science* 4: 733–740.

Morgan, C. Lloyd (1896b). *Habitat and Instinct.* London: E. Arnold Press.

Morgan, C. Lloyd (1900). *Animal Behaviour.* London: E. Arnold Press.

Osborn, H. F. (1896). A mode of evolution requiring neither natural selection nor the inheritance of acquired characters. *Transactions of the New York Academy of Science* 15: 141–142, 148.

Osborn, H. F. (1897a). Organic selection. *Science* (October 15): 583–587.

Osborn, H. F. (1897b). The limits of organic selection. *American Naturalist* 31: 944–951.

Papaj, D. R. (1994). Optimizing learning and its effect on evolutionary change in behavior. In L. A. Real (ed.), *Behavioral Mechanisms in Evolutionary Ecology,* pp. 133–153. Chicago: The University of Chicago Press.

Parsons, P. A. (1981). Habitat selection and speciation in *Drosophila.* In W. R. Atchley and D. Woodra (eds.), *Evolution and Speciation,* pp. 219–240. Cambridge: Cambridge University Press.

Pearson, R. D. (1988). Reviews. *Acta Biotheoretica* 37: 31–32.

Piaget, J. (1929a). Les races lacustres de la "Limnaea stagnalis" L. Recherches sur les rapports de l'adaptation hereditaires avec le milieu. *Bulletin de Biologie, France et Belgique* 63: 424–455.

Piaget, J. (1929b). L'adaptation de la *Limnaea stagnalis* au milieu lacustres de la Suisse Romande. Etude biométrique et génétique. *Revue Suisse Zoologie* 36: 263–531.

Piaget, J. (1966). Observations sur le mode d'insertion et la chute des rameaux secondaires chez les Sedum. *Candollea* 21–22: 137–239.

Piaget, J. (1978). *Behavior and Evolution.* New York: Pantheon Books.

Piaget, J. (1980). *Adaptation and Intelligence: Organic Selection and Phenocopy.* Chicago: University of Chicago Press. (Translation of *Adaptation vitale et psychologie de l'intelligence: Sélection organique et phénocopie,* Paris: Hermann, 1974.)

Piatelli-Palmerini, M. (ed.) (1980). *Language and Learning: The Debate between Jean Piaget and Noam Chomsky.* London: Routledge and Kegan Paul.

Polikoff, D. (1981). C. H. Waddington and modern evolutionary theory. *Evolutionary Theory* 5: 143–168.

Provine, W. B. (1986). *Sewall Wright and Evolutionary Biology.* Chicago: The University of Chicago Press.

Raff, R. A. (1996). *The Shape of Life. Genes, Development, and the Evolution of Animal Form.* Chicago: The University of Chicago Press.

Rainger, R. (1991). *An Agenda for Antiquity: Henry Fairfield Osborn and Vertebrate Paleontology at the American Museum of Natural History, 1890–1935.* Tuscaloosa, Ala.: The University of Alabama Press.

Rendel, J. M. (1968). Genetic control of developmental processes. In R. C. Lewontin (ed.), *Population Biology and Evolution,* pp. 47–68. Syracuse, N.Y.: Syracuse University Press.

Richards, R. J. (1987). *Darwin and the Emergence of Evolutionary Theories of Mind and Behavior.* Chicago: The University of Chicago Press.

Robert, J. S., B. K. Hall, and W. M. Olson (2001). Bridging the gap between developmental systems theory and evolutionary developmental biology. *BioEssays* 23: 954–962.

Robertson, A. (1977). Conrad Hal Waddington. *Biographical Memoirs of Fellows of the Royal Society* 23: 575–622.

Rollo, C. D. (1995). *Phenotypes: Their Epigenetics, Ecology, and Evolution.* London: Chapman and Hall.

Russell, J. (1978). *The Acquisition of Knowledge.* London: Macmillan.

Sarkar, S. (1999). From the *Reaktionsnorm* to the adaptive norm: The norm of reaction, 1909–1960. *Biology and Philosophy* 14: 235–252.

Scharloo, W. (1991). Canalization: Genetic and developmental aspects. *Annual Reviews in Ecology and Systematics* 22: 65–93.

Schmalhausen, I. I. (1938). *The Integrating Factors of Evolution.* Leningrad: Nature (Priroda).

Schmalhausen, I. I. (1942). *The Organism as a Whole in Development and Evolution,* second edition. Moscow.

Schmalhausen, I. I. (1949). *Factors of Evolution. The Theory of Stabilizing Selection.* Translated by I. Dordick, edited by T. Dobzhansky. Philadelphia, Penn.: Blakiston. (Reprinted with a new foreword by David B. Wake, Chicago: The University of Chicago Press, 1986.)

Schwenk, K. (1994/95). A utilitarian approach to evolutionary constraint. *Zoology* 98: 251–262.

Sewyn, V. D. (1945). *The Social Theory of James Mark Baldwin.* New York: King's Crown Press.

Shine, R. and L. J. Guillette, Jr. (1988). The evolution of viviparity in reptiles: A physiological model and its ecological consequences. *Journal of Theoretical Biology* 132: 43–50.

Simpson, G. G. (1953). The Baldwin effect. *Evolution* 7: 110–117.

Sinha, C. (1984). A socio-naturalistic approach to human development. In M.-W. Ho and P. J. Saunders (eds.), *Beyond Neo-Darwinism: An Introduction to the New Evolutionary Paradigm,* pp. 331–362. London: Academic Press.

Stearns, S. C. (1989). The evolutionary significance of phenotypic plasticity. *BioScience* 37: 436–445.

Stearns, S. C. (1992). *The Evolution of Life Histories.* Oxford: Oxford University Press.

Stern, C. (1958). Selection for subthreshold differences and the origin of pseudoexogenous adaptations. *American Naturalist* 92: 313–316.

Stern, C. (1959). Variation and heredity transmission. *Proceedings of the American Philosophical Society* 103: 183–189.

Stern, C. D. (2000). Conrad H. Waddington's contribution to avian and mammalian development, 1930–1940. *International Journal of Developmental Biology* 44 (special issue): 15–22.

Thom, R. (1989). An inventory of Waddingtonian concepts. In B. C. Goodwin and P. Saunders (eds.), *Theoretical Biology. Epigenetic and Evolutionary Order from Complex Systems,* pp. 1–7. Edinburgh: Edinburgh University Press.

Thompson, J. N. and J. M. Thoday (1975). Genetic assimilation of part of a mutant phenotype. *Genetical Research* 26: 149–162.

Thomson, K. S. (1988). *Morphogenesis and Evolution.* Oxford: Oxford University Press.

Thorpe, W. H. (1930). Biological races in insects and allied groups. *Biological Reviews of the Cambridge Philosophical Society* 5: 177–212.

Thorpe, W. H. (1940). Ecology and the future of systematics. In J. Huxley (ed.), *The New Systematics,* pp. 341–364. Oxford: Oxford University Press.

Thorpe, W. H. (1945). The evolutionary significance of habitat selection. *Journal of Animal Ecology* 14: 67–70.

Van der Weele, C. (1999). *Images of Development. Environmental Causes in Ontogeny.* Albany, N.Y.: SUNY Press.

Vonèche, J. (1982). Evolution, development and the growth of knowledge. In J. Broughton and D. Freeman-Noir (eds.), *The Cognitive-Developmental Psychology of James Mark Baldwin,* pp. 51–79. Norwood, N.J.: Ablex.

Vorobyeva, E. I. (1987). I. I. Schmalhausen's conception of orthogenesis evolution. In V. P. Delfino (ed.), *International Symposium on Biological Evolution,* pp. 369–381. Bari: Adriatica Editrice.

Vorobyeva, E. I. (1989). The evolutionary principle of dynamic stability. *Rivista di Biologia—Biology Forum* 82: 313–315.

Waddington, C. H. (1940). *Organisers and Genes.* Cambridge: Cambridge University Press.

Waddington, C. H. (1942). Canalization of development and the inheritance of acquired characters. *Nature* 150: 563.

Waddington, C. H. (1953a). Genetic assimilation of an acquired character. *Evolution* 7: 118–126.

Waddington, C. H. (1953b). The "Baldwin effect," "genetic assimilation," and "homeostasis." *Evolution* 7: 386–387.

Waddington, C. H. (1956a). Genetic assimilation of the *bithorax* phenotype. *Evolution* 10: 1–13.

Waddington, C. H. (1956b). The genetic basis of the 'assimilated bithorax' stock. *Journal of Genetics* 55: 241–245.

Waddington, C. H. (1958). Inheritance of acquired characters. *Proceedings of the Linnean Society of London* 169: 41–62.

Waddington, C. H. (1959). Canalisation of development and genetic assimilation of acquired characters. *Nature* 183: 1654–1655.

Waddington, C. H. (1961). Genetic assimilation. *Advances in Genetics* 10: 257–293.

Waddington, C. H. (1975). *The Evolution of an Evolutionist.* Ithaca, N.Y.: Cornell University Press.

Wagner, G. P. and L. Altenberg, L. (1996). Complex adaptations and the evolution of evolvability. *Evolution* 50: 967–976.

Wagner, G. P., G. Booth, and H. Bagheri-Chaichian (1997). A population genetic theory of canalization. *Evolution* 51: 329–347.

Wagner, G. P. and K. Schwenk (2000). Evolutionary stable configurations: Functional integration and the evolution of phenotypic stability. *Evolutionary Biology* 31: 155–217.

Wake, D. B. (1986). Foreword to *Factors of Evolution. The Theory of Stabilizing Selection* (I. I. Schmalhausen), pp. v–xii. Chicago: The University of Chicago Press.

Wake, D. B. (1996). Schmalhausen's evolutionary morphology and its value in formulating research strategies. *Memorie della Società Italiano di Scienze Naturali e del Museo Civico di Storia Naturale di Milano* 28: 129–132.

Watanabe, M. (1966). John Thomas Gulick: American evolutionist and missionary in Japan. *Japan Studies in the History of Science* 5: 140–149.

Watkins, J. (1999). *Human Freedom after Darwin. A Critical Rationalists View.* La Salle: Open Court.

Weber, B. and T. Deacon (2000). Thermodynamic cycles, developmental systems, and emergence. *Cybernetics and Human Knowing* 7: 21–43.

West-Eberhard, M. J. (1986). Alternative adaptations, speciation, and phylogeny (a review). *Proceedings of the National Academy of Science USA* 83: 1388–1392.

West-Eberhard, M. J. (1989). Phenotypic plasticity and the origins of diversity. *Annual Reviews in Ecology and Systematics* 20: 249–278.

Wilkins, A. S. (1997). Canalization: A molecular genetic perspective. *BioEssays* 19: 257–262.

Wright, S. (1968). *Evolution and the Genetics of Populations,* volume 1. Chicago: The University of Chicago Press.

Yoxen, E. (1986). Form and strategy in biology: reflections on the career of C. H. Waddington. In T. J. Horder, J. A. Witkowski, and C. C. Wylie (eds.), *A History of Embryology,* pp. 309–329. Cambridge: Cambridge University Press.

Zelditch, M. (ed.) (2001). *Beyond Heterochrony: The Evolution of Development.* London: John Wiley.

9

On Having a Hammer

Susan Oyama

1 Introduction

Some wise wag once observed that when you have a hammer, the whole world looks like a nail. I've been wielding my particular hammer, a preoccupation with the nature-nurture problem, for so long that the tool is now virtually fused to my hand, and the Baldwin effect presents a broad vista of tempting nailheads that make my hammer hand itch. This bit of intellectual autobiography informs much of my discussion of the Baldwin effect. The recent renewal of interest in the roles of development and behavior in evolution, in fact, provides an opportunity to reexamine the conceptual frame within which that literature has developed. Especially significant features of this frame are the dualisms of nature and nurture and of body and mind. Many of the links holding this background of assumptions and oppositions together are not logically necessary, however compelling their historical and philosophical relations. In fact, they complicate theorists' attempts to relate developmental processes to evolutionary ones, and to do justice to both. I submit that it is possible to place development and evolution in a different frame, one that does not rest on traditional dualities, but instead incorporates the full range of organisms' developmental and behavioral relations with their surroundings. Once this is done, the need to transform the "acquired" into the "innate" or otherwise inject organismic activity and mind into the evolutionary process is seen to be as spurious as the distinctions on which the traditional conceptual structure rests. I am accordingly less concerned with whether or how frequently some version of the Baldwin effect occurs, or what the man really may have written or thought, than with his place in past and present evolutionary thinking. Scientific, philosophical, and popular understandings of life processes continue to turn on overly global and irregularly intertwined contrasts, and it is primarily these, and their consequences, that occupy me in this chapter.

The distinction between nature and nurture is just one of the broad polarities built into the scaffolding of much of our intellectual discourse. Such polarities, it has often been noted, can exert a powerful influence (not always benign) on theory and practice; in fact they supply much of the common ground for our disputes. As an example of the sort of mischief that can be spawned by such related distinctions, consider an ambiguity that arises repeatedly in this volume. Discussions of the Baldwin effect, like those of many other literatures, are characterized by frequent conflation of learning in particular with phenotypic flexibility in general. When Daniel Lehrman reviewed arguments over biology and behavior long ago, in fact, he complained about ethologist Konrad Lorenz's failure to distinguish between learning and the much broader class of "experiential" effects (Lehrman 1970).[1] An organism, after all, may learn something that allows it to survive until a favorable mutation can appear, but it may alternatively be changed in some other way that does not involve learning but that has an equivalent selective consequence.

The association between the innate-learned distinction and the one between genes and environment encourages just this kind of slippage: The innate is identified with the genes, whose contrast class consists of a breathtakingly global "environment" encompassing everything else in the cosmos. As a result there seems to be a parallel tendency to contrast the innate not only with the learned, but more broadly with some ill-defined notion of "caused not by genes but by the environment." When this occurs, an opposition that is already suspect (more or less so depending on how the terms are defined) becomes enmeshed with an even worse one. The situation is further exacerbated if consciousness is added to the equation. Assuming the possibility of learning without consciousness (a possibility for humans as well as other species), there are then three classes of phenomena being invoked—learning, consciousness, and general developmental plasticity—and, therefore, that much more room for unproductive cross-talk. The identification of learning with consciousness intrigues even as it vexes, given the historical tendency for explanations by conditioning (often characterized as "automatic" or "mechanical," especially by those hostile to such explanations) to be presented as an *alternative* to the attribution of "higher" cognitive processes, including conscious reflection. It is common, for example, to counter a claim about "animal mind" with one about conditioned learning. Unless it is simply identified by, or with, learning, consciousness would seem to be beside the point in discussions of the Baldwin effect.

2   The Terrible Two: Lamarck and Darwin

Consider table 9.1, a not-very-systematic sampling of what I have called *developmental dualisms*. The evolutionary contrasts in table 9.2 are less familiar, less orderly; yet they overlap the developmental ones and are related to them in interesting ways. (For more on the relations between developmental and evolutionary dichotomies, see Oyama 2000b, chaps. 4 and 5.) All the contrast pairs can be variously read, though the possible readings will not be rehearsed here.

The Baldwin effect turns on a distinction between the innate and the acquired, as does the contrast between Darwinian and Lamarckian evolution that is so often invoked in discussions of it. Hall observes that many

Table 9.1
Developmental dichotomies

Nature	Nurture
Inherited traits	Acquired traits
Innateness/instinct	Learning
Genes	Environment
Transmission	Development
Biology	Culture
Body	Mind
Insides	Outsides
The physical	The mental
Mechanism	Intelligence
Fate	Will
Rigidity	Flexibility
Passivity	Activity
Essence	Appearance
Genotype	Phenotype

Table 9.2
Associated evolutionary dichotomies

Darwin	Lamarck
Natural selection	Orthogenesis
Randomness	Progressiveness
Selectional model	Developmental model
Body	Mind
Outsides	Insides
External selection	Internal constraints
Direction by environment	Direction by organisms
Genotype	Phenotype
Nature	Nurture
Passivity	Activity
Rigidity	Flexibility

theorists have attempted to reconcile Darwin and Lamarck (chap. 8, this volume). This would not, of course, be such a chore had their differences not been so selectively exaggerated in the first place.[2] Once Lamarck was firmly identified with the inheritance of acquired characters, and once the inheritance of acquired characters was set in place as the defining contrast to Darwinian natural selection, all sorts of other things followed. Whether Lamarck's heresy was ruled out of bounds altogether (perhaps defined anachronistically as reverse translation from protein to DNA) or safely confined to the "transmission of culture," anyone wishing to explore the evolutionary roles of organismic activity, phenotypic plasticity in general, or learning in particular was obliged to engage in some theoretical acrobatics to do so. These might involve invoking a separate informational "channel," relying on hidden genetic variation, or hoping for fortunate mutations, but there seemed to be a need for fancy footwork to avoid the dreaded charge of Lamarckism.

My point is not that activity and developmental variability, with or without genetic variability, are unimportant in evolution; quite the contrary. Rather, I wish to indicate the forced moves a theorist is constrained to make in order to address them. Something special became necessary once evolutionists had accepted the Weismannian barrier as a barrier to Lamarckian inheritance (and once they had accepted the definition of evolution as genetic change, as did the founders of the mid-century Modern Synthesis). As several authors in this volume have suggested, these were unnecessarily narrow readings of both Darwin and Lamarck, and the restrictions have left traces on current thinking. The felt need for an "out" shows us something about the way the conceptual field is structured.

3   More Troublesome Pairs

The contrast between the innate and the acquired, then, or the genetic and the environmental (or the learned, or the cultural, and so on—the indeterminacy is one of the problems with which this chapter began) is certainly central to most contemporary comparisons of Darwinian and Lamarckian evolution. But there is another major feature of the ideational terrain: the familiar division between bodies and minds. At times this fault line nearly parallels the nature-nurture rift. In fact, discussions of the Baldwin effect are full of questions and assertions about the role of mind in evolution. Certainly the idea of a will—an agency guiding or directing evolution, possibly able to "look ahead" rather than cluelessly awaiting its selective fate—fits into the sequence of intelligences people have credited with the shaping of life: if not God, then a vigilantly selecting Nature, and if not Mother Nature, then, as in the case of the Baldwin effect, the organism itself. Instincts, on the other hand, are thought to be products of the body—the site of Cartesian mechanical movement, mindless and automatic, built by genes. And because the standard account of evolution is gene-based (only genes, or in slightly more generous treatments, the germ cell, are transmitted, and genetic change is typically the sole criterion of evolutionary change), the "mind" side of the body-mind pair needs a lever to exert some sort of mental force on the all-important chromosomal mass, to nudge it into the next generation.

Perhaps it is obvious that there is an intimate alliance between these two great oppositions (body vs. mind on the one hand, and on the other, the one that is variously termed nature vs. nurture, genes vs. environment, biology vs. learning or culture, etc.). For the doubtful, however, it might help to consider the fact that when people are pressed to explain just what they mean by "innate," "genetic," "biological," or "evolutionary," their first response is often, "It's *physical*." I can also say, after many years of dealing with written and spoken arguments on these issues, that virtually every time I've hammered in a nature-nurture nail, there's been a body-mind one within easy striking distance.

Another grand opposition is the one between insides and outsides. It sometimes runs alongside the others, but in complicated ways, so that the mind may in one context be used as a kind of internal counterweight to "external" natural selection, while in another (instinct vs. learning, for instance), it can be the point of entry for "information" from the outside (see note 2). This in turn suggests the use of the inside-outside boundary by anti-neo-Darwinist structuralists, who tend to see developmental factors as internal: as constraining, or, more positively, *channeling,* an external selection (Oyama 2000b, chaps. 4 and 5). A noteworthy feature of the contrasts sampled in tables 9.1 and 9.2, in fact, is that standard wisdom credits internal forces with primary (developmental) authorship of the organism and external ones with the (evolutionary) shaping of populations. In each case mentality is a contrasting factor, which puts mind on the outside in the first list and on the inside in the second. All this is consistent with a tradition of seeing the history of evolutionary theory in terms of a clash between the "developmental" model described by Lewontin (1982, 1983) and Sober (1984, 1985)—internalist, progressivist, even orthogenetic—and the externalist "selectional" one.[3] It is selection from the outside, of course, that triumphs in the neo-Darwinian synthesis. These are intricate and weighty matters, and one could easily become terminally lost in the maze of interwoven polarities. I mention them here in order to suggest that the oppositions are not just connected to each other in fascinating ways, but that seeing them as a backdrop to contemporary debates about Baldwin effects may help us understand why those debates take the shape they do, and why there may be a general misapprehension of what is actually at stake.

Philosophers and scientists tend to be quite hostile to mind-body dualism, though they disagree on how to make it go away. In contrast, the developmental and evolutionary oppositions between internal and external causation, as well as those between the innate and the acquired, are not only tolerated, they are crucial to the definitions of whole fields, categories, and perspectives. Mainstream evolutionary theory has these dualities built into it—I mentioned the triumphant vanquishing of the internalist developmental model of change by the externalist selectional model of the Modern Synthesis. (See Godfrey-Smith 1996 for more on internalism and externalism.) Consider also the importance of the Weismannian barrier in shielding the germ line from corruption from the outside. This barrier not only protects the DNA from the world; in the standard story, as we saw, it also separates Darwin from Lamarck, hard science from wishful thinking.

Because oppositional positions help to shape, and are partially shaped by, the traditions they challenge, they often bear the negative images of the very arguments against which they struggle. A natural selection construed as a capricious force acting on populations from the outside is thus countered by a structuralist emphasis on necessity: perhaps ahistorical developmental laws that can push back from the inside. Or a neo-Darwinism construed in terms of selection for genes, and thus, by the associations just mentioned, the body and instinct, must be tempered with a dose of mind and learning. In the second case, failure to question the very definition of evolution in terms of genetic change, and of inheritance as inheritance of DNA or germ cells, means that theorists must posit a second channel of "information" to supplement the genetic one. Thus we have a variety of dual channel gene-culture coevolution schemes (e.g., Boyd and Richerson 1985; Durham 1979; Lumsden and Wilson 1981), while Deacon offers us three transmission processes for the Baldwin effect: "genetic inheritance . . . social transmission by learning . . . and persistence of physical changes in the environment produced by behavioral changes" (1997: 323). Eva Jablonka and colleagues give us four: genetic, epigenetic, behavioral, and symbolic (Avital and Jablonka 2000; Jablonka and Lamb 1995).[4] This alone—the sheer proliferation of channels—should make us wonder whether a conceptual scheme is being stretched beyond its useful capacity. In general, channels for information flow are, I suggest, anti- (or at least non) developmental devices. More and more are invoked as theorists look more seriously at development—at what happens between those moments of reproduction. To put it more provocatively, perhaps theorists are remembering that *re-production*—the reconstruction of an organism—is not a moment, but a process inseparable from development (Griesemer 2000). To capture this process, we require not more channels but a different way of thinking about intergenerational relations.

Look again at tables 9.1 and 9.2. Notice that behavior occurs on one side of these joined contrasts if it is learned and on the other if it is "instinctive." In his contribution to this volume, Downes cites Richards's talk of "ontogenetic behaviors." This is not an unusual usage, but it raises a question (if we let it): Could there be behavior that has no ontogenetic history? Once the question is asked out loud, its absurdity is inescapable, but of course this is exactly how innateness is conceived—as something that need not develop because it is *already there,* in the genes. A kind of essentialism permeates not just standard gene-talk, but much of the oppositional literature as well. Elsewhere I have considered the distinction between essence and appearance that is implicit in much current thinking about genotypes and phenotypes (Oyama 2000c, 2002). A substantial part of the lure of the Baldwin effect, however defined, is that it legitimates the evolutionarily illegitimate, by transforming the learned into the innate, allowing acquired traits to switch channels, if you will, to *pass,* to enter the next generation by the other entrance, to become "assimilated" to the species essence.

You were warned about my hammer.

4   Baldwin (Over)Burdened: Channels and Systems

Current theories need "information flow" to recreate the next generation. Because we have been taught to see phenotypes themselves as evolutionary dead-ends,[5] that information must pass by means of the germ cells, diminutive reproductive life boats that must, if they can, abandon the doomed body before it goes down. Development, will, mind, learning, intelligence, activity, and consciousness all belong to the dead-end phenotype, out there interacting with the world, and therefore on the wrong side of the crucial dichotomies. Bearers of environmental influence, they are properties of the expiring organism, not the potentially immortal genes (Williams 1966: 24). I suspect that this massing of opposing forces—mechanical, improbably static, nonconscious bodies on one side, and mind, activity, and flexibility on the other—explains some of the conflation and slippage mentioned earlier—when one side is smooshed together, the other side tends to be, too. This loss of distinctions (and distinctions between distinctions) is one of the principle prices paid for the strategic simplification gained by aligning arguments with these grand dichotomies. Consider the difference between *mind* as staying alive by dint of behavioral flexibility and as "directing" evolution, consciously or not. Or between learning and culture, or, as mentioned earlier, between developmental flexibility in general and the more specific processes of learning. Too often, where dichotomies dominate, differences disappear—and not all of those disappearences are conceptually innocent, as is evident when findings relevant to one distinction are used to argue for another, to which they are not so properly applied (P. Bateson 1991; Johnston 1987; Lehrman 1970; Oyama 2000b,c).

Several of my co-contributors find Baldwin confusing. This may simply be owing to garden-variety sloppiness but (more interesting for my purposes) it could also be a partial consequence of inadequate conceptual space for a more synthetic formulation. Suppose we were to move from the vision of information flowing through discrete and limited channels to a more inclusive view of the entities and processes that make transgenerational continuity and variation possible, indeed, without which "gene flow" would be unthinkable. I am obviously not in a position to guess what Baldwin or his contemporaries would have thought of what I am about to say. My principle concern, as indicated earlier, is with the framing of present debates, rather than with what Baldwin really thought, what the Baldwin effect really is, or how often it really occurs. (That is why I have not floated a definition of my own.) While I welcome investigation of these topics, I do wonder whether the poor gentleman's ghost is being asked to bear rather more theoretical weight than is strictly necessary.

Today these "effects" are recruited to transform the acquired into the innate, the cultural into the biological. Baldwin is seen as offering a means whereby the merely learned can gain evolutionary significance, rendered really real and given natural selection's seal of approval, perhaps by a genetic assimilation that makes an acquired response part of "the genotype." But what if there is actually no substantial, necessary wall separating the two sides of the entwined dichotomies I have been alluding to? Is there then such a pressing need for a canny Baldwin to find a crack in the masonry, widen it, and keep it open so his latter-day cohorts can scramble through to the other side?

This is where I would recommend the concept of the developmental system: organism-environment complexes changing over developmental and evolutionary time, in which the means or resources for development are inherited, but phenotypes are constructed (Oyama, Griffiths, and Gray 2001). I second with enthusiasm many of my co-contributors' points on organismic activity, development and flexibility, and my misgivings should not be misconstrued as a lack of appreciation for the phenomena and models under discussion or their eventual significance. Insofar as students of development and evolution rely on the dichotomies in tables 9.1 and 9.2 to orient their theorizing, however, I contend that they may fail to do justice to the very interrelations they seek to elucidate. Boosters and skeptics alike (Godfrey-Smith, chap. 3, this volume) thereby help to maintain the very conceptual background that makes Baldwinian contortions necessary.

Environmental constancy (or recurrence, as in seasonal cycles) is critical in maintaining (or better, reconstructing) species characteristics, and extraorganismic regularities are frequently quite closely tied to organismic ones. A developmental system accordingly includes the organism and many aspects of its surroundings, both nonliving and living, conspecific and other. (This is not quite the same as considering the *organism* to be a system that exists in and interacts with an environment.) Organisms are embedded in their environmental surrounds. They can neither develop nor function without an adequate milieu, and as they develop and function, they change those milieux even as they are being changed. Variations in these exchanges (which may or may not involve changes in germline DNA sequences) in turn may have short- and long-term consequences, both developmental and evolutionary, as variant systems are differentially reproduced. If the genetic material is always and only viewed in its developmental matrix, the insistence that evolutionary adaptation must be defined by, or initiated by, genetic change can be seen for what it is: an insistence on maintaining pride of place for one category among many, despite the difficulty of justifying that privileged place (Oyama 2000a).

Taking the step of conceiving the system as composed of the organism and relevant aspects of its environment, and further, of including in the notion of heredity *a spatially and temporally extended interacting complex* effectively eliminates a significant number of the forced choices posed by our grand oppositions: the need to decide just how many transmission channels there really are (and a good thing, too, since as I have suggested, the sorts of lively interactions described by many theorists who use this terminology actually point up the limitations of the metaphor). Nor need we decide whether the organism or the environment "drives" evolution, say, or counter external selective forces with internal mental or developmental ones.

Writing in a quite different (but not unrelated) context, behavior analyst Howard Rachlin notes that mentalist and behaviorist explanations in psychology stop in different places; the former halts when "a current internal cause" has been found (perhaps a desire or a belief), while the other continues until "a previous external cause" (past reinforcement) is identified (1987: 177). These are hardly arbitrary choices, either for the theorists or for their audiences. The deeply felt methodological and ontological commitments they express can lead people to make rather less measured comments than Rachlin's about what it takes to study behavior in a scientifically respectable way. Despite the occasional perfunctory nod in the direction of factors on the other side of the skin (external influences for the mentalist, internal for the behaviorist), those comments may well include claims about what *really* drives, controls, causes, or explains an organism's behavior. In such situations, phenomena that threaten the canonical explanatory form acquire a special charge, as, for instance, certain species differences in learning did in psychology (see discussions in Hinde and Stevenson-Hinde 1973). In the skirmishes that follow, it sometimes happens that prior positions (whether actually held or merely attributed) are disavowed or denied (We never excluded . . . We have always acknowledged . . . Of course it is understood that . . .) as it becomes clear that some dictum or other has become a liability. Such things need not be viewed cynically. As conceptual environments change, previously indispensable stances may wane in significance. Perhaps the debates about development and evolution have reached such a moment.

If oil flowing through one tube and water in another simply meet at some point and mix (only to a limited extent, retaining their identities), speaking of channels might make sense (though it could also encourage odd talk of behavior that is partly biological and partly learned, or of genes interacting with culture). But what if the very character, volume, and reactions of the contents of one of the tubes are affected by what is contained in the others, as well as being altered by processes taking place within each one? I contend that the information-theoretic approach handles such shenanigans about as well as cognitive psychologists' language of item storage and transfer can handle, say, the dynamic constructive processes of memory. Given the standard assumption, furthermore, that "transmission" of both genes and culture must be from parent generations to their successors, the influence of young organisms' innovations on older members of a group, for instance, may go untheorized. (A moment's reflection on our own youth-dominated popular culture should be enough to suggest how adequate an exclusively old-to-young transmission scheme of cultural change would be.) A systems framework, however, raises no barriers to such effects.[6] The influence of the immature on adults, including influences of offspring on parents, is not limited to behavioral contagion or indeed to postnatal effects; even in egg-laying species, an embryo is for a time part of its mother's developmental system, a source of significant chemical, mechanical, and sometimes sensory effects. While influences on other adults will not always appear as early, depending on the species, they can have great developmental impact, as any self-aware human father can attest, and embryonic offspring can affect others through their effects on the parents. I wonder whether discussion of older organisms learning from younger ones, for instance, is rare (as it seems to me) in the literature because it happens infrequently or because it does not fit well with the image of items being conducted down the generational slope by a series of ducts, or, indeed, with the whole apparatus of evolutionary transmission. Such against-the-generational-current influences can both help to maintain evolutionary stability (mothering often improves with practice, for instance) and serve as potential sources of evolutionary novelty.

In a developmental system, evolutionary change need not begin with genetic change. More fundamentally, evolutionary change itself is not defined by genetic change. Elevating one constituent of the system to this definitional role is like declaring all inhabitants of a territory to be citizens (and taxpayers, to be sure) but stipulating that only the aristocracy may vote, say, or be counted in a census. One thing that falls out from the developmental systems perspective is that there is no warrant for using exclusively genetic criteria for evolution and adaptation (Johnston and Gottlieb 1990). From this point of view, adaptation would be identified, not by contrasting learning or other developmental flexibility with innateness or some other stand-in for the genes, but by asking whether, and how, the interactions of organisms with their surroundings increase the probability that similar interactional patterns will recur in successive generations of offspring. The same reasoning can be used for other interactants in the system (Griffiths and Gray 2001; Oyama 2000c: 141).

None of this deprives us of the possibility of studying the effects of particular environmental factors, stable or variable, on other aspects of a system. The same goes for particular behaviors, social patterns, or alleles. On the contrary, thinking in terms of developmental systems opens up new research possibilities (Oyama 2000b, Intro.; Oyama, Griffiths, and Gray 2001). The language of transmission, after all, formalizes a series of decisions scientists have made to individuate certain objects and patterns, tracking them across generations, noting their reappearance (or absence) at the appropriate point in the next life cycle. The objects and patterns themselves, the phenotypic traits, the patterns of behavior, whether classified as learned or instinctive, whether species-characteristic or unusual, must all be reconstructed from the changing complex of developmental interactants or resources at hand, and not all these developmental influences will be contained within the organism itself. Construction in this sense is simply developmental emergence, and it is emergence from continuous, multileveled processes, not a manifestation of a preexisting representation. *Construction* should not be taken as a code word for the acquired, the culturally variable, or any other variant of a "nurture" that can be contrasted with "nature" (recall my earlier remarks on the incoherence of speaking of "ontogenetic behavior," as though there were another kind of behavior that lacked an ontogeny). Some of those ontogenetic resources will contribute to features that appear regularly; some may even be invariant across individuals in a population, or many populations. Others will be associated with variations. Some variations will be evanescent, while others will reappear in the population again and again.

For Downes, a Lamarckian view is one in which an organism strives to meet its needs, with the resulting morphological changes being passed to offspring (chap. 2, this volume). This is certainly truer to the original sense than the reverse translation and culture mentioned earlier. But no morphological feature is literally passed on, whether it is a "modification"[7] or the "wild type." Instead, according to the view being advanced here, the means or resources for developmental construction are "transmitted" to the next (or same, or previous—see previous discussion of the influence of youth on age) generation in the sense that they are made available to that life cycle. Sometimes they are supplied in the germ cell—the standard locus of inheritance—but often they become available in some other way. Some would distinguish between "direct" (genetic) transmission and "indirect" transmission, but it is not even clear what this could mean. If directness means bypassing developmental processes, a magical bolus moving across generations independently of other constituents of the system, then no phenotypic feature qualifies, even endosymbionts. I've argued, in fact, that while the transmission metaphor purports to explain development, it actually *assumes* reliable development. The patterns of appearance and reappearance in successive generations that are the data (etymologically, the "givens") for transmission genetics require developmental courses that are not only sufficiently reliable to produce all those organisms whose features are being tracked, but transgenerationally uniform enough that small variations in resources (what I have also called *interactants* or *means*) can be reliably correlated with traits.[8] In other words, most of the constituents and processes must be stable enough to provide a background against which a difference in interactant will consistently make the same difference in successive phenotypes—be *informative* in the way the analyst desires.[9] But notice that this notion of information, in Gregory Bateson's sense of a difference that makes a difference, diverges radically from the ways the term is used in most biology and social science (G. Bateson 1972; Oyama 2000c). The kind of interactively stable repetition referred to here has nothing to do with disembodied, matter-free, formal representations or instructions travelling through isolated channels (consider that the whole point of a channel is to isolate) and everything to do with three-dimensional, moving organisms in their three-dimensional, changing surroundings.[10] It is precisely the embodiment, the embeddedness, of interactants that allows them to generate the differences against stable backgrounds that can constitute "information" in Bateson's sense. This is also the sense that is operative in the correlations used in information theory (Johnston 1987; Johnston, personal communication, March 1998).

5   Baldwin Unburdened, Darwin Depolarized

Rather than attributing the reconstruction of organisms to the transmission of disembodied information, we can ask not only how the reconstructions occur (the usual stuff of developmental analysis), but how the means for those repeated developmental cycles are, or are not, brought together. Typically many conspecifics and members of other species are involved in the provision of developmentally important resources for any organism, as are many aspects of the nonliving milieu; thus not only developmental inquiry is called for, but also work in ecology, population and behavioral biology, and the social sciences (Gilbert 2001; van der Weele 1999; West, King, and White in press).

The long-term saga of these life cycles is the saga of evolution, and it necessarily involves the organism's development (one aspect of which is any learning that occurs), its activities, its alterations of its surround, its choices, and its differential sensitivities, all of which in turn can contribute to its further development and reproductive fortunes. The phantom wall separating morphology from behavior, body from mind, gene from environment, biology from culture, and all the rest, comes tumbling down, even as we dimly and belatedly recall our own role in putting it up. We need no longer dwell in a world in which psychologists study learning, consciousness, choice, and mind because they are "not biological" at the same time that their colleagues down the hall study the biology of learning (not to speak of a world in which the subject matters of cultural and biological anthropologists are so disjunct that what used to be two branches of a single discipline are apt to be housed as far apart on campus as possible).

That said, perhaps it bears repeating that I very much appreciate the efforts reported in this collection. My critical remarks about the conceptual landscape notwithstanding, I am not minimizing the importance of such explorations. I would suggest, though, that looking at development and evolution in terms of the systems of developmental construction that produce repeated life cycles lightens the theoretical load old Baldwin must bear. I would hardly downplay the significance of organisms' roles in selecting and altering their own niches, for instance, and therefore, of organisms' influence on their own selective contexts, or of the evolutionary importance of development and behavior in general. In fact, I devote a fair amount of my time doing what many of my fellow contributors do: trying to bring such phenomena to others' notice, and to fashion an effective way to frame them.[11]

Still, redrawing boundaries along developmental systems lines casts these phenomena in a different light, in a way making them look less remarkable, less special, although not less worthy of attention. Or, better, by stressing the context-sensitive dynamics and ecological embeddedness of the developmental processes that produce the "biological," a developmental systems perspective diminishes the theoretical distance between those processes and the ones that form the subject matter of the present volume. This last point is important. Part of the problem with the nature-nurture complex is that what develops most reliably has tended to be treated as though it didn't really need to develop at all. This is why the cryptopreformationism of genetic programs, instructions, and blueprints has been at once so hard to recognize and so hard to do without.

Theorists disagree about whether "new" mechanisms are needed to accommodate Baldwin and his ilk. My aim is to show that a view of evolution that is more expansive than the standard one but that is nevertheless implied by it, and indeed could be said to be demanded by its logic (Oyama 2000a), renders the phenomena themselves less anomalous. The argument, then, is not that these effects do or do not occur, or that they are unimportant if they do, but that what makes them appear to be in need of a special mechanism is precisely the standard evolutionary story whose narrow compass legislates, as does any definition, *de facto* or *de jure,* what falls within its limits. We might want to think about what counts as special (in need of special explanation), and why. It may well be that we will find that many traditional ways of distinguishing between the columns in tables 9.1 and 9.2 do not stand much scrutiny. This has a positive side, however. In addition to the considerable benefit of doing away with a good deal of nature-nurture befuddlement, it should sharpen and highlight whatever distinctions remain, leaving us with a more usable set of tools. (I might even retire my hammer.) It is not that everything in the left-hand columns is "just like" everything on the right, but that some legitimate differences are not clearly distinguished from each other, and, what is worse, are mixed willy nilly with distinctions that make no sense at all.

I have argued that at least some characteristics of Baldwinesque phenomena, viewed in a developmental systems framework, are not as special as they seem. The loose-jointedness we often observe between adjacent levels of a system means it should not be unusual to see developmental outcomes that are similar at one level but produced by quite different processes at another level. This may occur in cases of developmental compensation. Developmental psychologists sometimes call this "catch-up": A developmental trajectory that has been deflected nevertheless ends up where it would have gone without the perturbation. (Bateson and Martin [1999 chap. 6] give some examples.) Such cases can involve compensation at the neural level, so that normal psychological functioning is served by atypical cortical areas. We can also speak of equifinality, which was the point of Waddington's canalization (1975). Phenocopies present us with similar products of dissimilar developmental pathways, giving us both degenerate between-level mapping, from the two genotypes to the same phenotype, and ambiguous mapping, from the normal genotype to the normal and phenocopying phenotypes (Gilbert, chap. 12, this volume; Hall, chap. 8, this volume; Ho 1984; Newman and Müller 1999; Oyama 2000b, chap. 2). This kind of partial uncoupling is fundamental to genetic assimilation and the Baldwin effect, but is not restricted to them. Over evolutionary time the developmental processes producing a feature may change more rapidly than the feature itself, and "phenotypic plasticity," so important to theorizing about Baldwin effects, is hardly the exception.

Active organisms are also integral to the developmental systems perspective. They alter their own developmental and selective contexts, as they are altered by them. But it is not just whole organisms that do this. Mutual construction occurs at lower and higher levels as well, as when a developing tissue brings about changes in an adjacent tissue, which changes then feed back upon the first, or when shifts in one body part over evolutionary time alter the adaptiveness of another. The notion of niche building, so productive when employed with whole organisms (Laland, Odling-Smee, and Feldman 2001) can usefully be deployed at these suborganismic levels, including that of cells (Jablonka 2001).

Consider the changing relationship between a mammalian fetus and its mother during gestation, or any of Moore's lovely examples (chap. 7, this volume), or the influence of younger organisms on older ones, discussed above. The reciprocal developmental effects are multifarious and complex, and similar analyses can be done on parts of a single organism (though it may be difficult to say just what a "single organism" is—a fruitful puzzle in itself). Change in any of these relationships, within a body, between an organism and its surround, or among entities of larger scale, could be the leading edge of an evolutionary cascade (Gray 1988).

In any case, it is evident that scholars are increasingly testing the limits of conventional theorizing; whether or not Baldwin is adopted as a crucial forerunner of current developments, a discussion of his writings provides a hospitable space within which to air interpretation, criticism, and speculation on such issues.

Acknowledgments

This chapter is based on a commentary on talks presented at the Bennington Workshop on the Baldwin Effect at Bennington College. I thank the other participants at the workshop and the student commentators for their thoughtful remarks. I am also grateful to Eva Jablonka, Tim Johnston, and Rasmus Winther for their critical reading of an earlier version of the chapter, and to the editors of the volume for their suggestions and support.

Notes

1. "Experiential" in Schneirla's (1966) sense, for instance, which seems roughly equivalent to the "phenotypic plasticity" of the present discussions. See Moore (chap. 7, this volume).

2. That is, had Darwin and Lamarck not been made to represent the Synthesis's One True Account, on the one hand, and the vanquished heresy on the other. Barbara Herrnstein Smith refers to "constitutive heresies," which, by giving improbably sharp and suitably horrifying contours to a doctrinal enemy, define by contrast the developing orthodoxy we are meant to embrace (2002). For more on this use of the Lamarckian boogeyman, see Avital and Jablonka (2000), who allow both Darwinian natural selection and (a certain version of) Lamarckian inheritance of acquired characters; Jablonka and Lamb (1995); Jordanova (1984); and Oyama (2000b, chap. 1). For further discussion of these matters, including the pros and cons of using the phrase *inheritance of acquired characters* to refer to the kinds of phenomena presented in Jablonka and Lamb's *Epigenetic Inheritance and Evolution* (1998), see the exchange between those authors and reviewers Griesemer (1998) and Keller (1998).

3. This description is simplified from the original sources; selectional processes are a subset of variational ones and the "developmental" model is sometimes referred to as "transformational" (Oyama 2000b, chap. 5). It is also incomplete; Lamarck is sometimes associated with a third, "instructional" model of change, which is distinctly undercharacterized in the literature.

4. Elsewhere Jablonka writes, "There is also another type of phenotypic information transfer between generations, which is more difficult to categorize because it does not occur at the cellular level, but at the level of the whole organism" (2001: 109). She goes on to discuss phenomena such as transgenerationally repeating prenatal hormonal effects, which, as she notes, are not captured satisfactorily by her typology. (In simpler gene-culture theories they are simply invisible—literally un-thinkable with the conceptual resources at hand.) In mentioning her four-channel scheme here, I do not mean to minimize its importance in systematizing a

large and important mass of literature. Nor am I questioning the desirability of bringing developmental, ecological, and sociocultural dimensions of life into the evolutionary narrative, as Deacon does; on the contrary, I consider this crucial. I am, however, questioning the wisdom of continuing to rely on a communication-theoretic vocabulary to do so. Given the number of subtypes that appear in the four-channel model (and therefore the channels-within-channels they imply), and given the fact that channels are described as interacting and affecting each other, I would ask whether the image of conduits conveying discrete quantities of fluid (or even the more abstract transmission channels of telecommunications) is equal to the task. In fact, Jablonka has affirmed her view of biological processes as thoroughly interactive and systemic, and has emphasized that talk of channels is an analytical expedient that lifts certain phenomena out from that background (personal communication, March 2001; Jablonka in press).

5. Griesemer and Wimsatt have written illuminating accounts of the influential diagrams that show genes (originally Weismann's *germ*) moving through time in an unbroken line, while organisms (Weismann's *soma*) are oblique offshoots, leading nowhere: only the DNA is passed on to the next generation (1989). Like Winther (2001), they argue that Weismann has been poorly served by these snapshots and soundbites, much to the detriment of our current treatments of development and heredity. See also Goodwin (1984) for a less sympathetic treatment of Weismann that nonetheless touches on some of the issues raised here, and Johnston (1995) for some remarks on Weismann and developmental dichotomies.

6. When, in the preface to my *The Ontogeny of Information* (2000c: xxi) I thanked my children for raising me so well, it was not just the usual authorial acknowledgment. It was also a dead-serious theoretical point.

7. Notice the movement, common enough, between individual and population marked by the use of "modification." A phenotype can be modified by interventions and perturbations, but more to the point, in the absence of any such interventions, it is still being developmentally modified (changed), at every moment. The modification of which Downes speaks, however, presumably refers to a variant phenotype in a population of phenotypes, not change in an individual.

8. See Nijhout for some complications (2001). It is risky to assume that gene-feature correlations that are reliable in some senses (statistically significant, repeatable) will be reliable in another (linking the feature in question with the same DNA sequence, generation after generation), so that easy reference to selection for "a gene for X" becomes suspect. Students are taught that a statistic that does not show what it purports to is not *valid,* even if it is *reliable* in the sense of being statistically significant.

9. This background includes, of course, the genetic background of any alleles that may be the object of inquiry, as well as other aspects of that "background"—that is, the rest of the developmental system. Those features of organisms that are so predictable that they qualify as species-typical are no less the result of constructive interaction than the novel ones. Hence my reformulation of the opposition, nature vs. nurture (or even the conjunction, nature *and* nurture): instead of two kinds of

developmental causation, they are the *product* and *process* of development (Oyama 2000b,c). This is a reformulation to make a point, not an argument for redeployment of these two words in a new-and-improved way. To wish for the latter, I suspect, would be to indulge in fantasy.

10. It hardly needs saying that standard uses of information, along with the rest of the terminological escapees from cognitive and computer science, fill the need for the organizing mind that is required once one separates executive genes from the mindless, motionless matter that is needed to make an organism—or, not to put too fine a point on it—the body of an organism, since, as we have seen, *its* mind (if it has one, and in contrast to the mind in its DNA) is at least partially attributed to "the environment." My discussion of *homunculoid genes* was an attempt to capture this tendency to parcel out (active) organizing and (passive) raw-material functions along mind-body lines (2000b, especially chap. 6). In the kind of system being described here, of course, there is no possibility of assigning these functions to different components. Rather, organized matter in interaction is both the "cause" of its future organization and the "effect" of its prior organization.

11. Many examples of this kind of work are to be found in Oyama, Griffiths, and Gray (2001), which includes a classic paper on organism-environment relations by Richard Lewontin, who has persistently stressed the mutual influences of organisms and environments.

References

Avital, E. and E. Jablonka (2000). *Animal Traditions: Behavioural Inheritance in Evolution*. Cambridge: Cambridge University Press.

Bateson, G. (1972). *Steps to an Ecology of Mind*. New York: Ballantine.

Bateson, P. (1991). Are there principles of behavioural development? In P. Bateson (ed.), *The Development and Integration of Behaviour*, pp. 19–39. Cambridge: Cambridge University Press.

Bateson, P. and P. Martin (1999). *Design for a Life*. London: Jonathan Cape.

Boyd, R. and P. J. Richerson (1985). *Culture and the Evolutionary Process*. Chicago: The University of Chicago Press.

Deacon, T. W. (1997). *The Symbolic Species: The Co-evolution of Language and the Brain*. New York: Norton.

Durham, W. H. (1979). Toward a coevolutionary theory of human biology and culture. In N. A. Chagnon and W. Irons (eds.), *Evolutionary Biology and Human Social Behavior: An Anthropological Perspective*, pp. 4–39. North Scituate, Mass.: Duxbury Press.

Gilbert, S. F. (2001). Ecological developmental biology: Developmental biology meets the real world. *Developmental Biology* 233: 1–12.

Godfrey-Smith, P. (1996). *Complexity and the Function of Mind in Nature*. Cambridge: Cambridge University Press.

Goodwin, B. C. (1984). A relational or field theory of reproduction and its evolutionary implications. In M.-W. Ho and P. T. Saunders (eds.), *Beyond Neo-Darwinism: Introduction to the New Evolutionary Paradigm*, pp. 219–241. London: Academic Press.

Gray, R. D. (1988). Metaphors and methods: Behavioural ecology, panbiogeography and the evolving synthesis. In M.-W. Ho and S. W. Fox (eds.), *Evolutionary Processes and Metaphors*, pp. 209–242. London: John Wiley.

Griesemer, J. (1998). Turning back to go forward. *Biology and Philosophy* 13: 103–112.

Griesemer, J. (2000). Reproduction and the reduction of genetics. In P. J. Beurton, R. Falk, and H.-J. Rheinberger (eds.), *The Concept of the Gene in Development and Evolution: Historical and Epistemological Perspectives*, pp. 240–285. Cambridge: Cambridge University Press.

Griesemer, J. and W. Wimsatt (1989). Picturing Weismannism: A case study of conceptual evolution. In M. Ruse (ed.), *What the Philosophy of Biology Is: Essays for David Hull*, pp. 75–137. Dordrecht: Kluwer.

Griffiths, P. E. and R. D. Gray (2001). Darwinism and developmental systems. In Oyama, Griffiths, and Gray (2001), pp. 195–218.

Hinde, R. A. and J. Stevenson-Hinde (1973). *Constraints on Learning: Limitations and Predispositions*. New York: Academic Press.

Ho, M.-W. (1984). Environment and heredity in development and evolution. In M.-W. Ho and P. T. Saunders (eds.), *Beyond Neo-Darwinism: Introduction to the New Evolutionary Paradigm*, pp. 267–289. London: Academic Press.

Jablonka, E. (2001). The systems of inheritance. In Oyama, Griffiths, and Gray (2001), pp. 99–116.

Jablonka, E. (in press). Information: Interpretation, sharing and heredity. *Philosophy of Science*.

Jablonka, E. and M. Lamb (1995). *Epigenetic Inheritance and Evolution: The Lamarckian Dimension*. Oxford: Oxford University Press.

Jablonka, E. and M. Lamb (1998). Bridges between development and evolution. *Biology and Philosophy* 13: 119–124.

Johnston, T. D. (1987). The persistence of dichotomies in the study of behavioral development. *Developmental Review* 7: 149–182.

Johnston, T. D. (1995). The influence of Weismann's germ-plasm theory on the distinction between learned and innate behavior. *Journal of the History of the Behavioral Sciences* 31: 115–128.

Johnston, T. D. and G. Gottlieb (1990). Neophenogenesis: A developmental theory of phenotypic evolution. *Journal of Theoretical Biology* 147: 471–495.

Jordanova, L. J. (1984). *Lamarck*. Oxford: Oxford University Press.

Keller, E. F. (1998). Structures of heredity. *Biology and Philosophy* 13: 113–118.

Laland, F., J. Odling-Smee, and M. F. Feldman (2001). Niche-construction, ecological inheritance, and cycles of contingency in evolution. In Oyama, Griffiths, and Gray (2001), pp. 117–126.

Lehrman, D. S. (1970). Semantic and conceptual issues in the nature-nurture problem. In L. R. Aronson, E. Tobach, D. S. Lehrman, and J. S. Rosenblatt (eds.), *Development and Evolution of Behavior: Essays in Memory of T. C. Schneirla*, pp. 17–52. San Francisco: Freeman.

Lewontin, R. C. (1982). Organism and environment. In H. C. Plotkin (ed.), *Learning, Development, and Culture*, pp. 151–170. New York: Wiley.

Lewontin, R. (1983). Darwin's revolution. *New York Review of Books* 30(10): 21–27.

Lumsden, C. J. and E. O. Wilson (1981). *Genes, Mind, and Culture*. Cambridge, Mass.: Harvard University Press.

Newman, S. A. and G. B. Müller (1999). Morphological evolution: Epigenetic mechanisms. *Encyclopedia of Life Sciences*. (www.els.net.) London: Nature Publishing Group.

Nijhout, H. F. (2001). The ontogeny of phenotypes. In Oyama, Griffiths, and Gray (2001), pp. 129–140.

Oyama, S. (2000a). Causal democracy and causal contributions in DST. *Philosophy of Science* 67 (proceedings): S332–347.

Oyama, S. (2000b). *Evolution's Eye: A Systems View of the Biology-Culture Divide*. Durham, N.C.: Duke University Press.

Oyama, S. (2000c). *The Ontogeny of Information: Developmental Systems and Evolution*, second edition. Durham, N.C.: Duke University Press. (Originally published 1985, Cambridge University Press.)

Oyama, S. (2002). The nurturing of natures. In A. Grunwald, M. Gutmann, and E. M. Neumann-Held (eds.), *On Human Nature: Biological and Philosophical Foundations of Anthropology*, pp. 163–170. Studienreihe der Europäischen Akademie, New York: Springer Verlag.

Oyama, S., P. E. Griffiths, and R. D. Gray (eds.). (2001). *Cycles of Contingency: Developmental Systems and Evolution*. Cambridge, MA: MIT Press/Bradford Books.

Rachlin, H. (1987). Rachlin replies to Lacey and Schwartz. In S. Modgil and C. Modgil (eds.), *B. F. Skinner: Consensus and Controversy*, pp. 177–178. London: Falmer Press.

Schneirla, T. C. (1966). Behavioral development and comparative psychology. *Quarterly Review of Biology* 41: 283–302.

Smith, B. H. (2002). Cutting-edge equivocation: Conceptual moves and rhetorical strategies in contemporary anti-epistemology. *South Atlantic Quarterly* 101 (1): 187–212.

Sober, E. (1984). *The Nature of Selection*. Cambridge, MA: MIT Press/Bradford Books.

Sober, E. (1985). Darwin on natural selection: A philosophical perspective. In D. Kohn (ed.), *The Darwinian Heritage,* pp. 867–899. Princeton, N.J.: Princeton University Press.

van der Weele, C. (1999). *Images of Development: Environmental Causes in Ontogeny.* Albany, N.Y.: SUNY Press.

Waddington, C. H. (1975). *The Evolution of an Evolutionist.* Ithaca, N.Y.: Cornell University Press.

West, M. J., A. P. King, and D. J. White (in press). Discovering culture in birds: The role of learning and development. In F. DeWaal and P. Tyack (eds.), *Animal Complexity and Social Intelligence.* Cambridge, Mass.: Harvard University Press.

Williams, G. C. (1966). *Adaptation and Natural Selection.* Princeton, N.J.: Princeton University Press.

Winther, R. G. (2001). August Weismann on germ-plasm variation. *Journal of the History of Biology* 34: 517–555.

10

Beyond the Baldwin Effect: James Mark Baldwin's "Social Heredity," Epigenetic Inheritance, and Niche Construction

Paul E. Griffiths

1 Introduction

James Mark Baldwin is remembered today almost exclusively for his paper "A New Factor in Evolution" (Baldwin 1896a). The new factor, which he called "organic selection," and which later became known as the Baldwin effect, was a process that could cause "accommodations"—the acquired adaptive responses of individual organisms—to become hereditary. "Accommodations" include physiological adaptations like calluses, and, of much greater interest to Baldwin, learned behaviors. The Baldwin effect differed from classic Lamarckian inheritance because it respected August Weismann's doctrine of the "continuity of the germ plasm," according to which modifications to somatic cell-lines can have no influence on the state of the germ cells. Viewed at the population level, the Baldwin effect would give the impression that the Lamarckian inheritance of acquired characters was taking place, but this impression would be an illusion—no individual organism would actually inherit an acquired character from a parent. I am not going to describe how the Baldwin effect is meant to occur. Baldwin himself never had a fully satisfactory theory and his contemporaries offered a number of significantly different theories. Later authors have offered many more. The details of these proposals are described by David Depew (chap. 1, this volume), Stephen Downes (chap. 2, this volume) and Peter Godfrey-Smith (chap. 3, this volume). Rather, in this essay I argue that too much attention has been paid to the Baldwin effect. George Gaylord Simpson was probably right when he said that the effect is theoretically possible and may have actually occurred, but that this has no major implications for evolutionary theory (Simpson 1953). The Baldwin effect is not even central to Baldwin's own account of "social heredity" and biology-culture coevolution, an account that in important respects resembles the modern ideas of epigenetic inheritance and niche-construction.

There are two reasons for the excessive attention that has been paid to the Baldwin effect. The first is the confused but enduring idea that the Baldwin effect allows "mind" to "direct" evolution and thus saves us from the barren Darwinian vision of a world ruled by chance and necessity. The second motive is less well known and far more interesting. Ever since Weismann, biologists interested in causes of adaptation other than natural selection acting on the germ line—causes which include physiological adaptation, learning and its relatives, and epigenetic, ecological, and cultural factors in individual development—have faced the challenge that the processes they study can be of no *evolutionary* significance because any changes in form produced by these means will not be preserved on evolutionary timescales. The Baldwin effect allows these processes to leave a record in the germ line and this explains the continuing interest in (and redefinition of) the Baldwin effect by biologists and psychobiologists. I will argue, however, that this way of gaining recognition for these processes merely obscures their real evolutionary role. As Celia Moore (chap. 7, this volume) shows, epigenetic inheritance can play an important role in evolution without a Baldwin effect to transfer its effects to the germ line. In section 5, I examine a number of recent arguments designed to minimize the evolutionary significance of epigenetic inheritance. I suggest that, at best, these arguments leave the evolutionary significance of epigenetic inheritance undetermined and a matter for (long overdue) empirical enquiry. In section 6, I turn from epigenetic inheritance to "niche construction": the reciprocal influence of evolving lineages on the ecological forces that impinge on those lineages. The importance of niche construction has become increasingly widely recognized in recent years, owing largely to the work of John F. Odling-Smee and his collaborators. As Peter Godfrey-Smith (chap. 3, this volume) argues, the potentially important evolutionary mechanism described by Terence Deacon as the Baldwin effect (Deacon 1997) is much closer to niche construction than to the Baldwin effect as conceived by its earlier advocates.

Before entering into these contemporary disputes, however, I want to reexamine the role of the Baldwin effect in Baldwin's own work. I will argue that his primary interests were "accommodation" as a phenomena in its own right, "social heredity," and the influence of social heredity on natural selection via the process we now call niche construction. Even the term Baldwin used for the effect now named after him—"organic selection"—meant something else in the rest of Baldwin's writings and was merely opportunistically redefined when Baldwin attempted to assert his priority with respect to the "new factor in evolution."

2   Baldwin's Opportunistic Redefinition of "Organic Selection"

In "A New Factor in Evolution," Baldwin defines organic selection as "The process of ontogenetic adaptation considered as keeping single organisms alive and so securing determinate lines of variation in subsequent generations" (Baldwin,1996: 78).[1] In an April 1897 letter to *Nature,* organic selection is "the perpetuation and development of congenital variations in consequence of accommodation" (Baldwin 1897a: 558). In an almost identical contribution to *Science* that same month, he repeats this definition, but with the word "congenital" in brackets (Baldwin 1897b: 635). So in 1896–1897, Baldwin consistently defines organic selection as the process in which a characteristic that was initially produced by the action on the individual organism of its developmental environment becomes a hereditary characteristic in descendants of that organism. Read literally, the *Nature/Science* definition of 1897 would encompass not only the Baldwin effect, but also the straightforward neo-Lamarckian inheritance advocated by Baldwin's sparring partner Edwin Drinker Cope (Baldwin 1896c; Cope 1896) and rejected by Baldwin by this date, although it was presumably not Baldwin's intention to be so inclusive.

The almost identical contributions to *Nature* and *Science* in April 1897 were designed to defuse a priority dispute between Baldwin, Conwy Lloyd Morgan, and the paleontologist Henry F. Osborn. In these short articles Baldwin lists papers published by the three men in 1896 discussing very similar mechanisms by which acquired characteristics could become hereditary without violating Weismann's doctrine of the continuity of the germ plasm. The three authors had introduced a host of neologisms in their accounts of the new evolutionary process. Baldwin lists nine of these terms and suggests that they be adopted as standard. He attributes four terms to himself, three to Lloyd Morgan, and treats the remaining two—

"variation" and "accommodation"—as needing no special attribution. Despite making a great show of even-handedness, however, Baldwin subtly emphasizes his own priority. Osborn had the first published paper (by eleven days), but the earliest date in the list of papers relating to the new theory is that of Baldwin's verbal presentation at the New York Academy of Sciences on January 31, 1896. Among the terms Baldwin attributes to himself is "organic selection," which is the name he suggests for the new factor in evolution as a whole and the title of both the articles.

Naming the new factor in evolution "organic selection" reinforced Baldwin's claim to priority in another way, since he had introduced this term some years earlier. This fact is heavily emphasized in "A New Factor in Evolution" where he remarks, "I have noted in print . . . that Prof. Lloyd Morgan and Prof. H.F Osborn have reached conclusions similar to my main one on Organic Selection. I do not know whether they approve of this name for the 'factor'; but as I suggested it in the first edition of my book (April 1895) and used it earlier, I venture to hope that it may be approved by the biologists" (Baldwin 1896: 79, n. 9). Earlier in the same article Baldwin cites the source of the concept of organic selection as chapter 7 of his *Mental Development in the Child and the Race: Methods and Processes* (Baldwin 1895). The clear implication of these passages is that Baldwin has known about the new factor for some years and has, indeed, described it in print. Why, then, in the two short contributions to *Science* and *Nature* in the next year, does Baldwin not cite the chapter-long discussion of organic selection published in 1895 and thus put his priority beyond doubt? The reason is that, as Robert J. Richards has noted (1987: 488), in his 1895 book Baldwin used the term to mean something quite different. The insinuation of priority in "A New Factor in Evolution" would not have stood up to the scrutiny generated by a dispute with two established scientists.

Chapter 7 of *Mental Development* . . . is entitled "Organic Adaptation in General" and in it Baldwin is concerned to improve on Alexander Bain and Herbert Spencer's explanation of how animals can acquire new, adaptive behaviors in a single lifetime: "How is it that we, or the brute, or the amoeba, *can learn to do anything*?" (Baldwin 1900: 181, his italics).[2] These adaptive responses cannot be explained by "*Natural selection as operative directly upon individual organisms*" (Baldwin 1900: 172, his italics), by which Baldwin means the conventional Darwinian process of natural selection acting on random variations in congenital behavior. Instead, adaptive responses that arise during a single lifetime must be explained by "*Natural selection as operative upon different reactions of the same organism,*" and it is this process that Baldwin terms "organic selection":

It is necessary to consider further how certain reactions of one single organism can be selected so as to adapt the organism better and give it a life-history. Let us at the outset call this process "organic selection," in contrast with the "natural selection" of whole organisms. (Baldwin 1900: 174)

The largest part of chapter 7 is devoted to establishing Baldwin's views of the origin of "the excess process itself, which gives the movements from which 'organic selection' selects the fittest" (Baldwin 1900: 205); the origin, to speak anachronistically, of operant behaviors. Baldwin is concerned to grant natural selection a larger role than he finds in the accounts of Spencer and Bain in explaining the origin of these "excess" behaviors and the origin of the ability to respond to pleasure and pain by repeating one "excess" behavior and suppressing another. In 1895, then, it seems that Baldwin meant by "organic selection" the acquisition of behaviors through reinforcement learning, and that his concern was to establish that this ability arose through natural selection rather than being in some way intrinsic to sensible matter.

Section 3 of chapter 7 is titled "*Development and Heredity,*" but despite this promising title, it contains no mention of the Baldwin effect. Baldwin's concern in this section is to show that his "theory would not be affected by the truth or falsity of either of the opposed views of heredity now so bitterly opposed to each other in biological circles" (Baldwin 1900: 204), these two theories being the "neo-Darwinian" (e.g., Weismannian) and the "neo-Lamarckian." Baldwin argues that his theory can be accepted by "neo-Darwinians [*who*] hold that natural selection, operating upon congenital variations, is adequate to explain all progressive race gains," because, "granting the ontogenetic progress required by the Spencer-Bain theory and adopted in my own,—the learning of new movements in the way which I have called 'organic selection,'—yet the ability to do it may be a congenital variation" (Baldwin 1900: 204–205). In 1895, it seems, Baldwin merely held that the congenital ability to learn from experience allowed organisms to adapt in ontogeny—hardly a "new factor in evolution." There is only one passage in section 3 that might be read as prefiguring the Baldwin effect, a passage where he argues that:

all the later acquirements of individual organisms may likewise be considered only the evidence of additional variations from these earlier variations *[those conferring ability to learn]*. So it is only necessary to hold to a view by which variations are cumulative to secure the same results by natural selection as would have been secured by the inheritance of acquired characters from father to son. (Baldwin 1900: 205)

However, the following sentences reveal that this has nothing to do with the Baldwin effect. He informs us that "Mr. Spencer and others seem to me to be quite wide of the mark in saying that the only alternative to the inheritance of acquired characters is a doctrine of 'special creation' " (Baldwin 1900: 205) and goes on to remark that in the recapitulation of phylogeny by ontogeny we see each feature emerge at the same stage that it emerged in the ancestor. The remark that seemed to prefigure the Baldwin effect is in fact an attack on the neo-Lamarckians. Baldwin is arguing that we should not be surprised that sons exhibit the behaviors their fathers learned, since the congenital variation that allowed the father to learn those behaviors will be inherited by the son and will allow him to learn them too. Hence this phenomenon does not compel us to accept the neo-Lamarckian theory of heredity.[3]

As late as May 1896, two months after the publication of part one of "Heredity and Instinct," in which the Baldwin effect is moderately clearly described (Baldwin 1896b, see esp. 439 and 440–441), Baldwin was still defining "organic selection" in a way that makes no reference to the Baldwin effect. Describing the theory of his 1895 book, he says:

Its main thought is this, that all new movements that are adaptive or "fit" are selected from overproduced movements or movement variations, just as creatures are selected from overproduced variations by the natural selection of those which are fit. This process, as I conceive it, I have called "organic selection," a phrase which emphasizes the fact that it is the organism which selects from all its overproduced movements those which are adaptive and beneficial. (Baldwin 1896c: 427)

3   Baldwin and "Social Heredity"

Viewed in the broader context of Baldwin's work, the Baldwin effect is primarily an addendum to Baldwin's theory of social heredity. The initial significance of social heredity for Baldwin may have been mainly as a counter to the arguments of the neo-Lamarckians, who argued that neo-Darwinism was insufficient to account for the progressive tendencies that they saw in evolution:

I have recently argued that Spencer and others are in error in holding that social progress demands the use hypothesis* since the socially-acquired actions of a species, notably man, are socially handed down; giving a sort of "social heredity" which supplements natural heredity. . . .
    *SCIENCE, August 23, 1895, summarised in Nature, Vol. LII, 1895, p. 627. (Baldwin 1896b: 439)

By the time he wrote *Social and Ethical Interpretations in Mental Development: A Study in Social Psychology* (Baldwin 1897), however, social heredity loomed large in Baldwin's thought:

It is as inexorable as the colour of his eyes and the shape of his nose. He is born into a system of social relationships just as he is born into a certain quality of air. As he grows in body by breathing the one, so he grows in mind by absorbing the other. (Baldwin 1906: 69–70)[4]

The increased importance of social heredity in human beings as compared to other animals plays a key role in Baldwin's typically optimistic Edwardian account of social progress. Individuals who fail to acquire the level of civilization of the society around them because of some defect in their "physical heredity" are eliminated by "social suppression of the unfit." Anti-social mental traits are eliminated by criminal sanctions—execution and imprisonment—and also by reproductive isolation, since the instincts of anti-social individuals are abnormal and do not "fit" with the instincts of potential mates. Meanwhile, pro-social mental traits flourish. By this means, once social heredity has evolved, evolution has an intrinsic tendency to move to higher and higher levels of social organization (Baldwin 1906: 80–90). Leaving aside the theme of "onwards and upwards" that was common to so many evolutionary theorists at this time (Ruse 1996), Baldwin's account of social heredity was a theory of what would today be called "niche-construction" (Odling-Smee 1988). Social heredity alters the selective forces that act on the units of biological heredity so as to alter the course of biological evolution. This general theory of social heredity figures prominently even in Baldwin's papers devoted specifically to the Baldwin effect. In the *Nature* and *Science* papers of 1897, he argues that his term "social heredity" is to be preferred to Lloyd Morgan's term "tradition" because it emphasizes the causal relationship between one human mind and the next (Baldwin 1897a: 558; 1897b: 636). In "A New Factor in Evolution," he argues that not only does social heredity facilitate the Baldwin effect, "it has a farther value. *It keeps alive a series of functions which either are not yet, or never do become, congenital at all"* (Baldwin 1996: 67, his italics). Most striking of all, when Baldwin describes how social heredity "tends to set the direction of phylogenetic progess" (Baldwin 1996: 67), he does not describe a case in which a character initially transmitted by social heredity later becomes congenital (the Baldwin effect), but instead describes a case in which social heredity of one character changes the selection pressures on other, quite different characters of the organism (niche construction). The separation of human racial types now living together in the American South, he argues, is due to the social transmission of "a repugnance to black-white marriages," which is the *"influence of education, imitation, etc."* Yet the effects of this process of social heredity will "appear in our fossils when they are dug up long hence by the paleontologist of the succeeding aeons!" (Baldwin 1996: 67–68, his italics).[5]

Not only did Baldwin continue to discuss social heredity and its impact on biological evolution by means other than the Baldwin effect in the years 1896–1897, his work after 1897 show no sign that he felt that the Baldwin effect had replaced his more general account of the interaction between biological and social heredity. He discusses the Baldwin effect in two later works, but with no sign that he has worked the process out in more detail or applied it to specific cases (Baldwin 1902, 1909). The primary focus of Baldwin's writing after 1897 continued to be the psychological processes by which the child comes to cope with its individual environment, processes discussed with a mass of detail in his multivolume *Genetic Logic* (Baldwin 1906–1911). Simpson claims that Baldwin's period of active interest in the Baldwin effect ended around 1903 (Simpson 1996: 100, n. 1), and this seems a reasonable assessment.

The prominence Baldwin gave to the Baldwin effect in 1896–1897 and his redefinition of "organic selection" to refer to the "new factor in evolution" can perhaps best be explained by his interest in obtaining scientific priority. The Baldwin effect was obviously an idea whose time had come and Baldwin wanted credit as its inventor. His tendency to claim priority rather too readily was evident elsewhere in his career. Baldwin was accused in print of having taken his theory of imitation—the core of his theory of mental development—from the work of the French sociologist M. G. Tarde without adequate acknowledgment (Baldwin 1906: viii, xi–xiv). Perhaps Baldwin's tendency to aggressively assert his priority explains the fact that the rest of American psychology showed more than the usual degree of *schadenfreude* in the face of his disgrace and dismissal in 1908 (but see Richards 1987, esp. 489–490 and 501–503 for a different view).

4   Why Has the Baldwin Effect Been Remembered?

As David Depew (chap. 1, this volume) makes clear, the Baldwin effect has been substantially redefined more than once in its century-long career as a controversial, but never completely disreputable aspect of evolutionary theory. Authors including C. H. Waddington, G. G. Simpson, I. I. Schmalhausen, R. Matsuda, and M. J. West-Eberhard have described diverse mechanisms by which acquired characters could become hereditary consistently with Weismann's doctrine, and all of these mechanisms have been described as Baldwin effects. Clearly, it is not the details of Baldwin's theory that have commanded such sustained interest, but rather the possibility of some mechanism or other filling the abstract role he identified.

There are two reasons for the continuing interest in finding some mechanism to fill this role. The first, and better known, is the idea that the Baldwin effect gives "mind" the chance to "direct" evolution and thus saves us from the barren Darwinian vision of a world ruled by chance and necessity. It was this prospect that attracted cultural critics such as George Bernard Shaw (Shaw 1939) and Arthur Koestler (Koestler 1972) to the Baldwin effect. But it is entirely unclear to me how, absent some prior commitment to an immaterialist account of mind, the fact that the evolution of intelligence has influenced future evolution is challenging to conventional Darwinism. That fact is exactly on a par with the fact that the evolution of plants led to an increase in atmospheric oxygen and so influenced future evolution. The tendency to find the influence of intelligence on evolution vaguely reassuring persists even today. The evolutionary psychologist Geoffrey Miller, commenting on his theory that human intelligence evolved by sexual selection, reassured a journalist that his "is probably the least reductionist theory of the mind's evolution one could hope for. . . . It doesn't reduce psychology to biology, but sees psychology as a driving force in biological evolution" (Smith 2000: 7s). But, like the Baldwin effect, sexual selection is no less biological than any other selection process, and the sexual preferences that drive it are material biological products like any other. The only

Darwinian account of mind that could reasonably be described as more "reductionistic" than Miller's would be Thomas Henry Huxley's epiphenomenalism, according to which minds are ineffectual side-effects of the brains that have been produced by evolution (Huxley 1896). But if epiphenomenalism was ever a live option for Darwinists,[6] it has not been so for many decades. The idea that the Baldwin effect will save the mind from evolutionary irrelevance is a confused solution to a nonexistent problem.

The second motive for the continuing interest in the Baldwin effect is both more sensible and more important since it is the motive that has drawn many significant biologists to consider the effect. Ever since Weismann asserted that the germ plasm is passed on from generation to generation unaffected by the bodies that house it, many well-known causes of individual variation have been excluded from playing a role in evolution, as opposed to individual development. Developmental biologists, and developmental psychologists like Baldwin, have had to accept that only phenotypic differences caused by genetic changes can provide the raw material for evolution. Furthermore, since natural selection acts only on the genes, an understanding of evolutionary dynamics seems to require only an understanding of selection and an understanding of genetic heredity. Phenotypic differences are selected and the genes responsible for those differences are differentially replicated. Developmental biology and psychology may be interesting in their own rights, but they are not important topics for a student of evolution. Richard Dawkins makes this point in a well-known passage:

when we are talking about development it is appropriate to emphasise nongenetic as well as genetic factors. But when we are talking about units of selection a different emphasis is called for, an emphasis on the properties of replicators. . . . The special status of genetic factors is deserved for one reason only: genetic factors replicate themselves, blemishes and all, but non-genetic factors do not. (Dawkins 1982: 98–99)

The view that organisms inherit nothing but their genes is often explained using a diagram distantly related to the cell-lineage diagrams that Weismann used to explain his doctrine of the continuity of the germ plasm (Griesemer and Wimsatt 1989). In the familiar diagram of "molecular Weismannism," there is a causal arrow from the genes of one generation to those of the next, and a causal arrow from the genes of each generation to the phenotype of that generation. There is, however, no causal arrow from the phenotype of one generation to the phenotype of the next. The diagram

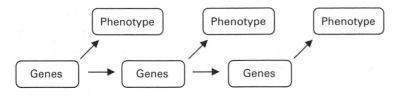

Figure 10.1
A visual representation of the idea that organisms inherit nothing but genes from their parents, a view often described as "molecular Weismannism."

is so familiar that it is hard to look at it with a naive eye. If one were to do so, however, it would pose an immediate puzzle. Everyone knows that in many species parents feed and nurture their offspring and that differences in feeding and nurturing lead to differences in the phenotype. Every biologist knows that parents pass on DNA methylation patterns and maternal DNA products in the cytoplasm of the egg, not to mention membranes, microtubule organizing centers, and many other essential features of a functioning cell that cannot be generated *de novo* by a set of naked chromosomes. Many of these features are sources of significant variation in the offspring's phenotype. What has happened to the causal arrows representing these processes? They are omitted from the diagram because they are taken to be real *developmental* phenomena but not real *evolutionary* phenomena. These causal influences may have an effect on the phenotype of the next generation, but they will not endure for long enough to play a significant role in evolution. John Maynard Smith has made this point in a characteristically forthright manner:

Differences due to nature are likely to be inherited whereas those due to nurture are not; evolutionary changes are changes in nature, not nurture. (Maynard Smith 2000: 189)

The Baldwin effect has continued to excite interest, I suggest, because it allows students of development to draw evolutionary implications from their developmental studies. If acquired traits can become hereditary then knowledge of how such traits are acquired in development is relevant to the construction of evolutionary scenarios. Furthermore, understanding evolutionary dynamics will involve understanding development as well as selection and genetic heredity. But the Baldwin effect is neither necessary nor sufficient to make development evolutionarily relevant. It is not *sufficient* because, as Simpson argued, even if it occurs, there is no reason to suppose that it is ubiquitous. The conventional neo-Darwinian approach of which Simpson was an advocate would probably remain a good approximation to the truth, and the Baldwin effect would be a mere footnote to that theory (Simpson 1953). The Baldwin effect is not *necessary* to establish the relevance of developmental to evolutionary studies for two reasons. First, as I will argue in the next section, there is good reason to think that epigenetic inheritance is an important factor in evolution even if the phenotypic differences thus transmitted never become incorporated in the germ line. Baldwin's "social heredity," of course, was a form of epigenetic inheritance. Second, as I discuss in section 6, one way in which parents influence their offspring is by constructing the niche that the offspring will occupy. Niche construction fundamentally influences evolutionary dynamics because it implies that organisms are not so much adapted to their niches as coevolved with them (Brandon and Antonovics 1996; Lewontin 1982, 1983). Baldwin anticipated this idea, in a primitive way, in his discussion of how social heredity could "set the direction of phylogenetic progress" without the operation of the Baldwin effect.

5   Three Ways to Marginalize Epigenetic Inheritance

The first way to marginalize epigenetic inheritance is, as discussed above, to assume that it is too unstable and fluctuating to be the basis of cumulative change by natural selection. Since it is cumulative selection, rather than one-step selection, that produces complex adaptation, this would seem to relegate epigenetic inheritance to a minor role at best. Kim Sterelny has suggested that this is likely to be particularly true of cultural inheritance: Baldwin's social heredity may exist, but it does not lead to adaptations (Sterelny 2001). This deflationary view of cultural inheritance may quite possibly be correct, but our current state of knowledge about the longevity of cultural traditions in animals and the degree to which they have involved cumulative changes is too inadequate to allow any substantial conclusion to be drawn. There is considerable cultural variation in tool use, grooming, and courtship behaviors between populations of wild chimpanzees (Whiten et al. 1999). However, there is little evidence that these variations have persisted for long periods of time, nor that they are a product of cumulative cultural change. It is possible that sensitive periods and social and ecological scaffolding may facilitate reliable cultural inheritance. One example is the reliability of human linguistic inheritance, which is supported by a host of such psychological adaptations. Language-like features in other species may be supported in the same way and thus exhibit reliable cultural inheritance. A study on chaffinches in Atlantic islands found substantial congruence between a tree based on morphology and a tree constructed from song syllables, indicating a common evolutionary history going back 1 to 2 million years (Lynch and Baker 1986). A study on the possible effect of cultural selection on mtDNA diversity in whales suggests that cultural inheritance has exhibited considerable longevity and fidelity in those species with matrilineal social systems. The results of computer simulations indicate that, assuming a 10 percent reproductive advantage is culturally transmitted down maternal lineages, it would take over 200 generations to produce the observed tenfold reduction in mtDNA diversity observed in lineages with matrilineal social systems (Whitehead 1998). We know of at least one case in which a process of social heredity in insects has persisted for long enough to create an adaptation. The morphology of queens and the colony structure of the fire ant *Solenopsis invicta* differ radically between different lineages because of stably replicated pheremonal nest "cultures" (Keller and Ross 1993). Some lineages have nests with several small queens, while others have nests with a single large queen. Moving eggs from one colony type to another reveals that a queen raised in a colony with a particular "culture" will develop the body type appropriate to her adopted culture and found a new colony with the same culture. This—pheremone transmitted—difference between colony types has persisted long enough for genes affecting growth rates in queens to diverge as each lineage adapts its growth rate to the demands of either the monogynous or polygynous lifestyle. These cases and others like them suggest that the ability of cultural inheritance—and of epigenetic inheritance more generally—to reliably reproduce features over evolutionarily significant periods of time is an open empirical question and one whose investigation is overdue.

But even if epigenetic inheritance sometimes exhibits high copying fidelity over long timespans, this may not mean that it can play a similar evolutionary role to genetic inheritance, generating the kind of variation on which natural selection can feed to produce complex adaptations.

In *The Major Transitions in Evolution,* John Maynard Smith and Eörs Szathmáry assign a vital role to membrane heredity and the inheritance of endosymbionts as sources of the evolutionary innovations in cell-compartmentalization and cell organelles that created the fundamentally different types of organism we see today—the various types of bacteria, and the animals, plants, and fungi (Maynard Smith and Szathmáry 1995). These epigenetic inheritance systems play a major role in Maynard Smith and Szathmáry's account of evolution, but, they argue, it is not a role that puts these systems on a par with the genes. The genetic inheritance system and cultural transmission in humans are the only two systems that display what they call "unlimited heredity," the form of heredity that makes possible the evolution of complex adaptation. Most inheritance systems, they argue, can only mutate between a limited number of heritable states, which can be specified in advance. Habitat imprinting, for example, can only lead organisms to choose different habitats. DNA methylation can only choose whether existing genes will be switched on or off. The genome and language, however, both have a recursive syntactic structure. Their basic constituents can be put together in many different combinations and these combinations can be of any length. Hence these inheritance systems have an unlimited number of possible heritable states.

The distinction between limited and unlimited heredity systems is an interesting one, and may provide insights into one of the key innovations—an inheritance system with this sort of recursive structure—that enabled the diversification of early life into the vast range of forms we see today. However, it is possible to take issue with the idea that unlimited heredity is a function of the genes, and limited heredity a function of methylation, membranes, and other nongenetic, heritable, developmental resources. A developmental systems interpretation, according to which the capacity for unlimited heredity is a property of the whole matrix of material resources, is equally defensible (Gray 2001; Griffiths 2001). The way Maynard Smith and Szathmáry interpret the limited/unlimited heredity distinction involves, in effect, partitioning the total number of developmental outcomes that can be generated by a developmental system between the various inheritance systems that make up that system. The number of outcomes allotted to an inheritance system measures its "limitedness," and the genetic inheritance system is allotted massively more outcomes than any other system. To derive this result, Maynard Smith and Szathmáry assume that the number of permutations of DNA codons is the relevant measure of "limitedness" for the genetic inheritance system and that some corresponding measure of the number of permutations of physical parts is the appropriate measure for other inheritance systems. But this is not the only way to partition the developmental outcomes among the inheritance systems, nor is it obviously the right way. For any one inheritance system, the range of physical changes that count as evolutionary changes is restricted to those that can be made use of by the rest of the developmental system. This point can be easily grasped by looking at the syntactic structure of human languages—the analogue to which Maynard Smith and Szathmáry are appealing. Not all physical differences between syntactic objects are *syntactic* differences. Differences in handwriting or in the accent with which one speaks, for example, are not syntactic differences. Syntactic differences are those physical differences that are treated as differences by the broader system for which this set of physical objects constitutes a set of linguistic inscriptions. The main lesson of the major evolutionary transitions that are the focus of Maynard Smith and Szathmáry's work is that evolution creates entirely new kinds of developmental systems that massively expand the possible interpretations of existing developmental resources, including genes. Think how many evolutionary possibilities can be caused by a base pair substitution in the DNA of a eukaryote cell that could not be caused by those same substitutions in a prokaryote cell. As Maynard Smith and Szathmáry themselves describe, that vast swathe of evolutionary possibilities came into existence through evolutionary change mediated by a limited heredity system. Membranes cannot be constructed without an existing membrane template into which to insert newly synthesized proteins. Hence, major changes to the partitioning of the cell require variation to arise through the membrane heredity system, not through mutations of the DNA. In effect, the measure of "limitedness" that Maynard Smith and Szathmáry adopt allots to the genetic inheritance system all the outcomes that can be generated by making changes to that system across the full range of possibilities for the other systems while allocating to the other systems only the number of outcomes they could produce given one possible genome. That is why it is not an appropriate measure. It would be no less reasonable to allocate to the genetic inheritance system only the range of outcomes it

could generate given one state of the other inheritance systems and to allocate to some other heredity system all the outcomes it could generate given
the whole range of possible genomes. What I want to suggest, however, is
not that we should engage in such reverse discrimination, but that we
should recognize that "unlimitedness" is a property of a developmental
system, not of any one of its physical components.

This conclusion can be reinforced by an independent argument. The potential of differences in genes, language, and perhaps pheremones in social
insects to cause a large number of phenotypic outcomes stems from the fact
that these differences "mean something" to the rest of the developmental
system. If the rest of the system surrounding the genes were such that indefinitely many base-pair combinations collapsed into only a few developmental outcomes, then the genetic inheritance system would not be
unlimited. It is not hard to imagine cellular machinery with this result—the
existing genetic code is substantially redundant in just this way, with several codons corresponding to the same amino acids. Hence, the unlimited
nature of the genetic inheritance system is more accurately seen as a property of the developmental system as a whole and not of the genome in
isolation.

A third way to marginalize epigenetic inheritance is to argue that only
genes have the capacity to generate a fine-grained response to selection and
thus to give rise to adaptation. Many epigenetic inheritance systems, such
as habitat imprinting or the inheritance of gut endosymbionts, seem to
change state in a way that corresponds not to the genetic micromutations
that conventional neo-Darwinians take to be the fuel of natural selection,
but rather to macromutations. Like genetically induced macromutations,
single changes in these inheritance systems produce large changes in the
phenotype, such as a whole new habitat or a whole new symbiont lineage.
It is widely believed that this kind of discontinuous change cannot give rise
to adaptation. However, as Russell Gray has pointed out, this argument
implicitly assumes that epigenetic inheritance systems must have evolutionary potential separately from one another and that only discrete, as opposed to continuous, variations count as alternative states of an inheritance
system. Gray argues that:

Extragenetic changes can also be piecemeal and incremental. Just as natural selection can favor combinations of genes at different loci, so selection may favor com-

binations of endosymbionts. Quantitative variations in cytoplasmic factors, nest design, and habitat preferences could also all be passed on extragenetically. Thus, although combinations of these factors are not unlimited, they can be quite large enough to allow a fine-grained response to selection. (Gray 2001: 197)

I have considered three arguments designed to show that epigenetic inheritance has only a marginal role in evolution. The first, the claim that epigenetic inheritance is too unstable to allow cumulative selection of its products, was inconclusive, pointing only to the need for empirical investigation of the actual properties of epigenetic inheritance systems. The other two arguments simply devised inappropriate criteria against which to assess epigenetic inheritance, requiring that it have a significant evolutionary role not in the actual world, in which epigenetic inheritance systems exist as part of a larger developmental system, but in imaginary scenarios in which evolution must proceed using one, decoupled epigenetic inheritance system at a time. These two arguments may show that epigenetic inheritance systems could not have evolutionary significance in the absence of the genetic inheritance system, but that is not at issue. The real evolutionary significance of epigenetic inheritance remains to be determined.

6   Niche Construction and Evolution

Richard Lewontin's critique of the "lock and key" model of adaptation is well known (Lewontin 1982, 1983). In that metaphorical conception of natural selection, adaptations are solutions (keys) to the problems posed by the environment (locks). Organisms are adapted to their ways of life because they have evolved to fit those ways of life. In place of this traditional metaphor, Lewontin suggested a metaphor of construction. Organisms and their ecological niches are co-constructing and codefining. Organisms both physically shape their environments (co-construction) and determine which factors in the external environment are relevant to their evolution (codefinition), thus assembling some subset of the biotic and abiotic factors in their physical environment into a niche. Organisms are adapted to their ways of life because organisms and their way of life were constructed for (and by) one another.

The most detailed attempt to develop the metaphor of construction into a program of actual biological research is that of F. J. Odling-Smee and his collaborators (Laland, Odling-Smee, and Feldman 2001; Odling-Smee

1988, 1996; Odling-Smee, Laland, and Feldman 1996). The current prominence of the term "niche construction" is due to this group. Odling-Smee's treatment differs significantly from Lewontin's in that he is concerned not to represent the organism-environment system as a closed system. It is well known that in Australian eucalypt forests, which require frequent bushfires to maintain themselves, and where the trees have many features that make bushfires more prevalent, the trees themselves have co-evolved with the bush-fire prone landscape in which they thrive. Nevertheless, the evolution of this organism-environment system was exogenously driven by the progressive drying of the Australian continent. Organisms do, of course, feel the impact of changes in the environment in its traditional sense of their total biotic and abiotic surroundings, but they experience these impacts via the environment as it appears in relation to them, and thus different lineages experience "the same changes" quite differently. Odling-Smee tries to respect this situation by assigning separate roles to the environment of a particular lineage of organisms and what he calls the "universal physical environment." The former, organism-referent description of the environment is the source of evolutionary pressures on that organism, and the organism is the source of niche-constructing pressures on that environment. The latter, universal physical environment is a source of exogenous change in the organism's environment.

Robert Brandon's theory of the role of the environment in adaptation is a useful complement to Lewontin and Odling-Smee's ideas. Brandon distinguishes not two but three senses of "environment" (Brandon 1990). His "external environment" corresponds to Odling-Smee's universal, physical environment. All organisms in a particular region of space and time share one external environment. The "ecological environment," however, must be described with reference to a particular evolving lineage. It consists of those environmental parameters whose value affects the reproductive output of members of the lineage. The idea that only these parameters are part of the organism's niche corresponds to Lewontin's claim that organisms and niches are codefining. Finally, the "selective environment" is that part of the ecological environment which *differentially* affects the reproductive output of variant forms in the evolving lineage. It is in this last sense of "environment" that the environment contains the sources of adaptive evolutionary pressures on the lineage. Brandon has used these ideas in his own exploration of organism-environment coevolution (Brandon and Antonovics 1996). Organisms modify the selective and ecological environments in numerous ways that can potentially influence their evolution. Only some of these modifications of the selective and ecological environments also constitute modifications of the external environment (actual co-construction rather than codefinition), but whether they do so is unimportant when determining their role in the future evolution of the organism-environment system. This is why the simple notion of the "external" or "universal physical" environment is inadequate for understanding organism-environment relationships. Many changes in the external environment do not constitute change from the point of view of the organism and, conversely, an organism can transform its environment without actually changing the universal physical environment (by becoming arboreal or troglobytic, for example). It is what Brandon calls the ecological environment and Lewontin calls an "organism-referent description of the environment" that defines what counts as a "change" in the environment for that organism.

The phenomena of epigenetic inheritance and niche-construction are closely related. Both the co-constructing and codefining relationships between organisms and their environments are frequently mediated by epigenetic inheritance. Inheritance mechanisms such as habitat and host imprinting create associations between an evolving lineage and one aspect rather than another of the external environment, defining an ecological environment out of that wider set of available environmental parameters. The actual, physical construction of aspects of the niche is an epigenetic inheritance mechanism in its own right: the inheritance by the offspring generation of modifications made to the environment by the parental generation. The recognition of the importance of niche construction in evolution thus reinforces the conclusions of sections 4 and 5, that no Baldwin effects are necessary to allow causal relationships between parent and offspring other than those through the germ line to be of evolutionary significance.

7   Conclusion

I have suggested that the role of the Baldwin effect in Baldwin's own biological thought was as an addendum to a more general theory of social heredity and its possible impact on biological heredity. Baldwin conceived social heredity as an alternative, parallel causal channel creating resemblance between parent and offspring—what we would now call an epigenetic inheritance system. He also understood that social heredity could alter the ecological forces impinging on the organism as a whole, and thus affect the fate of the biological hereditary material—an idea now referred to as niche construction. Even in his period of greatest enthusiasm for the Baldwin effect, he saw that process as only one way in which social heredity could affect the future of biological heredity. The other way in which this could occur—niche construction—is there right alongside the Baldwin effect in "A New Factor in Evolution." In a limited way and in the context of a very dated, Edwardian, progressive conception of the evolutionary process as a whole, Baldwin anticipated these contemporary "new factors" in evolution.

I have suggested that biologists have continued to show interest in the Baldwin effect because of the conviction that unless epigenetic inheritance can leave traces in DNA, it cannot make a significant contribution on an evolutionary timescale. But I have argued that this conviction is mistaken and that the significance of epigenetic inheritance is, at the very least, an open empirical question (see also Moore, chap. 7, this volume). Baldwin effects are very likely not necessary for epigenetic inheritance and niche construction to play a significant role in evolution. Nor would the existence of Baldwin effects guarantee those two processes a significant role. If Baldwin effects occur, there is, as Simpson argued, no reason to suppose that they are a major mechanism of evolutionary change. Baldwin effects are thus of limited interest and should not be allowed to distract attention from the more general significance of epigenetic inheritance and niche construction.

Notes

1. This issue of *American Naturalist* in the University of Pittsburgh library having succumbed to the usual fate of acid-rich Victorian paper, citations are to the centenary reprint.

2. Citations are to the second edition, of which Baldwin remarks in the preface that he has made "minor corrections throughout. The only important alteration is to be found in the tables (I. and II.) on p. 52." In the third edition, Baldwin did "emend the text and sprinkle in footnotes which urged the reader to find the new factor in the original text" (Richards 1987: 489).

3. This reading is reinforced by the fact that in his exchange with Cope in *American Naturalist,* Baldwin describes Cope's neo-Lamarckian view of the origin of adaptive behavior in the individual, using exactly the same language. Cope's view is "the doctrine of the special creation of ontogenetic adaptations by consciousness," and contrasts unfavorably with Baldwin's own Darwinian theory of the "organic selection" of adaptive behaviors in the individual (Baldwin 1896c: 427).

4. Page references are to the fourth edition. Chapter 2, "The Social Person," was not substantially revised in these later editions. As Baldwin notes in the prefaces to these later editions, he is publishing new books all the time, so it is not important to revise the old ones to keep up with his changing views (although he is gratified they are still being reprinted).

5. This example occurs elsewhere in Baldwin's writing. In *Social and Ethical Interpretations,* he enlarges on it and adds that this repugnance is not shared by "Northern whites" (Baldwin 1906: 87–88). It is hard not to read these passages in the light of the fact that Baldwin—a Southerner—was dismissed from the Johns Hopkins University in 1908 after being detained in a police raid on "a black house of prostitution in Baltimore" (Richards 1987, 496).

6. Huxley himself may not have held the view usually attributed to him (Campbell 2001).

References

Baldwin, J. M. (1895). *Mental Development in the Race and the Child: Methods and Processes.* London: Macmillan.

Baldwin, J. M. (1896a). A new factor in evolution. *American Naturalist* 30 (June, July): 441–451, 536–553.

Baldwin, J. M. (1896b). Heredity and instinct. *Science* 3 (March 20 and April 10): 438–441, 558–561.

Baldwin, J. M. (1896c). Physical and social heredity. *American Naturalist* 30 (May): 422–428.

Baldwin, J. M. (1897). *Social and Ethical Interpretations in Mental Development: A Study in Social Psychology.* London: Macmillan.

Baldwin, J. M. (1897a). Organic selection. *Nature* 55 (April 15): 558.

Baldwin, J. M. (1897b). Organic selection. *Science* 5 (April 23): 634–636.

Baldwin, J. M. (1900). *Mental Development in the Race and the Child: Methods and Processes,* second edition. London: Macmillan.

Baldwin, J. M. (1902). *Development and Evolution.* New York: Macmillan.

Baldwin, J. M. (1906). *Social and Ethical Interpretations in Mental Development: A Study in Social Psychology,* fourth edition. London: Macmillan.

Baldwin, J. M. (1906–1911). *Thoughts and Things or Genetic Logic,* vols. 1–3. London: Swann Sonnenschein.

Baldwin, J. M. (1909). *Darwin and the Humanities.* Baltimore, Md.: Review Publishing.

Baldwin, J. M. (1996). A new factor in evolution. In R. K. Belew and M. Mitchell (eds.), *Adaptive Individuals in Evolving Populations,* pp. 59–80. Reading, Mass.: Addison-Wesley.

Brandon, R. (1990). *Adaptation and Environment.* Princeton, N.J.: Princeton University Press.

Brandon, R. and J. Antonovics (1996). The coevolution of organism and environment. In R. Brandon (ed.), *Concepts and Methods in Evolutionary Biology,* pp. 161–178. Cambridge: Cambridge University Press.

Campbell, N. (2001). What was Huxley's epiphenomenalism? *Biology and Philosophy* 16(3): 357–375.

Cope, E. D. (1896). Observations on Prof. Baldwin's reply. *American Zoologist* 30 (May): 428–430.

Dawkins, R. (1982). *The Extended Phenotype.* New York: Freeman.

Deacon, T. W. (1997). *The Symbolic Species: The Co-evolution of Language and the Brain.* New York: W.W. Norton.

Gray, R. D. (2001). Selfish genes or developmental systems? In R. S. Singh, C. B. Krimbas, D. B. Paul, and J. Beatty (eds.), *Thinking about Evolution: Historical, Philosophical, and Political Perspectives,* pp. 184–207. Cambridge: Cambridge University Press.

Griesemer, J. R. and W. C. Wimsatt (1989). Picturing Weismannism: A case sudy of conceptual evolution. In M. Ruse (ed.), *What the Philosophy of Biology Is,* pp. 75–137. Dordecht: Kluwer.

Griffiths, P. E. (2001). Genetic information: A metaphor in search of a theory. *Philosophy of Science* 68(3): 394–412.

Keller, L. and K. G. Ross (1993). Phenotypic plasticity and "cultural transmission" of alternative social organisations in the fire ant *solenopsis invicta. Behavioural Ecology and Sociobiology* 33: 121–129.

Koestler, A. (1972). *The Case of the Midwife Toad.* New York: Random House.

Laland, K. N., F. J. Odling-Smee, and M. W. Feldman (2001). Niche construction, ecological inheritance, and cycles of contingency in evolution. In S. Oyama, P. E. Griffiths, and R. D. Gray (eds.), *Cycles of Contingency: Developmental Systems and Evolution,* pp. 117–126. Cambridge, Mass.: MIT Press.

Lewontin, R. C. (1982). Organism and environment. In H. Plotkin (ed.), *Learning, Development, Culture,* pp. 151–170. New York: John Wiley.

Lewontin, R. C. (1983). Gene, organism, and environment. In D. S. Bendall (ed.), *Evolution: From Molecules to Man,* pp. 273–285. Cambridge: Cambridge University Press.

Lynch, A. and A. J. Baker (1986). Congruence of morphological and cultural evolution in Atlantic island chaffinch populations. *Canadian Journal of Zoology* 64: 1576–1580.

Maynard Smith, J. (2000). The concept of information in biology. *Philosophy of Science* 67(2): 177–194.

Maynard Smith, J. and E. Szathmáry (1995). *The Major Transitions in Evolution.* Oxford, New York, Heidelberg: W. H. Freeman.

Odling-Smee, F. J. (1988). Niche-constructing phenotypes. In H. C. Plotkin (ed.), *The Role of Behavior in Evolution,* pp. 73–132. Cambridge, Mass.: MIT Press.

Odling-Smee, F. J. (1996). Niche-construction, genetic evolution, and cultural change. *Behavioural Processes* 35: 196–205.

Odling-Smee, F. J., K. N. Laland, and F. W. Feldman (1996). Niche construction. *American Naturalist* 147(4): 641–648.

Richards, R. J. (1987). *Darwin and the Emergence of Evolutionary Theories of Mind and Behavior.* Chicago: The University of Chicago Press.

Ruse, M. (1996). *Monad to Man: The Concept of Progress in Evolutionary Biology.* Cambridge, Mass.: Harvard University Press.

Shaw, G. B. (1939). *Back to Methuselah (A Metabiological Pentateuch).* New York: The Limited Editions Club.

Simpson, G. G. (1953). The Baldwin effect. *Evolution* 7 (June): 110–117.

Simpson, G. G. (1996). The Baldwin effect. In R. K. Belew and M. Mitchell (eds.), *Adaptive Individuals in Evolving Populations.* Reading, Mass.: Addison-Wesley.

Smith, D. (2000). Mind over matter. *Sydney Morning Herald,* May 20, p. 7s.

Sterelny, K. (2001). Niche construction, developmental systems, and the extended replicator. In S. Oyama, P. E. Griffiths, and R. D. Gray (eds.), *Cycles of Contingency: Developmental Systems and Evolution,* pp. 333–349. Cambridge, Mass.: MIT Press.

Whitehead, H. (1998). Cultural selection and genetic diversity in matrilineal whales. *Science* 282: 1708–1711.

Whiten, A., J. Goodall, W. C. McGrew, T. Nishida, V. Reynolds, Y. Sugiyama, C. E. G. Tutin, R. W. Wrangham, and C. Boes (1999). Culture in chimpanzees. *Nature* 399: 682–685.

III

Beyond Baldwinism

11

The Baldwin Effect in the Age of Computation

Ruben R. Puentedura

1 Introduction—The Baldwin Effect

Baldwin (1896) introduced the notion that animals might, via plastic learning within their lifetimes, affect their subsequent evolutionary path in areas related to this plastic learning. Baldwin's proposal was not constructed as an exemplar of Lamarckian thought, but was rather designed as a viable alternative to it. Thus, the plastic learning involved is not incorporated directly into the germ line (à la Lamarck), but rather serves as an "in-life" crutch that allows animals that have learned a "good trick" to outcompete the others. While Baldwin clearly thought of his theory in terms of Mind as the source of plastic learning, it is generally applicable to scenarios invoking only a rudiment of neural thought—see, for instance Dennett (1995)—and in fact could be reasonably applicable to scenarios invoking no neural interaction at all, but only a modicum of in-lifetime behavioral plasticity. I will leave a more detailed description of the general mechanism of the Baldwin effect to other authors in this volume (see, for instance, Paul E. Griffiths's chapter in this volume). The specifics of one nonbiological incarnation of the Baldwin effect—the computational model developed by Hinton and Nowlan (1987)—will instead be the focus of this essay. The rationale for the interest in computational models such as this one is twofold: first, given the difficulty of determining unequivocally the presence of the Baldwin effect in biological systems (Waddington 1942), it is desirable to provide a model that can be investigated directly and might hence shed some light on the actual activities of its biological counterparts. Second, the Baldwin effect may in fact provide a tool that may prove of considerable use in computer modeling. Genetic algorithms on their own having proven in many cases somewhat disappointing, a mechanism that would allow a neural network component to aid the genetic algorithm's evolutionary path would indeed be warmly welcomed.

2   The Hinton and Nowlan Model

The task defined in the model is the following: start out with a string containing twenty loci, all set to 1: this will provide a "fitness target." Next, create a population of 1000 strings (the "organisms"), all containing twenty loci, all set at random to either 1 or 0. Compare the strings to the fitness target—if any string matches the target exactly, assign it a fitness value of 20; otherwise, assign it a fitness of 1. Assign a probability of reproduction to the organisms based upon their fitness value (i.e., the higher the fitness value, the greater the reproductive probability), then create a new generation by random crossover among the fitter organisms. Repeat the process, until a majority of the population has found the target.

Clearly, the problem is insoluble in any reasonable fashion by this mechanism—the space to be explored yields only $1/2^{20}$ as the probability of a correct string match for any given randomly selected string, a negligible percentage. However, now assume that the "digital critter" is allowed to apply an in-lifetime "guessing approach" to some of the locations. The coding used by Hinton and Nowlan takes the form:

1: definitely set

0: definitely not set

?: available to guessing

In other words, locations with a ? in them allow for a set of lifetime guesses by the organism (with a lifetime set by Hinton and Nowlan at 1000 tries) at the correct fitness target. A possible coding gene for the organism then looks like:

1100?11?001??1?0?110

Hinton and Nowlan set the average distribution of 1s, 0s, and ?s in the starting population at 25 percent, 25 percent, and 50 percent, respectively. Furthermore, to go along with this "plastic genome," matching to the fitness target also needs to be adjusted. The fitness is now given by a function F, where

$$F = 1 + 19 \cdot n/1000$$

and n is the number of trials remaining (out of 1000) for a particular organism after it stumbles upon the correct result. As can be readily seen, organisms that start out with all twenty locations set to 1 have a fitness of 20, while those with any location set to 0 have a fitness of 1. Organisms with a number q of locations in their genome set to ? and all other locations set to 1 have a probability p of matching the string in any given round given by:

$$p = 1/2^q$$

Remarkably, with this change, the task goes from being impossible to being readily achievable in a few generations. The result of a standard run of this model is depicted in figure 11.1a—as can be seen, the solution is reached in roughly 15 generations.

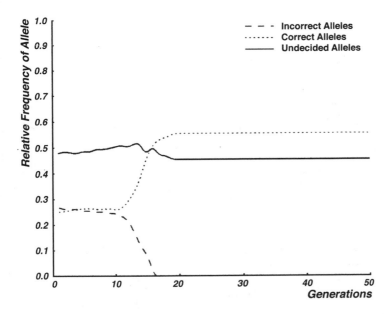

Figure 11.1a
The frequency in the population of "correct" (1) alleles rises sharply at around the 15th generation, indicating that a partial solution has been found; the frequency of "incorrect" (0) alleles drops sharply at this same point, while that of "undecided" alleles drops only slightly, indicating that the "correctness" is achieved primarily at the expense of the absolutely incorrect alleles, rather than the undecided ones. Note that: $\text{Freq}_1 + \text{Freq}_0 + \text{Freq}_? = 1$. (From Hinton and Nowlan 1987.)

3   What Does This Mean?

The Hinton and Nowlan model clearly establishes that, under some very specific and stringent limitations, the Baldwin effect can be observed in computational systems. The task, clearly impossible under the conditions originally stated for the system, becomes eminently possible. This is done via a "smoothing" of the evolutionary landscape: the plasticity transforms the single spike into a gentler curve, as shown in figure 11.1b.

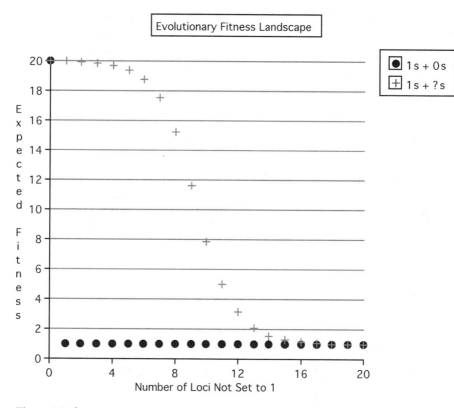

Figure 11.1b
The expected fitness for the nonguessing setup is a single sharp spike, corresponding to all 20 loci being correctly set. By contrast, the probabilistic element introduced by the guessing loci allows for reasonably high fitness results for up to about 10 loci being set to ?.

4   What Does It Not Mean?

Some aspects of the original model have been overinterpreted, and given far too much prominence. By a long shot, the worst of these is the question of what have been called the "persistent question marks" (Harvey 1993). This refers to the fact that, as can be seen in the diagram above, the fitness "levels off" before all the question marks have been replaced by ones. A common misreading of this aspect of the model is that this implies that the Baldwin effect cannot, in fact, yield the global optimum (i.e., a population with all genetic loci set to 1) for the problem, a misinterpretation further confused by some erroneous results of Belew (1989). As pointed out by Harvey (1993), the observed leveling off is nothing more than the result of "hitchhiking" in the genome with a limited population. Consider the fact that no mutation at all is allowed in the Hinton and Nowlan model; therefore, in a population where all 1000 members have a specific locus with ? in it, there is no possibility that it will be replaced by a 1. A simple probabilistic analysis reveals that this would not be the result of an aberrant run, and in fact runs such as this are guaranteed to be the norm (again, for the details, see Harvey 1993). Adding even a minute amount of mutational probability quickly rectifies the situation.

5   Critiques and Responses

Interestingly, some possible critiques of the model have merited little or no serious commentary in the literature. In the remainder of this paper, I will deal with three of these problems: the coupled genome problem, the autonomous learning function problem, and the teleological problem.

6   The Coupled Genome Problem

The coding used by Hinton and Nowlan suffers from one significant problem in terms of its applicability to the broader biological picture: the allele that codes for plasticity (?) is a replacement for the allele that codes for a fixed location (1 or 0). In other words, one necessarily replaces the other. This is a weak aspect of the model: it militates against the likelihood that

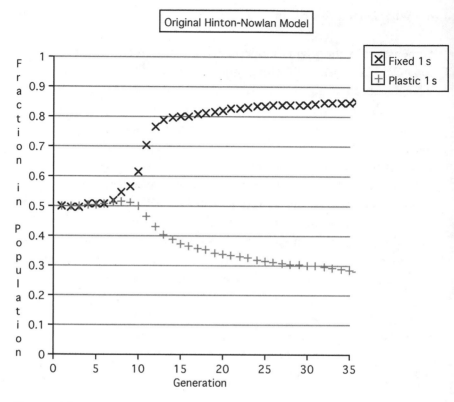

Figure 11.2a
The curves shown here are akin to those displayed above in the original Hinton and Nowlan experiment; for exact interpretation purposes, it should be noted that some of the "fixed" 1s here are overlaid with "plastic" 1s. The exact frequencies observed in this run are somewhat different from those obtained by Hinton and Nowlan, but fully compatible with those subsequently obtained by Harvey (1993).

this would be a mechanism of significant biological import—consider that this would mean that the key gene for the "good trick" learning potential in the organism's lifetime, and the "hard-coded" version would have to be one and the same. Fortunately, this is an easily soluble problem. We adopt the following "two gene" model:

Fixed location gene: 20 sites, all 1 or 0

Plasticity gene: 20 sites, all 1 (plastic) or 0 (fixed)

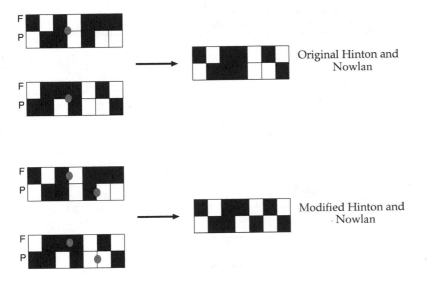

Original Hinton and Nowlan

Modified Hinton and Nowlan

Figure 11.2b
The dots represent the crossover point for the creation of a "child" gene from two parents; in this diagram we assume the first part of the child gene comes from the top "parent," the second part from the bottom one. In the original Hinton and Nowlan model, the crossover point for both the fixed (F) and plastic (P) genes is forced to be the same, since plastic genes are not autonomous from fixed genes; in the modified model, this restriction is lifted.

This new coding can easily be mapped onto the old Hinton and Nowlan model:

Fixed: 1101101...

Plastic: 1001110...

Hinton and Nowlan: ?10???1...

Note that, when the crossover location in both genes is forced to be the same, and the percentage of ones in each gene is set to 50 percent, we recover the original Hinton-Nowlan model. A run with this constraint is illustrated in figure 11.2a. However, if we loosen this constraint—in other words, if we allow the two crossover points to vary independently, we obtain a new model, not subject to the preceding critique. Again, figure 11.2b should help clarify this point. It is gratifying to note that the results for a typical run for this model are akin to those already noted for the original Hinton and Nowlan model, as shown in figure 11.2c.

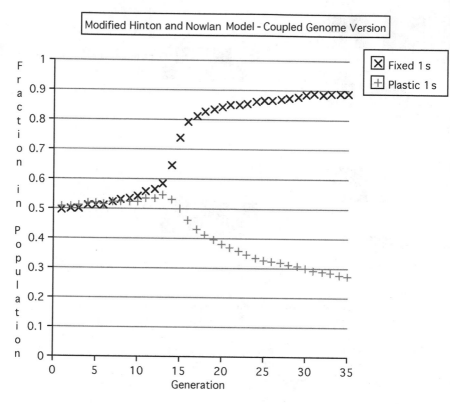

Figure 11.2c
While the onset of the sharp rise in the fraction of fixed 1s in the population is delayed (by about 5 generations) from that observed in the original Hinton and Nowlan model, the overall curve profiles, and hence conclusions, are essentially similar.

7   The Autonomous Learning Function Problem

It can be argued that the Hinton and Nowlan model may have made the search task of its critter a little too easy by making the learning function too autonomous. In other words, the fact that an independent coin toss occurs for each ?-locus, regardless of the "hard-coded" aspects of other gene sites, indicates that the hard-coding has no effect at all on the plastic behavior— again, not that likely an assumption if we would like to apply our results to the biological domain. Fortunately, the modification from the preceding

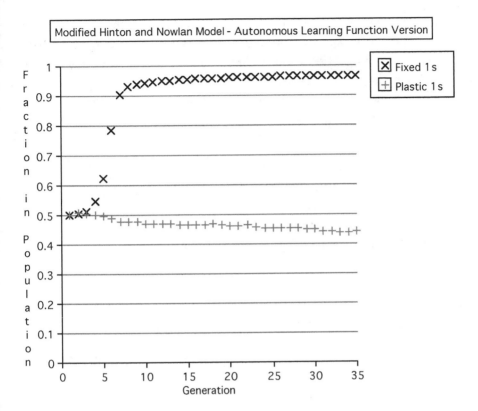

Figure 11.3
Again, the sharp rise in the population of fixed 1s is observed. Two interesting features differ from the Hinton and Nowlan model: first, the onset of the sharp rise in the population of fixed 1s occurs about 5 generations earlier than in the original model, and reaches higher values earlier. Second, the fraction of plastic 1s drops off at a slower rate than in the original model. These two observations, taken together, indicate that there is a higher evolutionary premium for having "good" underlying fixed behavior in this model, but less of a penalty for retaining plasticity.

step allows us to sidestep this difficulty. We now make the dependence of the fixed/plastic genes to be probabilistic, rather than deterministic (in fashion akin to Turney 1997). That is, loci in the plastic gene will not determine uniquely the resulting behavior, but will rather interact probabilistically with the underlying fixed gene according to the following table:

If locus in plastic gene is off -> use the unmodified original fixed gene when determining fitness.

If locus in plastic gene is on -> 50 percent of the time "flip a coin," 50 percent of the time use the unmodified original fixed gene when determining fitness.

It is rewarding to report that the results of the basic model survive this modification, as can be seen in the sample run shown in figure 11.3.

8   The Teleological Problem

Even after the preceding modifications have been incorporated into it, it can be argued that the Hinton and Nowlan model is unrealistic in a different fashion. To a very large extent, one of the key aspects of the problem at hand is the length of the string to be determined. By hard coding the length of their original gene at 20 loci—identical to the length of the string to be found—Hinton and Nowlan essentially predefined this aspect of the question in a fashion that can only be called teleological. Putting the question in biological terms, how would the organism conveniently know beforehand that the length of its plastic and fixed genes should be "just right" for a question it has not even encountered yet? Fortunately, the preceding modifications can be adapted to deal with this question. We now allow our dual genes to now vary independently in length such that they can both be too short (in which case the organism will always fail to find an answer), just right, or too long (in which case the organism may find an answer, but it will carry "junk" unused baggage in its genome). Yet again, the basic model proves fundamentally stable. While there are limits to how much this particular variation may be pushed—fixed genes of length one are clearly outside the bound of anything that could reasonably work—it is nonetheless gratifying to report that the basic model survives even this. As can be seen in the sample run in figure 11.4, a 20 percent variation still allows for reasonable goal-achievement by our digital critters.

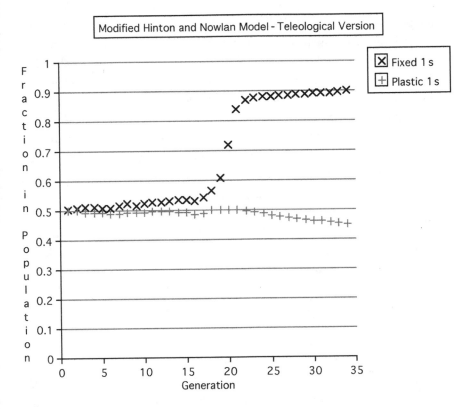

Figure 11.4
The familiar sharp rise is still present here, albeit with an onset delayed by about 10 generations, and a slower drop-off in the plasticity fraction. This latter point may be interpreted as indicating an even more significant role for plasticity in providing a good search path in the context of the increased difficulty of this problem.

9   Issues Still Ahead

From my expansion of the original Hinton and Nowlan model, it can be seen that many basic questions can be successfully answered without doing violence to the results or simplicity of the model. Simple extensions and uses of the model in computational questions are therefore both safe and desirable. However, in terms of what the results mean for biological systems, I believe a fundamental question is yet to be answered. Thus far, the model has operated on a one-dimensional landscape, with strict homology between the plastic and fixed universes. Furthermore, the distance between genotype and phenotype in the model is minimal. In a biological system, this twin situation is much less likely to arise. It may be indeed at the heart of Waddington's canalization phenomena (Waddington 1942), but probably not elsewhere. In particular, it would be desirable to have a multidimensional problem landscape that would allow for the fixed/plastic aspects to scan directions of exploration that are not strictly collinear, like the one shown in figure 11.5a. A few models have been proposed that attempt to deal with this, but unfortunately it is not clear that any of them has quite risen to the challenge. The work done, among others, by Ackley and Littman (1992), Parisi, Nolfi, and Cecconi (1992), Menczer and Belew (1996), and Nolfi, Elman, and Parisi (1994) sets its digital critters the task of surviving in a two-dimensional landscape, riddled with sources of food and poison. In each "animat" a set of plastic neurons dedicated to the predictive evaluation/determination of actions on the landscape based on a set of sensory inputs is coupled to a genetically determined set of parameters, describable as tendencies/goals (see fig. 11.5b). Reproductive fitness is not determined by a fixed fitness function, but rather is determined by the "energy level" of the animat and its survival capacity. These models generally show poor results when animats lack the capacity to learn plastically in their lifetime, far better results when animats can learn plastically, but lack any form of genetic evolution, and (sometimes) very modest improvements over this latter category when learning is coupled to evolution (see fig. 11.5c). From these results, coupled to the greater observed variability in the learning gene when the third case is compared to the second, many authors have designated this a "better" example of the Baldwin effect than the Hinton and Nowlan model (see, for instance, Mitchell 1996). However, as Harvey (1997) points out, there exist significant flaws in considering this as a Baldwin effect model: two separate tasks (plastic and fixed) are required; the plastic and fixed tasks are completely uncorrelated, and the plastic "good trick" is not assimilated into the genome; at-birth performance of the animat is not improved; too much learning causes the effect to disappear. Harvey claims a different effect, which he terms "Another New Factor (ANF)," is responsible for the observed results here, one which he attributes to the recovery of weight perturbations in a neural network via the learning of uncorrelated tasks. This latter element of Harvey's interpretation has recently been

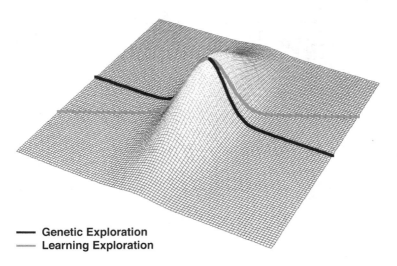

—— **Genetic Exploration**
—— **Learning Exploration**

Figure 11.5a
The diagram illustrates a two-dimensional analogue of figure 11.1b above. The dark line indicates the more sharply spiked path available to genetic exploration, while the white line indicates the more softly curved path accessible to learning exploration. The problem to be solved is assumed to be essentially the same, but the exploratory approaches are partially different.

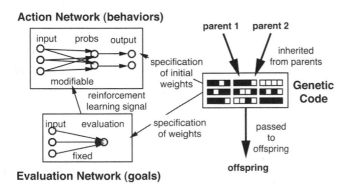

Figure 11.5b
A schematic diagram of the Ackley-Littman model. The "action network" is modifiable within the lifetime of the animat, and hence corresponds to the learning component, while the "evaluation network" is modifiable only genetically via reproduction. (From Ackley and Littman 1992.)

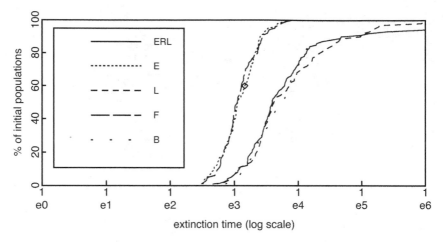

ERL = Evolution Plus Learning
E = Evolution Only
L = Learning Only
F = Fixed Random Weights
B = Random (Brownian) Movements

Figure 11.5c
Ackley and Littman's results. The sooner a population goes extinct, the less fit it is. Note that there is roughly an order of magnitude in difference between the evolution-only results and the learning-only and learning plus evolution results, but only very small differences between these latter two. (From Ackley and Littman 1992.)

challenged by Nolfi (2000), although his results in no way reestablish the observed effect as being Baldwinian in nature.

Thus, the question of a generalized computational Baldwin effect is still very much open. Further work in this field will require careful model definition, in order to avoid having the peculiarities of specific neural network setups (such as are encountered in the training of feedforward neural nets) swamp out any potential observation of the Baldwin effect. A paper by Giles Mayley (1997) has two important implications in terms of any future research in this area. First, any future model must clearly establish the role of the cost of learning within it as a source of evolutionary pressure for genetic assimilation. Second, the existence of correlation between learned/innate distances in phenotypic space and learned/innate distances in genotypic space must also be clearly parametrized, since it defines the path by which assimilation might occur. It is clear that we have so far only scratched the surface of the understanding that the age of computation might bring to the Baldwin effect.

Acknowledgments

My thanks go to Bruce Weber and David Depew for inviting me to participate in the current volume. Also, my thanks go to Stacy D. Evans for her helpful suggestions and sharp eye when reading early drafts of this essay—any remaining awkward spots are, needless to say, my responsibility alone. Finally, I would like to acknowledge the generous support of my colleagues and Bennington College.

References

Ackley, D. and M. Littman (1992). Interaction between learning and evolution. In C. Langton (ed.), *Artificial Life II*. Reading, Mass.: Addison-Wesley.

Baldwin, J. M. (1896). A new factor in evolution. *American Naturalist* 30: 441–451, 536–553.

Belew, R. K. (1989). When both individuals and populations search. In J. D. Schaffer (ed.), *Proceedings of the Third International Conference on Genetic Algorithms*. San Mateo, Calif.: Morgan Kaufmann.

Dennett, D. C. (1995). *Darwin's Dangerous Idea*. New York: Simon and Schuster.

Griffiths, P. E. (2002). Beyond the Baldwin effect: James Mark Baldwin's social heredity, epigenetic inheritance, and niche-construction. In D. J. Depew and B. H. Weber (eds.), *Evolution and Learning*. Cambridge, Mass.: MIT Press.

Harvey, I. (1993). The puzzle of the persistent question marks: A case study of genetic drift. In S. Forrest (ed.), *Proceedings of the Fifth International Conference on Genetic Algorithms, ICGA-93*. San Mateo, Calif.: Morgan Kaufmann.

Harvey, I. (1997). Is there another new factor in evolution? *Evolutionary Computation* 4 (3): 313–329.

Hinton, G. E. and S. J. Nowlan. (1987). How learning can guide evolution. *Complex Systems* 1: 495–502.

Mayley, G. (1997). Landscapes, learning costs, and genetic assimilation. *Evolutionary Computation* 4(3): 213–234.

Menczer F. and R. K. Belew. (1996). Latent energy environments. In R. K. Belew and M. Mitchell (eds.), *Adaptive Individuals in Evolving Populations: Models and Algorithms*, SFI Studies in the Sciences of Complexity vol. 23. Reading, Mass.: Addison-Wesley.

Mitchell, M. (1996). *An Introduction to Genetic Algorithms*. Cambridge, Mass.: MIT Press.

Nolfi, S. (2000). How learning and evolution interact: The case of a learning task which differs from the evolutionary task. *Adaptive Behavior* 7(2): 231–236.

Nolfi, S., J. L. Elman, and D. Parisi. (1994). Learning and evolution in neural networks. *Adaptive Behavior* 3(1): 5–28.

Parisi, D., N. Nolfi, and F. Cecconi. (1992). Learning, behavior, and evolution. In C. Langton (ed.), *Artificial Life*. Reading, Mass.: Addison-Wesley.

Turney, P. (1997). How to shift bias: Lessons from the Baldwin effect. *Evolutionary Computation* 4(3): 271–295.

Waddington, C. H. (1942). Canalization of development and the inheritance of acquired characters. *Nature* 150: 563–565.

12

The Role of Predator-Induced Polyphenism in the Evolution of Cognition: A Baldwinian Speculation

Scott F. Gilbert

1 Development and the Baldwin Effect

Developmental biology is not often called upon to relate mind and body. However, the Baldwin effect almost demands that it be considered. The Baldwin effect (Baldwin 1896) was formulated to explain how psychological characteristics that made an individual more fit in a particular environment could be fixed in the genome. One way of restating this (see Marcos 2000) is to say that the greater the ability of an individual to adapt to external conditions, the greater its fitness (i.e., the production of progeny). This ability, which was originally a physiological response to particular conditions, will eventually be inherited even if the original initiating conditions are no longer present. Whereas Baldwin believed that a single mutation could transfer the inducing signal from the environment to the genotype, Ivan Schmalhausen and Conrad Waddington found that the transfer of competence from an environmental inducer to an internal inducer could also arise through the cryptic variation already present in the population. Waddington (1953, 1956) called this transfer "genetic assimilation."

The first tenet of the Baldwin effect and genetic assimilation is phenotypic plasticity. This idea that environment can induce phenotypic variation is now very well established. Reaction norms, dietary polyphenisms, seasonal polyphenisms, and predator-induced polyphenisms have become more familiar to biologists, especially as life history strategies research has begun to enter developmental biology (Gilbert 1997, 2001; Schlicting and Pigliucci 1998; Tollrian and Harvell 1998). Moreover, environmentally regulated gene expression has now been demonstrated. Physical stress, for instance, has been known to effect bone density, both positively and negatively. It is now known that physical load activates certain osteoblast genes involved in increasing bone mass (Sato et al. 1999; Nomura and Takano-Yamamoto 2000; Zaman et al. 2000), and weightlessness downregulates the genes involved in maintaining bone density (Hammond et al. 2000; Wassersug 2000). Similarly, genes for erythropoietin and angiogenetic factors (which generate more blood cells and blood vessels) are activated by low oxygen pressure (Brunn et al. 1998; Wenger et al. 1998).

The second tenet of the Baldwin effect and genetic assimilation—that environmental stimuli can become replaced by embryological inducers—is now being shown on a molecular level as well. This has been demonstrated experimentally by numerous researchers including Waddington (1953, 1956, 1957), Ho et al. (1983), and Matsuda (1982, 1987). Waddington (1953), for instance, found that in certain strains of wild-type *Drosophila melanogaster*, heat shock of 40°C during the pupal period caused disruptions in the posterior wing crossvein. Two selection regimens were followed, one where the aberrant flies were bred to one another, and another where the non-aberrant flies were bred to one another. By generation 14, in the crossveinless-selection line, some crossveinless individuals were found even if they did not treat the pupae. More were found in each succeeding generation. A response (and not necessarily an adaptive one) induced by the environment could be assimilated into the genotype. A similar situation was seen when ether shock caused a phenocopy of the bithorax mutation. Waddington's studies on bithorax phenocopy were confirmed and extended in 1996 by Gibson and Hogness. Ether exposure caused numerous flies to have the bithorax phenotype. Selection procedures then generated flies whose bithorax phenotypes were independent of ether exposure. Using polymerase chain reactions, they found that a large percentage of these phenotypes were due to at least four polymorphisms in the *Ultrabithorax* gene, the gene that naturally regulates the bithorax phenotype. Moreover, this example of genetic assimilation can be simulated by computer (Behera and Nanjundiah 1997). Genetic assimilation definitely can occur in the laboratory.

However, the idea that genetic assimilation occurs in nature remained controversial until Rutherford and Lindquist (1998) demonstrated a possible molecular mechanism for it. The abnormalities that they observed when the *Hsp83* was mutated, or the Hsp90 protein (the product of the

Hsp83 gene) inactivated, did not show simple Mendelian inheritance, but were the outcome of the interactions of several gene products. Selective breeding of the flies with the abnormalities led over a few generations to populations where 80–90 percent of the progeny had the mutant phenotype. Moreover, these mutants did not keep the *Hsp83* mutation. In other words, once the mutation in *Hsp83* allowed the cryptic mutants to become expressed, selective matings could retain the abnormal phenotype even in the absence of abnormal Hsp90. Hsp90 appears to be responsible for allowing mutations to accumulate but keeping them from being expressed until the environment changes. Each individual mutation might not change the phenotype, and mating would allow these mutations to be "collected" by members of the population. An environmental change (anything that might stress the cells) would thereby release the hidden phenotypic possibilities of a population. In other words, transient decreases in Hsp90 (resulting from its aiding stress-damaged proteins) would uncover preexisting genetic interactions that would produce morphological variations. Most of these morphological variations would probably be deleterious, but some might be selected for in the new environment. Continued selection will enable the fixation of adaptive physiological responses to the environment.

2   Predator-Induced Polyphenism and the Immune System

Baldwin's "new factor for evolution" was, of course, polyphenism. But Baldwin was more interested in the behavioral than in the physical phenotypes. Recent studies suggest that the two may not be all that different when we look at a particular type of developmental change that is induced by the external environment, predator-induced polyphenism. Predator-induced polyphenism is the ability of the developing organism to respond to the presence of a predator by changing its morphology and behavior in such a way as to make it less susceptible to predation. To demonstrate predator-induced polyphenisms, one has to show that the phenotypic change is caused by the predator (usually from kairomones, soluble chemicals released by the predator), and that the induced phenotypic modification increases the fitness of its bearers when the predator is present. For instance, juvenile *Daphnia* and other invertebrate species will alter their morphology when they develop in pond water in which their predators have been cultured. The water in which the predatory larvae of the dipteran *Chaoborus* have been cultured can induce a "neck spine" or a "helmet" during *Daphnia* development. These allow the *Daphnia* to escape from their predator more effectively. The induced *Daphnia* suffer lower mortality from these predators (Tollrian and Dodson 1999; Agrawal et al. 1999). This induction is even transferred to the parthenogenetic offspring of these *Daphnia*. Those *Daphnia* whose mothers had been exposed to predation cues were born with large helmets, even if the mothers had been transferred to water that lacked the caged predators. Thus, progeny born in a precarious environment (i.e., an environment where the kairomone concentration is high enough to induce helmet growth in their mothers) are thereby born with a defense against predation.

Predator-induced polyphenism has been documented throughout the animal kingdom, and it is seen in vertebrates, as well as in invertebrates. There are usually trade-offs that prevent the fixation of one phenotype as the best in all environments. Usually, in a predator-induced polyphenism, the induced phenotype can better survive the predator, but the phenotype may be less adaptive in other ways. In *Daphnia,* the production of helmets appears to lessen the amount of resources that can provision eggs (Riessen et al. 1984, 1992). If the induced phenotype were not only more successful in avoiding predators but also had no significant trade-offs, one might expect that it would become the dominant morph of the population. To have this happen, the more fit phenotype would have to be formed even in the absence of the environmental inducer. In other words, the same phenotype would be induced by internal rather than external factors. This replacement of external inducers by internal inducers would cause the Baldwin effect or genetic assimilation. However, what is usually inherited is the potential to respond if predation abounds.

In vertebrates, structural predator-induced polyphenisms are often accompanied by behavioral polyphenisms as well (Relyea 2001a,b). This has been documented in amphibians, where tadpoles exposed to the water in which predators have been swimming show not only different morphologies than they would have in predator-free water, but also show different predator-avoidance behaviors that go with these new structures. Interestingly, the behavioral phenotypes seem as plastic as the structural phenotypes, and different sets of behavioral and structural phenoypes are inherited together. It seems that Baldwin's prediction of behavioral plasticity was correct. What may have been a learned response for predator avoidance is now part of the genetic repertoire of the amphibian species.

Human predator-induced polyphenism is on a scale unimaginable in invertebrates. Our major predators, of course, are microbes, and our mechanism for predator-induced polyphenism is called the immune system. We respond to microbial predators through an immune system based on the clonal selection of lymphocytes that recognize specific predators and their products. Our immune system recognizes a particular microbe such as a cholera bacterium or a poliovirus by expanding precisely those lymphocytes that can defend the body against them. When a B-cell binds its foreign substance (the antigen), it enters a pathway that causes that B-cell to divide repeatedly and to differentiate into an antibody-secreting cell that secretes the same antibody that originally bound the antigen. Moreover, some of the descendants of that stimulated B-cell remain in the body as sentinels against further infection by the same microorganism. Thus, identical twins are not identical with respect to their immune systems. Their phenotypes (in this case, the lymphocytes in their lymph nodes and their ability to respond against an infectious microorganism) have been altered by the environment. Our immune system also provides transgenerational immunity against common predators. The IgG antibodies produced by our mothers during pregnancy can cross the placenta and give us passive immunity when we are born. In birds, a similar antibody is placed into the eggs. The cells of our respective immune systems are not specified solely by our genetic endowment. (Even the genes for the antibodies and T-cell receptors aren't present in the zygote.) Rather, experience is added to endowment. The environment, in this case, antigens, directs the development of our lymphocytes.

The immune network is a remarkable semiotic system wherein each molecular shape outside the body has a molecular image within the body (see Chernyak and Tauber 1992). Interestingly, the only things we are unable to recognize through the immune system is the body, itself. In order to recognize something as foreign (i.e., as an antigen), we must see this foreignness in the context of a self-protein. The protein receptors on our T-lymphocytes do not recognize foreignness out of context. Only when a foreign substance is bound to a particular class of self-proteins can it be recognized as being something from outside the body. Our immune systems recognized "altered self" better than "nonself."

Moreover, according to Matzinger (1994; 1998), the immune system has evolved not to discriminate self from nonself, but to recognize "danger" from "nondanger." This view looks less at the specificity of the immune response and more at inflammation and the context of antigen presentation, wherein a substance provided in one context elicits an immune response, while the same substance presented in a less dangerous context does not. It builds on the antigen presenting cell (which does not distinguish self from nonself) as the arbiter of the immune reaction, and Matzinger links this phylogenetically to the origins of the immune system in avoiding danger. This model has been seen as central for the re-evaluation of the evolutionary role of the immune system (Tauber 2000).

So humans have the ability to respond to predation by having evolved an immune system that is constantly in the state of developing. It has the capacity to change the population of lymphocytes based on which microbes are present in its environment; and this immune system may have arisen as a mechanism of predator-induced polyphenism to escape dangerous situations. This has important implications when we look at the body's other sensory network, the nervous system.

3   The Plastic Nervous System

So far, we have looked at the immune system as having evolved as a way of evading predators by changing development. I now wish to look at the nervous system in a similar light—as a system that monitors the external environment and that can adaptively alter its development in response to that environment. The plasticity of the nervous system has long been appreciated by behavioral biologists, and the relationship between neural plasticity and behavior has been the foundation of evolutionary hypotheses by Baldwin (1896; 1902) and more recently by Dennett (1991), and Gottlieb (1992). Molecular analyses have confirmed many of their intuitions.

There is extensive evidence that experience does create more neurons and neuronal connections. The cerebral cortices of young rats reared in stimulating environments are packed with more neurons, synapses, and dendrites than are found in rats reared in isolation (Turner and Greenough

1983). Even the adult brain is developing in response to new experiences. When adult rats learn to keep their balance on dowels, their cerebellar Purkinje cell neurons develop new synapses (Black et al. 1990). Studies on rats and mice indicate that environmental stimulation can increase the number of new neurons in the dentate gyrus (Kemperman et al. 1997; Gould et al. 1999; Praag et al. 1999), and it appears that these neurons formed in the adult rat hippocampus are associated with memory (Shors et al. 2001). Several thousands of these neurons are produced each day, and experience appears to protect them from apoptosis. These neurons appear to integrate into the adult brain where they respond to regionally specific cues and differentiate into site-specific types of neurons (Gage et al. 1995; Suhonen et al. 1996). Behavior can even modify the neuroanatomy, as shown by Breedlove's experiments (Breedlove 1997) on the SNB region of the spinal cord. Here, a specific behavior (copulation) altered the morphology of a particular region of the central nervous system.

Neuronal plasticity appears to be an extremely significant part of the human phenotype. If there is any important developmental trait that distinguishes us from the rest of the animal kingdom, it is the retention of the fetal neural growth rate. During early postnatal development, we add approximately 250,000 neurons per minute (Purves and Lichtman 1985). Apes' brains have a high rate of growth before birth. After birth, this rate slows greatly. In contrast, humans have rapid brain growth both before birth and for years thereafter (Martin 1990). By the time humans are adults, they are literally off the chart. The ratio of brain weight to body weight is similar for great apes and humans at birth. However, at adulthood, the human ratio is 3.5 that of apes (Bogin 1997). It is in this early postnatal stage that intervention can raise IQ (reviewed in Wickelgren 1999). This age also sees much of the maturation of the neural circuitry as determined by axon diameter and myelination.

The retention of the fetal neural growth rate gives us a remarkable number of new neurons, and we can only speculate that these will be utilized in ways that allow us to think and act. It is thought that this increase in neurons may (1) generate new modules (addressable sites) that can acquire new functions, (2) store new memories for use in thinking and forecasting possible scenarios, and (3) learn by interconnecting among themselves and with prenatally generated neurons. It should provide a new level of plasticity, one that adds experience to endowment; for the nervous system, like the other sensory network, the immune system, can develop according to environmental needs. Its repertoire is enormous, and we can each learn different skills and have different memories. Indeed, it is during this childhood stage that we learn how to learn. As Childs (1999) has concluded:

Extended exposure of a gradually maturing nervous system to experiences of a variable environment, together with the mental resiliency to continue to learn at all ages, is a recipe for the adaptive agility that has enabled human beings to live in all latitudes and so to exploit the earth's resources to construct civilizations and to be aesthetically creative.

We retain our plasticity into adulthood. Cortical reorganization is still possible in adults, and the "phantom limb" syndrome appears to be due to such "rewiring" of the nervous system (Flor et al. 1995; Davis et al. 1998; Montoya et al. 1998). Thus, the human brain is not an anatomical fait accompli at birth (or even after childhood). Like the immune system making new lymphocytes from its stem cells, so the nervous system keeps making new neurons. Purves and Lichtman (1985) have concluded, "The interaction of individual animals and their world continues to shape the nervous system throughout life in ways that could never have been programmed. Modification of the nervous system by experience is thus the last and most subtle developmental strategy."

4   The Nervous System and the Immune System

The immune system monitors the outside environment. It has the ability to recognize all possible shapes in the external world. It has memory such that once it has been exposed to an antigen, it "recalls" seeing it and can react to it more rapidly and efficiently. The same features, of course, are seen in the nervous system. I will propose (as others have before me) that the immune system and the nervous system are actually different components of an integrated sensory network. Hoffmeyer (1995) has seen the immune system as metaphor for the nervous system, taking the nervous system into the body. There is now evidence that the connections between the immune system and neural system are quite real.

First, classical "neuromodulators" of the nervous system also affect the immune system, while classical "cytokines" of the immune system also affect the nervous system. Several cytokines can function in the nervous system. Interleukin-2, the prototypical T-cell growth factor and immunoregulatory cytokine, can function as a neurotrophic factor (Petitto et al. 1999). The hypothalamus is rich in IL-2 receptors, and mice having genetic defects of IL-2 synthesis have reductions in hippocampal mossy fiber length and in spatial learning and memory (as assayed by the Morris water maze). Interleukin-1 receptors are also present in the hypothalamus, and IL-1 is able to produce several CNS effects, including fever and lethargy. IL-1 has also been implicated in the hippocampus, where it appears to play an inhibitory role in long-term potentiation (O'Connor and Coogan 1999; Hammond et al. 1999).

Conversely, several neuromodulators have important effects in the immune system. Since the 1980s, we have known that stress has important effects on the CNS. Physiological stress reduces lymphocyte number and function, and both ACTH and alpha-endorphins severely reduced T-cell-dependent immune responses (Keller et al. 1981; Johnson et al. 1982). Beta-endorphins appear to enhance the T-cell response (Gilman et al. 1982). These interactions between the neural and immune systems have given rise to new scientific disciplines (such as neuropsychopharmacology) as well as a burgeoning popular literature on how to stay healthy (as in Bernie and Siegel 1992). T-cells respond to serotonin by proliferating (Sibella-Arguelles 2001), and even nerve growth factor (NGF) appears to be involved as a cytokine (Solomon et al. 1998; Turrini et al. 2001). Eosinophils have NGF receptors and they make and store NGF. NGF can induce eosinophils to selectively release peroxidase (but not IL-6).

One remarkable phenomenon showing the integration of the immune and neural systems is the ability to use Pavlovian operant conditioning to induce allergies by odors. When paired with an audiovisual or odor cue, the injection of an allergen can induce an allergic immune response in rodents. After several paired trials of allergen and sensory cue, the allergic response can be triggered solely by the audiovisual or odor cue. The entire immune response has become regulated by the nervous system. The actual allergen is no longer needed (Metalnikov and Chorine 1926; Russell et al. 1984; Palermo-Neto and Guimaraes 2000).

Even the expression of major histocompatability genes can be regulated by neural activity. Carla Shatz's laboratory has shown that in the murine lateral geniculate nucleus, the genes encoding class I major histocompatibility complex (MHC) proteins were significantly repressed upon neural stimulation (Cooriveau et al. 1998; Huh et al. 2000; Boulanger et al. 2001). While class I MHC proteins are the critical molecules used to display certain antigens, these proteins also appear to be necessary for developmental plasticity and synaptic modification. If these brain neurons fail to synthesize MCH class I proteins, several memory functions are impaired or enhanced. One of the papers concluded, "These observations indicate that class I MHC molecules, classically thought to mediate cell-cell interactions exclusively in immune function, may play a novel role in neuronal signaling and activity-dependent changes in synaptic connectivity." Another classic set of immune molecules, the immunoglobulins, may also play roles in the nervous system. Immunoglobulin synthesis has been detected in the mammalian brain cortex (Upender et al. 1997; Weiner and Chun 1997), and Upender and Naegele (1999) provide evidence that neural immunoglobulin may be involved in regulating phagocytosis in the CNS.

There is even an "immune synapse" between T-lymphocytes and B-lymphocytes. While this term was originally used as a metaphor, suggesting that the contact points between T lymphocytes and antigen-presenting B cells were like the neuromuscular junction, research by Khan and colleagues (2001) has shown that the neuromuscular junction organizing protein, agrin, is also found in these "immune synapses," and it is important for the restructuring of the membranes and signaling proteins of this region, just as it is in the neuromuscular junction. Trautmann and Vivier (2001) speculate that just as agrin appears to be important for the establishment of neural memories, it might also be critical for the establishment of immune memory.

Last, another possible, though not as mechanistically grounded, area where the immune system and nervous system can be seen to interact may be in the pathogenesis of autism. Studies looking at the relationships between autoimmune diseases and mental health suggest that in some families, immune dysfunction may be interacting with other environmental factors to play a role in the development of autism (van Gent et al. 1997; Comi et al. 1999).

Therefore, it is misleading to consider the immune system as something distinct from the neural system. There is as much an immunoneural system as there is a neuroendocrine system. But as the neuroendocrine system monitors the internal milieu, the immunoneural system is a sensory network that monitors the external environment, remembers what it has perceived, and can react upon that memory when it perceives the outside signal again. These are not merely metaphorical terms. As has been shown with operant conditioning of allergic responses, histamine release from mast cells can be taken from immune function to neural function; monitoring the external environment can give you the same result through either pathway. One cannot make an antibody to an idea; but the ability to mount an immune response to a noise or an odor perception indicates a remarkable synergy between the immune and neural sensory networks. Both these networks have the capacity for simple learning and memory. Their synergism might lead to the emergence of unexpected properties.

5   *Quid significat?*

So far, we have shown that predator-induced polyphenism is prevalent in the animal kingdom, and that the immune system can be viewed as an elaboration of this ability to defend oneself against predators by changing cellular development. We have shown that, like the immune system, the nervous system retains its plasticity throughout development. We have also shown that the immune system and the nervous system are so tightly integrated that molecules active in the signaling of one system are also active in signaling in the other system. Moreover, these cross-signaling properties are physiologically relevant. There exists an immunoneural sensory network.

What does it all mean? Most all hypotheses concerning the evolution of cognition describe the evolution of the nervous system. Thus, nervous system-specific phenotypes such as language acquisition or childhood have been foregrounded as being essential to becoming human. But if the entire sensory network (not just the nervous system) is involved with plasticity and cognition, perhaps other phenotypes were equally important. Let me leave the data for the moment and enjoy some speculation. I'll suggest as a hypothesis that a major role of the sensory network (ie., the immunoneural system) was that of predator defense. In other words, the neural portion of the sensory network was (and is) also involved in what the immune portion was doing. How does the neural portion of the sensory network help us avoid predators? There are two ways. The first is the obvious way of seeing, smelling, tasting, touching, and hearing. These we share with any other preyed-upon species. But I had always learned (indeed, since elementary school) that humans were weak animals, and that it was our brains that allowed us to prevail in nature. So our brains are involved in particularly human ways of escaping from predation. There are two ways this could be done. One way is the manufacture of weapons. The other way is more primary. It is to fantasize that which isn't there or even possible. Humans can imagine alternatives and fantasize what would happen if one follows them. Our brain can fantasize how we would feel in different situations, and then we could choose, having imagined ourselves in these alternatives scenarios. This ability to fantasize may be critical in our becoming human, for humans are those animals who can visualize alternatives and make plans to enhance the odds of certain alternatives happening.

In our most basic metaphor of choosing, we envision two paths diverging from where we stand. Which path do we follow? This is perhaps the key to fantasy, for the roads will rarely be equal. We must imagine what lies beyond the horizon on each path. Here is where our mind must act to avoid predators. While our immune system acts to avoid the micropredators, the brain acts to avoid the lions, tigers, and bears. We are not good fighters or runners. As any martial arts instructor will tell us, the first rule of self-defense is to avoid the confrontation. We must fantasize which path is the safest. And then we must choose, based on these fantasies. Paul Tillich and other existentialist philosophers have also located the essence of humans in their ability to choose between alternatives. To choose is an act of will. But in order to choose, we must first be able to visualize the consequences of our choices before making the decisions. In other words, we have to be able to fantasize the counterfactual, the not-yet-brought-into-being. Fantasy becomes a prerequisite for our humanness.

The next step is to take an active part in realizing what one has only imagined. In the above metaphor, humans are the choosers, but the diverging paths lie before us, already made. But what if there is but one path, and one can imagine it going into a place fraught with danger. One can imagine oneself being chased, mutilated, or eaten there. One can imagine making another, safer, path. One can envision a better destination, and make plans for reaching it. One, literally as well as metaphorically, can make one's own path. This means that humans can plan. In this model of the sensory network as a predator-avoidance system, the first step is to fantasize, the second step is to choose, and the third step is to plan. They are not far apart, and one event might lead quickly into the others. As the philosopher A. J. Heschel (1965) has noted, we are event-planning animals. We can avoid danger by imagining what would happen if we pursued certain paths; and we can attempt to manipulate events such that certain outcomes become more probable than others. The immune function and the neural function are combined in this critical act of cognition.

The ability to fantasize is incredibly well developed in humans. We can be lying on a sofa, a loved one or a pizza by our side, while watching an action movie on television. When the hero is in peril, we undergo all the flight-or-fight responses—even though we are in a safe, even loving, environment. Our sympathetic nervous system is pumping hormones into our blood to give us strength to run away from the perilous situation. The mind has the ability to fool itself. Perhaps given the enormous responsibilities of life, the mind needs to fool itself if only to allow us to continue our daily existence. Denial is also a fundamental fact of human cognition, and it is a consequence of our ability to fantasize the counterfactual. Indeed, the ability to avoid reality may be both prerequisite and perquisite of being human. The ability to fantasize is probably selected, and other animals probably share it with us in rudimentary form. Dreaming and erotic fantasy certainly show that the mind can fool itself (and the body), and other mammals also seem to be able to partake in both these types of exercise. Rabbits and other easy prey make their burrows with several escape routes. Perhaps they can imagine a time when they will be needed; and those that did not have probably been eliminated by natural selection.

It may be possible that cognition and mind originated in the context of predator-induced polyphenism, the ability of the organism to alter development in a manner that would increase its fitness. Baldwin would have certainly understood this. The ability to avoid predators by sensing them immunologically and neurally emerged early during evolution. What forms a cognitive mind would be the combination of these elements to form a joint immune and neural sensory network that interacted in such a manner that one part of the system would synergistically aid the other. Both the human immune system and the human nervous system are able to continue growth for a long duration. Unlike all other primates, the human nervous system grows significantly after birth. It is in this period of childhood that fantasy is learned. And it may be that fantasy, as much as or even more so than language, is what makes us human.

Acknowledgments

The author thanks the NSF for its support. Moreover, I would like to thank Sabine Braukmann, Bill Bug, and the editors for their comments on earlier versions of this essay.

References

Agrawal, A. A. (1998). Induced responses to herbivory and increased plant performance. *Science* 279: 1201–1202.

Agrawal, A. A., C. Laforsch, and R.Tollrian (1999). Transgenerational induction of defenses in animals and plants. *Nature* 401: 60–63.

Baldwin, J. M. (1896). A new factor in evolution. *American Naturalist* 30: 441–451.

Baldwin, J. M. (1902). *Development and Evolution.* New York: Macmillan.

Behera, N. and V. Nanjundiah. (1997). *Trans*-gene regulation in adaptive evolution: A genetic algorithm model. *Journal of Theoretical Biology* 188: 153–162.

Bernie, S. and Siegel, M. D. (1992). *Meditations for Enhancing Your Immune System: Strengthen Your Body's Ability to Heal.* Hay House Publishing, Carlsbad, Calif.

Black, J. E., K. R. Issacs, B. J. Anderson, A. A. Alcantara, and W. T. Greenough (1990). Learning causes synaptogenesis, whereas motor activity causes angiogenesis, in cerebellar cortex of adult rats. *Proceedings of the National Academy of Science USA* 87: 5568–5572.

Bogin, B. (1997). Evolutionary hypotheses for human childhood. *Yearbook of Physical Anthropology* 40: 63–89.

Boulanger, L. M., G. S. Huh, and C. J. Shatz (2001). Neuronal plasticity and cellular immunity: Shared molecular mechanisms. *Current Opinions in Neurobiology* 11: 568–578.

Breedlove, S. M. (1997). Sex on the brain. *Nature* 389: 801.

Brunn, H. F., J. Gu, L. E. Huang, J. W. Park, and H. Zhu (1998). Erythropoietin: A model system for studying oxygen-dependent gene regulation. *Journal of Experimental Biology* 201: 1197–1201.

Chernyak, L. and A. I. Tauber (1992). The dialectical self: Immunology's contribution. In A. I. Tauber (ed.), *Organism and the Origins of Self,* pp. 109–156. Dordrecht: Kluwer.

Childs, B. (1999). *Genetic Medicine.* Baltimore, Md.: Johns Hopkins University Press.

Comi, A. M., A. W. Zimmerman, V. H. Frye, P. A. Law, and J. N. Peeden (1999). Familial clustering of autoimmune disorders and evaluation of medical risk factors in autism. *Journal of Child Neurology* 14: 388–394.

Corriveau, R. A., G. S. Huh, and C. J. Shatz (1998). Regulation of class I MHC gene expression in the developing and mature CNS by neural activity. *Neuron* 21: 505–520.

Davis, K. D., Z. H. Kiss, L. Luo, R. R. Tasker, A. M. Lozano, and J. O. Dostrovsky (1998). Phantom sensations generated by thalamic microstimulation. *Nature* 391: 385–387.

Dennett, D. C. (1991). *Consciousness Explained.* Boston: Little, Brown.

Flor, H. et al. (1995). Phantom-limb pain as a perceptual correlate of cortical reorganization following arm amputation. *Nature* 375: 482–484.

Gage, F. H. et al. (1995). Survival and differentiation of adult neuronal progenitor cells transplanted into an adult brain. *Proceedings of the National Academy of Science USA* 92: 11879–11883.

Gibson, G. and D. S. Hogness (1996). Effect of polymorphism in the *Drosophila* regulatory gene *Ultrabithorax* on homeotic stability. *Science* 271: 200–203.

Gilbert, S. F. 1997. *Developmental Biology,* fifth edition. Sunderland, Mass.: Sinauer.

Gilbert, S. F. 2001. Ecological developmental biology: Developmental biology meets the real world. *Developmental Biology* 233: 1–12.

Gilman, S. C., J. M. Schwartz, R. J. Milner, F. E. Bloom, and J. D. Feldman (1982). Beta-endorphin enhances lymphocyte proliferative responses. *Proceedings of the National Academy of Science USA* 79: 4226–4230.

Gottlieb, G. (1992). *Individual Development and Evolution.* New York: Oxford University Press.

Gould, E., A. Beylin, P. Tanapat, A. Reeves, and T. J. Shors (1999). Learning enhances adult neurogenesis in the hippocampal formation. *Nature Neuroscience* 2: 260–265.

Hammond, E. A., D. Smart, S. Toulmond, N. Suman-Chauhan, J. Hughes, and M. D. Hall (1999). The interleukin-1 type I receptor is expressed in human hypothalamus. *Brain* 122: 1697–1707.

Hammond, T. G., E. Benes, K. C. O'Reilly, D. A. Wolf, R. M. Linnehan, A. Taher, J. H. Kaysen, P. L. Allen, and T. J. Goodwin (2000). Mechanical culture conditions effect gene expression: gravity-induced changes on the space shuttle. *Physiological Genomics* 3: 163–173.

Heschel, A. J. (1965). *Who Is Man?* Berkeley: University of California Press.

Ho, M.-W., E. Bolton, and P. T. Saunders (1983). The bithorax phenocopy and pattern formation. I. Spatiotemporal characteristics of the phenocopy response. *Experimental Cellular Research* 51: 282–290.

Hoffmeyer, J. (1995). The swarming cyberspace of the body. *Cybernetics & Human Knowing* 3: 16–25.

Huh, G. S., L. M. Boulanger, H. Du, P. A. Riquelme, T. M. Brotz, and C. J. Shatz (2000). Functional requirement for class I MHC in CNS development and plasticity. *Science* 290: 2155–2159.

Johnson, H. M., E. M. Smith, B. A. Torres, and J. E. Blalock (1982). Regulation of the in vitro antibody response by neuroendocrine hormones. *Proceedings of the National Academy of Science USA* 79: 4171–4174.

Keller, S. E., J. M. Weiss, S. J. Schleifer, N. E. Miller, and M. Stein (1981). Suppression of immunity by stress: Effect of a graded series of stressors on lymphocyte stimulation in the rat. *Science* 213: 1397–1399.

Kempermann, G., H. G. Kuhn, and F. H. Gage (1997). More hippocampal neurons in adult mice living in an enriched environment. *Nature* 386: 493–495.

Khan, A. A., C. Bose, L. S. Yam, M. J. Soloski, and F. Rupp (2001). Physiological regulation of immunological synapse by agrin. *Science Express* (May 10).

Marcos, A. (2000). *Tajemstvi Hladiny. Hermeneutika Ziveho.* Prague: Vesmir.

Martin, R. D. (1990). *Primate Origins and Evolution: A Phylogenetic Reconstruction.* Princeton, N.J.: Princeton University Press.

Matsuda, R. (1982). The evolutionary process in talitrid amphipods and salamanders in changing environments, with a discussion of "genetic assimilation" and some evolutionary concepts. *Canadian Journal of Zoology* 60: 733–749.

Matsuda, R. (1987). *Animal Evolution in Changing Environments with Special Reference to Abnormal Metamorphosis.* London: John Wiley.

Matzinger, P. (1994). Tolerance, danger, and the extended family. *Annual Review of Immunology* 12: 991–1045.

Matzinger, P. (1998). An innate sense of danger. *Seminars in Immunology* 10: 399–415.

Metalnikov, S. and V. Chorine (1926). Role des réflexes conditionnels dans l'immunité. *Annales de l'Institut Pasteur* 40: 893–900.

Montoya, P., K. Ritter, E. Huse, W. Larbig, C. Braun, S. Topfner, W. Lutzenberger, W. Grodd, H. Flor, and N. Birbaumer (1998). The cortical somatotopic map and phantom phenomena in subjects with congenital limb atrophy and traumatic amputees with phantom limb pain. *European Journal of Neuroscience* 10: 1095–1102.

Nomura, S. and T. Takano-Yamamoto (2000). Molecular events caused by mechanical stress in bone. *Matrix Biology* 19: 91–96.

O'Connor, J. J. and A. N. Coogan (1999). Actions of the pro-inflammatory cytokine IL-1 beta on central synaptic transmission. *Experimental Physiology* 84: 601–614.

Palermo-Neto, J. and R. K. Guimaraes (2000). Pavlovian conditioning of lung anaphylactic response in rats. *Life Sciences* 68: 611–623.

Petitto, J. M., R. K. McNamara, P. L. Gendreau, Z. Huang, and A. J. Jackson (1999). Impaired learning and memory and altered hippocampal neurodevelopment resulting from interleukin-2 gene deletion. *Journal of Neuroscience Research* 56: 441–446.

Praag, H. van, G. Kempermann, and F. H. Gage (1999). Running increases cell proliferation and neurogenesis in the adult mouse gentate gyrus. *Nature Neuroscience* 2: 266–270.

Purves, D. and J. W. Lichtman (1985). *Principles of Neural Development*. Sunderland, Mass.: Sinauer.

Relyea, R. A. (2001a). Morphological and behavioral plasticity of larval anurans in response to different predators. *Ecology* 82: 541–554.

Relyea, R. A. (2001b). The relationship between predation risk and antipredator responses in larval anurans. *Ecology* 82: 523–540.

Riessen, H. P. (1984). The other side of cyclomorphosis: Why *Daphnia* lose their helmets. *Limnology and Oceanography* 29: 1123–1127.

Riessen, H. P. (1992). Cost-benefit model for the induction of an antipredator defense. *American Naturalist* 140: 349–362.

Rutherford, S. L. and S. Lindquist. (1998). Hsp90 as a capacitor for morphological evolution. *Nature* 396: 336–342.

Russell, M., K. A. Dark, R. W. Cumins, G. Ellman, E. Callaway, and H. V. Peeke (1984). Learned histamine release. *Science* 225: 733–734.

Sato, M., T. Ochi, T. Nakase, S. Hirota, Y. Kitamura, S. Nomura, and N. Yasui (1999). Mechanical tension-stress induces expression of bone morphogenetic protein BMP-2 and BMP-4, but not BMP-6, BMP-7, and GDF-5 mRNA, during distraction osteogenesis. *Journal of Bone and Mineral Research* 14: 1084–1095.

Schlichling, C. D. and M. Pigliucci (1998). *Phenotypic Evolution: A Reaction Norm Perspective*. Sunderland, Mass.: Sinauer.

Shors, T. J., G. Miesagaes, A. Beylin, M. Zhao, T. Rydel, and E. Gould (2001). Neurogenesis in the adult is involved in the formation of trace memories. *Nature* 410: 372–376.

Sibella-Arguelles, C. (2001). The proliferation of human T lymphoblastic cells induced by 5–HT1B receptors activation is regulated by 5–HT-moduline. *Comptes Rendus de l'Academie des Sciences* III. 324: 365–372.

Solomon, A., L. Aloe, J. Pe'er, J. Frucht-Pery, S. Bonini, F. Levi-Schaffer (1998). Nerve growth factor is preformed in and activates human peripheral blood eosinophils. *Journal of Allergy and Clinical Immunology* 102: 454–460.

Suhonen, J. O., D. A. Peterson, J. Ray, and F. H. Gage (1996). Differentiation of adult hippocampus-derived progenitors into olfactory neurons in vivo. *Nature* 383: 624–627.

Tauber, A. I. (2000). Moving beyond the immune self. *Seminars in Immunology* 12: 241–248.

Tollrian, R. and S. I. Dodson (1999). Inducible defenses in cladocera: Constraints, costs, and multipredator environments. In R. Tollrian and C. D. Harvell (eds.), *The Ecology and Evolution of Inducible Defenses,* pp. 177–202. Princeton, N.J.: Princeton University Press.

Tollrian, R. and C. D. Harvell (1999). *The Ecology and Evolution of Inducible Defenses.* Princeton, N.J.: Princeton University Press.

Trautmann, A. and E. Vivier (2001). Agrin: A bridge between the nervous and immune systems. *Science Express* (May 10).

Turner, A. M. and W. T. Greenough (1983). Synapses per neuron and synaptic dimensions in occipital cortex of rats reared in complex, social, or isolation housing. *Acta Stereologica* 2 (suppl. 1): 239–244.

Turrini, P., M. L. Zaccaria, and L. Aloe (2001). Presence and possible functional role of nerve growth factor in the thymus. *Cellular and Molecular Biology* 47: 55–64.

Upender, M. B., J. A. Dunn, S. M. Wilson, and J. R. Naegele (1997). Immunoglobulin molecules are present in early-generated neuronal populations in the rat cerebral cortex and retina. *Journal of Comparative Neurology* 384: 271–282.

Upender, M. B. and J. A. Naegele (1999). Activation of microglia during developmentally regulated cell death in the cerebral cortex. *Developmental Neuroscience* 21: 491–505.

van Gent, T., C. J. Heijnen, and P. D. Treffers (1997). Autism and the immune system. *Journal of Child Psychological Psychiatry* 38: 337–349.

Waddington, C. H. (1953). Genetic assimilation of an acquired character. *Evolution* 7: 118–126.

Waddington, C. H. (1956). Genetic assimilation of the bithorax phenotype. *Evolution* 10: 1–13.

Waddington, C. H. (1957). The genetic basis of the assimilated bithorax stock. *Journal of Genetics* 55: 240–245.

Wassersug, R. J. (2000). Vertebrate biology in microgravity. *American Science* 89: 46–53.

Weiner, J. A. and J. Chun (1997). Maternally derived immunoglobulin light chain is present in fetal mammalian CNS. *Journal of Neuroscience* 17: 3148–3158.

Wenger, R. H., I. Kvietikova, A. Rolfs, G. Camrenisch, and M. Gassmann (1998). Oxygen-indicible erythropoietin gene expression is dependent on a CpG hypoxia-inducible factor-1 DNA-binding site. *European Journal of Biochemistry* 253: 771–777.

Wickelgren, I. (1999). Nurture helps mold able minds. *Science* 283: 1832–1834.

Zaman, G., M. Z. Cheng, H. L. Jessop, R. White, and L. E. Lanyon (2000). Mechanical strain activates estrogen response elements in bone cells. *Bone* 27: 233–239.

13

Baldwin and Biosemiotics: What Intelligence Is For

Jesper Hoffmeyer and Kalevi Kull

1 Introduction

That the species of this world are products of evolution is a fact we no longer have to defend, and thus we no longer need to agree on some unitary, simple mechanism to justify its belonging inside well-established scientific knowledge. Rather we should try to grasp the evolutionary process on Earth as a multifaceted play of creative life processes. That such a process has ultimately created intelligence is a striking fact, which is not easily explained in the absence of a theory of natural intentionality ("aboutness"). Biosemiotics, by positing interpretation in the center of its focus, necessarily admits semiosis as an inescapable feature of life and claims that semiosis (i.e., sign action,[1] see below) was the root-form of intentionality and intelligence. Biosemiotics shares with Baldwinism an ambition to widen up evolutionary theory by putting explicit emphasis on the influence of mental processes in the broadest sense possible of this term, in other words, as comprising semiotic interactions even at the cellular level.

2 The Child as Model Organism

Baldwin's own theory is perhaps best understood and explained from the vantage point of the child. As a child psychologist, James Mark Baldwin was acutely aware of the phenomenon he termed "social heredity": "that in the child's personal development, his ontogenesis, his life history, he works out a faithful reproduction of his social conditions. He is, from childhood up, excessively receptive to social suggestions; his entire learning is a process of conforming to social patterns. The essential to this, in his heredity, is very great plasticity, cerebral balance and equilibrium, a readiness to overflow into the new channels which his social environment dictates" (Baldwin 1902: 53).

Baldwin was also a persuaded Darwinian and in essence what he suggested was that social heredity was operational not only in children but in the animal world at large, although to a lesser extent. In this way he could synthesize child psychology and his belief in Darwinism. He saw the intellectual plasticity of the child, or—in general—the young, as a trait for natural selection to work on, and since "social transmission" is enough to explain the likeness of the father and his son, there is no need for a theory of acquired mental characteristics. Quite to the contrary: "The only apparent hindrance to the child's learning everything that his life in society requires would be just the thing that the advocates of Lamarckism argue for—the inheritance of acquired characters. For such inheritance would tend so to bind up the child's nervous substance in fixed forms that he would have less or possibly no plastic substance left to learn anything with" (Baldwin 1902: 55).

It is instructive to see how Baldwin's Lamarckian opponent, the paleontologist E. D. Cope, responds to the idea of social heredity. First he puts forward the obvious objection that intelligence and social heredity as a factor in psychic evolution is mainly restricted to the higher animals and to man. Then he goes on to assert his belief in the inheritance of mental characteristics, offering the following example as support: "One does not believe in either education or imitation as a cause of the repetition of insanity in family lines. We rather believe in a defective brain mechanism, which is inheritable, though fortunately not always inherited" (Cope 1896: 430).

Thus, in the nature-nurture controversy, strict Lamarckians were no less nature hard-liners than are the Darwinian "fundamentalists" of our days. In fact, one way to conceive of Baldwinism is to see it as a reconciliatory strategy in the nature-nurture controversy: Through his idea of *organic selection,* Baldwin thought that he had shown "that the ordinary antithesis between 'nature and nurture', endowment and education, is largely artificial, since the two are in the main concurrent in direction" (Baldwin 1902: 106). Baldwin illustrated this by reference to complex instincts where physical heredity and social transmission are mixed up. Thus, in certain instincts "we find only partial coördinations given ready-made by heredity, and the creature actually depending upon some conscious resource (imitation, instruction, etc.) to bring the Instinct into actual operation." In animals, he says "social heredity serves physical heredity, while in man we find the reverse" (Baldwin 1902: 107).

The controversial point here is Baldwin's belief in "organic selection" as the mechanism by which this concurrence of nature and nurture is effectuated. The essence of organic selection is that "physico-genetic," "neurogenetic," and "psycho-genetic" adaptations in the life of each single individual allows the individual to survive even under odd conditions, and this survival prevents "the incidence of natural selection," in other words, the destruction of the otherwise unfit. "Thus kept alive, the species has all the time necessary to perfect the variations required by a complete instinct" (Baldwin 1902: 97). Or, in other words, the plasticity of the child's brain, as proved by the fact of social heredity, implied to Baldwin that the necessary genetic settings behind the child's success must have been tuned to facilitate a mentally guided ontogenetic dynamics. Thus, social heredity blurs the outcome of any single genetic variation and institutes a holistic "mental" bond on fitness. And Baldwin speculated that what counts in the child will also count in other animals, although to a lesser extent.

The idea that nature and nurture are not opponents in the ontogenetic process but rather "concurrent in direction" is, in fact, strikingly modern. For illustration let us consider a recent study of the interaction of innate and learned behavior in the cuckoo *Clamator glandarius* (Soler and Soler 1999). Cuckoos are well-known brood parasites—they lay their eggs in the nests of other bird species that incubate the parasitic eggs and rear the young. This may—on Darwinian assumptions—be seen as an elegant way of freeing oneself from the burden of child rearing. The cuckoos have a problem though, for how does a cuckoo young that has been imprinted upon foster parents from a quite different host species become sexually imprinted on conspecifics? Following Lorenz it has generally been assumed that brood parasites were exceptional among bird species in that conspecific recognition was innate, and the main reason for this assumption has been that young brood parasites are assumed never to encounter adult conspecifics but nevertheless to become sexually imprinted on conspecifics (Lorenz 1935).

This last assumption is exactly what Soler and Soler's study seems to reject. When single fledglings of the great spotted cuckoo were artificially introduced into magpie *Pica pica* nests in areas of allopatry with cuckoos, they did not form groups, whereas they did so if two fledglings were introduced into the same nest. This was taken to show that fledgling cuckoos did not recognize conspecifics when they were reared without any other cuckoo nestling. When the experiment was conducted in the areas of sympatry of magpie and cuckoo, the single fledglings could later on also aggregate normally. It was found that this coincided with the appearance of completely unrelated adult cuckoos who made contact with the fledglings.

It was concluded that sexual imprinting in this species is not an instantaneous and irreversible process. Taken together with observational evidence, the experiments supported the view that adult cuckoos are visiting parasitized nests in the late phase of the nestling period and making contact with fledgling cuckoos. In so doing they imprint young cuckoos (or re-imprint if the chicks had already been imprinted on foster parents), implying that the onset of the sensitive phase for imprinting is delayed in this species, and is still open when contact is made as late as two weeks after fledglings leave the nest (Soler and Soler 1999).

Generalizing these results, we may speculate that avian brood parasites have developed a genetically changed dependence of imprinting on a rather sophisticated scheme of inter-generational semiotic exchanges, and this would seem to perfectly exemplify Baldwin's claim that " 'nature and nurture'... are in the main concurrent in direction" (Baldwin 1902: 106). Nature in this case certainly may be said to have taken advantage of the semiotic means at disposal to the birds.

Another pertinent example of how genetic and cognitive factors have evolved to interact in ontogeny is kin discrimination for inbreeding avoidance in higher animals. As we saw in the cuckoo case, birds often give care to foreign offspring that is placed in the nest, which seems to imply that they do not possess the capacity for direct discrimination between kin and non-kin. Based on reported evidence from a range of different animals, including humans, Swedish anthropologist Bo Gräslund recently concluded that genetical kin discrimination is of limited importance, whereas imprinting through early close contact seems to be the main mechanism for inbreeding avoidance (Gräslund 1998).

This runs somewhat counter to the theory of kin selection that presupposes that animals, in a statistical sense, behave as though they can identify their genetic kin, determine the degree of this kinship, and estimate whether help to relatives is genetically profitable or not. Several studies have shown that among monogamous species of birds, 25–30 percent of offspring may be the result of extra-pair copulation (references given in Gräslund 1998). Extra-pair offspring are common also among many other monogamous and polygamous animals, including humans and west-African chimpanzees: "This means that a substantial number of males unwittingly feed and care for other males' offspring as if they were their own," writes Gräslund, and he concludes that "reproductive altruism does not operate through allelic identification but through discrimination based on imprinting by early close contact" (Gräslund 1998: 83).

The question of inbreeding avoidance in the human species has had an interesting history. In 1891, the Finnish sociologist Edward Westermarck published ethnographic and sociological data, supporting the idea that taboos against sexual contact within human families, which are found in all societies, are based on an innate inhibition that is activated when small children grow up close to each other and adults live close to small children, in the way that children and mothers, sisters and brothers, and, in general, children and fathers normally do (Westermarck 1891). This idea was fiercely opposed by Sigmund Freud who maintained that incest in humans is basically a reflection of an atavistic instinct inherited from a precultural stage of human evolution, the "primal horde," when reproduction was wholly promiscuously incestuous. Later Freudians found it necessary to dispense with this idea of the "primal horde" as a prehistorical event, but they retained the notions of unconscious desire, guilt, and repression to account for an incest taboo (Stone 1997). Mainstream social science has tended to follow Freud and to reject Westermarck's idea as an undue biologism.

However, as we saw, inbreeding avoidance (the so-called Knight-Darwin law) is widespread in the animal world and Freud's hypothesis of a repressed instinctual basis for incest would place the human animal in a unique reproductive position. Gräslund presents overwhelming empirical evidence for the thesis that early close contact is associated with inbreeding avoidance in human populations. Furthermore, when incest, infanticide, and violence against small children does in fact occur, such acts are statistically committed mainly by men who have not lived close to the child in question during its early years. "That they are more often stepfathers than genetic fathers is usually seen as an expression of kin selection," writes Gräslund, but, "At the proximal level, it can be explained by the fact that stepfathers generally have experienced the least amount of early close contact with children in question" (Gräslund 1998: 79–80).

According to Westermarck, incest is avoided in human populations because early close contact with children activates an innate inhibition mechanism. One might perhaps speculate that the avoidance was caused by a more general emotional logic pertaining to human sexual schemata, but this does nothing to detract from the general Baldwinian conclusion that the productive interplay of the hereditary component and the cognitive component is indeed a central theme of human ontogeny. And it can hardly be denied that this interplay is also important in the ontogeny of mammals and birds.

For Baldwin nurture is not just feeding and protecting, but a grand social process of individuation:

The society into which the child is born is, therefore, not to be conceived merely as a loose aggregate, made up of a number of biological individuals. It is rather a body of mental products, an established network of psychical relationships. By this the new person is molded and shaped to his maturity. He enters into this network as a new cell in the social tissue, joining in its movement, revealing its nature, and contributing to its growth. It is literally a tissue, psychological in character, in the development of which the new individual is differentiated. He does not *enter it* as an individual; on the contrary, he is only an individual when he comes out of it . . . . In the personal self, the social is individualized. (Baldwin 1913, quoted in Doise 1996)

We think it is fair to say that biologists have tended to underestimate the intricacies of the nurture project, thus failing to see the true challenge it poses to the understanding of genetics, in other words, to see, as Baldwin did, the true complexity of ontogeny as subtly determined by a nonadditive interplay between genes and social minds.

3   Intelligence and Semiosis

The term intelligence was used by Baldwin and his contemporaries in a very broad sense. In fact, Baldwin juxtaposes intelligence to instinct to the effect that either an activity is instinctual or it is intelligent. Here again he is explicitly opposing the Neo-Lamarckian idea that instincts are cases of so-called lapsed intelligence. Toward this view Baldwin holds that "intelligent adaptation does not create coördinations; it only makes functional use of coördinations which were alternatively present already in the creature's equipment . . . in instinct the muscular coördination is brought into play *directly* by a sense stimulation; while in intelligence it is brought into play *indirectly, i.e.,* through association of brain processes, with selection of fortunate combinations" (Baldwin 1902: 63–64).

Needless to say, the extent to which different animals possess intelligence has been highly disputed. It has often been overlooked, however, that intelligence is not just something you have "between the ears," but is very much a social skill, an ability to use physical marks as well as social relations to scaffold and organize your knowledge.

From the very beginning nerves were developed as tools for movement. Their task was to facilitate "long-distance communication" between cells in different parts of a moving animal. But the presence of fast-moving animals implied the creation of fast-moving environments, and brains developed to allow certain animals to cope with this situation in new ways. The combinatorial possibilities of moving in a moving world are enormous, of course, and from the beginning the task of brains was to help the animal to make proximal decisions that might be assisted by learning but that could not possibly be based on genetic anticipation. Brains were means for nurturing nature.

One aspect of brain action that may deserve special emphasis is proprioception, that is, the awareness of movement and position. Even the simplest movements presuppose a continuous feedback from proprioceptive organs in the body measuring muscle tensions and displacements of cell layers including the sense of gravitational orientation. The American philosopher Maxine Sheets-Johnstone has recently suggested that the proprioceptive sense serves as a "corporeal consciousness": "Any creature that *moves itself,* i.e., that is not sessile, senses itself moving;[2] by the same token, it senses when it is still. Distinguishing movement from stillness, motion from rest, is indeed a fundamental natural discrimination of living creatures that is vital to survival" (Sheets-Johnstone 1998: 284). It was the French philosopher Maurice Merleau-Ponty who first, in 1945, observed that "originally consciousness is not a 'I think that' but a 'I can'" (Merleau-Ponty 1945: 160). Sheets-Johnstone echoes this insight when she writes that "A creature's initiation of movement is coincident with its kinesthetic motivation, its dispositions to do this or that—turn, pause, crouch, freeze, run, or constrict; its kinesthetic motivations fall within the range of its species-specific movement possibilities . . . [which] are the basis of its particular repertoire of 'I cans,' " and further: "any item within its repertoire of 'I cans' is undergirded proprioceptively (kinesthetically) by a sense of agency" (Sheets-Johnstone 1998: 285).

It is a well-known fact that animals can and do dream. This implies that the mental states may sometimes be uncoupled from bodily action. But the extent of uncoupling between behavior and mental activity that characterizes the human mind is probably unique to that specific animal. The uncoupling has made philosophers wonder how it can be that mental states are always "about" something. But seen in the perspective of biology, this is no wonder, since mental "aboutness," human intentionality, grew out of a bodily "aboutness" (Hoffmeyer 1996). Whatever an organism senses also means something to it: food, escape, sexual reproduction, and so forth. This is one of the major insights brought to light through the work of Jakob von Uexküll: "Every action, therefore, that consists of perception and operation imprints its meaning on the meaningless object and thereby makes it into a subject-related meaning-carrier in the respective Umwelt" (Uexküll [1940] 1982). "Umwelt" was Uexküll's term for the phenomenal worlds of animals, the subjective universe in which the animals live, or, in other words, the ecological niche as the organism itself perceives it.

Seeing the "I can" as the center around which mental processes are evolutionarily organized has the effect of blurring the traditional mind-body dichotomy. Body action and mind action are not entirely separate categories but are essentially connected through the intentionality of the animal in which they occur, and mental activity is just one peculiarly sophisticated extension of traditional animal behavior. It follows from this understanding that we do not necessarily have to operate with two quite different categories such as "phenotypic flexibility" versus "learning." Again, learning is just one particularly sophisticated kind of phenotypic flexibility.

The embodiment of mental processes has been a recurrent theme in cognitive science and neural biology during the latest decade and paradoxically even in robotics (Lakoff 1987; Varela et al. 1991; Damasio 1994; Deacon 1997; Lakoff and Johnson 1999; Hendriks-Jansen 1996; Clark

1997). But the coin has two sides, and while the naturalization of human intelligence has attracted much attention, the other side of the coin, the inherent intelligence of nature, has not drawn such attention.

Biosemiotics can be seen as an attempt to operationalize this neglected part of the insight in the embodied nature of the mental sphere (Hoffmeyer 1992; 1995; 1996). That mental life is embodied has the implication that its natural history cannot be separated from embodied life. Mental life is grounded in bodily intentionality as manifested in perception-action cycles, and thus ultimately in semiosis. Semiosis, in the understanding of the American philosopher and scientist Charles S. Peirce, is a triadic process whereby a *sign* provokes the formation of an *interpretant* to stand in a relation to an object that somehow reflects the relation in which the sign itself stands to this same object.[3] For illustration, smoke can be seen as a sign that normally provokes the formation of an interpretant (neural processes) in the mind of a human observer, which relates to fire in a way echoing the way smoke itself relates to fire. Likewise a certain concentration of adrenaline may become a sign to the extent it provokes the formation of an interpretant in a liver cell (a cascade of enzymatic processes ultimately releasing free glucose molecules), which relates to an actual stress situation in the same way that the hormone production itself relates to the stress situation.

People from science and humanities alike often object to such an idea by pointing to the interpretative freedom of the human observer compared to the law-bound nature of the adrenaline-caused cellular response. Thus the human observer may know that the smoke he is observing is probably faked since he is just watching a piece of drama, but the liver cell, so the argument goes, does not have any possibilities for not responding to the adrenaline. But is not this argument hiding a strange lapse of logic? Or do we really believe that some mysterious soul-factor enters the man's brain cells and induces an element of freedom not else seen in cellular life?

We prefer thinking that already the liver cell is underdetermined to the extent that the contextual situation in which it finds itself does—if ever so weakly—enter the myriad relational connections making up for cellular control. For instance a diversity of cellular recognition processes are mediated by the same G-proteins, and different G proteins can occasionally be utilized by the same receptor. This enables the cell to vary its response to a given signal. As Maurine Linder and Alfred Gilman have put it : "The ability of receptors, G proteins, and effectors to interact with more than one species of molecule inside the cell also means that a cell can make different *choices* from time to time—now sending a signal down one pathway and now directing it along a somewhat different route" (italics added; Linder and Gilman 1992).

Biosemiotics searches the precursor processes out of which mental life arose and claims that cellular and organismic, semiotic processes predate the appearance of genuine intelligence and mental life, and that semiosis should be seen as a germ form of intelligence. The social nature of intelligence immediately become apparent in this approach, since semiosis transcends traditional (efficient) causality by its triadic nature, that is, by its inclusion of the contextual situation in which the causal processes unfold.

In an attempt to transcend the tradition of idealistic philosophy, American philosopher John Dewey observed that

The true stuff of experience is recognized to be adaptive courses of action, habits, active functions, connections of doing and undergoing; sensori-motor coordinations. Experience carries principles of connection and organization within itself. . . . These principles are none the worse because they are vital and practical rather than epistemological. Some degree of organization is indispensable to even the lowest grade of life. Even an amoebae must have some continuity in time in its activity and some adaptation to its environment in space. Its life and experience cannot possibly consist in momentary, atomic, and self-enclosed sensations. Its activity has reference to its surroundings and to what goes before and what comes after. This organization intrinsic to life renders unnecessary a super-natural and super-empirical synthesis. It affords the basis and material for a positive evolution of intelligence as an organizing factor within experience. (Dewey 1948: 91)

Thus, by allowing a semiotization of nature, the subject-object separation that has marred European philosophy may be softened. Organisms, and the cells and tissues of which they are built, are not just objects but also subjects in the sense that they are semiotic agents capable of interacting with their surroundings in "clever" ways. The history of how these semiotic interaction patterns have been scaffolded into the myriads of ontogenetically consistent dynamics of this world, that is, the life cycles of organisms, is what evolution is about. Genetic fixation of course plays a crucial role in such scaffolding but we believe that there are countless semiotic ways of obtaining a relatively secure scaffolding of intra- and interspecific interaction patterns (called semethic interactions by Hoffmeyer 1995). We see no reason to believe that all—or even most—of these semiotic scaffolding mechanisms are unambiguously coded for in the genomic set-up. On the contrary, we think there are serious reasons to believe they are not, since flexibility is the core of such semiotic scaffolding (Bateson 1963).

4   Nonselective Adaptation: Semiosis as a Factor of Evolution

All organisms have at least some capacity for making distinctions and for making choices. Whether this ability to distinguish and to choose may be a factor in evolution has been a subject for long debates in the theory of evolution. Darwinian evolutionism has generally rejected it, for instance, when stating that all adaptive evolution is a result of natural selection exclusively; according to this view, an ability to use sign processes may turn out to be an advantage in the struggle for existence (like many other features, e.g., an ability to move quickly), but it cannot be itself a factor that is sufficient for creating evolutionary adaptations.

However, since one of the fundamental biosemiotic views states that semiosis is a creative process also in an evolutionary sense, it will be highly interesting to analyze the possible evolutionary mechanisms that include sign processes from the very beginning. On this basis, a model has been suggested to account for adaptive evolution in the absence of natural selection (Kull 2000). Basically this model depends on the fact that nonfunctional parts of the genome undergo a much more rapid change than do functional parts of the genome. It is further assumed that whenever a population finds itself in a state of changed conditions, the "reading" of the genome will change, so that certain genomic sections will now be less expressed, or not at all, whereas others will become functional. Given these assumptions, it follows that if the changed state is maintained for many generations, the formerly functional but now nonfunctional parts of the genome risk being damaged. Eventually this may block the way for a return to the original state. The implication of this is that an irreversible adaptive specialization has taken place in the absence of any differential reproduction of genotypes. This mechanism can be called "evolution via forgetting of unused," and it was concluded "that adaptive evolution is a more general process than the adaptive evolution via natural selection" (Kull 2000: 48).

Theoretically, this kind of nonselective evolution "allows a much higher speed of adaptive evolutionary specialization than when evolution is restricted by the mechanism of differential reproduction" (Kull 2000: 50). Thus, the appearance of a new adaptation may occur simultaneously for the whole population during just one generation as a response to the self-organizational and communicative capacities of organisms. The eventual genetic fixation of the change will of course take many generations, but the mechanism will nevertheless allow for a fast evolutionary change compared to the traditional case where the new adaptation first appears as a mutation in single organism, which then gradually via the competitive advantage become distributed over the population.

The occurrence of nonselective adaptations may also indicate a solution to the debate on punctualism and gradualism. The data that led to the formulation of punctualism came from morphological studies of phylogeny, showing alternating periods of stasis and change. Evidence from molecular data, on the contrary, shows that lineages change gradually. This is exactly what the mechanism as described above predicts—the morphological change and the genetic change may not necessarily be concurrent. That is, morphological change may begin as an ontogenetic adaptation that is quickly developed compared to the subsequent genetic fixation, which may typically depend on a large number of generations.

The main statements from which the conclusions given here follow is that (a) organisms have many different ways to behave and build oneself from the exact same genome; and (b) organisms may behave in the same particular (constant) way for quite a large variety of genomes. In other words, (a) an organism has many ways to interpret its genome; and (b) there are other inheritance mechanisms than the genetic one (e.g., epigenetic, or just the stability of the environment), which enables organisms to keep some features of their structure and behavior unchanged even if some changes in the genome take place.

In other words, the organism's phenotype and genotype are not so strictly coupled as is often assumed because in general an organism does not make use of its whole genome for living, and there exist potentially more functionally expressible parts in the genome than those that are currently in use. And also, there are many different ways to live using the same genome, as is for instance dramatically illustrated by the dreaded locust, which most of the time lives its life as an ordinary, harmless grasshopper, but which under certain conditions, generates new generations with a markedly changed morphology and behavior, causing these locusts to form enormous flocks flying many thousand kilometers, and devouring every green thing in their path (Hoffmeyer 1996: 20).

Essentially this phenotypic flexibility depends on semiotic activity (which includes perception and operation, i.e., the functional cycle, according to Uexküll 1928), and particularly, on the mobility of populations causing changes in both selection and environment, that is, niche construction (Laland, Odling-Smee et al. 1996; Odling-Smee, Laland et al. 1996). Thus, the uncoupling is a result of the cooperation between two levels of functional circles possessed by cells (or phenomes)—one of these acting via the genome, the other via the environment.

A cell may not only interpret its genotype in different ways, it also has several ways to preserve a particular interpretation over a number of generations through epigenetic inheritance mechanisms, or due to a permanent change of environmental conditions. This may eventually supply the time needed for stochastic genetic changes to accumulate in unused segments of the genotype and thus to fix the otherwise only phenotypic changes. For instance, this means that if for many generations a particular organic structure has not been formed, it may not be possible for this particular organic structure to be formed at a later time, due to stochastic changes in the part of the genome which normally scaffolded this particular step in cellular differentiation.

It is important to notice that a similar interpretational shift may take place simultaneously in many individuals of a population (e.g., as a result of invasion of the population into a new environment, for instance in the case of monophage or oligophage insects when they inhabit a new host species). The phenetic shift that this implies may be sufficient to decrease the efficiency of recognition of the source population specimens (which is needed for mating) down to the level that guarantees the sufficient isolation and provides time to the mutation processes to fix this separation also at the level of genome or cytoplasm incompatibility (Kull 1988; 1993; Paterson 1993).

Here, we would like to draw attention to an interesting paradox of natural selection, which was called the *paradox of the unique child* (Kull 2000). That is, in the case of sexual reproduction, almost every descendant has a genotype that has never been present before (e.g., in the sense of a new combination of alleles of the whole genome) and whose capacity for survival and reproduction has therefore never been checked by natural selection. Nevertheless, a considerable percentage of the offspring—particularly in the species that have a low reproduction rate—will usually stay alive.

The explanation for this apparent paradox is that every organism has many ways to carry out the tasks they need to fulfill. Structures or processes that happen to be corrupted can most often be substituted by others or repaired in some way or other. For instance small quantitative changes in efficiency of one particular enzyme can often be compensated by small changes in the production of other enzymes, without this having any real influence upon reproduction. Also, for the most part, it is not necessary for a living organism to be a hundred percent precise at the digital level (DNA).

For a new character to appear in the phylogeny of species, it is not necessary to assume that there had to be one specimen who gained this character first due to mutation, and that then this mutation became spread over the species to all those whose grandparent that first mutant individual is. This would be required only if digital preciseness in the determination of the character is assumed. As far as this is not the case, many different genetic changes in many individuals of the population may simultaneously give rise to the same new character. And the final genetic fixations of the new character (in the sense of making its appearance irreversible) may have taken place only a long time after the first appearance of this character in the paleontological record.

The Baldwin effect implies that evolution may take place without differential reproduction of genotypes. Assuming that mutations in the expressed part of the genome cause inviability of a near equal percentage of the offspring from all individuals of the population involved in an interpretational shift, we have a mechanism of evolution that works without the differential reproduction of genotypes. The neo-Darwinian mechanism is thus a special case of this mechanism, since it requires an additional assumption (e.g., that the percentage of inviable offspring is systematically different in different individuals, and this difference is correlated with a particular genetic character of parents).

The stochastic (entropic) changes in genotype preferentially lead to the forgetting of "unused" and the storing of "used." Owing to the large size of genomes in terms of the number of genes, many mutations are always simultaneously distributed among individuals via sexual reproduction, thereby enabling the ontogenetic change to become fixed for the whole population (making the phenotypic change irreversible); theoretically, this is a much faster mechanism than the classical one, which requires a distribution of new mutations to take place across the population through competitive advantage.

The proposed "Baldwin effect" mechanism is supported by recent studies on epigenetic inheritance mechanisms, and on the stability of morphogenetic mechanisms (Jablonka and Lamb 1995; Webster and Goodwin 1996).

We conclude that an organism is itself a subject in the continued evolution of the lineage to which it belongs. This is exactly what was originally implied by the so-called Baldwin effect. As an obvious implication of this understanding, we need to direct our attention toward the evolutionary function of interpretations and semiosis.

5   Phenotypic Plasticity for Semiotic Competence

The term organism immediately implies the term environment—the one cannot exist without the other—and therefore to ask for the origin of life is also to ask for the origin of the environment (Hoffmeyer 1998). Or to state this differently, life is process in context, and one major theme in organic evolution has been the interiorization of the context into the organism, that is, in the course of evolution, organisms have learned to make more and more sophisticated internal representations of selective aspects of their external situations. This representational activity is the root of biosemiosis and since it is deeply integrated into the survival strategies of the organisms, it is an intentional activity, that is, a precursor for that dimension of the life process we find exhibited in higher animals as intelligence, semiotic control, and eventually consciousness.

Even bacteria continuously measure the presence of bacterial waste products or nutrients in their surroundings, compare such measurements through time, and interpret these compared measurements through the execution of historically acquired activity patterns such as attraction or repulsion. To the extent these historically acquired activity patterns have become fixed as solutions to survival challenges of ancestral organisms, they can be conceived of as virtual realities, just like the virtual realities produced by patterns of firing neurons in our brains. Our virtual realities have an experiential quality to them that is probably absent in bacteria and other brainless animals or plants, but one cannot be sure that this aspect of our mental processes have no precursors in bacteria.

When Conrad Waddington introduced his image of *canalization*, that is, of development as a ball running down through the valleys of an epigenetic landscape whose features are largely determined as a concerted effect of a multitude of genes, he tried to establish an autonomous role for embryology in evolutionary theory. Genes according to this idea do not directly cause traits; they rather assist in laying out the features of the epigenetic landscape, and, therefore, in the pattern of canalizations open to embryonic development. By emphasizing the autonomous role of this dynamic intermediate level, the epigenetic landscape, between genotype and phenotype, he attempted to transcend the behavioristic black-box conception of the organism.

Not only genes but also environmental factors might influence the features of the epigenetic landscape making phenotypic plasticity possible. Waddington thought that natural selection would tend toward some kind of balance between genetic fixation and phenotypic plasticity, and this was the key to his idea of "genetic assimilation" (Waddington 1957: 168). A crucial factor for the evolution of phenotypic plasticity is now thought to be the relation between the time scale of environmental change and the generation time. Phenotypic plasticity is believed to be beneficial only if this ratio is low, that is, if the environment may be expected to change a lot in the lifetime of every single individual (Gordon 1992).

All of these discussions take on a new dimension when considered in the light of semiotically controlled behavior or, in general, activity. Behavior is what the organism needs the Umwelt for; that is, their trajectories into the real world are guided by their *virtual realities*. If the Umwelt does not guide the activity of the organism successfully, the organism's chance of leaving offspring is hampered, and it follows that the assurance of the production of well-tuned umwelt is one important focus for the evolutionary process.

An implication of this is that there is not only one layer pushed in between the genotype and the phenotype, as Waddington suggested, but that in addition to the epigenetic landscape guiding the pattern of developmental canalizations, there must also be an epi-developmental, semiotic *umwelt landscape* canalizing the learning processes whereby a particular umwelt is calibrated to the actual environmental circumstances (Hoffmeyer 2001).

The reality of the organism's virtual reality is assured by a calibration process in the combined or integrated epigenetic and Umwelt landscapes whereby the rigidities of genetic predisposition are transcended. For that same reason the Umwelt cannot be strictly bound by its genetic basis but must to some extent reflect the unpredictability of endless semiotic recombinations between adaptive developmental elements and environmental elements (what Bateson 1979 called a double stochastic system).

Another way to state this is by the observation that phenotypic plasticity at the level of semiotic competence may be orders of magnitude bigger and not well-correlated with phenotypic plasticity at the morphological level. For instance, morphological plasticity is predominant in most unicellulars as well as in plants and fungi, but much less so in insects, mammals, or birds. Ultimately, this is because the semiotic niche (i.e., that subset of the local semiosphere which the species must be capable of controlling [Hoffmeyer 1996]) is both a more subtle and a much richer concept than the ecological niche since it encompasses all latently relevant cues that have to be correctly interpreted by the organism if its success shall be assured. Since the number of features of the world, which may in some situation or other become relevant cues governing the behavior of an organism, is infinite, or at least orders of magnitudes bigger than the number of features with which the organism has to interact physically, the semiotic aspect opens the door to a very versatile adaptive landscape. Thus a bird, to take an example, not only has to deal with a range of items for food or shelter, but also with patterns of sounds, directions, and speeds of wind, differences in temperature of air or wind, changing intensities and wavelengths of light, and so on—or even, as is the case with some migratory birds, with the shifting constellations of stars. And clearly at this level, many kinds of environmental changes are to be expected in the lifetime of an individual organism.

We conclude that the inclusion of life's semiotic dimension into the evolutionary theory complex considerably strengthens the case for Baldwinian thinking. It becomes obvious that organisms do not passively succumb to the severity of environmental judgment. Instead, they perceive, interpret, and act in the environment in ways that creatively and unpredictably change the whole setting for selection and evolution.

Notes

1. "If we ask what it is that semiotic studies investigate, the answer is, in a word, action. The action of signs" (Deely 1990: 22).

2. Unicellular organisms who can move themselves (e.g., using flagellum), may not always be able to distinguish between the moving of the body and the changes or movements in their surrounding. In that respect, Sheets-Johnstone's statement is slightly overstrained. However, the principal meaning of her statement is clearly correct.

3. According to Peirce, "A sign, or Representamen, is a First which stands in such a genuine triadic relation to a Second, called its Object, as to be capable of determining a Third, called its Interpretant, to assume the same triadic relation to its Object in which it stands itself to the same Object" (Peirce 1931–1935: vol. 2, no. 274). Thus, in Peirce's philosophy the interpretant represents a category of "thirdness" that transcends mere causality, which he saw as "secondness."

References

Baldwin, J. M. (1902). *Development and Evolution*. New York: Macmillan.

Baldwin, J. M. (1913). *History of Psychology:* From John Locke to the Present Time, vol. 2. London: Wats.

Bateson, G. (1963). The role of somatic change in evolution. *Evolution* 17(4): 529–539. Reprinted in Bateson (1972).

Bateson, G. (1972). *Steps to an Ecology of Mind*. New York: Ballantine.

Bateson, G. (1979). *Mind and Nature. A Necessary Unity*. New York: Bantam.

Clark, A. (1997). *Being There: Putting Brain, Body, and World Together Again*. Cambridge, Mass.: MIT Press /Bradford Books.

Cope, E. D. (1896). Observations on Prof. Baldwin's reply. *American Naturalist* 30: 428–430.

Damasio, A. (1994). *Descartes' Error: Emotion, Reason, and the Human Brain*. New York: Putnam.

Deacon, T. (1997). *The Symbolic Species*. New York: Norton.

Deely, J. (1990). *Basics of Semiotics*. Bloomington: Indiana University Press.

Dewey, J. (1948). *Reconstruction in Philosophy,* enlarged edition. Boston: Beacon Press.

Doise, W. (1996). The origins of developmental social psychology: Baldwin, Cattaneo, Piaget, and Vygotsky. *Swiss Journal of Psychology* 55(2/3): 139–149.

Gordon, D. M. (1992). Phenotypic plasticity. In E. F. Keller and A. L. Elisabeth (eds.), *Keywords in Evolutionary Biology*, pp. 255–262. Cambridge, Mass.: Harvard University Press.

Gräslund, B. (1998). The biological basis of social behaviour. In L. Larsson and B. Stjernquist (eds.), *The World-View of Prehistoric Man*. Stockholm: Almqvist and Wiksell.

Hendriks-Jansen, H. (1996). *Catching Ourselves in the Act. Situated Activity, Interactive Emergence, and Human Thought*. Cambridge, Mass.: MIT Press.

Hoffmeyer, J. (1992). Some semiotic aspects of the psycho-physical relation: The endo-exosemiotic boundary. In T. A. Sebeok and J. Umiker-Sebeok (eds.), *Biosemiotics: The Semiotic Web 1991*, pp. 101–123. Berlin: Mouton de Gruyter.

Hoffmeyer, J. (1995). The semiotic body-mind. In N. Tasca (ed.), *Essays in Honour of Thomas Sebeok (Cruzeiro Semiótico 22/25)*, pp. 367–383. Porto.

Hoffmeyer, J. (1995). The swarming cyberspace of the body. *Cybernetics and Human Knowing* 3(1): 16–25.

Hoffmeyer, J. (1996). Evolutionary intentionality. In E. Pessa, M. P. Penna, A. Montesanto (eds.), *Third European Congress on Systems Science*, pp. 699–703. Rome: Edizioni Kappa.

Hoffmeyer, J. (1996). *Signs of Meaning in the Universe*. Bloomington: Indiana University Press.

Hoffmeyer, J. (1998). Semiosis and biohistory: A reply. *Semiotica* 120(3/4): 455–482.

Hoffmeyer, J. (2001). Seeing virtuality in nature. *Semiotica* 134 (1/4): 381–398.

Jablonka, E. and M. Lamb (1995). *Epigenetic Inheritance and Evolution: The Lamarckian Dimension*. Oxford: Oxford University Press.

Kull, K. (1988). The origin of species: A new view. In K. Kull and T. Tiivel (eds.), *Lectures in Theoretical Biology*, pp. 73–77. Tallinn: Valgus.

Kull, K. (1993). The recognition concept of species and a mechanism of speciation. *Folia Baeriana* 6: 133–140.

Kull, K. (2000). Organisms can be proud to have been their own designers. *Cybernetics and Human Knowing* 7(1): 45–55.

Lakoff, G. (1987). *Woman, Fire, and Dangerous Things. What Categories Reveal about the Mind*. Chicago: The University of Chicago Press.

Lakoff, G. and M. Johnson (1999). *Philosophy in the Flesh*. New York: Basic Books.

Laland, K. N., F. J. Odling-Smee, and M. W. Feldman (1996). On the evolutionary consequences of niche construction. *Journal of Evolutionary Biology* 9: 293–316.

Linder, M. E. and A. G. Gilman (1992). G proteins. *Scientific American* 267: 36–43.

Lorenz, K. (1935). Der Kumpan in der Umwelt des Vogels. *Journal für Ornithologie* 83: 137–213, 289–413.

Merleau-Ponty, M. (1945). *Phénoménologie de la Perception*. Paris: Gallimard.

Odling-Smee, F. J., K. N. Laland, et al. (1996). Niche construction. *American Naturalist* 147(4): 641–648.

Paterson, H. E. H. (1993). Collected writings. In S. F. McEvey (ed.), *Evolution and the Recognition Concept of Species*. Baltimore, Md.: The Johns Hopkins University Press.

Peirce, C. S. (1931–35). *Collected Papers I–IV*. C. Hartstone and P. Weiss (eds.). Cambridge, Mass.: Harvard University Press.

Sheets-Johnstone, M. (1998). Consciousness: A natural history. *Journal of Consciousness Studies* 5(3): 260–294.

Soler, M. and J. J. Soler (1999). Innate versus learned recognition of conspecifics in great spotted cuckoos *Clamator glandarius*. *Animal Cognition* 2(2): 97–102.

Stone, L. (1997). *Kinship and Gender*. Boulder: Westview Press, Harper-Collins.

Uexküll, J. v. (1928). *Theoretische Biologie*. Berlin: Verlag von Julius Springer.

Uexküll, J. v. ([1940]1982). The theory of meaning. *Semiotica* 42(1): 25–87.

Varela, F. J., E. Thompson, and E. Rosch (1991). *The Embodied Mind: Cognitive Science and Human Experience*. Cambridge, Mass.: MIT Press.

Waddington, C. H. (1957). *The Strategy of the Genes*. London: Allen and Unwin.

Webster, G. and B. Goodwin (1996). *Form and Transformation: Generative and Relational Principles in Biology*. Cambridge: Cambridge University Press.

Westermarck, E. (1891). *The History of Human Marriage*. London: Macmillan.

14

The Hierarchic Logic of Emergence: Untangling the Interdependence of Evolution and Self-Organization

Terrence W. Deacon

1 Introduction

[... *something more from nothing but.*[1]]

Biological evolution is characterized by a collection of highly convoluted processes that produce a remarkably complex kind of combinatorial novelty. The contention of this paper is that biological evolution and evolutionary processes in general are a subset of processes drawn from a much larger set of novelty-producing processes that also includes self-assembly and self-organizing processes. Not only does it appear that these are related concepts, I think it is also clear that they are interdependent in complex and subtle ways that have yet to be fully delineated, especially in the processes of life and mind. It is also suspected by many writers that a synthesis that successfully integrates the logic of these various kinds of creative processes will do more than significantly advance our understanding of how life came about and how thoughts and experiences are generated. It could possibly also provide new insights into the very nature of physical causality. But there are some broad theoretical issues that stand in the way of this outcome. These issues derive from a set of unresolved problems about the nature of physical novelty itself, and how we conceive of its origination in terms of current theories of causality. These most enigmatic physical phenomena all have something to do with creative or originative processes in nature, and for this reason seem inevitably to come in conflict with our otherwise quite successful, reductionistic account of most other aspects of the world.

A more general term often used to describe this larger class of spontaneous, and only weakly predictable, order-generating processes is "emergence."[2] This is a promising abstract explanatory concept, but one that is at
risk of becoming overused and too vague for any technical purposes, precisely because of its generality and only partially specified meanings. The
purpose of this essay is to take the concept apart and to attempt to discern
what (if any) features about physical causal processes it accurately reflects,
so that it contributes to the empirical investigation of biological and mental processes, and not just to philosophizing about them.

The concept of emergence probably has gained its worst reputation
when it has been used in a primarily negative sense—to point to something
missing in reductionistic explanations. In explicitly anti-reductionistic criticisms of standard accounts of such phenomena as life and mind, it has
come to be a code word identified with a complex systems theoretic perspective. In this use, the concept of emergence is a place-marker intended to
indicate points where standard reductionistic accounts fail or seem incompletely to explain apparent discontinuities in properties exhibited at different levels of physical scale. This negative usage has unfortunately led many
more orthodox thinkers to suspect that there is no underlying phenomenon
to be described, only a vague suspicion due to incomplete analysis. On the
other hand, in examples where it has been more precisely described (e.g.,
the emergence of liquidity or surface tensions from the interactions of
water molecules), it is seen as adding nothing of empirical significance to
standard physical reductionistic accounts. And finally, where it is used to
describe more complex phenomena (e.g., emergence of life or mind), the details and logic are sufficiently obscured by incomplete scientific investigation to be of much use. Incautious uses allow critics to rightfully claim that
it mostly serves only as a sort of philosophically motivated promissory note.

Nevertheless, the term emergence has become a kind of signal for research paradigms sensitive to systemic factors. There is growing awareness
among biologists, physicists, and computation scientists studying diverse
kinds of complex phenomena that many of these share a curious general
feature in common. Complex dynamical ensembles can spontaneously assume ordered patterns of behavior that are not prefigured in the properties
of their component elements or in their interaction patterns. Moreover, unprecedented global forms can develop along parallel lines to reach similar

patterns of behavior despite arising from components of radically different constitution, interacting according to quite diverse physical principles. Thus, retrospectively at least, the "cause" of such unprecedented forms appears to be attributable to properties that can only be described at the level of the whole ensemble. Systems that behave this way are often described as "self-organized," since the most relevant antecedent condition is at the same level of description and scale as the consequent ordered behavior.

The appearance of this general form of systemic causal dynamic in diverse domains motivates the suspicion that phenomena like this may be related in some underlying ways to one another, independently of their material composition and interactions. There is also a sense, however, that living phenomena exhibit a mode of unpredictability in their self-organization that is something more than mere self-organization. It is also becoming clear that the kinds of processes we call "evolutionary" are potentially quite diverse and of varying levels of complexity. In this volume alone, diverse views about the relative importance of the Darwinian account of natural selection are expressed, with a few authors significantly departing from the orthodoxy. Others (including this author) suggest that, in cases of complex organisms able permanently to alter their environment, or, in cases where higher-order evolutionary phenomena (like language and culture) contribute influences to biological evolution, it becomes difficult to distinguish where evolution leaves off and self-organization begins.

The term "emergence" connotes the image of something coming out of hiding, coming into view for the first time, something without precedent and perhaps a bit surprising. But is there some new physical quality emerging in the physical processes we are considering or merely some change that allows us to see something that previously was in a cryptic form and is now unmasked? In other words, we need to be clear about whether we are investigating a limitation of scientific description or something about actual physical processes in the world. There will always be gaps in our understanding. Phenomena that we cannot predict often merely reflect limitations of theory or of modeling and computing power. It should come as no surprise that we encounter difficulties producing commensurate descriptions that are adequate at very different levels of scale. And something that defies continuity of description with respect to current tools across levels of scale is an artifact of science, a descriptive discontinuity, not a causal one.

Many scientists suspect that most things described as emergent phenomena are actually matters of descriptive inadequacy across levels of scale. To the extent that new kinds of descriptive methodologies are forced upon us by the scale-dependent features of our analytical tools, the novelty we encounter can be described as *epistemological emergent*. The question is whether there is something we might, in contrast, call *ontological emergence*. We need to distinguish between recognizing a descriptive discontinuity and the generation of true physical novelty. This distinction has been made by many others, and is at the heart of a long-running philosophical debate. I enter this discussion with the hypothesis that true physical novelty can be generated by many natural processes including evolutionary and mental processes, but also with the suspicion that we tend to look for the wrong sort of novelty. So I take my challenge to be the task of trying to be as explicit and concrete as I can be about what "emerges" in these cases. This also means trying to make explicit the connection between emergent processes and those we think of as plain old garden-variety mechanical processes.

A good place to start is to ask "what" emerges? The answer is not some "thing" but rather something like a form, or pattern, or function. The concept of emergence seems to apply to phenomena in which relational properties tend to dominate over constituent properties in determining aggregate features. To some extent the modern conception of physical "cause" tends to combine and confuse what might be called *constituent* or *material* features of things and events with what might be called *topological* or relational features.[3] This contributes to confusion about emergence because it is with respect to the *configurations* and *topologies*, not the specific properties of constituents that we trace processes of emergence. Global topological properties are often shared by many systems irrespective of any particular physical laws or any particular constituent properties. Correspondingly, it is the spontaneous, unprecedented production of new relational properties that constitutes emergence, not the production of new kinds of substance or physical law.

2   Synchronic and Diachronic Senses of Emergence

The conception of novelty implicit in all senses of emergence can implicitly or explicitly involve a "before and after" comparison, even when the major focus is on phenomena involving differences of scale. Emergent phenomena are always defined with respect to time in some regard, but the constitutive role played by temporal change differs with different *senses* of emergence. As a further preliminary, we need to distinguish forms of emergence in which development in time leads to a kind of self-similarity across time, allowing us to treat it as synchronic, and self-similarity that is not in the outcome, but instead is in the developmental process from moment to moment. This requires us to consider it as irreducibly diachronic.

Synchronic uses of the concept of emergence are usually restricted to properties of matter that become evident with ascent in scale. Consider water: H_2O molecules in large aggregates in the right conditions exhibit a set of dynamical properties we refer to as liquidity. These higher-order properties depend only on the specific properties of the constituent molecules, determining what might be called parameters of liquidity (e.g., viscosity, vaporization point, etc.), but in some sense not for the generic property of liquidity itself. At appropriate temperatures and pressures and time domains (e.g., glass is a "slow," i.e., viscous liquid), many different kinds of molecular constituents can exhibit the same general behavioral properties. But liquid properties are only one of a few phases of matter (solid, gas, and plasma being others) and transitions from one to another can occur with changes of boundary conditions affecting the aggregate. Specific details of the boundary conditions are determined by the molecular constituents, but, again, not the existence of these phases themselves. A general characteristic of all types of molecular constituents is that they can exhibit these phases under the right conditions. So we can consider these phasic behavioral regimes to be *generic* properties irrespective of the material. Whereas the specific conditions at which phase transitions occur depend on the material properties of the constituents, the form of these phases depends on something more, and yet not more. Phase "states" are a sort of oxymoron in a microscopic sense since they are dynamic processes. But they are processes with a special kind of temporal topology. They are "attractors," in the lingo of complexity theory: highly self-similar ensembles of configurations of the global dynamics that tend to lead to one another "neighboring" configurations with very high probability. And these attractors are separated from each other by unstable intermediate transients.

The existence of multiple regular higher-order attractors means that they can come into existence and fall out of existence over time. One might be tempted to treat the coming into being of a new phase as emergent in a different, diachronic sense than when self-similar dynamics (in effect) cycle. But this would ignore the fact that in some sense the new configuration of the material remaining in the same phase is also being diachronically "generated" anew, and so forth, in each ensuing microsecond. This might suggest that it is an artificial distinction to say that, for example, the emergence of liquidity is synchronic whereas the evolution of life on earth is diachronic. The first unfolds in time as well. But I want to argue that in this comparison an important distinction about this unfolding is missed.

Evolution is a historical phenomenon in ways that liquidity isn't. I would even want to say that evolution is, in some sense, "more" emergent than liquidity. Evolution involves time in a convoluted way. It is not self-similar in any simple way. A raindrop analyzed two hundred million years ago and another analyzed five minutes ago would be vastly more similar than two individual vertebrates even from the same lineage. There is self-similarity to life across time but there is also a similar trend of difference. Life and mind are, similarly, more temporally convoluted than liquidity, although in a very vague sense they each are emergent. Attending to this kind of difference in mode of development when comparing different kinds of emergent phenomena is thus important. I believe that failure to do so has been the most consistent reason this concept has more often obfuscated than clarified the causal logic of the most vexing scientific questions of the past century. Its long use as an explanatory term despite little advance in the sophistication of its scientific use appears to attest to this. (See for example its early use in Lewes's "Problems of Life and Mind.")

Francis Crick, co-discoverer of the structure of DNA, calls the realization that thoughts, feelings, passions, and so forth are the results of chemical processes in the brain an "Astonishing Hypothesis." One has the suspicion, however, that the astonishing part of this is to be found in what is not stated in Crick's reductionistic claim. Mind can't be "nothing but" this, and yet isn't exactly "something in addition" to these chemical processes either. But here is where an indiscriminate use of the concept of emergence can be unhelpful. Many who feel uncomfortable with the "nothing but" characterization express this by arguing along the following lines: "Consciousness is an emergent property of the cellular and molecular processes within a brain in the same sense as surface tension is an emergent property of the interactions of water molecules."[4] By invoking this analogy, an implicit claim about a presumably well-understood relationship is meant to inform our understanding of the general logic that can be applied to a much less well-understood (indeed deeply mysterious) relationship. Unfortunately, it is precisely the huge number of unstated details on both sides of the analogy that turns this into an exercise in question-begging.

What motivates the analogy is that both surface tension and consciousness are in some sense compositional. Both, too, involve a contrast between levels of description for which quite different descriptive tools are required. But that fact is pretty self-evident. The question is whether these are analogous in any other way. By hypothesis, water molecule collisions (obeying lower-order component properties) stand in relation to surface tension as neuro-chemical reactions stand in relation to conscious experience: both exhibit higher-order aggregate properties. Without question, activities supported by whole living brains must at the same time be supported by the component processes of these brains, since the brain is also a composite or aggregate dynamic entity. Beyond that of mere aggregate form, however, we are left with little confidence that the kind of causal relationships implicitly being compared allows for any further extension of the analogy. It is a bit like the comparison of the production of liquidity to the evolution of living forms.

It becomes obvious that we are actually comparing different kinds or modes or levels of emergence, however, when we consider comparing different properties. Notice, for example, that we would be on pretty solid ground comparing the viscosity or the opacity of brains to the relative viscosity or opacity of a liquid, and we would feel confident treating both cases as similar forms of emergent properties from their molecular interactional properties. It is apparent that we implicitly recognize that there can be different "species" of emergence. And if there are, then cross-category comparisons of emergent relationships, such as this, may not be as informative as we might hope.

Whatever we mean by "emergence," there can be no doubt that mental phenomena are emergent from the subordinate neuro-chemical interactions occurring in a brain in a more complex way than liquid phenomena are emergent from water molecule interactions. The fact that we can identify similar kinds of properties in brains to those of liquids (e.g., viscosity) also suggests that the brain-mind kind of emergence might at least be described as of a higher order. The same can be said of life as an emergent phenomenon. Living metabolism is not emergent from its constituent chemical processes in the same way that a flame's dynamical features are emergent from its component chemical processes, even though a metabolic process shares some features in common with burning. The critical features that make metabolism emergent, and sets it apart from, and at least a level above, those features that make flames emergent, can be traced to the fact that, in some sense, flamelike emergence is one component in lifelike emergence.

At the very least, then, we need to articulate a more elaborate and hierarchically organized taxonomy of emergence relationships that unpacks the temporal complexity of the issue a bit more clearly. This can at least aid us in avoiding these sorts of too-simplistic comparisons. Though I hope to finesse philosophical debate about the reality of irreducible emergence—ontological emergence—I hope to provide explicit positive definitions and categories of emergence to counter the current vagueness in its usage, so that irrespective of whether we believe there is something like "true" emergence, we will be more clear about what we are claiming in either case. Though by describing as precisely as possible a causal logic distinguishing specific examples, we risk sacrificing the strong sense of emergence implied by proponents of antireductionism, I think we do not necessarily lose the constructive sense it contributes to explanations of natural creativity that is behind its most important uses. At the very least, an explicit analytic categorization of types of emergence can help to distinguish among theoretical claims that are commonly confused in discussions of evolutionary and mental phenomena.

Although I will offer only a qualitative descriptive account of what I mean by "levels of emergence," I believe it can be made sufficiently precise and unambiguous to be easily rendered in mathematical terms using current theoretical tools.

3   Compound Interest

What is it about certain phenomena we label as emergent that prompts us to consider them novel and unprecedented? It is not the energy that courses through them nor the material they are composed of that matters. It is rather their topology or configuration, that is, how the matter and energy is organized, and how it behaves. Emergence is about the *topology of causality*. What I believe to be critical for explaining the emergent properties of some system is an account of the origins and development of the *configurational* or *topological* regularities of both the constituent interactions and also of whole aggregates. This account must also address the fact that these topological relationships between levels of phenomena can be multiply realized by different physical systems, and are thus neither *only* nor *merely* expressions of substrate properties.

A related point is made by researchers simulating complex systemic dynamics in computers and by computational theorists in the cognitive sciences. In many of these model systems, the large scale configurations that are produced more often reflect configurational properties of the whole ensemble (e.g., number of elements and their interactional connectivity) rather than properties derived only from interactional dynamics of constituents. The point is that similar systemic properties can be exhibited by systems made up of unrelated elements with very different component dynamics. This is a specific case of a much more common phenomenon that is axiomatic in the computer sciences. Radically different machine architectures can "run" the "same" program or algorithm (e.g., a high-level description of some entire class of input-output relations) even if the physical mechanism involved is different in different cases of its running. There is, of course, a mundane, commonsense version of this in the case of arithmetic done with the aid of an abacus, a slide-rule, or with paper and pencil manipulations of scribblings. All of these embodiments can assist us in "doing" the same arithmetic operation in some sense. By analogy, cognitive scientists have argued that the "functional" properties that define a given cognitive operation are like the logical architecture of a computer program. A given thought may also be the same in certain critical respects irrespective of the device that embodies it.

Philosophically, this general form of argument is known as functionalism, and although I think there are problems with this view of mind, I nevertheless think the general logic is relevant to the problem of emergence. Claiming the existence and relative autonomy of higher-order ensemble properties of physical systems and arguing that they are consitituted by some sort of global influence over the properties and dynamics of system constituents is a claim for a kind of physical-causal analogue to functionalism. In functionalist accounts, only certain substrate details are essential; others may vary without functional consequence. But function is defined extrinsically, at least in computer science and cognitive theories, because function is a semiotic distinction, not a physical one. What is the physical analogue? It is, as I suggested above, something like topology: the form, configuration, or distribution of component features. In these terms, my argument will not be grounded on any more radical assumption than the claim that the same topology can be differently instantiated. This is noncontroversial. But two additional points need to be made about this assumption, and about the analogy I am drawing.

First, topology is not just a descriptive feature of a physical system, it is a constitutive fact about the spatial-temporal relationships among component elements and interactions with intrinsic causal consequences. Second, it is not a single relationship, but a space of relationships, or perhaps more accurately the space of spaces of relationships. There are various levels of abstraction we might use to describe a system configuration. Each might include more or ignore certain details, but the description is irrelevant, it is the way that these topological features contribute to future topological features and influence those in adjacent systems that matters. This propagation of effect is selective and relational and always subject to higher-order topological factors or boundary conditions. What is gained in a physical theory of causality by noting that, under certain reduced descriptions, multiple physical systems with divergent details are isomorphic in some respects? It matters, of course, only if it is not just description, but a matter of dynamical importance. It matters if certain aspects of topology at some level are more relevant for an account of topology at that or some other level or stage of development. It matters, then, if topology at one level of scale or locus affects topology at some other level or locus, irrespective of the physical substrate. Topology is a global or ensemble relationship. So it may also include whole-to-part influences that are the most cited characteristic of emergent phenomena. The "top-down" character is both the key defining character and yet the most criticized aspect of the concept of emergence. Reframing it in terms of topological influences and constraints is a first step toward removing the confusion of "causality" claims associated with it.

What needs to be explained, then, is not a new form of causality, but how some systems come to be dominated by their higher-order topological properties so that these appear to "drag along" component constituent dynamics, even though, at the same time, these higher-order regularities are also constituted by lower-order interactions. In other words, an explanation of how topologies come to make a difference is required. I believe that the secret to explaining this lies in what can be called amplification processes. I believe that we can understand emergent phenomena as all being variant forms of what might be called *topological reinforcement* or *amplification in pattern formation*.

Albert Einstein once quipped that "compound interest" is the most powerful force in the universe.[5] Perhaps he was thinking of nonlinear field dynamics, like the compounding effects of gravitation, or possibly he was just sardonically reflecting on his house payments. In any case, it is a useful metaphor for explaining many kinds of amplification effects. I will argue that a kind of compound interest of topologies is the basis for all forms of emergence. We are justified in calling something "emergent," I will suggest, if it is the result of a recurrent amplification of configuration or topology. This recurrent architecture is itself a topological concept, so in some sense emergence is a special case of topological transformation of topologies.

Wherever it occurs, amplification is accomplished by a kind of repeated superimposition of similar forms. Amplification can be achieved by mathematical recursion in a computation, by recycling of a signal that reinforces itself and cancels the background in electronic sound amplification or other signal processing circuits, or by repetitively sampling the same biased set of phenomena in a statistical analysis. In each of these cases, the formal or configurational regularities of the medium are what serve as the basis for the amplification. The "stuff" that constitutes the medium in which amplification is exhibited is largely irrelevant, as is the electricity in an audio amplifier. (Audio amplification can for example be achieved using a liquid medium flowing through pipes or light beaming through light guides.) Amplification can be a merely physical process or an informational process— the latter usually depends on the former—as in statistics and certain computations. In all cases, it is a form that is amplified; repetition either multiplies the number of its appearances in some physical medium or else gets it embodied in a progressively larger fraction of the physical medium (as in sound amplification). Thus amplification is a kind of compound interest of physical form.

The relevance of "compound interest logic" in the analysis of emergence is that it helps explain how certain minor or even incidental aspects of a complex phenomenon can come to be the source of its dominant features. In this analysis, then, emergence will be treated as a form of amplification of certain topological features within a physical system. Specifically, I will argue that amplification occurs because of iterated superimposition of events sharing the same form occurring across levels of scale. Using the logic of compound interest in physically-embodied forms as my guide, I will argue that we can distinguish three hierarchically related classes of emergent phenomena on the basis of their constraint architectures. Specifically, I will suggest that the most useful architectonic feature is whether there is recurrent or circular redundancy of the influence of constraints or biases exhibiting the same form across levels of scale. In the history of the development of theories of complexity and emergence, writers have regularly recognized the important role of "circular causality" in some form or other.[6] Problems of recursion and self-reference have also regularly been the basis for emergent concepts in mathematics: from the calculus, to the concept of imaginary numbers, to the inspiration for Gödel's incompleteness proof. To date, however, I know of no effort to formalize this intuition with respect to a theory of ontological emergence, or to apply it as a general analytic tool for describing the common features of all forms of emergent phenomena.

4   Circular Definition

Not all cases of circular causality may qualify as full instances of emergence, at least in the sense that it is most often invoked in physical systems. A simple and well-known example of "circular causality" is embodied in a thermostatic control system. By connecting a heating and/or cooling device to a temperature-sensitive switch, the coupled devices can be configured to respond to temperature in a manner that will eventually invert the state of the switch and with it the state of the device that heats or cools the environment. In other words, there is a self-undermining pattern of cause and effect—so-called negative feedback—that tends to produce behavioral oscillation around some set-point. If this causal linkage is reversed, of course, so that deviation away from the set-point activates mechanisms that cause the environmental temperature to deviate yet further, a very different and unstable behavior results—so-called positive feedback. This runaway effect is checked only by outside constraints. Even simple deterministic engineering devices, in which a number of such feedback control devices are coupled, can produce highly complex, quasi-periodic behaviors—or even "deterministic chaos," in which long-term prediction is essentially impossible. So feedback effects of this sort can be quite complicated, and even deeply unpredictable, in complex dynamical systems. They produce higher-order quasi-regularities whose patterning can only be understood in terms of the whole causal system, and are only produced when the whole ensemble of components is assembled.

Emergent effects in most contexts inherit their surprising characteristics from some version of this logic. This basic feedback servomechanism design has a self-undermining architecture in terms of the transformation of energy and the "signals" this energy conveys. This self-undermining logic is a bit like the famous liars' paradox—"This statement is false." In a servomechanism, internal self-contradiction of this kind serves a sort of self-correcting or self-compensating function, although higher-order loops of servomechanisms can produce complicated mixtures of asynchronous positive and negative feedback effects.

The importance of circularity in positive feedback is that it is deviation amplifying in the same way that compound interest is by operating on an outcome of that same operation performed previously. In general, it takes relatively little in the way of circular architecture in physical or computational systems to produce highly complex and convoluted behaviors. The effect is quite general and is entirely a consequence of the global architecture or topology of this causal closure. Indeed, some degree of causal "circling back," so to speak, is inevitable in the real world because of finiteness and aggregation.

The first component of my definition, then, is that nearly every sort of phenomenon that we are inclined to agree is emergent is considered so because it manifests some variant of this kind of circular causality. What we consider emergent about such phenomena are the consequences of this circularity. What emerges are certain configurational properties that become amplified via circular topology. By "amplified" I mean something like "come to be more coherently expressed over ever more extensive scales of both space and time."

Deterministic feedback in servomechanisms or finite recurrence in recursive computations exemplify the limiting cases of this architecture. Their behaviors are often referred to as emergent, but this is so only when both phenomena are considered in abstraction. By design, such systems exhibit closure to the world of the physical details of their embodiment. In working with reliable machines we can effectively ignore any undesigned influences; and we ignore their physicalness by abstraction in computational models. So we should probably describe them as exhibiting "computational emergence" to distinguish this from the ontological emergence characteristic of open physical systems. Higher-order emergent behaviors of complex servo-mechanisms occur in a deterministic single-level architecture, and this precisely limits their dynamics to a narrow, even if sometimes near chaotic, range. As a result, any higher-order transformation of this dynamics is not possible. For example, there is no recruitment of noise from microscopic physical tolerance variations to become "signal," except for situations where amplified perturbations exceed some physical limits of the device and it "fails." Precisely because they are idealized either in the form of *representations* (e.g., computation) or as engineered devices that we only operate within set tolerances (which are also embodiments of representations), they cannot actually produce ontological emergence, only highly unpredictable, nonregular behaviors.

In the natural world, however, where forms and physical interactions grade into one another, circular causal architectures can spontaneously amplify form relationships originating from anywhere at any scale and as a result of any contingency, depending on the architecture. This openness to physical influence is missing from simulations and is minimized by design in electronic or mechanical feedback devices. It is typically a source of smoothing effects because of the uncorrelated nature of such factors, including everything from extrinsic environmental changes to quantum fluctuations. But if any given contingency, no matter how minute, can be amplified in its effect by some deviation amplifying causal architecture, then a kind of unpredictability that isn't merely the result of exceeding computability can result. In this case, even in principle, it may be impossible also to predict what specific physical contingency will become selectively amplified. However, as complexity theorists and systems theorists have shown, despite the details, there may still be convergent development to predictable attractor patterns, which will have more to do with the general causal architecture of the system in question than with which contingent event was amplified.

5 Ascent in Scale

These considerations point to one more critical feature that is typically a correlate of emergence in physical systems, and which is nearly ubiquitous with spontaneous emergence: *ascent in scale*. The critical role played by ascent in scale in physical emergence is that it creates the context for causal circularity and amplification. It affords the substrate for structural influences to recirculate, so to speak. It is the physical analogue of repeated sampling from the same population in statistics. Ascent in scale increases the probability that potentially reinforcing regularities will compound and that nonreinforcing regularities will wash out. Although we must design and engineer simple systems to achieve the amplifying effects of circular causality, it almost inevitably occurs, in at least minimal form, with an ascent in scale that includes very large numbers of interactions. The numbers of ways that various physical effects can "circle back around" to the same locus in a fixed period of time increases rapidly with size and density of the population of interacting parts, whether in a physical medium or a randomly constructed network. My implication is a simple one: an ascent in scale that correlates with greater numbers of components and their interactions increases the probability that potential canceling and amplifying effects will be manifested in that collection. A subset of these effects are what we recognize as emergent.

The causal architectonic feature I will use as my central diagnostic feature might be described as trans-scale causal recursion, that is, circles of deviation amplifying causality that develop up levels of scale. My question is this: What happens when the global topological regularities of a locally bounded open physical system are in some way "fed back" into that system? Following Einstein's more familiar characterization of nonlinearity in terms of compound interest, then, one might describe the taxonomy of emergence I have in mind as a categorization based on a sort of "compound interest" of form as a consequence of expansion in scale.

By distinguishing the causal topology by which these influences propagate through a system, three general categories of emergence can be derived. The three highly general ways that causal architectures can be topologically recurrent across levels of scale are (1) as nonrecurrent-architectures, (2) as simple recurrent-architectures, and (3) as recurrent-architectures of recurrent architectures. These produce phenomena that can correspondingly be called first-, second-, and third-order emergence, respectively, reflecting the progressive embedding of recurrent causal effects.

6   Simple Emergence

The most basic sense of emergence can be called *first-order emergence*. It corresponds to the way the term "emergence" is often applied to descriptively "simple" higher-order properties of an aggregate, such as the statistically- or stochastically-determined phase states of matter I have discussed above. Statistical thermodynamics and quantum theory have provided a remarkably complete theory of how the properties of water molecules can produce liquid properties in aggregate. Thus, in one sense, these higher-order properties are considered to be fully reducible to molecular properties and their effects on molecular interactions in aggregate. But such relational properties, as opposed to intrinsic molecular properties (e.g., mass, charge, configuration of electron shells, etc.), are not symmetric across levels of description. Precisely because they are relational, they are not applicable to descriptions of water molecules in isolation, for instance, and many will not be discernable in just any large aggregate. It is only when certain of the regularities of molecular interaction relationships add up rather than cancel one another that certain *between*-molecule relationships can produce aggregate behaviors with ascent in scale. So in this case, although the diversity of momenta, directions of relative movement, and orientation geometries of molecular interactions cancel one another out in aggregate, the ratio of hydrogen bond strength to energy of collision and its effect on molecular distances expresses itself as large-scale aggregate properties because these features produce an average net effect.

Philosophers of science have used the term "supervenience"[7] to refer to the dependence of higher-order phenomena on lower-order phenomena, or rather for the more subtle relationship that exists between higher-order phenomena that are not exactly just scaled-up, lower-order phenomena, and yet are products of them. Though the aggregate effects that consist in liquid properties are unlike any of the molecular interaction properties, there is a direct correspondence between the summation of these and some aggregate property. Because of the cancellation effects, in the aggregate much of the detail at the micro-level can be ignored without loss of descriptive adequacy. Micro-level events don't matter with respect to interactions at the macroscopic level, such as bouyancy of certain materials, surface tension, viscosity, and so forth. The higher-order properties nevertheless "supervene" on specific lower-order interactions to the extent that the former always entail the latter but not vice versa.

Not all aggregate properties can be considered emergent, however, even in this most reduced sense. For example, consider weight or density. Weight has a descriptive adequacy almost irrespective of level of analysis. The force of gravity exerts an effect on matter irrespective of scale, even if its effect may be scale-dependent in some ways. It is scale-dependent in that it has a relatively minor contribution to make to the trajectory followed by any individual water molecule in solution, but a major effect on the behavior of large bodies of water. Nevertheless, it is the same force and the same effect at both levels of scale. Nothing more needs to be added to the account of the aggregate behavior except that aggregate properties also are affected (e.g., surface tension and surface shape).

In contrast, other liquid properties develop out of the properties of water molecules in more complex ways. This occurs in cases where the lower-order *relational* properties are the constitutive factor determining the higher-order property. In these cases, the account is fundamentally incomplete without including specific "configurational" and/or distributional information concerning the relationships between the components (e.g., quantity of constituents, their relative positions and momenta, their molecular geometry, their hydrogen bond strengths in different orientations, etc.). To represent all of this would produce a description with a very high dimensionality (many degrees of freedom, roughly corresponding to the relevant properties of each molecule with respect to the others, times the number of molecules) at the lower level. At the higher level of description, this dimensional complexity can often be ignored and little descriptive adequacy will be lost.

But this is not merely a descriptive matter. The astronomically many details cancel out due to the relative linearity of the stochastic processes and the evenly distributed diversity of these details. This results in a sort of phenomenological simplification with ascent in scale. This simplification tends to be nonuniform with respect to scale, often exhibiting threshold effects, or steps, of increasing size as regularities begin to dominate the messiness. The vast amount and diversity in causal detail that is distributed among the components and their interaction histories simply has little impact on the aggregate behavior if the aggregate is very large. The micro-effects are not just buried among the vast numbers of interactions; their differences cause some to get revealed in aggregate and others to get obscured.[8] Net effects matter, but some, like mass, merely matter via the aggregation of the tiny effects, while others matter because of the specific form of the aggregate effect. Where the form of aggregate effect is critical, the form itself becomes, in some cases, an additional physical dimension. Although not independent from the details, and despite the fact that it can be given a potentially exhaustive, reductive description in terms of them, it can have other form-altering effects on other systems, not because of the details, but because of the aggregate form.

Wave propagation in a fluid is such an example. Although the nature of the wave and its detailed underlying dynamical realization in each may differ depending on whether the fluid is water, air, or an electromagnetic field, the ability to propagate a wave is a first-order emergent feature they all share in common. It is this emergent commonality that enables sound waves in air, for example, to be transformed into electric current fluctuations, transmitted through space as electromagnetic fluctuations, and converted via a radio receiver back into sound waves halfway around the globe. It is for this reason that first-order emergent phenomena, although minimalistically emergent, are an essential part of the concept: they are the basis for relationships that can be far more than merely supervenient.

7   Diachronic Symmetry-Breaking

Philosophical and scientific discussions of the mind-brain mystery often invoke some implicit version of supervenient emergence to model the presumed relationship between higher-order, mental phenomena and the lower-order, cellular-molecular processes on which they depend. But, as noted above, it is clear that the analogy is not nearly adequate. At the very least it fails to capture an essential distinguishing feature: temporal development or symmetry-breaking. There is a simple self-similarity to liquid properties across time and position that is further "smoothed" by stochastic processes. In contrast, there is a self-differentiating feature to living and mental processes, which both retains and undermines aspects of self-similarity despite (or rather ironically because of) stochastic features. This characteristic breakdown of self-similarity, or symmetry-breaking, is now recognized in numerous kinds of complex phenomena, including systems far simpler than living systems. Complex emergent phenomena of these sorts share a characteristic change of ensemble properties across time, and are often computationally unpredictable as well. So it would be useful to distinguish first-order emergence from these more complex forms of emergent phenomena in which the cumulative stochastic canceling of configurational interactions exhibited by simple entropic systems is undermined, and where this contributes to development and change of both micro- and macro-properties across time.

At first glance, it may appear as though distinguishing between synchronic and diachronic classes of emergent phenomena can capture this difference. First-order emergence is typically described in synchronic terms, and, although it is recognized that this is a short-hand descriptive trick, there is very little descriptive loss in this heuristic. But in many discussions, the synchronic and diachronic uses of the concept must be made explicit. For example, biological scientists now feel comfortable with the notion that life is an emergent property of organic matter that supervenes on the properties of its constituent molecular interactions. Because life is a continuous property of an organism, one can describe it at any one moment as synchronically supervenient on the properties of the organism's constituent molecules and their relationships. But this fails to capture the vast and convoluted temporal depth of the causal account that would be necessary to understand the configurational details that constitute structures and behaviors that we intend to capture by the notion of "life." Specifically, biological aggregate properties that we consider "functions" implicitly require reference to a detailed history of at least the micro- and macro-configurational relationships. These histories link biological function with interactions among critical substrate variables, and, implicitly, with an evolutionary ensemble of reproductively related individuals and their interactions with these substrates. In short, the synchronic shorthand account assumes far more than a simple diachronic restatement of first-order emergence.

This can be demonstrated easily by considering evolutionary examples. Consider the process by which life must have arisen from nonlife in the early history of the earth. Both a synchronic and a diachronic sense of emergence must be considered here. The higher-order properties of the molecular systems that constituted the first lifelike, self-organizing proto-metabolisms can be said to have supervened on the molecular interactions concurrently involved, since the present state of these very interactions is the basis for describing the whole ensemble as having the property of being alive. But, prior to the formation of the first molecular configuration of this kind, no living phenomena existed. So, in addition to being first-order emergent by way of interactions of lower-order constituents, a higher-order emergence relationship is also involved. The configurational properties of prebiotic systems are a part of the causal complex upon which the first biotic systems supervene—in time. In other words, evolutionary processes must be described as the successive emergence of new emergent phenomena from old: emergent phenomena constituted of other emergent phenomena. By this I do not mean to suggest that "life" itself is more than a re-description of this supervenience, but rather to note that there is a temporal component to this kind of emergence as well as ascent in scale. There is an asymmetry in configuration across time—a development.[9]

This difference is not merely a matter of adding levels upon levels, as in the way solid-state physics reduces to atomic interactions that in turn reduce to elementary particle interactions and so on (presumably to quarks, etc.). Rather, it involves nonlinear systems that exhibit an internal causal recursivity and ultimately a self-undermining dynamic that causes prior states of the system to be irreversibly replaced and superseded. This recursiveness is the basis of an irreducibly diachronic asymmetry. But for this reason the distinction is more complicated than merely distinguishing between synchronic systems with self-similar, simple, entropic development (e.g., behavior of a gas) and diachronic ones with difference-amplifying development. There is more than one way to change.

8   Self-Assembly and Self-Organization

Surface tension is an emergent property of a comparatively simple type. It is characterized by predictability so long as lower-order properties fall within certain parameters. But there are conditions where this is not the case: specifically under conditions where more or less chaotic or self-organized behaviors are produced. Under chaotic conditions, for example, certain higher-order regularities become unstable, and an unpredictability of higher-order dynamics results. In chaotic systems, unpredictability derives from the fact that regularities at lower levels have become strongly affected by regularities emerging at higher levels of organization. This can happen when configurational features at the ensemble level drastically change the probabilities of certain whole classes of component interactions.

This occurs in shock wave boundaries, for example, where relative movements of whole ensembles of gas molecules exceed the rate at which energy can be exchanged by typical elastic collisions between individual molecules. So breaks in symmetry appear that affect component molecular interactions. Those on one side or the other of this interactive threshold can have an inordinate influence over ensemble behaviors. The specific nonsystematic locations of these micro-symmetry-breaks become important since they become loci of major energy transfer for whole subsystems distinguished by sharing similar global features. The result is that these specific micro-configurations have macro-configurational consequences (e.g., local energetic "cascades" and irregularities) that in turn affect future micro-configurations, and so on. This hierarchical nonlinearity consequently produces a kind of self-undermining dynamic across levels that is expressed in a unique time series of configurations.

The signature feature of this complication of first-order emergence is that the configuration of individual components and unique interactions can exert an organizing effect on an entire ensemble. While in principle these examples still exhibit first-order emergence, we now must contend with an additional *second-order emergence* of behaviors and ensemble properties. Whereas micro-configuration can be ignored in first-order emergent systems, with minimal loss of descriptive adequacy, this is not the case for systems exhibiting second-order emergence. Chaotic and self-organized systems are generally of this type. Chaotic phenomena have become a major focus of "complexity" theory in its many forms. Such phenomena cannot be adequately described without incorporating a detailed history of the system and its components, whereas merely first-order emergent phenomena can. Moreover, as has come to be the hallmark of complex chaotic systems, initial conditions of system history can play critical roles in the ongoing global dynamics of the system.

This is often expressed as the apocryphal "butterfly effect," in which it is supposed that a butterfly flapping its wings in a particular pattern in one part of the globe is responsible for monsoons forming in another part of the globe, years later. Although in reality this is an implausible and misleading just-so story (since the highly entropic dynamics of the atmosphere tend to quickly smooth out such perturbations rather than amplify them; see below), it does capture the possibility that large-scale configurational properties of a system could conceivably be substantially affected by extremely miniscule differences in prior micro-configurations of the same system under certain special circumstances. What are these special circumstances? Whereas atmospheric dynamics can be chaotic and unpredictable, they are not systematic. As a result, and importantly, they do not tend to consistently amplify specific perturbations. Certain other kinds of highly organized physical systems can, however, exhibit what I will call an "ampliative character." This gets reflected in their critical dependency on historical contingency and complex unique individual structure.

Take, for example, snow crystal formation.[10] The structure of an individual snow crystal reflects the interaction of three major factors: (1) the hexagonal micro-structural biases of ice-crystal lattice growth, inherited from water molecule symmetry, (2) the radial symmetry of heat dissipation, and (3) the unique history of changing temperature and humidity regimes as a developing crystal falls through the air. Different temperatures and humidities interact with water molecule binding regularities to generate a handful of distinct patterns of ice-lattice formation. Since a snow crystal grows as it falls through different regions in a variable atmosphere, a record of the temperature and humidity differences it encounters literally gets frozen into the variant patterns of crystal structure at successive diameters.

In this way, the snow crystal is a sort of record of the conditions of its development. But it is more than merely a historical record. There is a "compound interest" effect as well. Prior patterns of crystal growth constrain subsequent patterns of crystal growth. So even identical conditions of temperature and humidity, which would otherwise determine identical lattice growth, can produce different global patterns depending on the current configuration of the crystal. The global configuration of this tiny developing system plays a critical causal role in its microscopic dynamics by excluding the vast majority of possible molecular accretions and growth points, and strongly predisposing accretion and growth at certain other sites.

Snow crystals are in this way at least minimally self-organizing (though not strictly speaking autopoietic; see below). The unique growth history of the crystal cannot be ignored. Indeed growth history is a dominant factor determining its final configuration. More importantly, these configurational properties of the system self-amplify. Each past configuration influences all subsequent configurations as well. This influence occurs by virtue of the progressive contraction of the potential growth options that results from past growth.[11]

Both self-undermining (divergent) chaotic systems, as in turbulent flow, and self-organizing (partially convergent) chaotic systems, as in snow crystal formation, exhibit causal circularity of a kind that links higher-order and lower-order configurational properties. These *feed-forward* circles of cause and effect, linking reciprocally reinforcing effects at different levels of scale, are the defining features distinguishing second-order emergence from first. It is "second order" because first-order emergent properties have become self-modifying, resulting in the emergence of new emergent phenomena.

More complex second-order emergence is exhibited by "autopoietic" systems. In autopoiesis the interaction dynamics of sets of different components is constrained both by the configurational properties of the whole collection and by configuration symmetries and asymmetries that exist between the micro-configurations of the different classes of its components. In snow crystal dynamics the micro-configuration of each component is essentially the same, producing symmetric interactions and strongly constrained structural consequences. When a system is composed of different kinds of components, however, it can also exhibit a more distributed inter-actional reflexivity. Because of the combinatorial possibilities the resultant properties can be quite complex.

For example, molecules that interact in highly allosteric fashion, that is, which bond selectively with some but not other types of molecules, can con-stitute interaction sets with more elaborate self-organizing features. Both the configurations of the different classes of individual interactions and the configuration of the whole set of possible interactions become critical or-ganizing influences. Processes of this sort can occur in a chemical "soup" that contains enough different kinds of molecules so that there is a subset of types that can each catalyze the formation of some other member in the set, constituting a closed loop of syntheses. (This is called an autocatalytic set; for a recent discussion see Kauffman 1995, 2000.) So long as sufficient en-ergy and other raw materials are available to keep reactions going (it must, that is to say, be an open system) the "autocatalytic" character of the set will play an inordinate role in determining both what chemical reactions can take place and how the whole soup will be constituted. It is the higher-order distributed circularity of the interactions of the different classes of constituents that matters. Such a system can generate far more complex micro-dynamics and macro-dynamics than if the interactions were sym-metric or canceling. The general theory of chemical reactions with these circular features was extensively investigated by Ilya Prigogine and by Manfred Eigen a generation ago. It has now become the basis for extensive research with both real and simulated chemical systems. (See Prigogine 1997, Eigen and Oswatitsch 1992 for their own accounts.) Ultimately, the metabolic molecular dynamics that constitute living cells depends on au-topoietic system dynamics constituted by numerous fully and partially au-tocatalytic sets of molecules.

What do these examples of second-order emergent phenomena have in common? The answer is: a kind of tangled hierarchy of causality where micro-configurational particularities can be amplified to determine macro-configurational regularities, and where these in turn further constrain and/or amplify subsequent micro-configurational regularities. In such cases, it is more appropriate to call the aggregate a "system" rather than a mere collection, since the specific reflexive configurational and recurrent causal architecture is paramount. So, although these systems must be open to the flow of energy and components—which is what enables their growth and/or development—they additionally include a kind of configurational closure as well. These material flows carry configurational constraints inherited from past states of the system that constrain future behaviors of its components. As material and energy flows on through and out again, *form* also recirculates and becomes amplified. In one sense, this form is nothing more than a set of restrictions and biases on possible future material and energetic events. In another sense, it is what defines and bounds the higher-order individual entity that we identify as the system.

Not surprisingly, quasi-crystalline and autopoietic, second-order, emergent systems are often found linked in living systems. For example, consider the configuration-constraining role of quasi-crystal-like molecular structures, such as the polymers and membranes in living cells. These can grow by self-assembly and also tend to play a critical role in constraining the interactions critical to living, autopoietic, chemical reactions. The configuration of such a substrate may both catalyze certain individual reactions and increase the probability of causal circularity of a reflexive set of other catalytic reactions, for example, by aligning multiple species of molecules with respect to one another. This kind of interaction between emergent phenomena turns out to be important for yet higher levels of emergent interaction.

9 Evolution and Semiosis: Third-Order Emergence

There is a further difference, however, between chaotic/self-organizing emergent phenomena, like snow crystal growth or chemical autopoeisis, and evolving emergent phenomena, such as living organisms. The latter additionally involve some form of *information* or *memory* (for example, as represented in nucleic acids) that is not seen in second-order systems. The result is that specific historical moments of higher-order regularity or of unique micro-causal configurations can exert an additional cumulative influence over the entire causal future of the system. In other words, via memory, constraints derived from specific, past, higher-order states can get repeatedly re-entered into the lower-order dynamics leading to future states, in addition to their effects mediated by second-order processes.

To get a sense of this additional loop of causality, imagine the following fanciful possibility: a kind of snow crystal that, instead of just melting, contributes some bias to the formation and ongoing growth of a new snow crystal.[12] It might perhaps provide a seed crystal that reflected some global aspect of its geometry to the new crystal growth (e.g., the relative predominance of spirelike or platelike geometry, the degree of structural heterogeneity, etc.). Each new generation of snow crystal would consequently be biased by the cumulative results of what happened to some prior snow crystal, and so on. Some trace of the history of cumulative biases would be repetitively updated and re-entered as an initial bias in each new snow crystal "generation." In this world, snow crystals in different eras would likely look different, and these differences would follow various trends. But to this fanciful example we need to add one more ingredient. There is now a whole class of new contingencies that can accumulate and amplify along another gradient of scale: the expansion of lineages (defined with respect to continuity of seeding) across generation-time. A lineage is an extended aggregate in both space and time. In this way, some contingent feature represented in an individual of an aggregate can give rise to its own temporally and spatially extended aggregate of individuals. Space and time get convolved together in this way, and a new type of amplification is possible.

In this way, larger scale extrinsic contingencies and boundary conditions will matter in ways not characteristic of second-order emergence. Analogous to the ampliative architectures that occur via ascent of scale in second-order emergence, there is now the possibility of ampliative architectures via ascent in temporal scale—historical extent—because greater and greater extended chunks of contingent events can be reentrantly compounded and fed-forward. In second-order emergence, a certain synergy between boundary conditions and the relational topologies of the constituents of a system results in the self-amplification of certain features as opposed to others. With this additional twist of causality, an analogous selective amplification bias can occur also with respect to these self-amplification conditions themselves. Contingent synergies between the conditions in which these fanciful snow crystals grow can now come to bias what aspects of snow crystal geometry will be passed on and amplified in the future. In other words, this allows for a process of selection among alternative second-order emergent processes. (The term "selection" is merely a post hoc short hand for the result of this spontaneous synergy-biased amplification, as it is also in evolutionary theory.)

In these systems, there is a kind of synergy between self-organization and representation. Even the topology of the "ampliative" architecture itself can be convoluted in unpredictable ways by a higher-order amplification in which such details come to play an inordinately important role in determining the causal architecture itself. For this kind of phenomena we must introduce a third-order of emergence, which recognizes the additional loop of recursive causality, enclosing the second-order recursive causality of self-organized systems. Capturing, condensing, and re-entering the effects of selected events distributed across a span of lineage history is what makes evolutionary processes both chaotically unpredictable in one sense and yet also historically organized, with an unfolding quasi-directionality.

Third-order emergence inevitably exhibits a developmental and/or evolutionary character. It occurs where there is both amplification of global influences on parts, but also redundant "sampling" of these influences and reintroduction of them redundantly across time and into different realizations of the same type of second-order system. Under these conditions there can be extensive amplification of lower-order emergent relationships and also lower-order chaotic/self-organizing relationships because their historical traces do not degrade. These traces get repeatedly re-entered into new iterations of the system in new contexts. Whereas second-order emergent phenomena exhibit locally and temporally restricted whole-to-part influences, third-order emergent phenomena can exhibit amplification of these effects as well, doubly convolving the link between levels and scales of causality.

This can be imagined as a sort of self-referential self-organization, an autopoiesis of autopoieses. Amplification of complexity and of self-organizational dynamics can be enormously complex under these conditions, forming into a maze of causal circularities, because every prior state is a potentially amplifiable initial condition contributing to all later states. Moreover, because there is a "re-membered" trace of each prior "self" state contributing to the dynamics of future states, such systems can develop with respect to this prior "self," rather than just with respect to the immediately prior state of the whole. This fact contributes to the characteristic differentiation and divergence from, and convergence back toward, some "reference" state, as exhibited in organisms.

The representation relationship implicit in third-order, emergent phenomena demands a combination of multi-scale, historical, and semiotic analyses for adequate description. This is why living and cognitive processes require us to introduce concepts such as representation, adaptation, information, and function in order to capture the logic of the most salient emergent phenomena. It is what makes the study of living forms qualitatively different from other physical sciences. It makes no sense to ask about the function of granite. Though the atoms composing a heart muscle fiber, or a neurotransmitter molecule, have no function in themselves, the particular configurations of the heart and its cell types, or the neurotransmitter molecule, do additionally beg for some sort of teleological assessment, some function. They do something for something. Organisms evolve and regulate the production of multiple second-order emergent phenomena with respect to some third-order phenomenon. Only a third-order emergent process has such an intrinsic identity.

So life, even in its simplest forms, is third-order emergent. This is why its products cannot be fully understood apart from either historical or functional concerns. Indeed, it may be that any third-order emergent system must be considered "alive" in some sense.[13] This suggests that third-order emergence may offer something like a definition of life in its broadest sense. If this is so, then the origins of life on the earth may also mark the initial emergence of third-order emergent phenomena on the earth. More generally, it constitutes the origination of information, semiosis, and teleological relationships on earth. It is the creation of an "epistemic cut" to use Howard Pattee's felicitous phrase: the point where physical causality acquires (or rather constitutes) significance. This is a complex and subtle issue, which I can only obliquely approach in this overview. Nonetheless, a few points are relevant to the purpose of this chapter.

The first is that third-order emergence serves as a sort of minimal account of what we mean by information. It is an implicit account of what constitutes the creation of information. The physical conveyance of configurational bias from one emergent context to another to generate third-order emergence constitutes the most primitive "aboutness" relationship. It is the embodiment of a "selection" among possible alternatives among some set of possible configurations of the same "type." Specifically it captures in a concrete way what might be called the potential amplifiability of some emergent features with respect to other emergent features and with respect to the ensemble of possible local boundary conditions. This progressively amplifies a correspondence relationship. Third-order emergence links the sampling over an ensemble of related emergent systems to sampling over an ensemble of likely boundary conditions. So in an evolutionary context we say that a given configuration of an organism is an adaptation to something. This is, implicitly, a representational relationship, even if the specific object of the representation is often somewhat vague.

Consider for example the dynamical organization of the molecular system that constitutes the ciliated pellicle, or skin, of a paramecium (the familiar sole-of-a-shoe-shaped, single-celled pond organism). The ciliated pellicle of the paramecium enables it to swim around obstacles by asymmetrically depolarizing, causing the cell to tumble, when it bumps up against something. I think it is appropriate to say that in some basic sense this complex configuration of molecular modules, with their linked molecular "tails," "motors," and mechano-receptors, is a representation of a cumulative past history of obstacles and their properties in terms of how these affected the reproduction of past versions of this mechanism. The configuration of the pellicle and its responsivity re-presents in the present system certain critical regularities of "obstacleness" that were sampled and amplified over billions of obstacle encounters and their outcomes in past generations. The "tokens" conveying this representation are ultimately genes, as interpreted with respect to the way the components tend to self-assemble and interact. The result is a system constituted so that it exhibits selective correspondent behaviors to classes of likely contextual conditions. It projects selective abstract regularities of the past onto potential future conditions. In this way the pellicle configuration is "about" obstacle avoidance. Evolution has produced the emergence of something like a functional category: "obstacle."

10   A Hierarchy of Emergent Phenomena

The three subcategories of emergent phenomena can be arranged into a hierarchy of increasing complexity, in which higher-order forms are composed of relationships between lower-order forms. Third-order (evolutionary) emergence contains second-order (self-organizing) emergence as a limiting case, which in turn contains first-order (supervenient) emergence as a limiting case. In this way, any given example of evolutionary emergence must also involve self-organizing and supervenient emergence as well, but not vice versa. Because higher-order emergent phenomena are dependent on and constituted by lower-order emergent phenomena, their probability of spontaneous occurrence is also substantially lower. Consequently there are vastly more examples of supervenient emergent phenomena than of self-organizing emergent phenomena and, in turn, vastly more examples of self-organizing emergent phenomena than of evolutionary emergent phenomena. So only a few generically supervenient phenomena are alive, but every living thing is a supervenient emergent phenomenon. Conversely, however, with the replication made possible by third-order emergence, the number of emergent phenomena of all types can rapidly increase, although the production of lower-order, subordinate, emergent phenomena produced to support the third-order will always be far more numerous.

This hierarchic categorization does not exhaust the possibilities of increasingly more complex forms of emergent phenomena. Evolutionary emergent systems can further interact to form multilayer systems of exceeding complexity. Indeed, this is the nature of complex organisms that is exemplified in the ascending levels of "self" that proceed from gene to cell to organism to lineage to species, and so on, in the living world. But this logic does not lead to what might have been called fourth-order emergence. Instead, I think we must rather analyze these more complex processes as first-, second-, and third-order emergent elaborations of third-order emergence, and so on, in recursive series. This is because third-order emergence includes the capacity to evolve new forms of emergence itself. This is implicit in its inherently representational or semiotic character. The introduction of referential relationship as the defining feature of third-order emergence creates a spatial and temporal boundedness that is able to encompass any physical system, and re-present any system with respect to its correspondences with another. So there is no upper, outer, past, or future bound to what can constitute a third-order emergent phenomenon. Representational capacity is ultimately unbounded.

One of the advantages of framing evolutionary processes in these quite abstract and general terms is that doing so helps us to delineate where the evolutionary and self-organizing processes of living systems can be distinguished and where they interact. For example, it makes explicit the dependence that evolutionary processes have on self-organizational processes, and provides important hints about how evolutionary processes might have themselves emerged from something simpler. So, for example, those approaches to the origins of life that emphasize the role of autocatalysis or autopoiesis as the necessary antecedent processes to living processes are consistent with this analysis. So are those that emphasize replication processes. But what might be called "replicator-first" models are not. The reason is that for replication to be ampliative it must occur as a part of and with respect to self-organization processes whose topologies are thus captured and conveyed to future iterations. Similarly, it also suggests a categorization of biological evolutionary processes that can encompass some of the complexities introduced by complex organisms and by the representational processes introduced into biology with the evolution of brains and symbolic communication.

Thus minimalist Darwinian conceptions of natural selection are a first-order variant of third-order emergence in the sense that the accumulation of the consequences of natural selection are treated as summed and integrated in individuals of succeeding lineages. There are no "top-down" effects. The adaptive self-organizing processes of the organism are not assumed to exert any feed-forward effect that biases what is subjected to selection in future generations.

However, the process described as "niche construction" and various forms of Baldwinian-like effects are more complex. (See Deacon, chap. 5, as well as others in this volume, for a critical reevaluation of the Baldwin effect.) In these cases, the effects of the organism's adaptive responses do feed-forward to affect what gets exposed to or hidden from the effects of selection. As a result, a kind of self-organizational dynamic can develop in which the specific form of the behavioral or physiological adaptability can become a bias on the future range of naturally selected, adaptive capacities. So, for example, beaver dam-building and pond creation create a condition in which selection favors the evolution of aquatic adaptations, and aquatic adaptations increase the advantage of having dam-building propensities, in an ever-increasing ratcheting of interdependence. The specific details of the behavioral adaptation become the initiating biases in a compound-interest effect that both amplifies and accumulates concordant adaptations. These effects then are second-order emergent variants on the third-order emergent process of natural selection, which, like the cumulative constraints of the growing snow crystal, are incrementally amplified in succeeding stages, creating a more and more idiosyncratically integrated and distinctive result.

Finally, consider the evolution of symbolic communication in hominids. (See my detailed discussion in Deacon, chap. 5, this volume.) This evolutionary transition marks the emergence of a new and partially decoupled evolutionary dynamic. Symbolic communication has evolved to be primarily exemplified in a highly specialized form—language—both by virtue of its influence on the evolution of the brain and by virtue of the evolution of an independently evolving and self-organizing system of symbols and their effects. Linguistic and cultural evolution have their own third-order emergent dynamic. The representational nature of this adaptation exemplifies its third-order character. The effects on human physiology and human consciousness have clearly become the tail that wagged the dog in many respects.

11   Conclusions

The insistent critique from a systems-theoretic perspective of both genetic-reductionism in evolutionary theories and computational reductionism in cognitive theories can now be more precisely paraphrased. Life and mind cannot be adequately described in terms that treat them as merely supervenient because this collapses innumerable convoluted levels of emergent relationships. Life is not mere chemical mechanism. Nor is cognition mere molecular computation. These analogies miss the most salient and descriptively important dynamics of these phenomena. To collapse descriptions of living and cognitive systems in this way inevitably ignores whole classes of causal topologies that are essential to their comprehensive explanation, and contribute their most robust and important characteristics. In living processes, for example, the sources of structure and function can become increasingly distributed in space and time over the course of evolution. Organizing processes may also extend to include progressively higher-level subsystems exhibiting progressively greater top-down control architecture; for instance, brains.

It is the capacity of evolutionary emergent processes to progressively embed evolutionary processes within one another via representations that amplify their information-handling power in ways that make the mythical butterfly-effect story trivially simplistic, and makes minds possible. The many levels of embedded evolutionary emergent processes characteristic of brains are what enable them rapidly and selectively to amplify such a vast range of possible forms of activity. Which particular molecular system configurations will become amplified to produce subsequent states of the brain is both essentially untraceable and largely irrelevant. The most salient, causal antecedents are themselves idiosyncratic, global, third-order, emergent configurations of neural activity of an exquisitely indirect and astronomically unlikely variety. The incorporation of language into this complex, convoluted hierarchy of emergent processes has further vastly amplified the emergent capacities of cognition, expanding the realm of represented forms into a truly limitless universe of emergent possibilities.

A living organism is the end product of a very elaborately convoluted history of recursive causal processes that cast a wider and wider net to capture sources of regularity and amplify them. The result is that locating any specific antecedent cause of functional organization is essentially impossible. This is one reason that evolutionary "explanations" of specific traits are inevitably vague and general in form. There is no clear causal trend from more local to more distributed, and from micro to macro scales. There are not even clear boundaries in space and time. Indeed the causes of living organization grade into molecular noise and distant past contingencies. An organism's functional properties may be currently instantiated by its molecular architecture (first-order, local). Yet this architecture emerges from a vast ensemble of molecular interactions with the world, generated by innumerable past members of a lineage (third-order, nonlocal).

Brain processes produce a further baroque convolution and temporal amplification of this logic. Brains might be characterized as "emergence machines," incessantly churning out complex, high-level, virtual functions, virtual environments, and virtual evolutionary lineages to track and adapt to the complexity of the world. The minds that result are marvels of high-level, holistic, causal loci. Subjective experience reflects this convergent holism. The experience of being a sentient agent is no less than being the locus of something that is incessantly and spontaneously emerging.

This experience is itself an emerging locus at the center of a vast but only weakly constraining, weakly determinate web of semiotic and physiological influences.

Language further distributes the convoluted trace of causality that constitutes human agency. Human minds that have become deeply entangled in the evolving, symbolic, communicative processes of culture—as all modern human minds are—may have an effective causal locus that extends across continents and back millennia, and which grows out of the experiences of hundreds of thousands of individuals. This immense convergence of causal determination is coupled with a vast capacity for selective amplification that has itself been amplified beyond recognition by our cognitive involvement in the super-organism of symbolic culture. Human consciousness is not merely an emergent phenomenon; it epitomizes the logic of emergence in its very form: the locus of an immense confluence, condensation, amplification, and dissemination of topological constraint and bias. Consciousness emerges as an incessant creation of something from nothing, a process continually transcending itself.

Acknowledgment

This essay includes material excerpted from a paper by Bruce Weber and Terrence Deacon published in *Cybernetics and Human Knowing* 7: 21–43, 2000.

Notes

1. From Ursula Goodenough, personal communication.

2. Much has been written about this notion. The interested reader can find a recent lay introduction to the general topic in *Emergence: The Connected Lives of Ants, Brains, Cities, and Software* by Steven Johnson (2001), and a slightly more sophisticated introduction in *Emergence: From Chaos to Order* by John Holland (1998).

3. Of course, this is a much more knotty problem than I can address here. To some extent, these concepts also reflect a levels-of-analysis distinction since constituent properties are to a large extent the result of lower-level topological features as well. For the sake of this discussion, I will treat these as distinguishable at any given level.

4. This is a composite statement I have assembled by borrowing from a number of sources.

5. This is quite possibly an apocryphal quote, since I can find no precise citation context among the dozen or so places it is mentioned in the literature and on web

sites. But I am inclined to believe it was something he could have said, given the sense of humor it conveys juxtaposed with the not immediately obvious mathematical profundity it captures. The author would be grateful to the reader who could supply the precise context and citation, if it exists.

6. Though it might be more accurate to use the metaphor of "spiral" causality, I will use the terms "circular" and "recursive" because they make it easier to visualize more complex and convoluted architectures. I have decided to use the term "cause" in this colloquial sense throughout, but with some reservation, because it ultimately begs the questions I am trying to answer. In most cases understanding it in terms of the expansion, recursion, or propagation of topological constraints captures the more precise meaning I have in mind.

7. I can't claim to even attempt to capture all the tortuous uses this term has been subject to in philosophical writings, and here I use only one of its most basic senses.

8. Consider momentum of molecules. Usually, in aggregate, momenta in different directions cancel. But imagine a body of water that suddenly lurches upward because a majority of the vectors of momenta of moving molecules just coincidentally happened to not be uniformly distributed.

9. This developmental asymmetry is often described as a trend that is opposed to entropy—sometimes called "negentropy"—though I consider it more appropriate to describe it as a very rare expression of entropy.

10. In the above account of snow crystal growth, I have omitted many details of the physics of this process for the sake of focusing on those most relevant to this discussion. These include the physics of the different modes of lattice formation and growth that vary with temperature and humidity, and also some poorly understood aspects of surface physics, including the quasi-liquid dynamics of the molecular surface of the growing crystal and how these affect the growth and symmetries of the crystal. These omissions do not substantially alter the description in any way that is relevant to this account.

11. Note that growth is not an essential factor since this same dynamic also obtains if during certain phases of snow crystal development, there is periodic partial melting—a common occurrence—which is similarly historically constrained, and which can lead to elaborately shaped, entrapped bubbles and pits with smooth, curved edges.

12. This fanciful analogy was first suggested to me by Don Favareau.

13. As mentioned previously, with respect to physical emergence versus the virtual emergence of computational and mechanical systems, a simulation of third-order emergence is possible, but, because it is a representation and the physical ground of its constituents are not constituents of the emergent dynamics, I do not consider them in themselves physically emergent. Perhaps they can be called computationally or symbolically emergent, although the principles are somewhat different. The simulation of complex systems and "artificial-life" ecosystems can nonetheless be highly instructive tools that capture many aspects of this dynamic in representational form.

References

Crick, Francis (1994). *The Astonishing Hypothesis: The Scientific Search for the Soul.* New York: Charles Scribner's Sons.

Eigen, Manfred and R. W. Oswatitsch (1992). *Steps Toward Life: A Perspective on Evolution.* New York: Oxford University Press.

Holland, John (1998). *Emergence: From Chaos to Order.* New York: Oxford University Press.

Johnson, Steven (2001). *Emergence: The Connected Lives of Ants, Brains, Cities, and Software.* New York: Scribner.

Kauffman, Stuart (1995). *At Home in the Universe: The Search for the laws of Self-Organization and Complexity.* New York: Oxford University Press.

Kauffman, Stuart (2000). *Investigations.* New York: Oxford University Press.

Prigogine, Ilya (1997). *The End of Certainty: Time, Chaos, and the New Laws of Nature.* New York: Free Press.

Weber, Bruce and T. Deacon (2000). *Cybernetics & Human Knowing* 7: 21–43.

15

Emergence of Mind and the Baldwin Effect

Bruce H. Weber

1 Introduction

Darwin laid the foundation for the program of a naturalistic, nondualistic account of mind by providing an evolutionary view of how the human mind might have originated (Darwin 1871).[1] Darwin's proposal was taken up by Chauncy Wright to account for the evolutionary origin of human self-consciousness (Wright 1873). Evolutionary theorizing of this sort played a crucial role in the growth of the philosophy and psychology developed by the American pragmatists (Wiener 1949; see also Godfrey-Smith 1996).

Recently, however, most theories of cognitive structures have been based upon contemporary human minds in literate, postindustrial societies and have stressed metaphors of the mind based upon computational and information-processing models, unconstrained by evolutionary biology (Donald 1991). Darwin's view of the mind as an evolutionary adaptation has receded from the view of many cognitive scientists as they have emphasized the discontinuity of human mind from its evolutionary origins (see, for example, Chomsky 1980; Fodor 1983). To the extent that evolutionary biologists have concerned themselves with such questions, they have assumed that the emergence of mind and human language is to be explained by the extrapolation of the microevolutionary processes described by neo-Darwinism to the creation of optimally adapted modules of neural and morphological function (Pinker and Bloom 1990). This assumption underlies the past decade of "evolutionary psychology" (see, e.g., Cosmides, 1989; Barkow, Cosmides, and Tooby 1992; and Pinker 1994, 1998).

A related line of speculation is informed by the evolutionary gene concept of Richard Dawkins. It gives a gene's-eye and meme's-eye view of how interacting replicators can give rise to ever more complex "interactor/vehicles" that serve to increase their own survival in the face of natural selection conceived algorithmically (Dawkins 1976, 1982; Dennett 1991, 1995; Blackmore 1999). Susan Blackmore, for example, speculates that meme/gene coevolution was important in the origin of language (Blackmore 1999). In this, she admits that she is following up in Dawkinsian terms on the suggestion of Merlin Donald, who attempted to shift the focus of inquiry onto the steps by which the emergence of symbolic reference became the selective pressure that drove the coevolution of mind and brain (Donald 1991). Indeed, some evolutionary theorists have invoked mechanisms to help account for the very rapid evolution of human language by either assuming a role for mind in evolution or by positing a coevolution of brain and language in which emerging linguistic ability produces a feedback loop upon which selection acts (Dennett 1991, 1995; Pinker 1994; Deacon 1997).

Currently popular approaches such as that of Pinker, however, make unrealistic assumptions about low amounts of human variance and cultural diversity. They also view the mind as a set of problem-solving modules of independent evolutionary origin, which are capable of independent optimization. This latter view perpetuates the atomistic description of traits assumed by Sir Ronald Fisher, a view challenged by Sewall Wright almost immediately (Wright 1935a,b, 1986; see also Dobzhansky 1937). In spite of these difficulties, Pinker goes even further by assuming that problem-solving modules behave analogously to genes, showing phenomena such as crossing over and recombination—an unsubstantiated assertion that reflects a misplaced concreteness as well as a case of mixed metaphor. I cannot help but feel that such use of evolutionary biology results in a view of mind that either falls far short of our experience of consciousness, or sets consciousness aside as an intractable epiphenomenon, thus negating the promise held out by Darwin's evolutionary perspective.

How, then, should we proceed to develop a robust theory of the emergence of mind? A starting point is to assume hypothetically that mind, language, consciousness are emergent phenomena and then ask whether the received evolutionary theory has an account of emergent phenomena in general. I mean this in the following sense. Sterelny and Griffiths argue that any theory of evolution must account for adaptation, pattern of life (diversity, disparity, and speciation), and development of organisms over their life cycles (Sterelny and Griffiths 1999). To this list I would add emergence of large-scale evolutionary novelties (see for example: Müller and Wagner 1996; Gerhart and Kirschner 1997; Hall 1999; Carroll, Grenier, and Weatherbee 2001; Weber and Depew 2001; Arthur 2002).

2 Why Emergence Is Important

Emergence occurs when new properties appear in a system that were not present in, and could not easily have been predictable from, the properties of the components of the system. Emergent phenomena obey laws that arise with the novel properties. Emergent phenomena impose conditions on their constituents that depend on the nature of the emergent phenomena (Collier and Muller 1998; Holland 1998). A related point has been made by Stuart Kauffman, whose simulations of a range of dynamical regimes shows that the order produced in emergent systems reflects system properties of the ensemble of constituents as a whole (Kauffman 1993).

Attempts to analyze emergent phenomena have been hindered both by the ambiguity of the concept of emergence and by the different ways it is used in different contexts (Weber and Deacon 2000; Deacon, chap. 5, this volume; Camizine et al. 2001). Deacon has made careful distinctions between *supervenient emergence,* which is time-independent (synchronic); *emergence through chaos/self-organization,* which is time-dependent (diachronic symmetry breaking), includes developmental systems, and occurs away from thermodynamic equilibrium; and *evolutionary emergence,* which involves specified information and memory instantiated in genetic systems imposing stability and constraints on accessible future states. Deacon terms these first, second, and third order emergence respectively (Deacon, chap. 5, this volume). This threefold pattern constitutes a hierarchy of increasing complexity: higher-order forms are composed of relationships between lower order forms. This means that evolutionary emergence occurs only in lineages of reproducing organisms and contains self-organizing emergence as a limiting case, just as self-organizing emergence in turn contains supervenience as its limiting case. Thus evolutionary emergent phenomena must include self-organization and supervenience, but not the reverse. The issue is not whether an emergent novel trait is an adaptation and an evolved phenomenon, but rather how such a novelty came into existence in the lineage at all (Deacon, chap. 5, this volume).

Ultimately the emergence of consciousness must in some sense take advantage of the possibility that evolutionary emergent systems build complexity over time by increasing the causal loops among information, semiosis, and teleology. Under approaches such as these, there is the hope that a theory of evolutionary emergence will prove sufficiently robust to provide a causal account of the emergence of consciousness and language. The steps toward such a theoretical framework are only beginning to become clear, however, as we will see in section 4 below.

Problems of emergence, such as that of life itself, have been only of remote interest to many neo-Darwinians. Indeed, Darwin himself set aside the issue of emergence, except in so far as he dealt with the appearance of a complex, sophisticated adaptive structure arising from a primitive one. In discussing the evolution of the eye—an exemplar of organs of extreme perfection—he wrote, "How a nerve becomes sensitive to light hardly concerns us more than how life itself originated. . . ." (Darwin 1859, 187). Although this was an appropriate strategy for Darwin's time, critics unfriendly to Darwinism charge that the Modern Evolutionary Synthesis continues to ignore such crucial issues as the origin of complex biochemical systems, including those involved in photosensitivity, blood clotting, and the immune system, as well as the origin of life (see, for example, Behe 1997; but also see a response in Weber 1999). Of late, Darwinians of various stripes have deployed information and ideas from biochemistry and molecular genetics to address these problems, including some who use the resources of complex systems dynamics (see discussion and references in Depew and Weber 1995; Weber and Depew 1996; Weber 1998, 2000; see also Maturana and Varela 1980; for a different approach to these problems see also Maynard Smith and Szathmáry 1995, 1999).

The question of how life began must, in any case, be part of any complete evolutionary theory. As the reduction-minded philosopher Kenneth

Schaffner has argued, the project of reducing Mendelian genetics to molecular genetics requires a plausible account of the origin of life if it is actually to explain the presence of the cellular structures that function to make DNA replication, transcription, and translation to protein possible (Schaffner 1969). Dawkins's invocation of an ur-replicator/interactor at the origin of life was deployed to make all-too-short work of this problem; he simply postulated the existence of a self-replicating RNA molecule in dilute solution in the ocean. An alternative scenario for the emergence of life is given below (section 4).

Even Darwinians who are committed to adaptive natural selection as the *only* significant causal and explanatory mechanism of evolutionary change, as well as genic reductionism, are beginning to address the general problem of emergence within their causal framework. For example, Maynard Smith and Szathmáry identify eight transformations in the history of life on earth (Maynard Smith and Szathmáry 1995, 1999). Three of these are involved in the process of the emergence of life from chemical systems, and hence can be regarded as aspects of a single process of the emergence of life. Another four involve transformations leading, respectively, from prokaryotes to eukaryotes, from unicellular to multicellular organisms (with the attendant appearance of developmental systems), and the appearance of organisms living in complex communities. Beyond that, they include one emergent process that is of special concern for this paper and this volume—the emergence of language and mind. Like Dawkins, Maynard Smith and Szathmáry assume a "replicator first" scenario for the origin of life (Dawkins 1976, 1989). Like Dawkins too, they say that DNA "lives" in cells. This is a position that is astonishing to most biochemists studying DNA replication in the context of cells. Cells alone fit the usual criteria of living entities. In them, replication is but one component of several interlinked processes including the dissipation of matter/energy gradients through metabolism, the ability to respond and adapt to changing circumstances, and signal transduction and information processing (Emmeche 1998; Whitesides and Ismagligov 1999).

Given this retrodictive enscription of "life" into base replicators, it is not surprising that Maynard Smith and Szathmáry should postulate that the emergence of all new levels of biological organization and phenomena is due solely to the power of natural selection, and that they should discount contributions from any kind of self-organization or other factor (Maynard Smith and Szathmáry 1995). Even then, however, real questions arise as to whether this account of emergence by Maynard Smith and Szathmáry is sufficiently robust to account for full range of the emergent phenomena they discuss, including both the origin of life and of mind.

3   Origin of Life and Natural Selection as Emergent Phenomena

Maynard Smith and Szathmáry, who are committed to the primacy of selection as sole causal and explanatory agent, as well as to a stress on replicators as the fundamental units of selection, avoid the term emergence, preferring instead "transformation" or "transition." To countenance emergence does not require commitment to holism. But it does mean that the call for explanatory reduction needs to be relaxed and/or that a causal pluralism that allows for parity among a variety of possible agents should be permitted.[2] The process of emergence of a new replicator, whether it be a gene or a meme, is really not addressed by Dawkins, Maynard Smith and Szathmáry, or Blackmore; rather they assume that once a replicator appears, no matter by what path or how unlikely, selection will take over and provide the explanation. This is really not any advance on Darwin's setting aside the question of the origin of a photosensitive nerve. As interesting as these approaches are, it is not clear that they provide any deep insight into the actual crucial events that lead to the emergence either of life or of language.

An alternative account for the emergence of life, which draws upon nonequilibrium thermodynamics and nonlinear dynamics (what might be characterized as complex systems dynamics), uses notions of self-organization and selection, and their *interaction*. Depew and I have argued that, rather than using natural selection to explain the origin of life, we might view natural selection itself as an emergent phenomenon that arises from the interplay between chemical selection and chemical self-organization in catalytically-closed, autocatalytic cycles in ensembles of protocells (Depew and Weber 1995; Weber and Depew 1996; Depew and Weber 1998; Weber 1998, 2000). That is, evolutionary emergence (in the sense used by Deacon, chap. 5, this volume) itself emerged from self-organizational emergence along with the emergence of life. As we have argued, this view about the origin of life constitutes a critique of the magic molecule theory, according to which life emerged once, and by accident, in the form of an improbable RNA molecule that thereupon acquired cellular survival machines. Our view of prebiotic, or what Depew and I have called "chemical," selection, also contains a critique of the rather promiscuous, substrate-neutral conception of natural selection that currently flourishes (see, for example, Dennett 1995). The implication is that natural selection can emerge in only a very specific range of physical and chemical systems, and that it is deeply dependent on the properties of its substrate.

In effect, this account of the natural selection as an emergent phenomenon addresses how third-order emergent phenomena could arise from second-order emergent systems. In this view, natural selection, properly so-called, is not primarily an explanatory model, or a universal mechanism, or algorithm. It is itself an *emergent* phenomenon uniquely characteristic of systems in which information retention and variation facilitates, coordinates, and regulates autocatalytic cycling of chemical systems within a set of thermodynamical constraints and imperatives. Further, any theory of natural selection worth its realistic salt must account for the fact that organisms, like the cells that make them up, are, in point of fact, informed, autocatalytic dissipative structures. It does not follow from this that natural selection is reducible to chemical selection.[3] What follows is that natural selection presupposes, and is uniquely predicable of, systems in which chemical selection, as we have described it, is at work. It also implies that in hierarchical, evolving systems, we might expect that other selective and self-organizational principles, such as neuronal group selection and reentry discussed below, will emerge and be differently instantiated at other levels.

4   Steps Toward a Theory of the Emergence of Mind

It seems at least intuitively reasonable, and by weak induction plausible, to expect that if natural selection emerged from an interplay of chemical selection and self-organization, this might provide clues about the dynamics and interactions that might produce appropriate, selective, and self-organizational principles at even more complex hierarchical levels.

A possible candidate for this sort of an emergent selection is Edelman's neuronal group selection. It was subsequently adopted by Deacon in his account of the origin of language and consciousness (Edelman 1987, 1989, 1992; Tononi and Edelman 1998; Edelman and Tononi 2000; Deacon 1997, and this volume). Edelman has been careful to distinguish neuronal group selection from natural selection, even if he uses it in an analogous fashion. Edelman does not explicitly consider whether neuronal group selection might be an emergent form of selection, but this seems a plausible interpretation given the complexity of the developmental biology and structure of the human brain.

The complexity of even simple nervous systems is vastly greater than that of cells or organs or anything else encountered in nature. It would not be surprising, then, if new dynamical principles occur in the development of brains (Koch and Laurent 1999). There is ample evidence of a wide variety of self-organizational phenomena in the dynamics of brain organization and action (Kelso 1995). We might well expect that selective and self-organizational principles are important not only for brain development, but for brain evolution itself. Any account along these lines will involve different and richer notions of what counts as heritable, the mechanisms by which adaptive selection occurs, and what the relevant units of selection are.

For his part, Edelman explicitly accepts that the brain is a self-organizing system characterized by nonlinear and massively parallel subsystems (Edelman 1992). The spatial/temporal constraints on axonal development, the role of chemical gradients and helper and target cells with their essential supply of nerve growth factor, introduce one new type of self-organizational and selective principles (Edelman 1987, 1989, 1992; Tononi and Edelman 1998; Edelman and Tononi 2000). These processes produce the primary repertoire of organized neurons; those cells not making synaptic connections and getting nerve growth factor die.

The processes that give rise to Edelman's secondary repertoire involve a kind of selection in which synaptic connections are strengthened or weakened by biochemical processes reflecting synaptic activity or disuse due to the activities and experiences of the organism. The resulting loss of synapses and cells gives rise to functional circuits. The primary and secondary repertoires produce maps of massively parallel and reciprocal connections. The diversity of the patterns and the number of interactions between neurons produced by the primary and secondary repertoires suggest a dynamical attractor on the (near) chaotic side of Kauffman's so-called edge of chaos. It should be noted, however, that although Edelman's formulation could well be framed in the discourse of complex systems dynamics, he has not chosen to employ such concepts explicitly in his published work. Rather he takes complex dynamical systems as the substrate upon which neuronal group selection acts.[4]

By the process of reentry, unique to neuronal dynamics, brain areas emerge that yield new functions. This process of reentry involves the rapid and massively parallel, reciprocal interaction of large numbers of neurons within and between neuronal groups. Such ongoing and recursive parallel interchanges between areas of the brain integrate and coordinate the neuronal activities in these neuronal groups both in space and time. What ultimately gets selected are neuronal groups as well as the reentry pathways within them and connecting them. As groups of neurons are selected, others in reentrantly connected, but different, maps may also be selected at the same time. The activity patterns of such neuronal groups are constantly changing and are significantly differentiated, due to the processes of developmental and experiential selection. They are integrated, through reentry, not only to coordinate widely dispersed perceptual and motor processes, but also to support the primary conscious experience present in animal brains. Primary consciousness, or the "remembered present" in William James's felicitous phrase, emerges from the functioning of a "dynamic core" of neuronal activity (Edelman 1989; Tononi and Edelman 1998; Edelman and Tononi 2000).

Pinker, along with many others, assumes that an expansion of brain capacity allowed an adaptation for language to emerge, that is, that brain evolution apparently preceded language acquisition and evolution (Pinker 1994). In contrast, Deacon envisions a coevolutionary emergence of both language and the brain capacity for language (Deacon 1997). Deacon describes this process in the dynamical language of Edelman. Deacon invokes the processes of neuronal group selection, developmental self-organization, and a Baldwin-type effect acting through reentry to provide a selection pressure operating for the organization of the brain for language (Deacon, chap. 5, this volume). Edelman sees language, as well as the sense of self, emerging from primary consciousness through novel elaboration of a special kind of reentrant connectivity between the expanding brain systems that became involved in language and those already existing areas of the primate brain devoted to conceptual activity (Edelman and Tononi 2000). The underlying mechanism is considered to be sufficiently plastic to have facilitated articulation of neuronal organizational changes and a range of accompanying phenotypic changes that supported speech. "This plasticity relieves us of the genetic and evolutionary dilemma of requiring simultaneous correlated mutations that are reflected both in altered body parts and in correspondingly altered neuronal mappings" (Edelman and Tononi 2000, p. 196). Subsequently, of course, there could be selection for both further phenotypic gene changes as well as mutations in neuronally significant genes that enhanced the evolutionary success of the organisms in the lineage leading to modern humans. Edelman posits a coevolution of body, brain, language, and higher consciousness in which social and affective relationships play a central role in the emergence of qualia (the subjective, qualitative aspects of consciousness), self-consciousness, and rational thought.

5   The Baldwin Effect and Emergence

These reflections about the emergence of life and of language suggest a possible role of some type of mechanism that might go by the name of the Baldwin effect, considered as a process that is emergent from a combination of selection and self-organization. The Baldwin effect has been invoked by both Dennett and Deacon as a factor in the evolutionary emergence of consciousness and language (Dennett 1991, 1995, and chap. 4, this volume; Deacon 1997, and chap. 5, this volume). The history of this notion is complex, and the effect has been redefined a number of times (Depew, chap. 1, this volume; Downes, chap. 2, this volume; Godfrey-Smith, chap. 6, this volume). Depew has argued that the Baldwin effect is not a theory-neutral empirical phenomenon nor is it a theoretical concept that maintains a fixity of reference across different theoretical backgrounds. Indeed, the idea was not homogeneous even in Baldwin's mind as it was reformulated several times by him, especially in response to the rise of genetics (Plotkin 1988). Against the background of the Modern Evolutionary Synthesis, the Baldwin effect seemed theoretically possible but of little significance and was easily conflated with Waddington's genetic assimilation—to the detriment of both (Depew, chap. 1, this volume; Deacon, chap. 5, this volume). Many phenomena that have been cited as evidence for the Baldwin effect are either examples of genetic assimilation or are adequately explainable by orthodox neo-Darwinian mechanisms. The Baldwin effect and genetic assimilation are conceptually distinct mechanisms and need to be evaluated separately (Gilbert 1997; Futuyma 1998; Downes, chap. 2, this volume).

The most noteworthy support for the Baldwin effect, as distinct from the mechanisms employed by Waddington and construed as effects that actually become genetically entrained, comes from computer simulation. Ackley and Littman combined genetic evolution with neural-network learning in an artificial life "experiment," demonstrating that learned adaptive behavior could, with a stability of both problem and adaptive solution, become encoded in the "genes" (Ackley and Littman 1992). The perceived advantage of the interplay of learning and genetics in this simulation is that the Baldwin effect allows the speed of Lamarckian evolution in a situation where acquisition of an acquired trait is specifically blocked. Hinton and Nowlan, in another simulation experiment, conclude that the Baldwin effect could be of selective advantage by speeding up the rate of evolutionary change (Hinton and Nowlan 1996; see also Puentedura, chap. 11, this volume).

As Peter Godfrey-Smith argues, there is a sense in which Deacon makes a novel extension of earlier conceptions of the Baldwin effect by extrapolating from Lewontin's notion of organismal niche construction to niche construction in the social ecology of humans (Godfrey-Smith, chap. 6, this volume; but see also Dennett, chap. 4, this volume, and Deacon, chap. 5, this volume, as well as the postscript at the end of section one). Two of the examples cited by Deacon—appearance of lactose tolerance in populations of herders of milk-producing animals, and sickle-cell hemoglobin conferring adaptive value against malaria in areas where agricultural practices fostered mosquitoes—involve selection pressures arising out of environmental niche alteration due to human activity. The change in gene frequency or selection for a mutant allele that arises subsequently allows an adaptive response to the changed niche due to human activity.

These examples are not, however, directly parallel to the simulations mentioned above. Although there is a changed environment due to human activity that is stable over generational time, the change in gene frequencies observed is not due to selection acting on or serving to support learned adaptive behavior. In a different example on which Deacon has reflected, the mechanism is more distinctly Baldwinian, but it does not involve the genetic encoding of learned behavior as implied in Hinton and Nowlan. Due to a proclivity to eat fruit, somewhere along the lineage leading to humans, there was loss of both alleles for the gene needed in the final step for the production of ascorbic acid. Deacon hypothesizes that the behavior that overcame this lethal mutation, namely eating fruit, was no longer elective but rather a necessary adaptation. Any traits that would support this adaptive response would have been favored by natural selection; populations in which this behavior was learned would have had a greatly enhanced frequency of survival of individuals. Over generational time, parallel mutations, which gave rise to genetic support of the adaptive behavior, such as taste and color preferences, would also have been selected. The moral of the story is that the adaptive behavior itself does not have to become entrained in the genome; the behavior (eating fruit in this case) can be indirectly underwritten by the genes.

Thus the Baldwin effect can be construed to refer to behavioral initiatives by an organism that have an effect on development of neonates through forms of cultural mimesis that are sustained and directional enough to result in a shift in gene frequencies over time by whatever mechanism that this might occur. The Baldwin effect, so construed, does not necessarily mean that the genetic change must mean loss of behavioral plasticity through "hard-wiring" adaptive behavior, a frequent criticism. Rather, gene-frequency changes are selected that underwrite adaptive behavior and stabilize it. Niche construction by the organisms' activities alter the environment in a stable fashion over generational time so that there is an adaptive reward to any changes in genetic regulation and/or gene frequency that supports behavior that is adaptive. This formulation is not only in the spirit of Baldwin's original vision, but can be considered Darwinian in a broad sense (Baldwin 1896, 1902; Depew and Weber 1995).

From this perspective, in their tendency to identify heritability with transgenerational selection at the genetic level, Darwinians such as Mayr can all too readily underestimate the possibility that mimesis and other forms of learning can be heritable over many generations at the phenotypic level and that variant behaviors can become adaptively established in a population before any shift in gene frequencies that stabilizes such an adaptation has taken hold. If there is a mechanism by which a selectively advantageous behavioral repertoire can become genetically entrained or underwritten, so much the better. However, there is some openness about when to call the resulting traits adaptations by natural selection (Weber and Depew 2001).

That behavior and even emotions could have an influence on natural selection was explored by Darwin. "Charles Darwin," says Edelman, "was the first to propose that natural selection alters behavior and vice versa" (Edelman 1987, p. 10). It is the "vice versa" that now needs to be included in any account of the evolutionary emergence of mind. Edelman himself goes on to argue that James Mark Baldwin "was the first to understand the importance of alterations of individuals during ontogeny, and he had the clarity of vision to see the issue in Darwinian terms" (Edelman 1987, p. 11).

The speculations of theorists such as Edelman and Deacon provide models of how consciousness, language, and culture may have emerged that might form the basis for research programs that will enable us to gain a deeper understanding of these phenomena. The neuronal group selection loop can be expected to ultimately modify the natural selection loop of organismic life cycles through the emergence of novel and complex patterns of behavior. Taken together the interaction of neural and organismic selection produces a genuinely emergent phenomenon in organisms with complex brains. Clues how to elaborate such theoretical approaches for this and other cases of emergent evolution (in Deacon's third sense) may come from an understanding of how the emergence of life itself resulted from an interplay between appropriate forms and modes of self-organization and selection.

To the extent that human agency and action played a role in the evolutionary emergence of the human mind, then mechanisms such as that implied in the Baldwin effect, as they are explored in this volume, need to be seriously considered. In contrast to genetic assimilation, which occurs over a wide phylogenetic range, it may well turn out that the Baldwin effect is an emergent phenomenon that arose in a lineage of primates when the brains of these primates evolved to such complexity that it played a role in the further emergence of minds capable of symbolic language and much more.

Acknowledgments

An earlier version of this paper was published in *Cybernetics and Human Knowing* (Weber and Deacon). I wish to thank the editor Soren Brier for permission to further develop material presented in his journal and for his helpful suggestions. I thank David Depew and Paul Griffiths for helpful ciriticism and suggestions on this subsequent version. I also wish to thank Susan Borden for helpful discussions about neuronal group selection theory.

Notes

1. Interestingly, a preliminary attempt to describe mind in terms of brain physiology, although not in evolutionary terms, was published in 1859 by the Edinburgh professor John Laycock (Laycock 1859). From Darwin's correspondence it is clear that he was aware of this work during the time he was preparing his *Descent of Man*. Of course Herbert Spencer's book on psychology from both naturalistic and evolutionary perspectives was published in 1855 (Spencer 1855). However, Spencer's version of evolution was not Darwinian and had little role for selection; even the subsequent revision of 1870 was little informed by Darwin or natural selection (Spencer 1870).

2. Such causal pluralism and parity is assumed in developmental systems theory (Griffiths and Gray 1994, 2001, and Oyama, Griffiths, and Gray 2001).

3. In the latter, information is not yet reliable enough, or sufficiently internalized, to produce adaptations. It merely facilitates certain energetic processes. Rather, natural selection arises when the very process that facilitates autocatalytic cycling in open systems by enhancing reproductive fidelity spins off, as it inevitably will, forms of variation whose differential retention leads to specifically biological fitness.

4. Indeed, current work in the Neurosciences Institute directed by Edelman is developing a theoretical account of the mechanism of reentry using explicit models from complex systems dynamimcs (Eugene Izhikevich and Gerald Edelman, personal communication).

References

Ackley, D. and M. Littman (1992). Interactions between learning and evolution. In C. G. Langston, C. Taylor, J. D. Farmer, and S. Rasmussen (eds.), *Artificial Life II*, pp. 487–509. Redwood City, Calif.: Addison-Wesley.

Arthur, W. (2002). The emerging conceptual framework of evolutionary developmental biology. *Nature* 415: 757–764.

Baldwin, J. M. (1896). A new factor in evolution. *American Naturalist* 30: 441–451.

Baldwin, J. M. (1902). *Development and Evolution*. New York: Macmillan.

Barkow, J. H., L. Cosmides, and J. Tooby (1992). *The Adapted Mind: Evolutionary Psychology and the Generation of Culture*. New York: Oxford University Press.

Behe, M. (1997). *Darwin's Black Box: The Biochemical Challenge to Evolution*. New York: Free Press.

Blackmore, S. (1999). *The Meme Machine*. Oxford: Oxford University Press.

Camazine, S., J.-L. Deneuborg, N. R. Franks, J. Sneyd, G. Theraulaz, and E. Bonabeau (2001). *Self-Organization in Biological Systems*. Princeton, N.J.: Princeton University Press.

Carroll, S. B., J. K. Grenier, and S. D. Weatherbee (2001). *From DNA to Diversity: Molecular Genetics and the Evolution of Animal Design*. Malden, Mass.: Blackwell Science.

Chomsky, N. (1980). *Rules and Representations*. New York: Columbia University Press.

Collier, J. and S. Muller (1998). The dynamical basis of emergence in natural hierarchies. In G. Farre and T. Oksala (eds.), *Emergence, Complexity, Hierarchy, and Organization*. Espee: Finish Academy of Technology.

Cosmides, L. (1989). The logic of social exchange: Has natural selection shaped how humans reason? *Cognition* 31: 187–276.

Darwin, C. (1859). *On the Origin of Species by Means of Natural Selection*. London: John Murray.

Darwin, C. (1871). *The Descent of Man*. London: John Murray.

Dawkins, R. (1976). *The Selfish Gene*. Oxford: Oxford University Press.

Dawkins, R. (1982). *The Extended Phenotype*. Oxford: Oxford University Press.

Dawkins, R. (1986). *The Blind Watchmaker*. New York: Norton.

Dawkins, R. (1989). *The Selfish Gene*, second edition. Oxford: Oxford University Press.

Deacon, T. W. (1997). *The Symbolic Species: The Co-Evolution of Language and the Brain*. New York: Norton.

Dennett, D. C. (1991). *Consciousness Explained*. Boston: Little, Brown.

Dennett, D. C. (1995). *Darwin's Dangerous Idea: Evolution and the Meanings of Life*. New York: Simon and Schuster.

Depew, D. J. and B. H. Weber (1995). *Darwinism Evolving: Systems Dynamics and the Genealogy of Natural Selection*. Cambridge, Mass.: MIT Press.

Depew, D. J. and B. H. Weber (1998). What does natural selection have to be like to work with self-organization? *Cybernetics and Human Knowing* 5: 18–31.

Dobzhansky, T. (1937). *Genetics and the Origin of Species.* New York: Columbia University Press.

Donald, M. (1991). *Origins of the Modern Mind: Three Stages in the Evolution of Culture and Cognition.* Cambridge, Mass.: Harvard University Press.

Edelman, G. M. (1987). *Neural Darwinism: The Theory of Neuronal Group Selection.* New York: Basic Books.

Edelman, G. M. (1989). *The Remembered Present: A Biological Theory of Consciousness.* New York: Basic Books.

Edelman, G. M. (1992). *Bright Air, Brilliant Fire: On the Matter of the Mind.* New York: Basic Books.

Edelman, G. M. and G. Tononi (2000). *A Universe of Consciousness: How Matter Become Imagination.* New York: Basic Books.

Emmeche, C. (1998). Defining life as a semiotic phenomenon. *Cybernetics and Human Knowing* 5: 3–17.

Fodor, J. A. (1983). *The Modularity of Mind.* Cambridge, Mass.: MIT Press.

Futuyma, D. J. (1998). *Evolutionary Biology,* third edition. Sunderland, Mass.: Sinauer.

Gerhart, J. and M. W. Kirschner (1997). *Cells, Embryos, and Evolution: Toward a Cellular and Developmental Understanding of Phenotypic Variation and Evolutionary Adaptability.* Malden, Mass.: Blackwell Scientific.

Gilbert, S. (1997). *Developmental Biology,* fifth edition. Sunderland, Mass.: Sinauer.

Godfrey-Smith, P. (1996). *Complexity and the Function of Mind in Nature.* Cambridge: Cambridge University Press.

Griffiths, P. E. and R. D. Gray (1994). Developmental systems and evolutionary explanations. *Journal of Philosophy* 91: 227–304.

Griffiths, P. E. and R. D. Gray (2001). Darwinism and developmental systems. In Oyama, Griffiths, and Gray (2001), pp. 195–218.

Hall, B. K. (1999). *Evolutionary Developmental Biology,* second edition. Dordrecht: Kluwer.

Hinton, G. E. and S. J. Nowlan (1996). How learning can guide evolution. In R. K. Belew and M. Mitchell (eds.), *Adaptive Individuals in Evolving Populations,* pp. 447–454. Reading, Mass.: Addison-Wesley.

Holland, J. H. (1998). *Emergence: From Chaos to Order.* Reading, Mass.: Addison-Wesley.

Kauffman, S. A. (1993). *The Origins of Order: Self-Organization and Selection in Evolution.* New York: Oxford University Press.

Kelso, J. A. S. (1995). *Dynamic Patterns: The Self-Organization of Brain and Behavior.* Cambridge, Mass.: MIT Press.

Koch, C. and G. Laurent (1999). Complexity and the nervous system. *Science* 284: 96–98.

Laycock, J. (1859). *Mind and Brain*. London.

Maturana, J. and F. Varela (1980). *Autopoiesis and Cognition: The Realization of Living*. Dordrecht: Reidel.

Maynard Smith, J. and E. Szathmáry (1995). *The Major Transitions in Evolution*. Oxford: Freeman.

Maynard Smith, J. and E. Szathmáry (1999). *The Origins of Life: From the Birth of Life to the Origin of Language*. Oxford: Oxford University Press.

Müller, G. B. and G. P. Wagner (1996). Homology, hox genes and developmental integration. *American Zoologist* 36: 4–13.

Oyama, S., P. E. Griffiths, and R. D. Gray (eds.) (2001). *Cycles of Contingency: Developmental Systems and Evolution*. Cambridge, MA: MIT Press/Bradford Books.

Pinker, S. (1994). *The Language Instinct*. New York: HarperCollins.

Pinker, S. (1998). *How the Mind Works*. New York: Norton.

Pinker, S. and P. Bloom (1990). Natural language and natural selection. *Behavioral and Brain Sciences* 13: 707–787.

Plotkin, H. C. (1988). Behavior and evolution. In H. C. Plotkin (ed.), *The Role of Behavior in Evolution*, pp. 1–17. Cambridge, Mass.: MIT Press.

Schaffner, K. F. (1969). Chemical systems and chemical evolution: The philosophy of molecular biology. *American Scientist* 57: 410–420.

Spencer, H. (1855). *Principles of Psychology*. London: Longman, Brown, Green, and Longmans.

Spencer, H. (1870). *Principles of Psychology*, second edition. London: Williams and Norgate.

Sterelny, K. and P. E. Griffiths (1999). *Sex and Death: An Introduction to Philosophy of Biology*. Chicago: The University of Chicago Press.

Tononi, G. and G. M. Edelman (1998). Consciousness and complexity. *Science* 282: 1846–1851.

Waddington, C. H. (1940). *Organisers and Genes*. Cambridge: Cambridge University Press.

Weber, B. H. (1998). Emergence of life and biological selection from the perspective of complex systems dynamics. In G. Van de Vijver, S. Salthe, and M. Delpos (eds.), *Evolutionary Systems*, pp. 59–66. Dordrecht: Kluwer.

Weber, B. H. (1999). Irreducible complexity and the problem of biochemical emergence. *Biology and Philosophy* 14: 593–605.

Weber, B. H. (2000). Closure in the emergence of life. In J. L. R. Chandler and G. Van de Vijver (eds.), *Closure: Emergent Organizations and Their Dynamics*, vol. 901 of the *Annals of the New York Academy of Sciences*, pp. 132–138. New York: The New York Academy of Sciences.

Weber, B. H. and Deacon, T. (2000). Thermodynamic cycles, developmental systems, and emergence. *Cybernetics and Human Knowing* 7: 21–43.

Weber, B. H. and D. J. Depew (1996). Natural selection and self-organization: Dynamical models as clues to a new evolutionary synthesis. *Biology and Philosophy* 11: 33–65.

Weber, B. H. and D. J. Depew (1999). Does the second law of thermodynamics refute the neo-Darwinian synthesis? In P. Koslowski (ed.), *Sociobiology and Bioeconomics: The Theory of Evolution in Biological and Economic Theory*, pp. 50–75. Heidelberg: Springer-Verlag.

Weber, B. H. and D. J. Depew (2001). Developmental systems, Darwinian evolution, and the unity of science. In Oyama, Griffiths, and Gray (2001), pp. 239–253.

Whitesides, G. M. and R. F. Ismagilov (1999). Complexity in chemistry. *Science* 284: 89–92.

Wiener, P. P. (1949). *Evolution and the Foundation of Pragmatism*. Cambridge, Mass.: Harvard University Press.

Wright, C. (1873). Evolution of self-consciousness. *North American Review* 116: 245–310.

Wright, S. (1935a). Evolution in populations in approximate equilibrium. *Journal of Genetics* 30: 257–266.

Wright, S. (1935b). The analysis of variance and the correlations between relatives with respect to deviations from an optimum. *Journal of Genetics* 30: 423–356.

Wright, S., 1986. *Evolution*. Chicago: The University of Chicago Press.

Index